AA003916

PATTERNS 2017

The Ninth International Conferences on Pervasive Patterns and Applications

February 19 - 23, 2017

Athens, Greece

PATTERNS 2017 Editors

Herwig Manaert, University of Antwerp, Belgium

Yuji Iwahori, Chubu University, Japan

Alexander Mirnig, University of Salzburg, Austria

Alessandro Ortis, University of Catania, Italy

Charles Perez, Paris School of Business, France

Jacqueline Daykin, Aberystwyth University (Mauritius Branch Camp), Mauritius

Printed from e-media with permission by:

Curran Associates, Inc.
57 Morehouse Lane
Red Hook, NY 12571

Some format issues inherent in the e-media version may also appear in this print version.

Printed by Curran Associates, Inc. (2017)

International Academy, Research, and Industry Association (IARIA)
412 Derby Way
Wilmington, DE 19810

Phone: (408) 893-6407
Fax: (408) 527-6351

petre@iaria.org

Additional copies of this publication are available from:

Curran Associates, Inc.
57 Morehouse Lane
Red Hook, NY 12571 USA
Phone: 845-758-0400
Fax: 845-758-2633
Email: curran@proceedings.com
Web: www.proceedings.com

Table of Contents

PATTERNS 2017

Forward

The Ninth International Conferences on Pervasive Patterns and Applications (PATTERNS 2017), held between February 19-23, 2017 in Athens, Greece, targeted the application of advanced patterns, at-large. In addition to support for patterns and pattern processing, special categories of patterns covering ubiquity, software, security, communications, discovery and decision were considered. As a special target, the domain-oriented patterns cover a variety of areas, from investing, dietary, forecast, to forensic and emotions. It is believed that patterns play an important role on cognition, automation, and service computation and orchestration areas. Antipatterns come as a normal output as needed lessons learned.

The conference had the following tracks:

- Patterns and Beyond
- Security Patterns
- Evolvable Modularity Patterns
- Patterns for Crowdsourced Media Analysis
- Patterns in Social Network Analysis and Mining
- Basics on Patterns
- Patterns in Combinatorial Structures and Algorithmic
- Computational Vision Systems and Applications of Pattern Recognition

We take here the opportunity to warmly thank all the members of the PATTERNS 2017 technical program committee, as well as all the reviewers. The creation of such a high quality conference program would not have been possible without their involvement. We also kindly thank all the authors that dedicated much of their time and effort to contribute to PATTERNS 2017. We truly believe that, thanks to all these efforts, the final conference program consisted of top quality contributions.

Also, this event could not have been a reality without the support of many individuals, organizations and sponsors. We also gratefully thank the members of the PATTERNS 2017 organizing committee for their help in handling the logistics and for their work that made this professional meeting a success.

We hope that PATTERNS 2017 was a successful international forum for the exchange of ideas and results between academia and industry and to promote further progress in the area of pervasive patterns and applications. We also hope that Athens, Greece provided a pleasant environment during the conference and everyone saved some time to enjoy the charm of the city.

PATTERNS 2017 Committee

PATTERNS 2017 Steering Committee

PATTERNS 2017

Committee

PATTERNS Steering Committee

Herwig Manaert, University of Antwerp, Belgium
Claudia Raibulet, University of Milano-Bicocca, Italy
Sneha Chaudhari, Carnegie Mellon University, Pittsburgh, USA
Valerie Gouet-Brunet, IGN, LaSTIG, MATIS, France
Wladyslaw Homenda, Warsaw University of Technology, Poland
Patrick Siarry, Université Paris-Est Créteil, France
Yuji Iwahori, Chubu University, Japan
Alexander Mirnig, University of Salzburg, Austria
Markus Goldstein, Ulm University of Applied Sciences, Germany

PATTERNS 2017 Technical Program Committee

Mourad Abbas, STRCDAL, Algeria
Adel Al-Jumaily, University of Technology, Sydney, Australia
Kamelia Aryafar, Etsy, USA
Hatem Ben Sta, Université de Tunis - El Manar, Tunisia
Silvia Biasotti, CNR – IMATI, Italy
Cristian Bonanomi, Università degli Studi di Milano, Italy
Julien Broisin, University of Toulouse - Institut de Recherche en Informatique de Toulouse (IRIT), France
Michaela Bunke, Universität Bremen, Germany
Amitava Chatterjee, Jadavpur University, India
Sneha Chaudhari, Carnegie Mellon University, Pittsburgh, USA
Sergio Cruces, University of Seville, Spain
Mohamed Dahchour, National Institute of Posts and Telecommunications, Rabat, Morocco
Jacqueline Daykin, King's College London, UK / Aberystwyth University, Mauritius Branch Campus
Danielly Cristina de Souza Costa Holmes, Federal Institute of Rio Grande do Sul, Brazil
Claudio De Stefano, University of Cassino and Southern Lazio, Italy
Vincenzo Deufemia, University of Salerno, Italy
Moussa Diaf, Mouloud MAMMERI University, Algeria
Susana C. Esquivel, Universidad Nacional de San Luis, Argentina
Francesco Fontanella, Università di Cassino e del Lazio Meridionale, Italy
Christos Gatzidis, Bournemouth University, UK
Markus Goldstein, Ulm University of Applied Sciences, Germany
Valerie Gouet-Brunet, IGN, LaSTIG, MATIS, France
Carmine Gravino, Università degli Studi di Salerno, Italy

Christos Grecos, Central Washington University, USA
Mannaert Herwig, University of Antwerp, Belgium
Wladyslaw Homenda, Warsaw University of Technology, Poland
Tzung-Pei Hong, National University of Kaohsiung, Taiwan
Wei-Chiang Hong, Nanjing Tech University, China
Chih-Cheng Hung, Kennesaw State University, USA
Shareeful Islam, University of East London, UK
Biju Issac, Teesside University, Middlesbrough, UK
Yuji Iwahori, Chubu University, Japan
Slinger Jansen, Utrecht University, Netherlands
Agnieszka Jastrzebska, Warsaw University of Technology, Poland
Maria João Ferreira, Universidade Portucalense, Portugal
Sylwia Kopczyńska, Poznan University of Technology, Poland
Sotiris Kotsiantis, University of Patras, Greece
Adam Krzyzak, Concordia University, Canada
Robert S. Laramee, Swansea University, UK
Fritz Laux, Reutlingen University, Germany
Gyu Myoung Lee, Liverpool John Moores University, UK
Haim Levkowitz, UMass Lowell, USA
Stan Z. Li, Institute of Automation - Chinese Academy of Sciences, China
Alex Po Leung, Macau University of Science and Technology, Macau
Alexander Mirnig, University of Salzburg, Austria
Hongwei Mo, Harbin Engineering University, China
Fernando Moreira, Universidade Portucalense, Portugal
Serena Nicolazzo, University Mediterranea of Reggio Calabria, Italy
Antonino Nocera, University Mediterranea of Reggio Calabria, Italy
Krzysztof Okarma, West Pomeranian University of Technology, Szczecin, Poland
Hélder Oliveira, INESC TEC, Portugal
Alessandro Ortis, University of Catania, Italy
Mrutyunjaya Panda, Utkal University, India
George A. Papakostas, Eastern Macedonia and Thrace Institute of Technology, Greece
Giuseppe Patane', CNR-IMATI, Italy
Christian Percebois, IRIT - University of Toulouse, France
Charles Perez, Paris School of Business, France
Agostino Poggi, DII - University of Parma, Italy
Giovanni Puglisi, University of Cagliari, Italy
Claudia Raibulet, University of Milano-Bicocca, Italy
José Raúl Romero, University of Córdoba, Spain
Theresa-Marie Rhyne, Independent Visualization Consultant, USA
Alessandro Rizzi, Università degli Studi di Milano, Italy
Gustavo Rossi, UNLP - La Plata, Argentina
Antonio-Jose Sanchez-Salmeron, Universitat Politecnica de Valencia, Spain
María-Isabel Sanchez-Segura, Carlos III University of Madrid, Spain
José Santos Reyes, University of A Coruña, Spain

Copyright Information

Embedding and Detecting Patterns in a 3D Printed Object

Kosuke Nakamura, Masahiro Suzuki, Hideyuki Torii, Kazutake Uehira
Kanagawa Institute of Technology
Atsugi, Japan
e-mail: gorisan_manju@yahoo.co.jp, msuzuki@ctr.kanagawa-it.ac.jp, {torii, uehira}@nw.kanagawa-it.ac.jp

Youichi Takashima
NTT Service Evolution Laboratories
Nippon Telegraph and Telephone Corporation
Yokosuka, Japan
e-mail: takashima.youichi@lab.ntt.co.jp

***Abstract*—This paper presents a technique for pattern embedding inside a real object fabricated with a 3D printer and a technique of detecting the pattern from inside the real object. The purpose of this technique is to hide information inside a real object by embedding patterns. The patterns are formed inside the object when the object is fabricated. The thermal conductivity of the pattern region differs from that of the other regions. Therefore, the pattern inside the object can be detected using thermography. In this study, we use plaster powder as the starting material, and the object is produced by sintering. However, the pattern region is formed by not sintering it, that is, the pattern region remains as powder. From the experiment, we find that we can detect patterns using thermography when the pattern size is 2 mm x 2 mm or larger, and we confirm the feasibility of this technique.**

Keywords-3D printer, information embedding, thermography, pattern detection.

I. Introduction

The 3D printer has become compact and inexpensive, and its use is expected to become widespread in the future.

We proposed a technique that embeds patterns inside real objects fabricated by 3D printers that cannot be observed from the outside [1][2]. The embedded patterns express certain information, that is, this technique can embed information inside a real object. We also proposed a technique that can non-destructively analyze the pattern inside real objects and read embedded information [1] [2]. We expect that this technique will be useful for applications such as embedding descriptions of objects inside the objects themselves. Moreover, it is possible to embed copyright information for the design data for a 3D object as a watermark. Related work was reported by K. D. D. Willis and A. D. Wilson [3]. They first made some product parts, one of which had visible pattern, and assembled these parts into one product such that patterned part was inside. However, with our technique, the product that includes patterns inside is formed as one unit, rather than several parts to be assembled later.

In our previous studies [1] [2], we used plastic resin as the material of the object, and patterns were formed by making cavities inside the object fabricated with a 3D printer. We could detect the embedded pattern from the image captured by thermography by utilizing the difference in the thermal conductivity between the cavity and the plastic resin.

This paper proposes a new technique to form patterns inside an object when using plaster as the material for 3D printing. This paper also presents an experiment we conducted to confirm the feasibility of the proposed technique.

II. Embedding and Detecting Pattern in an Object

Figure 1 shows the basic concept of the technique we proposed. Since the pattern region is formed inside the object, it is invisible from the outside. The heat conductivity of the pattern region is lower than that of the other regions of the object. Therefore, if the pattern region is formed near the surface of the object, the pattern appears in the thermal image of the surface when the surface is heated because the heat conduction from the surface to the inside is reduced by the pattern region.

Figure 2 indicates the method we propose to form a pattern region whose heat conductivity is lower than the other regions. This technique required the use of an inkjet 3D printer. First, a layer of plaster powder was paved, and it was solidified by jetting binder onto this layer in accordance with 3D data. However, the binder was not jetted on the powder in the pattern region. Therefore, the powder remained in the pattern region. This process was repeated. Finally, the

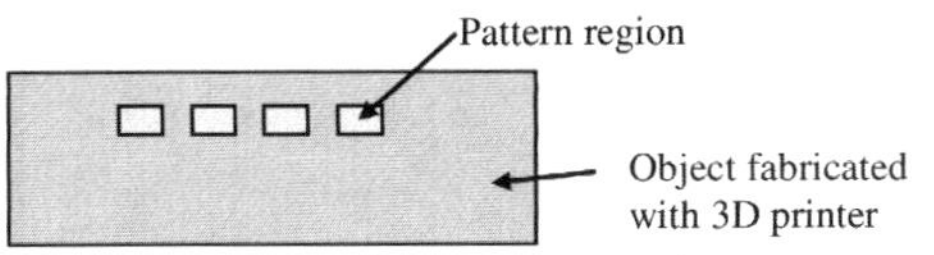

Figure 1. Basic concept of technique we proposed.

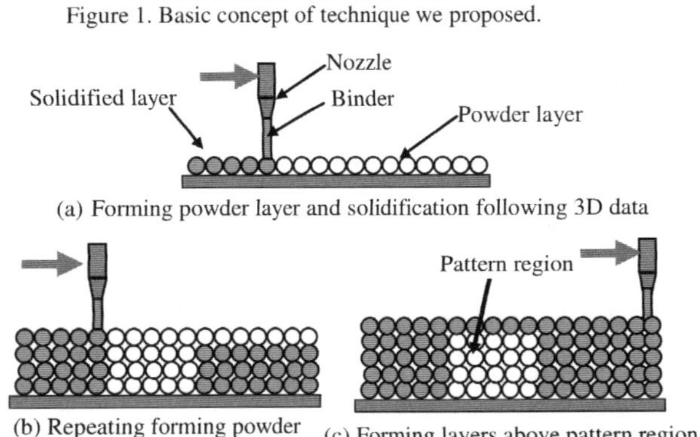

Figure 2. Forming pattern inside object fabricated with 3D printer.

pattern region was covered with a solidified layer.

The arrangement of the patterns express information although they are invisible from the outside of the object. Thermography is used to see the pattern inside. First, the temperature of the surface of the object rises by heating the object. This results in heat conduction from the surface to the inside of the object. Heat conduction is reduced by the pattern region because its heat conductivity is lower than that of the solidified region. This causes the temperature of the surface area above the pattern to increase, and the temperatures of such areas become slightly higher than those of the other areas. Therefore, if we obtain the temperature profile of the surface of the object using thermography, we can determine the arrangement of the patterns, i.e., we can read out the information embedded in the object.

III. EXPERIMENT

We evaluated the feasibility of the proposed technique. Figure 3 shows the sample used in the experiment, which was produced with an inkjet 3D printer. In this experiment, we embedded binary data using small rectangular patterns. That is, the existence or absence of a small rectangular pattern at 25 designated positions expresses "1" or "0". The size of the pattern was changed as one of the experimental parameters.

We investigated to determine if the embedded pattern could be detected in the sample image captured using thermography. If we could detect the pattern, we evaluated how small a pattern could be detected and how accurately the embedded patterns could be detected, that is, how accurately the embedded binary data could be read out.

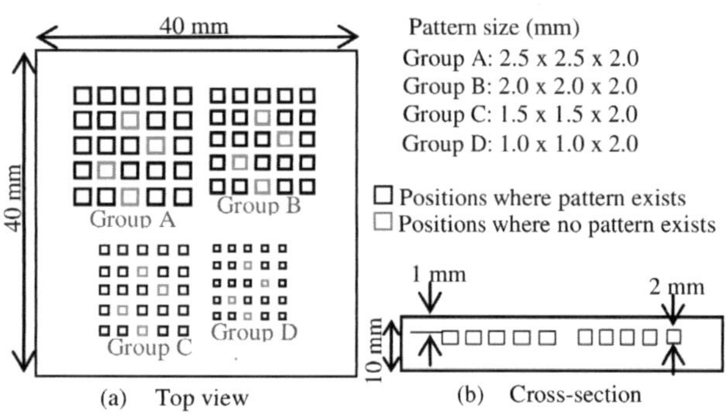

(a) Top view (b) Cross-section

Figure 3. Sample used in experiment

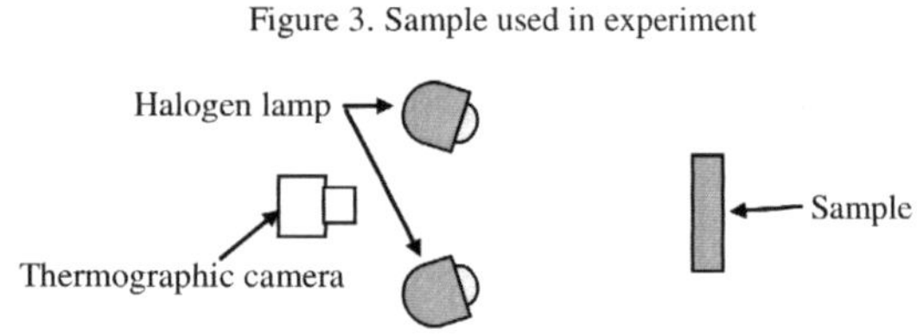

Figure 4. Experimental system

Figure 4 illustrates the experimental system. We used two 500-W halogen lamps to heat the object surface. The lamps were placed at a distance of 10 cm from the sample. Thermography with a resolution of 160 x 120 pixels was used to capture a thermal image of the surface of the object. The temperature resolution of the thermography was 0.1 degrees.

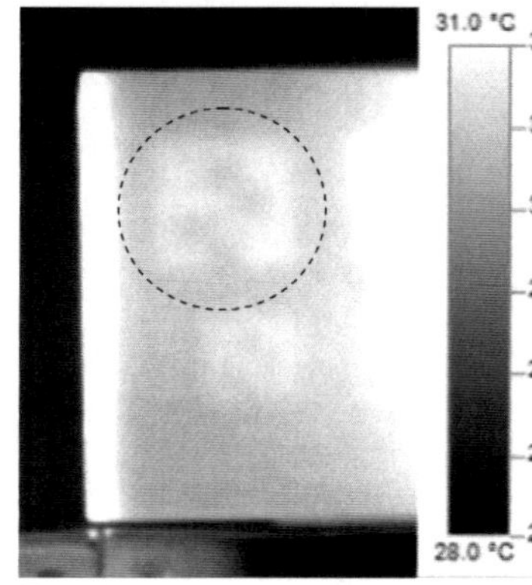

Figure 5. Image captured by thermography

TABLE I. ACCURACY IN READING OUT INOFRMATION

Group (size)	Accuracy (%)
A (2.5 mm x 2.5 mm)	100
B (2.0 mm x 2.0 mm)	100
C (1.5 mm x 1.5 mm)	72
D (1.0 mm x 1.0 mm)	76

IV. RESULTS AND DISCUSSION

Figure 5 shows part of the image captured by thermography. The embedded patterns can be seen in the image. The pattern in the dotted-line circle is that of Group A.

Table 1 indicates the accuracy for reading out 25 binary data for each group. For Groups A and B, we achieved an accuracy of 100%, that is, embedded information could be read out with an accuracy of 100% when we used a pattern with a size of 2 x 2 mm or more.

V. CONCLUSION

This paper proposes a new technique to form powder shape patterns inside an object fabricated with a 3D printer using plaster as the material. The purpose of this technique is to embed information using powder shape patterns and detecting them in the object. From the experiment using thermography, we confirmed that the embedded patterns can be detected from the outside and the embedded information could be read out correctly when patterns with a size of 2 x 2 mm or more are used.

REFERENCES

[1] M. Suzuki, P. Silapasuphakornwong, K. Uehira, H. Unno, and Y. Takashima, "Copyright Protection for 3D Printing by Embedding Information inside Real Fabricated Objects", Proceedings of the 10th International Conference on Computer Vision Theory and Applications, vol. 3, pp. 180–185, 2015

[2] P. Silapasuphakornwong, M. Suzuki, H. Unno, H, Torii, K. Uehira, and Y. Takashima, "Nondestructive Readout of Copyright Information Embedded in Object Fabricated with 3D Printers", Digital-Forensics and Watermarking LNCS 9569 Springer, pp. 232–238, 2015J

[3] K. D. D. Willis and A. D. Wilson, "Infrastructs: Fabricating information inside physical objects for imaging in the terahertz region," ACM Transactions on Graphics, vol. 32, no. 4, pp. 138:1–138:10, 2013.

Detection of Hidden Encrypted URL in Image Steganography

Moudhi Aljamea, Tanver Athar, Costas S. Iliopoulos, M Samiruzzaman
Department of Informatics,
Kings College London,
WC2R 2LS, London
Email: [mudhi.aljamea@kcl.ac.uk, tanver.athar@kcl.ac.uk, c.iliopoulos@kcl.ac.uk, mohammad.samiruzzaman@kcl.ac.uk]

***Abstract*—Steganography is the science of hiding data within the data, either for the good purpose of secret communication or for the bad intention of leaking confidential data, embedding malicious code or Uniform Resource Locator (URL). Various carrier file formats can be used to hide this data (network, audio, image etc.). The most common steganography carrier is embedding secret data within images. We can hide different formats (another image, text, video, virus, URL etc.) inside an image. To the human eye, the changes in the image appearance with the hidden data can be imperceptible. This paper proposes an implementation of a novel detection approach that will concentrate on detecting any kind of hidden URL in most types of images and extract the hidden URL from the carrier image using the Least Significant Bit (LSB) hiding technique. We have recently introduced an algorithm for *Detection of URL in Image steganography*. In addition, we have extended the algorithm to detect and extract encrypted URLs. In this paper, implement the proposed algorithm, successfully test it and compare it with various results, using different images.**

Keywords–Steganography; Image Steganography; Security; String Matching; Steganalysis; URL Detection.

I. INTRODUCTION

Steganography is the science of hiding data within data. The word steganography is derived from the Greek words stegos, meaning cover, and grafia, meaning writing [1]. There are some differences between steganography and cryptography. Cryptography is the art of scrambling messages to make them difficult to understand, whereas steganography is the art of hiding messages to make them difficult to find. Therefore, steganography is an extra layer that will support transferring secret information securely whereas, cryptography, in this case, is data protection. Besides, when steganography fails and the message can be detected, it is still of no use as it is encrypted using cryptography techniques [2].

Steganographic techniques started in ancient Greece. One early example consisted in writing text on wax-covered tablets. Another example involved shaving the head of a messenger and tattooing a message or an image on the messenger's head and let the hair grow back. The message would remain undetected until the head was shaved again [3].

The science of steganography has developed significantly to more sophisticated techniques, allowing a user to hide large amounts of information within images, audio files, and even networks. In fact, the main difference between the modern steganographic techniques and the previous ones is only the form of carrier for the secret information. Researchers are devising new steganographic applications and techniques and old methods are given new twists [3].

Our Contribution: We have recently introduced an algorithm for *Detection of URL in Image Steganography* [4]. In this paper, we extend the algorithm to detect and extract encrypted URLs. We implement the proposed algorithm and successfully test it and compare it to various results using different images.

Structure of the paper: In Section II, we present some background related to image steganography. In Section III, we discuss stegonalysis, which is the main component of detecting hidden messages inside the image. In Section IV, we discuss the problem of hiding URLs inside an image. In Section V, we discuss and present the algorithm, algorithm complexity analysis, implementation and results of the experiments. In Section VI, we present the conclusion and future work.

A. The Concept of Steganography

The concept of steganography is to embed data, which is to be hidden. However, this process will require three files:

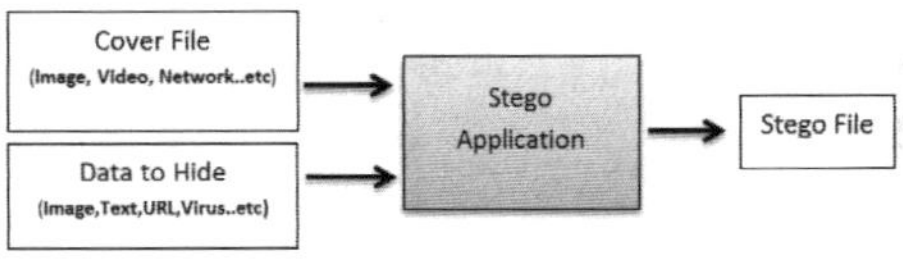

Figure 1. Stego application scenario

First, we have the secret message, which is the information to be hidden and, as mentioned before with the new steganography techniques, almost any kind of data can be hidden. *Second,* we have the cover file that will hold the hidden information and, similarly, almost any kind of file can be used as a carrier. *Finally,* we have the key file to find the hidden message and extract it from the cover file. The result of these three files is a file called stego file, as shown in Fig. 1.

The most common steganography technique is embedding messages within images, as it is considered the best carrier to hide all types of files within it. For example, it is possible to hide another image, virus, URL, text, exe file, audio etc. without changing its visible properties [5].

B. Steganography Applications

Steganography can be used in many useful ways. For example, to help in transferring secret data, copyrights control of materials and smart identity cards (IDs), where individuals' details are embedded in their photographs [6]. It can be used in printed images, where the data can be embedded after printing the image. The user can scan the printed image with a smart device and the embedded information will appear on his/her device. This technique is useful in exhibitions and displaying the product's information.

Cybercrime is believed to benefit from steganography in transferring illegal data or embedding viruses and malicious URLs. To counter this threat, new techniques and methods are being developed and this area is getting more attention among researchers.

There are many sophisticated steganography pieces of software available online, which can be used for cybercrime. Xiao steganography [7] is one such tool. Any user can use this tool to leak his/her company's confidential information.

For this reason, many companies are finding it difficult to detect the stego files even after scanning all their employees outgoing emails.

II. IMAGE STEGANOGRAPHY

Images can be more than what we see with our eyes. To use an image as a cover file is considered to be one of the most useful and cost effective techniques [8]. All image steganographic techniques to hide data are based on the structure of the most commonly used image format on the Internet: graphics interchange format (GIF), portable network groups (PNG) and Bit Map Picture (BMP).

- Cover Image: In steganography, the original image that was chosen as a carrier for the secret data is called a cover image.
- Stego Image: This is the result image of choosing the right cover image and embedding the secret data inside it.
- Stego Key: The sender should have an algorithm for create the stego image to embed the data, and the receiver should have the matching algorithm to extract the hidden data from that particular stego image. Sometimes, the process will require a key, which is similar to a key used in cryptography, to extract the hidden message, and that key is called stego key.

Image Embedding Process: Let C be the chosen cover image, and C' be the stego image, K be the stego key, and M be the hidden message then:

$$C \oplus M \oplus K \rightarrow C'$$

as shown in Fig. 2.

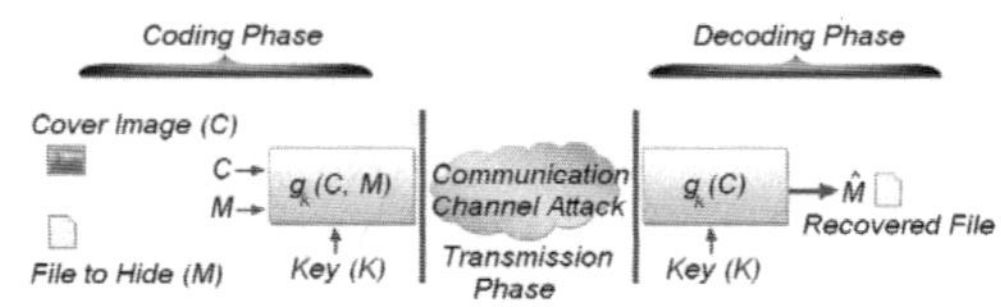

Figure 2. Image Steganography Embedding process

The main challenge in image steganography is that many image manipulation techniques might destroy the hidden message on any image, since it will change the feature of the stego image. Cropping might destroy or corrupt part of the hidden message if the hidden image is located where the image is cropped. Rotation might give the receiver difficulty in finding the hidden message. Filtering might destroy the hidden message completely.

A. Current Image Steganography Techniques

There are some naive implementations of image steganography, such as by feeding windows operating system (OS) command some code to embed the text file which contains the secret message into a specific image and produce the stego image (Fig. 3).

```
C:> Copy Cover.jpg /b + Message.txt /b Stego.jpg
```

Figure 3. Stegocode

Steganography embedding techniques can be divided into two groups. The first is the Spatial Domain, also known as Image Domain, which embeds the secret data directly in the intensity of the image pixels, usually the Least Significant Bit (LSB) in the image. The other is the Transform Domain, which is also known as Frequency Domain, where images are first transformed and then the secret data is embedded in the image [9].

The focus of this paper will be on the spatial domain. In the spatial domain, the steganographer modifies the secret data and the cover image, which involves re-encoding the LSBs in the carrier image. To the human eye, these changes in the image value of the LSB are imperceptible [10]. This technique can be applied for most image formats.

Least Significant Bits: This technique embeds bits of the secret data directly into the LSB plane of the cover image [6]. LSB is considered to be one of the simplest approaches of embedding data in a cover image. Yet, it is one of the most difficult approaches to detect.

On average, the changes will be only made on three bits with a byte. Only half of the bits within an image are modified to hide the secret data using the maximal cover size. The result of these changes is too small to be recognized by the human visual system (HVS) [1].

III. STEGAANALYSIS

Steganalysis is the main step in the steganography technique to discover the hidden messages. It is the way of identifying the suspected medium, determine whether or not they have an embedded data into it, and, if possible, recover that data. Steganalysis is the science of attacking steganography in a battle that never ends [6].

Steganlysis can sometimes be more challenging than cryptanalysis. The steganalyst first has to identify the suspected cover file, then locate the hidden message. The hidden message might be scattered in different locations inside the cover file. In some cases, the hidden message might be encrypted to make it more difficult to detect. The main mission of the cryptanalyst is to decrypt the encrypted message.

There are 4 types of Steganalysis listed below:

1) **If the steganography attack is known to the stegnalysis:** since the cover file, the hidden message and the steganography tool (algorithm) are all known to the steganlysis, the hidden message can be identified quite easily.
2) **Only the original file (before embedding the message) and the cover file are known to stegnalysis:** the objective will be to compare the two files, and using pattern difference between the two files, to identify the hidden message.
3) **If only the secret message is known to the stegnalysis:** the objective is to identify a known pattern in all the files. This is a difficult approach.
4) **Only the cover file is known to the stegnalysis:** similarly to the previous attack, it can be very challenging to identify the hidden message location, since it may be scattered to more than one place.

Image analysis forms the backbone of the image steganalysis programs. Image manipulations techniques, such as translating, filtering, cropping and rotation are used in steganalysis. Discrete cosine transform (DCT)-based image steganography hints can be identified using JPEG double compression and the DCT transform [6].

The focus of this paper will be a new kind of attack where the type of the hidden message is URL and the hiding technique LSB are both known.

A. URL in Image Steganography

Embedding data in images is not a new technique. This method is getting better and more sophisticated. One of the recent improvements is embedding a URL in the image LSBs (see Fig. 4). The objective of the URL is to direct the receiver to a web page. The web page might contain a virus that will harm the image receiver, either by destroying or stealing data.

The main reason behind embedding an URL in an image instead of the whole secret data is that the URL requires very little space in the carrier [11]. This ensures that the URL can be difficult to detect and there is less chance of losing the URL by image manipulations.

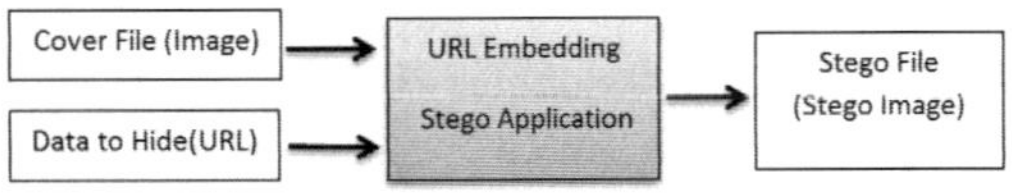

Figure 4. URL Stego Embedding Scenario

In [12], the authors discusses about stegoloader malware. It was noted that the malware authors are evolving their techniques to evade network and host-based detection mechanisms. Stegoloader could represent an emerging trend in malware, hiding malicious code inside a digital image. Stegoloader has a modular design and it uses digital steganography to hide its main module's code inside a legitimate PNG image.

One malware, Lurk Downloader [12] specifically embeds URLs into an image file by inconspicuously manipulating individual pixels. The resulting image contains additional data that are virtually invisible to an observer. Lurk's primary purpose is to download and execute secondary malware payloads [13].

IV. THE PROBLEM

There are various types of information that can be hidden in the LSB of an image. In this paper, we are dealing with an URL hidden inside an image. Any malicious code can be embedded by using LSB. To modify the LSB means to modify the colour, by using LSBs of an image.

There are different colour ranges which require different amounts of memory, such as 2 bits, 8 bits, 24 bits etc. They have both colour and grey scale. 8 bits colour means each pixel can have any of 256 (2^8) colours. The same calculation is applicable 8 bits grey scale or 24 bit colours. Since there are many colour combinations, modifying the LSB does not make much difference to the human eye. URL attack uses this weakness in colour LSB.

For example, an URL "http://exampleattack.com" has 24 characters. Each character of this URL takes 8 bits in ASCII format. The URL will require 192 significant bits from an image.

For simplicity, let us see how the first character 'h' of our example URL "http://exampleattack.com" can be added by using LSBs of an image. The ASCII value for 'h' is decimal 104 and binary 01101000

Before LSB insertion let us assume that 8 consecutive bytes of an image are:
10000010 10100110 11110101 10110101 10110011 10010111 10000100 10110001

After inserting 'h' (01101000) in LSBs, the result is below.
10000010 10100111 11110101 10110100 10110011 10010110 10000100 10110000

In this way, by using more significant bits of images, we can embed the rest of the characters of the intended URL.

V. URL DETECTION ALGORITHM

We are going to present an algorithm overview to detect a hidden URL from the LSBs of an image.

TABLE I. LIST OF TOP-LEVEL DOMAINS (TLD) BY THE ICANN FOR FULL LIST PLEASE REFER TO [14]

AAA	AARP	ABB	ABBOTT	ABOGADO
AC	ACADEMY	ACCENTURE	ACCOUNTANT	ACCOUNTANTS
ACO	ACTIVE	ACTOR	AD	ADS
ADULT	AE	AEG	AERO	AF
AFL	AG	AGENCY	AI	AIG
AIRFORCE	AIRTEL	AL	ALLFINANZ	ALSACE
AM	AMICA	AMSTERDAM	ANALYTICS	ANDROID
AO	APARTMENTS	APP	APPLE	AQ
AQUARELLE	AR	ARAMCO	ARCHI	ARMY
ARPA	ARTE	AS	ASIA	ASSOCIATES
AT	ATTORNEY	AU	AUCTION	AUDI
AUDIO	AUTHOR	AUTO	AUTOS	AW
AX	AXA	AZ	AZURE	..etc

A. Algorithm Overview

Step 1: Create a sorted list, DOMAIN[], from the static official top level domain list.

Step 2: Create an array called BITMAP[], from an image taking each bit in the array.

Step 3: Make a character array called, LSBCHARARRAY[] from an intermediate array of LSBARRAY[] by converting each 8 bits to an ASCII character.

Step 4: Loop through the LSBCHARARRAY[], find out possible hidden URL is formed by http or https, www, domain name and TLD.

B. Complexity Analyses

1) Step 1 (Create a sorted list from the static official top level domain):: **Space complexity**: We have a known TLD list [14]. So, in the pre-processing stage, we have created an indexed array, DOMAIN[] considering each TLD as a string. It is linear to the size of all characters plus the index of each string position in a sorted order. We have created a separate index list with just starting position of TLDs with a specific character.

For example, if .co and .com both starts with c, so if we know where the c starts on the whole sorted list, we just can look at the block starts with 'c'. The overall space complexity of the sorted list is O(M) +O(t) + O(i), where M is the total number of characters, it is the index on each TLD string which is limited to the official static list.

Time complexity: This step of computation can be a pre-processing step, so complexity is not a major issue. However, it is possible to build up a sorted list by radix sort [15] where an LSD radix sort operates in $O(nk)$ in all cases, where n is the number of keys, and k is the average key length.

2) Step 2 (Create a sorted list from the static official top level domain list):: **Space complexity:** O(M) where M is the number of bits.

Time complexity: O(n) where n is the number of bits. This means in just a single iteration the array is built.

3) Step 3 (Make a character array by converting each 8 bits to an ASCII character):: **Space complexity**: The complexity is $O(n)$ here where n=M/8 where M is the number of bits in BitMap and only one in each 8 bits are placed in a character array by converting 8 such Least Significant bits into character. So, the complexity here is sub linear. Although an intermediate LSBARRAY has been introduced in Step 3 for clarity purpose of the flow, it is possible to calculate the LSBCHARARRAY directly from BITMAP[] array. So LSBARRAY[] is not required in the implementation.

Time complexity. This is looping through the BitMap array just once and producing a character array by taking each 8 significant bits together and converting to ASCII. So, the time complexity is linear here with O(n) where looping n bits just once produces the result. Converting to ASCII and character has happened just 1 in 1/64 where 1 byte (8 consecutive LSB) comes from 64 bits. This operation produces a time complexity of O(n+n/64) which is linear.

4) Step 4 (Loop through the array, find out possible hidden URL is formed by http or https, www, domain name and TLD): **Space complexity**: The space complexity is linear with O(n), where n is the number of characters in the array.

Time complexity: This is a loop through the character array. Finding the first 3 parts of an URL (http/https and/or www, domain name) are done in one go in the single loop. They are part of the inside loop, used to find the position and calculation purpose for the string 'http', 'https' and 'www'. The actual counter of the characters array is incremented in each go whether it is inner loop or outer loop. The complexity holds linear for the operations because the whole character array are traversed just once.

Looking at the 4th part, TLD requires a short lookup in a sorted array described in Step 1. For the whole character array, this lookup is just done to complete the search in a sorted and indexed Top Level Domain array which we called in step 1 as DOMAIN[]. In a sorted list, the binary search works as log(n) complexity in the worst case where n is the number of items in an array. But, in our case, n is narrowed down by the index of each character. So, each block of searched area is n/m, where m is the number characters in the alphabet. So, the search takes log(n/m)time because we know the starting character what to lookup DOMAIN[] array. The overall complexity stays linear for step 4.

C. Next Level Detection (Detecting and Extracting Encrypted URL)

The previous tool can be considered as one of the first tools to detect the hidden text in images and extract these hidden messages. We have taken the algorithm to the next level, to detect and extract encrypted URLs.

In this new algorithm, the sender will encrypt and store the URL using the NOT encryption technique in the LSB of the image.

The following proposed algorithm is a linear time algorithm so, it terms of time and space, it does not add any more complexity compared to the previous algorithm.

D. The NOT Encryption Technique

This level of text encryption will not be detectable using the previous algorithm, since it will evade the URL detection through using the binary operation NOT to encrypt the plain text.

We continue with the example that was mentioned in the Problem Definition section:

The ASCII value for '*h*' is decimal 104 and binary 01101000

Before the LSB insertion, let us assume that 8 consecutive bytes of an image are below.

10000010 10100110 11110101 10110101
10110011 10010111 10000100 10110001

To add the extra encryption level to the plain text before embedding it in the image, the '*h*' binary NOT will transform from 01101000 to 10010111

Therefore, after inserting the encrypted '*h*' (10010111) in the LSBs the result is below.

10000011 10100110 11110100 10110101
10110010 10010111 10000101 10110001

The strength of this technique is that it will encrypt the URL, which is a very short text embedded in a very large number of pixels. It gives the sender the advantage of hiding the text without any key for the receiver to use to extract the text. The receiver will only need to know the hiding technique and the text location to extract the hidden text. There are many encryption mechanisms. The complement is one of the easiest mechanism to encrypt data.

E. Experiments

The solution was implemented using Visual Studio 2015 Studio, ASP.Net 4.5 and javascript. The solution is available her [18]. It was tested using BMP, PNG and GIF images of different sizes, colour depth, colour palettes and compression types. The solution has been tested using different browsers such as IE11, Firefox 4 and Chrome Ver 50.0. We have used 2 dozen different images with image size ranging from 300 bytes to 10 KB, colour depth ranging 2 bits to 24 bits, colour palettes ranging from 2 to 65K.

It uses javascript as a client side scripting language and it will work only on the browser where javascript is enabled. It also needs to access files from client machines or folders, so if there are restrictions on accessing image files, the browser will not be able to read the image files.

It cannot accept compressed and lossy images as there is a possibility that the URL data will be lost or corrupted when the images are compressed and the solution will not be able to extract the URL from the stego image [9].

Furthermore, for monochrome images, changing the LSB technique might alter the image in such a way that the changes are visible to the viewers and raise suspicion that the image have been altered, therefore, it will be eliminated.

F. Checking Experiment Results

1) Image Difference: We tested the generated images with the original images using a free image comparison website [16]. The website found no difference between the original and the image containing the hidden URL. In comparing the pixel value and colour between the images, there is a threshold (3 points) which the pixel must exceed in order to register as a difference. It confirms that the statistics steganalysis techniques will not be effective in detecting and extracting the hidden encrypted URLs since they are very short and the changes that they do to the images are imperceptible.

2) Histograms Analysis: We have analysed the histograms of the original image and the generated stego image using the website [17]. There was no difference between the histograms of both the original image and the stego image. It also confirmed that the steganalysis depending on the histograms of images will not detect the hidden URL even if the original image is known and the stego image is known as well.

VI. DISCUSSION AND FUTURE WORK

This paper describes in detail the existing research on how data can be hidden in an image. It also explains how to extract the hidden URL detection in images and the new algorithm to detect encrypted URL.

The URL detection problem in images was simplified with respect to string matching approach, which can be used in other kind of string matching problems in an image. For example, users may be interested to search for malicious commands or other kind of strings hidden in the image using the LSB of the image. The proposed solution has taken the previous URL detection algorithm to the next level, detecting and extracting encrypted hidden URLs. We have implemented and successfully tested this new algorithm using different images.

The experiments showed that the solution is very effective in detecting and extracting the URLs.

Detecting and extracting URL as it is, specifically in images, is a novel approach in image steganography analysis. The reason of concentrating on this problem is a response to the introduction of the new technique of embedding malicious URLs in images recently, and that is relatively a new technique for hiding/spreading viruses. The approach time and space complexity are promising. Therefore, as a future work the detection tool can be improved to cover more encrypting techniques.

VII. References

[1] M. Hariri, R. Karimi, and M. Nosrati, "An introduction to steganography methods," World Applied Programming, vol. 1, no. 3, 2011, pp. 191- 195

[2] R. Krenn, "Steganography and steganalysis," Retrieved September, vol. 8, 2004, p. 2007.

[3] N. F. Johnson and S. Jajodia, "Exploring steganography: Seeing the unseen," Computer, vol. 31, no. 2, 1998, pp. 26-34.

[4] M. M. Aljamea, C. S. Iliopoulos, and M. Samiruzzaman, "Detection of url in image steganography," in Proceedings of the International Conference on Internet of Things and Cloud Computing, ser. ICC 16. New York, NY, USA: ACM, 2016, pp. 23:1-23:6. [Online]. Available: http://doi.acm.org/10.1145/2896387.2896408

[5] N. Provos and P. Honeyman, "Hide and seek: An introduction to steganography," Security and Privacy, IEEE, vol. 1, no. 3, 2003, pp. 32- 44.

[6] A. Cheddad, J. Condell, K. Curran, and P. Mc Kevitt, "Digital image steganography: Survey and analysis of current methods," Signal pro-cessing, vol. 90, no. 3, 2010, pp. 727752.

[7] softonic. Xiao steganography. Accessed: 2017-01-15. [Online]. Available: http://xiao-steganography.en.softonic.com/ (2015)

[8] C. Mohapatra and M. Pandey, "A review on current methods and application of digital image steganography." International Journal of Multidisciplinary Approach and Studies, vol. 2, no. 2, 2015.

[9] T. Morkel, J. H. P. Eloff, and M. S. Olivier, "An overview of image steganography," in Proceedings of the Fifth Annual Information Security South Africa Conference (ISSA2005), H. S. Venter, J. H. P. Eloff, L. Labuschagne, and M. M. Eloff, Eds., Sandton, South Africa, 6 2005, published electronically.

[10] Y. J. Chanu, T. Tuithung, and K. Manglem Singh, "A short survey on image steganography and steganalysis techniques," in Emerging Trends and Applications in Computer Science (NCETACS), 2012 3rd National Conference on. IEEE, 2012, pp. 52-55.

[11] O. K. E. Satir, "A distortionless image steganography method via url," in The 7th International Conference Information Security and Cryptology, 2014.

[12] D.S.C.T.U.T. Intelligence Stegoloader: A stealthy information stealer.Accessed:2017-01-15. [Online]. Available: http://www.secureworks.com/cyber-threat-intelligence/threats/stegoloader-a-stealthy-information-stealer/ (2015)

[13] D.S.C.T.U.Brett Stone-Gross,Ph.D. Malware analysis of the lurk downloader. Accessed: 2017-01-15. [Online]. Available:http://www.secureworks.com/cyberthreat-intelligence/threats/malware-analysis-of-the-lurkdownloader/?view=Standard (2014)

[14] ICANN. List of top-level domains. https://www.icann.org/resources/pages/tlds-2012-02-25-en. [Online].Available:https://www.icann.org/resources/pages/tlds-2012-02-25-en (2016)

[15] R. Sedgewick and K. Wayne. Radix sorts. [Online]. Available: https://www.cs.princeton.edu/rs/AlgsDS07/18RadixSort.pdf (2014)

[16] J. Cryer. Image analysis and comparison. Accessed: 2017-01-15.[Online].Available: https://huddle.github.io/Resemble.js/ (2015)

[17] LunaPlc.com. Histogram of image colors.Accessed:2017-01-15. [Online]. Available: http://www169.lunapic.com/editor/?action=histogram (2017)

[18] http://tanvera-001-site2.htempurl.com (2017)

Optical Watermark Pattern Technique using Color–Difference Modulation

Kazutake Uehira and Hiroshi Unno
Kanagawa Institute of Technology
Atsugi, Japan
e-mail: uehira@nw.kanagawa-it.ac.jp

Abstract— **We propose a new optically written watermarking technique that produces a watermark pattern by modulating color difference. The illumination that contains such a watermark is projected onto an object. An image of the object taken by the camera contains the same watermark, which can be extracted by image processing. Therefore, this technique can protect portrait rights of real objects. We conducted a simulation where one-bit binary data were embedded in blocks that consisted of 8 x 8 pixels using the phase of the highest-frequency component. The simulation results revealed that a watermark pattern produced by modulating color difference could be accurately read out.**

Keywords-Watermark pattern, information embedding, portrait right.

I. INTRODUCTION

Digital watermarking has been widely used to protect the copyright of digital content, which includes images printed from digital data. This is to prevent the illegal use of images copied by digital cameras or scanners. However, printed images or other real objects that have a high value, such as paintings in museums, do not contain watermarks in themselves, and images taken of these with cameras can easily be utilized without copyright.

We developed a technique that can prevent the illegal use of images of real objects that do not have watermarks [1] [2] by using illumination that contains an embedded watermark pattern invisible to the naked eye. An image taken of an object illuminated with the watermark pattern by a camera would also contain the pattern.

We embedded the watermark pattern in the illumination by modulating its brightness, as documented in our previous study. In this current study, we produced a watermark pattern by modulating color differences and evaluated its readability from the captured image by comparing it with the previous method that modulates brightness.

II. EMBEDDING WATERMARK PATTERN IN THE ILLUMINATION

Figure 1 outlines the basic concept underlying our watermarking technique using light to embed a watermark. An object is illuminated by a projected light that contains an invisible watermark. A photograph taken of the object illuminated this way would also contain the watermark. The watermark can be extracted in the same way as that in conventional watermarking techniques for digital content.

Figure 2 illustrates the procedure for applying a watermark and reading it from a captured image.

The color difference signal Cb of Luminance, Chroma-blue and Chroma-red (YCbCr) signal was used to produce the watermark. Figure 2 (a) shows the original data of Cb as a frequency domain. The original data is divided into numerous blocks, each of which consists of 8 x 8 pixels. Each block has only the highest frequency component (HC)

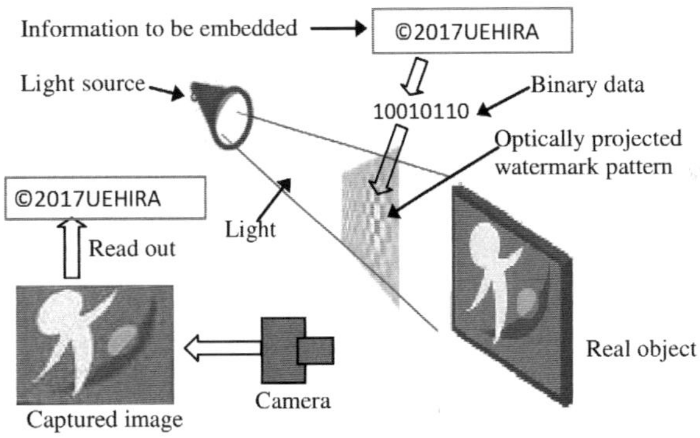

Figure 1. Basic concept underlying proposed

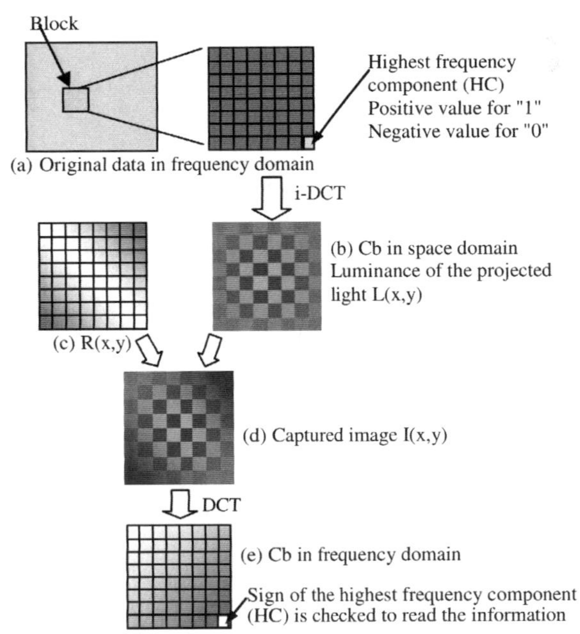

Figure 2. Procedure for watermarking

in both the x and y directions to express one-bit binary data. If the sign of the HC in a block is positive, it is expressed as "1", and if it is negative, it is expressed as "0". This original data in the frequency domain is converted into a signal in the space domain by making an inverse discreet cosine transform (i-DCT) (Fig. 2 (b)). Y and Cr signals are constant. After converting the YCbCr into an Red, Green and Blue (RGB) signal, the RGB signal is input to a projector, and the watermark pattern is projected onto the object.

The captured image of the object $I(x,y)$ is given as a product of the reflectance of the object surface $R(x,y)$ and luminance of the projected light $L(x,y)$, as shown in (1).

$$I(x,y) = R(x,y)\{L(x,y) + L_0\} \quad (1)$$

where L_0 is a bias luminance, such as one produced by room light.

A captured image is first converted into a YCbCr signal, and then Cb is converted into a signal in the frequency domain by DCT. Finally, the embedded data is read out by checking the sign of the HC of the Cb for each block.

The watermark pattern in the light and in the captured image cannot be seen by the human visual system because it is modulated at the highest frequency and the amplitude of the modulation is small.

III. SIMULATION

We simulated the captured images of objects using (1). We used RGB signal as $L(x,y)$, assuming that the brightness of the RGB component of the projected light was proportional to the component of the RGB signal. As for the objects $R(x,y)$, we used three standard images shown in Figure 3.

HC in the original data was changed from 1 to 20 as an experimental parameter, while Y, Cr, and L_0 were set to constant values of 200, 0, and 40, respectively. For reference, we embedded a watermark pattern by modulating Y. In this case, Cb and Cr were set to zero, and L_0 was set to 40.

(a) Image A (b) Image B (c) Image C

Figure 3. Images used as objects in the simulation.

IV. RESULTS AND DISCUSSION

Figure 4 shows the accuracy with which the binary data was read out. The accuracy is indicated by the percentage of the data read out correctly from the entire data. The results show that the accuracy when modulating Cb is higher than that when modulating Y with values over 99% for HC values set over 2

Figure 5 shows the captured images simulated using (1)

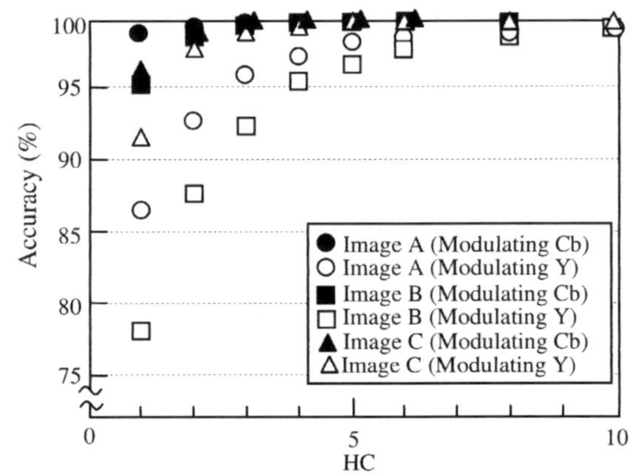

Figure 4. Accuracy in reading out binary data

Figure 5. Simulated captured images (HC=5)

when HC was set to 5. We could not see any watermark pattern in the images. These results indicate that we can satisfy both invisibility and readability of embedded data by using certain HC ranges.

V. CONCLUSION AND FUTURE WORK

We developed a technique that can embed an invisible watermark pattern into captured images of real objects using illumination that contains the pattern. We embedded the pattern into the illumination by modulating color difference.

We demonstrated from the simulation that an accurate reading of the watermark information is possible by modulating color difference, and embedded watermarks could be invisible.

In the future, we will examine the detailed conditions for invisibility of watermarks.

REFERENCES

[1] K. Uehira and M. Suzuki, "Digital watermarking technique using brightness-modulated light," Proceedings of the IEEE ICME2008, pp. 257–260, 2008

[2] Y. Ishikawa, K. Uehira, and K. Yanaka, "Practical Evaluation of Illumination Watermarking Technique Using Orthogonal Tranforms," Journal of Display Technology, Vol. 6, No. 9, pp. 351–358, 2010

Study Setup Optimization - Providing Solutions with Patterns

Artur Lupp*, Alexander G. Mirnig*, Andreas Uhl† and Manfred Tscheligi*

*Center for Human-Computer Interaction, University of Salzburg, Austria
Email: name.surename@sbg.ac.at
†Department of Computer Sciences, University of Salzburg, Austria
Email: uhl@cosy.sbg.ac.at

***Abstract*—This paper proposes the use of the contextual user experience (cUX) pattern approach for refining a study concept involving biometric image data. While the concept of a study may be clear from the beginning, external influences can not always be predicted beforehand. While designing a study concept for a thesis about the acquisition, inspection, and evaluation of Near Infrared (NIR) iris biometry images, certain problems arose, e.g., how to deal with the environmental light, which material to use for 3D printing or the problem of picking the right questionnaire. We used the cUX pattern approach to provide solutions in the form of patterns for the occurred problems during the refinement process of the study setup.**

Keywords–design patterns; pattern reuse.

I. Introduction & Related Work

In this paper, we will present three patterns, created to provide solutions for problems encountered during the improvement of a study setup. Patterns, in general, are a well acknowledged method in Human-Computer Interaction (HCI), providing reliable solutions for specific problems. They can be advantageously used to ease the communication between experts with different levels of expertise or even alternate disciplines. This is particularly useful in interdisciplinary areas, such as HCI research and design. Patterns were first introduced by Christopher Alexander [1][2] as a means to capture working solutions for reoccurring problems in the field of architecture. His methodology was adopted by Gamma et al. [3] for Software Engineering and related disciplines, and has been used as a tool in these domains since. Patterns were adopted to supplement guidelines and other general means of guidance, because such approaches are often either too simplistic or high level [5][4]. Pattern solutions are firmly embedded in the context their problems occur in. This makes a specific pattern less reapplicable, i.e., only when the problem contexts match to a sufficient degree. But it also makes the solutions they describe more specific, as well as practice relevant, and lends them to be used by novices and experts [6]. Patterns have been adopted by other domains as well, such as Web Design and HCI [7][8][9] and also suggested as a general, discipline-independent knowledge transfer tool [10].

In section 2, we will shortly describe the study setup we wanted to improve, followed by an overview of the approach we used for pattern creation. We will show how we discovered and summarized the problem statements for each pattern and give an insight to the pattern creation process.

Section 3 will illustrate three solution patterns with the following *Titles*:

1) Choosing the Right Light Sources to Examine NIR-Images Differences
2) Lens Holder Construction for a Mobile Phone
3) Finding and Adjusting the Right Usability Questionnaire

Apart from the *Title*, each pattern is divided into six sections. The *Intent* provides a short description and is followed by the *Problem* statement, which is, in our case, a question. After stating the problem, a *Scenario* is presented that is used as an example, for which a *Solution* is provided. The solution is backed up by *Examples*, usually illustrated with images. The pattern ends by providing *Keywords*, matching the subject of the pattern. Last, we will discuss our findings in Section 4 and conclude this work in Section 5.

II. Approach

We wanted to improve and optimize an existing study setup, dealing with biometric images. These biometric images had to be analyzed afterwards, with respect to image quality. The setup was divided into several steps. During the first step, test subjects have to capture videos with a customized Nexus 5 mobile phone. The IR-blocking filter was removed from the rear camera image sensor, to enable NIR image capturing. The built-in rear camera image sensor is a Sony Exmor R IMX 179. The sensor offers an Red-Green-Blue (RGB) sub pixel layout with $3264x2448$ (8 MegaPixel) pixels and a sensor size of $5.68mm$ $(1/3.2")$, leading to an effective pixel size of $1.4\mu m$. The pixel size is decent for a mobile phone released in 2013. Therefore, taking images or videos in twilight conditions is possible. However, a brighter environment is preferred due to less image noise. Each test subject had to record at least three frontal face videos using two different filters / lenses, mounted on the mobile phone, which takes a lot of time. Afterwards, the test subjects had to fill in a questionnaire. Due to the time consuming video capturing process, the questionnaire needed to be short, while still maintaining a decent reliability. We proposed patterns to refine the study concept using an approach similar to the pattern generation process for car user experience patterns described in detail by Mirnig et al. [11], with some minor changes. The first mandatory step in our approach was to analyze the study concept and the associated setup to extract the problem statements. This was done by organizing a workshop with the person responsible for the study concept and a group of HCI researchers accustomed with the pattern generation process. During the workshop, the study setup was explained as follows: Study participants have to capture three frontal face videos: one without any lens, for NIR and visible light images, one with the IR-blocking filter / lens and one with the NIR-only lens. As it is possible to extract high quality images from high resolution videos, it was decided, to capture only videos instead of pure frontal face images. The two different lenses forced the researcher responsible for the study, to change them after every recording, due to the current lens mounting method. To ensure a variety of captured videos, the test subjects had to record the videos in different light environments, which where not yet defined. The final step was the acquisition of data, relating to the usability of the video recording process. As the video capturing procedure was time consuming, the data acquisition had to be fast, whilst still reliable. This workshop brought up the following three main problems:

1) Which light sources and ambient environments need to be considered, to ensure a diversity of captured image or video data usually acquired during real life usage?
2) How can the lens / filter changing process be improved?
3) What questionnaire should be used to provide reliable results while not using much time to fill out?

For each of the three problems, a draft pattern was created. The draft pattern initially did not provide any final solutions. Thus, the draft pattern was iterated for the first time, in a second workshop. The original draft pattern was reworked, with respect to the feedback from the first iteration. This iteration resulted in a refined version of the pattern. Each iteration improved the pattern to a certain degree. After the second iteration and rework phase, the pattern was finalized. It is noted that, depending on the experience of the involved experts, more iterations are necessary to create a good pattern. The final pattern should provide an adequate solution for the predefined problem statement. In our case, two iterations were sufficient.

In the next section, we will present the three solution patterns we generated. Each pattern provides a solution for a certain problem statement, previously mentioned in this section.

III. Solution Patterns

A. Choosing the Right Light Sources to Examine NIR-Images Differences

Intent: There are several variables one needs to take into account when taking pictures or videos with a mobile phone. Due to the usually small built-in image sensor in mobile phones, sufficient environmental light is a crucial point. Insufficient light leads to higher image noise, which is generally not preferred. However, to analyze a wide area of possible real life conditions, selecting different environments for image capturing is important. This pattern presents three possible scenarios covering the most important lighting conditions. The scenarios were selected to provide images with a quality sufficient for subsequent analysis in mind.

Problem: Which scenarios are needed in order to acquire analyzable data, covering indoor, as well as outdoor, lighting conditions that enable NIR image acquisition?

Scenario: The study needed special image acquisition scenarios to reflect actual real life scenarios as closely as possible. Additionally, the ambient light in at least one of the scenarios had to cover the NIR wavelength ($>= 700nm$) spectrum to enable NIR imaging.

Solution: To cover most real life scenarios of possible image capturing conditions, we proposed three scenarios: one outdoor scenario using passive sunlight to enable NIR imaging and two indoor scenarios, using different light environments to challenge the imaging sensor of the mobile phone.

- **Outdoor (variable ambient light conditions)** - The outdoor scenario is and should be variable. In this condition, the sun is providing the ambient light. Therefore, the image quality is depending on time, weather, and location. To ensure the best possible conditions for NIR image acquisition, daylight is necessary. Therefore, image acquisition in this scenario should be done during daytime. An example of the outside condition is shown in Figure 2.
- **Indoor (dim light)** - The indoor scenario using a dim light source is intended to challenge the image sensor. The passive artificial light provides sufficient luminosity for images to be taken, as pictured in Figure 3. Nevertheless, the provided light is dark enough to force the image sensor to use a higher sensitivity setting (this is also referred to as ISO, which is derived from the International Organization for Standardization standard describing camera sensitivity settings), thus, resulting in more image noise. Note, that image noise is not desirable in general, but, if the main concept of the study is to analyze the whole range of possible image qualities, it is mandatory to include this unfavorable condition.
- **Indoor (bright light)** - In contrast to the dim light indoor scenario, the bright light indoor scenario uses a very bright artificial white light source to illuminate the frontal face area. This scenario complements the previously mentioned scenarios. The bright artificial light, covers the spectrum visible to the human eye (from about 390 to $700nm$), and provides a decent environment needed to capture regular frontal face images and can be observed in Figure 4. However, conventional light sources are usually not suitable for NIR imaging, as they do not cover the spectrum above $700nm$ (see Figure 1).

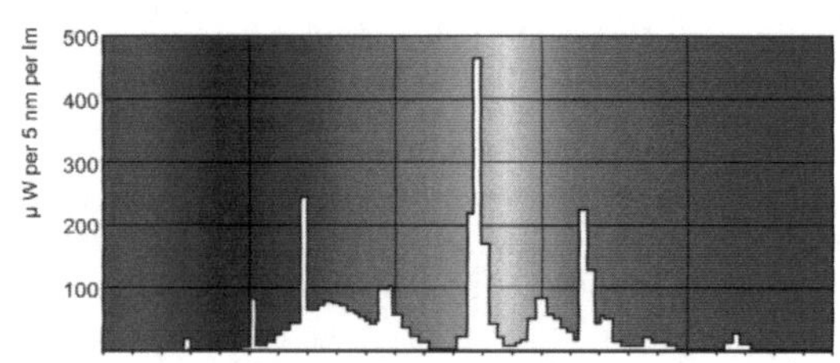

Figure 1. Philips TL5 HO 49W 865 Lamp [12] - Photometric Data.

Examples: This section shows nine sample images. They are grouped by the three proposed scenarios. Each group consists of three images: NIR only, NIR & visible light, and visible light only.

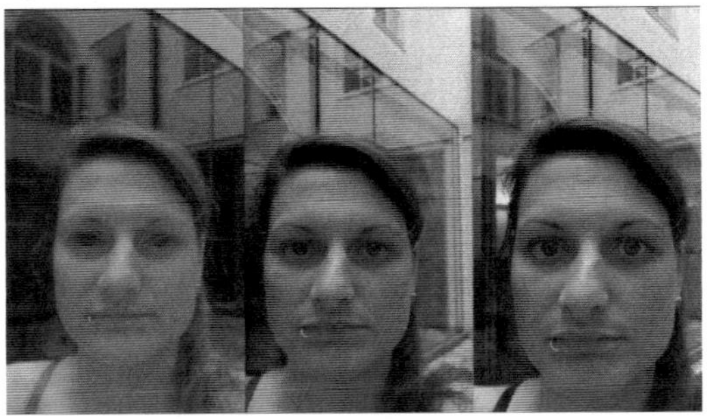

Figure 2. Outdoor - NIR only, NIR & visible light, visible light only (from left to right).

As mentioned in the solution section, the outdoor scenario provides sufficient light. This scenario provides the best NIR image quality, as the sunlight covers a wider spectrum compared to conventional light sources.

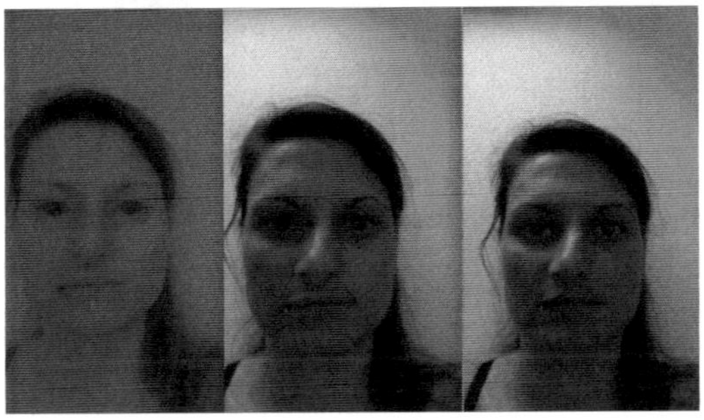

Figure 3. Indoor (dim light) - NIR only, NIR & visible light, visible light only (from left to right).

The indoor scenario with a dim passive light source tends to induce image noise and is not optimal for NIR imaging.

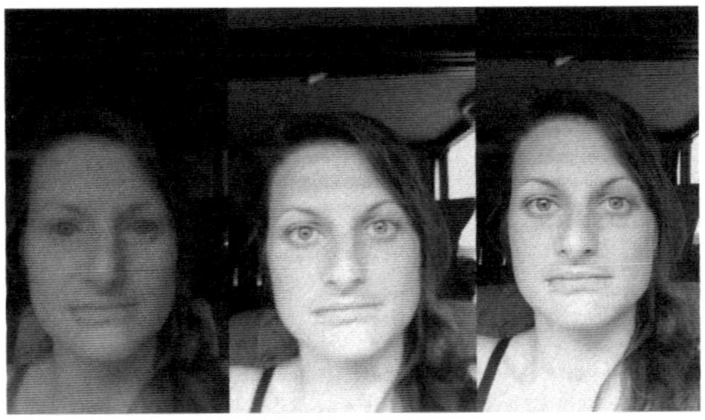

Figure 4. Indoor (bright light) - NIR only, NIR & visible light, visible light only (from left to right).

The last scenario provides a direct illumination of the facial area. It is very favorable for images captured in the visible spectrum, e.g., due to reduced image noise.

Keywords: NIR, visible light, wavelength, spectrum, image acquisition, illumination

B. *Lens Holder Construction for a Mobile Phone*

Intent: This pattern describes steps-by-step the construction of a lens holder for the Nexus 5 mobile phone.

Problem: Is it possible to create a method or item to reduced the lens change time and make the whole process more comfortable?

Scenario: Two different filters / lenses are each to be mounted on the mobile phone using a clip. This is very time consuming and elaborate. To ease the transition from one lens to another, they had to be mounted on a movable holder, with the possibility to be mounted on the mobile phone.

Solution: A custom made movable lens holder, mounted on a hard shell mobile phone case. The following points are describing a step-by-step guide to construct a lens holder for a mobile phone case:

- First, get a hard shell mobile phone case to work with. The case should be made of a robust material, e.g., polycarbonate. The easiest way to obtain a good mobile phone case is either by buying it or by printing one using a 3D printer. Note, that the camera lens of the mobile phone should not stick out of the case, when it is mounted on the phone, as it will be tough or impossible to rotate the custom made lens changer afterwards.
- Measure the phone case and the lens width, length, and depth. Measurements should be taken as precisely as possible.
- Sketch the available items (i.e., lenses and phone case), with the measurements from the previous step.
- The sketch is then used to figure out, how to arrange the lenses in a way, that allows them to cover the camera lens of the phone when the lens changer is being rotated.
- With the lenses arranged, pick a focus point between them. This is the pivot point of the lens changer. In our case, its the small circle in between the two bigger ones, as illustrated in Figure 6.
- Craft a paper prototype of the lens holder. Sketch the lens changer with the exact measurements and cut it out. This prototype can be used to simulate the finished product. Try it out, and see if it fits your expectations, as depicted in Figure 5.
- Digitize the sketch and construct a 3D model. Note that it may be beneficial to add some room to move, especially if using a 3D printer that is not 100% accurate. An example of the digitized model is pictured in Figures 6 and 7 (left).
- Print the 3D model with a material that allows editing with tools (i.e., a file or a multifunction rotary tool) later on. In this case, PVC was used.
- Deburr the edges whilst occasionally trying to fit in the lenses. When everything fits accordingly, proceed with the next step. If anything is odd or needs refinement, redo the 3D modeling and print the item again.
- Drill the pivot point holes into the 3D printed item, as well as in the phone case, to combine them later on.
- Temporarily mount the printed lens holder to the phone with a screw, as shown in Figure 7 (right).

- Double check if everything is according to your needs.
- Finally, install the lenses into the lens holder and mount it to the phone case. See Figure 8 for the final result.

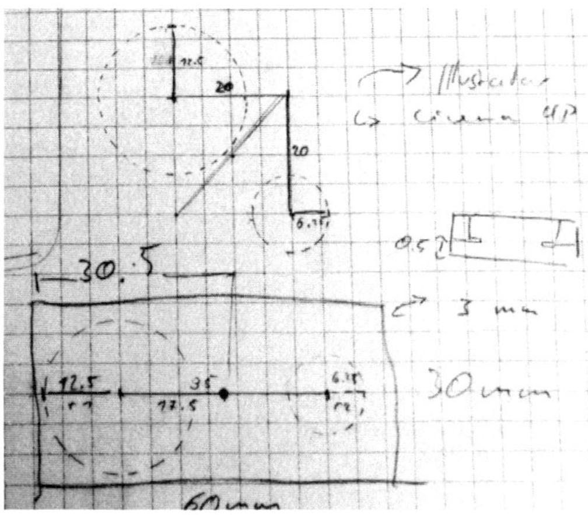

Figure 5. Sketch of the lens holder with exact measurements and radius.

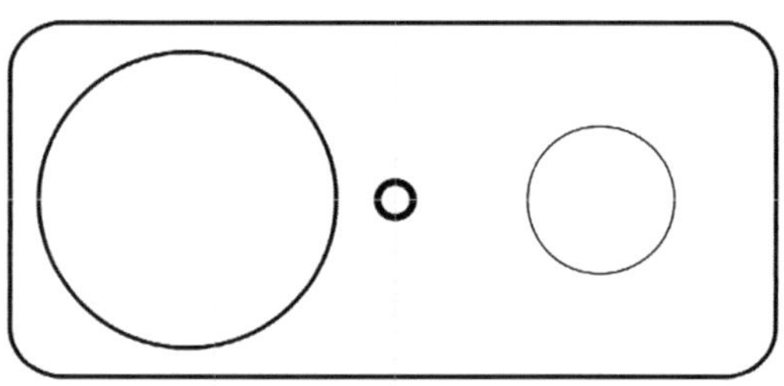

Figure 6. Digitized 2D model of the sketched lens holder.

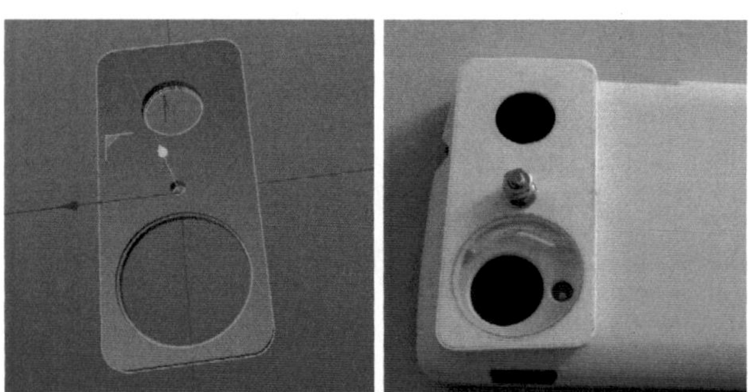

Figure 7. 3D model of the lens holder (left), already printed lens holder with installed lenses/filters (right).

Figure 8. Final lens holder mounted on the phone case.

Examples: Figure 9 holds a QR Code that is linked to a video showing the lens holder in action, whereas Figure 10 is picturing the effect of the different lenses on image acquisition.

Figure 9. YouTube Video - Nexus 5 Lens Holder Case [13].

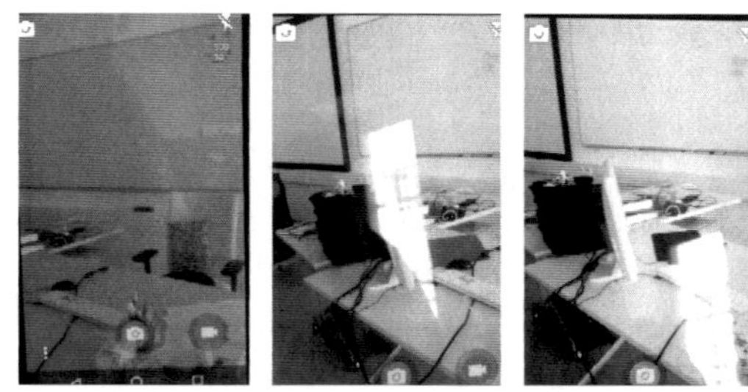

Figure 10. NIR, NIR and visible light, visible light only by using IR-blocking lens (from left to right).

Keywords: NIR, lens holder, phone case, PVC, polycarbonate, 3D modeling, 3D printing

C. Finding and Adjusting the Right Usability Questionnaire

Intent: This pattern tries to guide you how to find the right usability questionnaire for your needs and how to adjust it to your certain needs.

Problem: There are a couple of usability and user experience questionnaires available. Which one should be picked and how is it possible to adjust them to your needs?

Scenario: Due to our study setup, we want a short questionnaire that can be filled out quickly on paper. Thus, it needs to have fewer items, while maintaining statistical reliability (reliability values of 0.70 or more).

Solution:

- **Define**
  The first step, before even choosing a questionnaire, is to define what you want to evaluate. Try to think, which aspects a questionnaire needs to fulfill in order to benefit your research. These aspects should come directly from the research questions which are investigated in the study. For example, if there is a research question regarding *intention to buy after using a system*, then a questionnaire on *intention to buy* or one with *intention* to buy as a subscale is needed. Define your research questions first, then look for the appropriate questionnaires. Include only those aspects or constructs which pertain to your research questions.
- **Consider**
  It takes longer to fill in a questionnaire with complex items, especially if there are a lot of items. It is

usually difficult to hold a participant's attention for more than 15 minutes in most questionnaire situations (most important for online questionnaires). Thus, it is recommended to keep the complexity and number of items such that a comfortable amount of 10-15 minutes total for filling in the questionnaire is reached. Use open questions only when they can not be replaced by any other item, as they require more thought by the participant and take longer to fill in as a result.

- **Choose**
  After it is clear what to evaluate and how big the scope should be, before creating a questionnaire, try to search for common and reliable questionnaires fitting your needs.
  Here is a small example of reliable questionnaires used to evaluate, e.g., usability and technology acceptance:
  - Questionnaire for User Interface Satisfaction [14]
  - Perceived Usefulness and Ease of Use [15]
  - Nielsen's Attributes of Usability [17]
  - Computer System Usability Questionnaire [18]
  - Practical Heuristics for Usability Evaluation [19]
  - Pardue Usability Testing Questionnaire [20]
  - System Usability Scale (SUS) [21]
  - Technology Acceptance Model [16]

  If none of the common questionnaires fit your needs perfectly, either pick one that satisfies most of them or create your own. If you need to create your own questionnaire skip the next step and proceed to "Create".
- **Customize**
  After choosing a common questionnaire that fits your need, it may be necessary to customize it slightly. Customizing existing questionnaires, however, should be done with caution. If such a customization changes the meaning of a validated questionnaire's items, then the questionnaire requires revalidation. Customization most often happens to make a questionnaire easier to understand by the intended target audience or when they are translated to other languages. Here is an example extracted from the SUS questionnaire: "I found the system unnecessarily complex". Sometimes, e.g., when working with children, they might not know the word "complex" however they usually know the term "hard to understand". Thus, changing the question to "I found the system unnecessarily hard to understand" would be legitimate. However, changing the question or the meaning completely is not and would reduce the tests reliability. The same is true for translations, which should ideally be done or at least double-checked by a native speaker of the target language. Sometimes, which happens especially with larger multi-purpose questionnaires, such as the Unified Theory of Acceptance and Use of Technology (UTAUT) [23] or others, individual items might not make much sense for the study at hand. For example, the aforementioned *intention to buy* from an acceptance questionnaire would not make sense when applied to the evaluation of third party web interface, which can not be bought and is not intended to. Items, or even whole constructs, can and should be omitted in such cases. This also means, however, that not all calculations between constructs can be done like in the full questionnaire. Any omissions made should be kept to the necessary minimum and need to be explicitly stated when disseminating the results, in order to ensure comparability with other studies using the same questionnaire or subscale.

In general, the optimal questionnaire has to provide enough statements or items covering the most common shades of opinions about the to be evaluated subject.

Examples: An example of the translated SUS questionnaire (translated by David Wilfinger et al. [22]) that was used in the study setup, is presented in Figure 11.

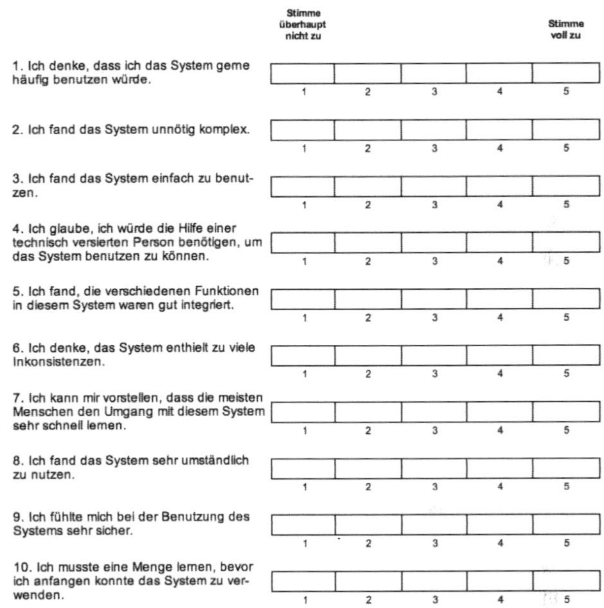

Figure 11. SUS questionnaire (German)

Keywords: questionnaire design, SUS, TAM, test theory, usability

IV. Discussion

Using the cUX pattern approach to create easy-to-use solutions, allowed us to adjust and improve the overall study concept and setup in several ways. Apart from that, we also acquired a deeper insight into the pattern creation process overall. This gave us a chance to notice certain weak points in the creation process, which, when improved, would help to generate better patterns. As mentioned at the end of Section 2, each iteration and the following rework phase, refines the pattern. The pattern is increasing in quality, with every feedback received during the iteration process. Bottom line, the more iterations processes a pattern runs through, the better it gets. In our case, we had a constant collaboration during the creation process of the patterns, which enabled us to get on demand feedback, if necessary. Due to active collaboration, we had the possibility of continuous iterations, allowing us to interplay between problem statements and solutions.

Usually, problem statements are defined in the beginning and changes can only be made during workshops. Solutions, however, are provided during the fist iteration, at the very earliest. Therefore, modifications can be made only after receiving feedback. Until then, the work on the pattern is on hold. The interplay showed us a huge advantage, due to the possibility to refine the problem statement, while at the same time, adjusting the solution. This induced the improvement of both the problem statement and the related solution leading to a higher quality pattern. The problem, however, was the recurring chance to rephrase the problem statement at any time. Thus, it was tempting to rephrase the problem statement to fit a certain solution, even when it was only covering a part of the statement. This behavior is not desired at all. Pattern are supposed to provide proven solutions. In the beginning, after describing the problem statements, we did not know if we could cover that criteria with our suggested solutions. However, we evaluated our patterns regarding that point, by trial and error. Each and every solution we provide in our patterns was tested before it was adopted into the patterns. This was, as well, only possible due to the interplay and instant feedback and, therefore, can not be applied in general. However, we found that this way of verification improved the provided solutions to a high degree.

The next point we want to discuss, is the use of a *Topics* section proposed by the cUX pattern approach. Topics, in this case, are predefined keywords, used to show scope of the problem and additionally, address one or more user experience factors. We willingly omitted that section, as we saw no need for them in our created patterns. Topics may be beneficial to organize a collection of patterns, providing a variety of solutions for a large main field. Each pattern can be assigned to at least one of the topics. However, in our case, we only had three problem statements that we wanted to address. Thus, creating a system in which we want to organize our patterns seemed unnecessary. Therefore, it was sufficient enough to provide keywords only at the end of the patterns. The keywords provide research topics and fields that may be related to the pattern and may be used to get more insight into certain areas covered or not sufficiently covered in the patterns.

V. CONCLUSION

This paper presents how patterns created by utilizing a slightly modified cUX patterns approach can be used to optimize a study setup for biometric image analysis. The pattern solutions were successfully used to optimize the study setup in question and document these for future applications. However, future work will have to focus on reapplying these patterns and refine them further, in order to provide more thorough solutions and to provide solutions, which have worked in more instances (i.e., as well-proven solutions, as should be the case for genuine patterns). The three patterns can be used to inform future study setups with solutions regarding (a) choice of the right lighting conditions, (b) construction of a custom lens holder, and (c) choice (and adaptation) of the right questionnaire for the study's purpose and research questions.

REFERENCES

[1] C. Alexander, "A Pattern Language: Towns, Buildings, Construction," Oxford University Press, New York, USA, 1997.

[2] C. Alexander, "The Timeless Way of Building," Oxford University Press, New York, USA, 1979.

[3] E. Gamma, R. Helm, R. Johnson, and J. Vlissides, "Design Patterns: Elements of Reusable Object-Oriented Software." Pearson, 1994.

[4] A. Dix, G. Abowd, R. Beale, and J. Finlay, "Human-Computer Interaction," Prentice Hall, Europe, 1998.

[5] M. J. Mahemoff and L. J. Johnston, "Principles for a Usability-Oriented Pattern Language," In Proc. Australian Computer Human Interaction Conference OZCHI98, IEEE Computer Society, 1998, pp. 132-139.

[6] D. May and P. Taylor, "Knowledge management with patterns," Commun. ACM 46, 7, July 2003, pp. 94-99.

[7] J. Borchers, "A Pattern Approach to Interaction Design," AI & Society, 12, Springer, 2001, pp. 359-376.

[8] A. F. Blackwell and S. Fincher, "PUX: Patterns of User Experience," Interactions, vol. 17, no. 2., NY, USA: ACM, 2010, pp. 27-31.

[9] M. Obrist, D. Wurhofer, E. Beck, A. Karahasanovic, and M. Tscheligi, "User experience (ux) patterns for audio-visual networked applications: Inspirations for design," in Proceedings of the 6th Nordic Conference on Human-Computer Interaction: Extending Boundaries, ser. NordiCHI 10. New York, NY, USA: ACM, 2010, pp. 343-352.

[10] A. G. Mirnig and M. Tscheligi, "Introducing a General Multi-Purpose Pattern Framework: Towards a Universal Pattern Approach," International Journal On Advances in Intelligent Systems, vol. 8, 2015, pp. 40-56.

[11] A. G. Mirnig et al., "User Experience Patterns from Scientific and Industry Knowledge: An Inclusive Pattern Approach," in PATTERNS 2015, Seventh International Conference on Pervasive Patterns and Applications. IARIA, 2015, pp. 38-44.

[12] Philips MASTER TL5 HO 49W/865 UNP/40 - Product Page. Available: http://bit.ly/2kDgmOV [Accessed: 11 - Jan - 2017]

[13] YouTube Video - Nexus 5 Lens Holder Case. Available: https://youtu.be/J3dParRRQJg [Accessed: 11 - Jan - 2017]

[14] J. P. Chin, V. A. Diehl, and K. L. Norman, "Development of an Instrument Measuring User Satisfaction of the Human-computer Interface," in Proceedings of the SIGCHI Conference on Human Factors in Computing Systems, New York, NY, USA, 1988, pp. 213218.

[15] F. D. Davis, "Perceived Usefulness, Perceived Ease of Use, and User Acceptance of Information Technology," MIS Q., vol. 13, no. 3, pp. 319340, Sep. 1989.

[16] F. D. Davis, R. P. Bagozzi, and P. R. Warshaw, "User Acceptance of Computer Technology: A Comparison of Two Theoretical Models," Manage. Sci., vol. 35, no. 8, pp. 9821003, Aug. 1989.

[17] J. Nielsen, Usability Engineering. San Francisco, CA, USA: Morgan Kaufmann Publishers Inc., 1993.

[18] J. R. Lewis, "IBM Computer Usability Satisfaction Questionnaires: Psychometric Evaluation and Instructions for Use," Int. J. Hum.-Comput. Interact., vol. 7, no. 1, pp. 5778, Jan. 1995.

[19] G. Perlman, "Practical Usability Evaluation," in CHI 97 Extended Abstracts on Human Factors in Computing Systems, New York, NY, USA, 1997, pp. 168-169.

[20] H. X. Lin, Y.-Y. Choong, and G. Salvendy, "A proposed index of usability: a method for comparing the relative usability of different software systems," Behaviour & information technology, vol. 16, no. 45, pp. 267277, 1997.

[21] J. Brooke, "SUS-A quick and dirty usability scale," Usability evaluation in industry, vol. 189, no. 194, pp. 47, 1996.

[22] D. Wilfinger, M. Pirker, R. Bernhaupt, and M. Tscheligi, "Evaluating and Investigating an iTV Interaction Concept in the Field," in Proceedings of the Seventh European Conference on European Interactive Television Conference, New York, NY, USA, 2009, pp. 175178.

[23] Venkatesh, M. G. Morris, G. B. Davis, and F. D. Davis, "User Acceptance of Information Technology: Toward a Unified View," MIS Q., vol. 27, no. 3, pp. 425478, Sep. 2003.

Patterns as Formulas:

Patterns in the Digital Humanities

Johanna Barzen and Frank Leymann
Institute of Architecture of Application Systems
University of Stuttgart
Stuttgart, Germany
e-mail: {barzen, leymann}@iaas.uni-stuttgart.de

Abstract—**During the last years, in particular due to the Digital Humanities, empirical processes, data capturing or data analysis got more and more popular as part of humanities research. In this paper, we want to show that even the complete scientific method of natural science can be applied in the humanities. By applying the scientific method to the humanities, certain kinds of problems can be solved in a confirmable and replicable manner. In particular, we will argue that patterns may be perceived as the analogon to formulas in natural science. This may provide a new way of representing solution-oriented knowledge in the humanities.**

Keywords-pattern; pattern languages; digital humanities; formalisation.

I. INTRODUCTION

A fundamental aspect of the scientific method (i.e., the method of the natural sciences) is repeatability. Repeatability allows to gain two key goals of research: objectivity and solvability.

Repeatability is the basis for verifiability of research results. Verifiability allows to establish objectivity in the sense of not having to rely on trusted authorities (i.e., well-accepted domain experts) expressing their subjective insights as research results. As a consequence, everybody can re-enact and track the way a research result has been achieved.

Often, a research result itself that has been obtained by applying the scientific method has an aspect of repeatability too. A corresponding result is represented as a procedure to solve recurring problems of a certain kind. Such a result is often expressed as a formula, and the solvability of the problem is achieved by applying this formula.

Also, the humanities, in particular the Digital Humanities [1], have domains in which objectivity and solvability (in the sense stated above) are important goals. As shown in the following, the scientific method may be applied in such domains to achieve both, verifiability of results as well as results that have a "solution character".

First, in Section II, we give evidence that the concept of patterns is a proper vehicle to establish the solvability facet of research results in the humanities. Second, in Section III, we show that applying the scientific method in data intensive domains of the humanities establishes the objectivity facet of research results. Section IV concludes the paper.

II. PATTERN AS FORMULAS

Solving problems in natural sciences by means of formulas is in close analogy to using patterns in other domains like architecture [2] or software engineering [3][4], for example. Applying a formula means to follow a certain proceeding: identifying the intent to solve a specific problem, determining the solution sketch and apply it to the actual context of the problem to be solved to result in the concrete solution of the problem.

A. Example: How to Solve Quadratic Equations

Assume that one has the **intent** to solve the problem of determining the roots of the following quadratic equation (1):

$$x^2 + 5x + 4 = 0 \tag{1}$$

What is done first is to consult a formulary to find the **sketch** of how to solve arbitrary quadratic equations $ax^2 + bx + c = 0$ and the quadratic formula (2)

$$x_{1,2} = \frac{-b \pm \sqrt{b^2 - 4ac}}{2a} \tag{2}$$

for solving (1) is found, i.e., for determining the roots x_1 and x_2.

Next, the ***context*** of the problem to solve the specific equation $x^2+5x+4=0$ needs to be determined, i.e., the actual coefficients (3) of the concrete equation have to be determined:

$$a=1,\ b=5,\ c=4 \tag{3}$$

After understanding the sketch and the context, the corresponding quadratic formula (2) and the actual coefficients (3) have to be combined, i.e., the coefficients a, b, c in the quadratic formula (1) have to be substituted by the actual values $a=1$, $b=5$, and $c=4$. Together, the ***solution*** description (4) of the problem has been determined:

$$x_{1,2} = \frac{-5 \pm \sqrt{5^2 - 4 \cdot 1 \cdot 4}}{2 \cdot 1} \tag{4}$$

This results in the ***concrete solution*** of the original problem, i.e., the roots of the quadratic equation (1), see (5):

$$x_1=-1,\ x_2=-4 \qquad (5)$$

B. Using a Formula Means Applying a Pattern

This proceeding of determining the roots of a quadratic equation can be described by a document that follows the template of a pattern (as introduced in [2][3][4]): First, a pattern has a name that uniquely identifies the **problem** to be solved. Second, it specifies the **intent** of solving the particular problem (e.g. finding the roots of a quadratic equation). Then, it describes in a **sketch** how to solve the problem (i.e., the quadratic formula). Next, it lays out how to determine the **context** in which the solution can be applied. Finally, the **solution** works out how the before-mentioned information is put together to solve the problem. Figure 1 depicts these elements of the corresponding pattern document (where the context-section and the solution-section are combined). Note, that these ingredients of the pattern document make use of only the essentials of a pattern template: pattern languages typically capture more information [2][3][4].

C. Example: Solving a Costume Design Problem

Patterns are used in different domains in the humanities. But the term "pattern" is often rather problematic because of the different meanings it refers to [5]. But used in the sense introduced by C. Alexander [2], patterns are a convincing tool to capture knowledge and make this knowledge easily accessible. In the MUSE (MUSE - MUster Suchen und Erkennen, engl.: pattern search and identification) project [6], patterns are used to document solutions of costume design problems in films.

This project is about solving a problem from the humanities (more specifically from the media studies), namely proving the existence of a costume language and providing such a costume language for several genres. The individual costumes found are documented as patterns (see Figure 2); note, that the pattern content shown is just an example and not yet a verified pattern.

As before, the pattern document begins with the name of the problem. It describes the intent of solving the problem. The sketch presents the essentials of the solution, and the context describes the circumstances of applying the solution. Finally, the solution discusses in details how the costume is built – in this case, a figure depicts all the primitives of the costume and the order in which they are worn.

By following the pattern, a solution to a certain costume design problem is constructed: just like following the pattern for solving quadratic equations. Thus, using patterns in the humanities to express research results brings the power of applying formulas to the humanities, i.e., it establishes the solvability facet of research result in the humanities.

III. THE SCIENTIFIC METHOD

In a nutshell (and admitting, this is a very simplified view), the scientific method consists of the following steps [7][8]: observation, data capture, data analysis, and formalization (or abstraction).

An *observation* can be based on planned experiments, systematically watching phenomena in nature etc. Often, observations are caused by a hypothesis resulting from theoretical reasoning. *Data capturing* refers to the stringent logging of information resulting from observations. *Data analysis* takes a close look to the captured data in order to find regularities. By means of *abstraction* or *formalization* found regularities are finally expressed as laws or formulas.

Problem	**Determine the roots of a quadratic equation**
Intent	The quadratic function $f(x) = ax^2 + bx + c$ is given and you want to determine its roots x_1, x_2, i.e. values such that $f(x_1)=0$ and $f(x_2)=0$.
Sketch	The roots x_1, x_2, are computed by the quadratic formula: $x_{1,2} = \frac{-b \pm \sqrt{b^2-4ac}}{2a}$
Context & Solution	The actual values of the coefficients a, b, c must be determined from the concrete quadratic equation to be solved. The corresponding variables of the quadratic formula must be substituted by these values. The first root x_1 is computed by using „+", and the second root x_2 is computed by using „-" in the quadratic formula.

Figure 1. Using a Formula as Applying a Pattern

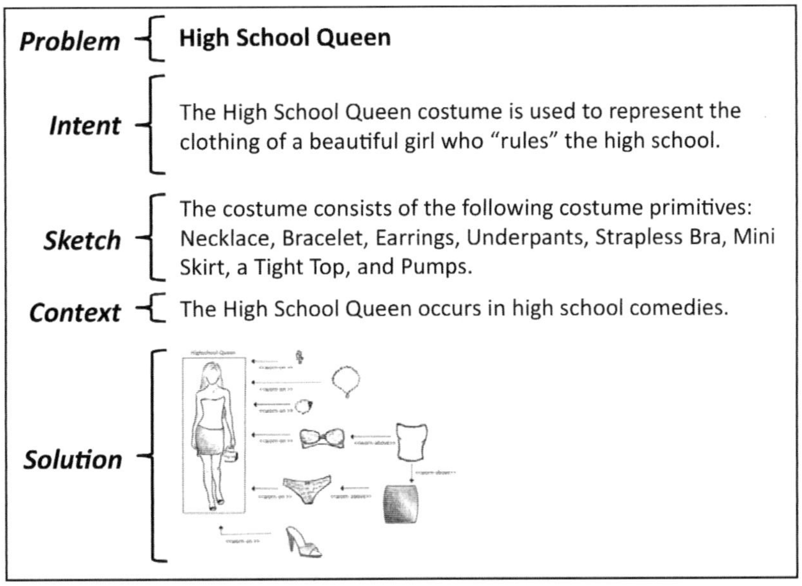

Figure 2. A Costume Described by a Pattern

A. Example: Determining Planetary Motion

Historically, Tycho Brahe observed celestial positions of planets (especially Mars) and captured the corresponding data in logs [9]. Johannes Kepler analyzed this data [9] and inferred Kepler's Laws of planetary motions [10]. For example, the first Kepler Law is: "The orbit of each planet is an ellipse with the sun in one of its foci." Kepler also formalized his laws, i.e., he abstracted his laws as mathematical formulas. The first Kepler Law, for example, is formalized as (6)

$$r = \frac{p}{1 + \varepsilon \cos\theta} \tag{6}$$

Thus, as Figure 3 depicts, the discovery of Kepler's Laws of planetary motions follows the proceeding of the scientific method sketched above: observation, data capture, data analysis, and formalization (or abstraction).

B. Example: Determining Costume Languages

The problem of determining costume languages has been described in [11]. In [12], a method (called the MUSE Method) has been described for deriving costume languages. This method is a refinement of the (simplified) scientific method sketched in Figure 3: The left-hand side of Figure 4 shows the MUSE method as described in [12] (ignoring aspects not relevant in the context of this paper), the right-hand side shows the scientific method, and the correspondence between steps in the MUSE method and steps in the scientific method are indicated as arrows.

In the MUSE method, characters of a film corpus are identified. This is done by watching the corresponding films – which means that observation is taking place. While watching the films, the cloths of the identified characters are described – which is data capturing. Based on the captured data about clothes, costumes are identified – which is data analysis. Identified costumes are then abstracted into patterns – which can be considered as formalization as argued above.

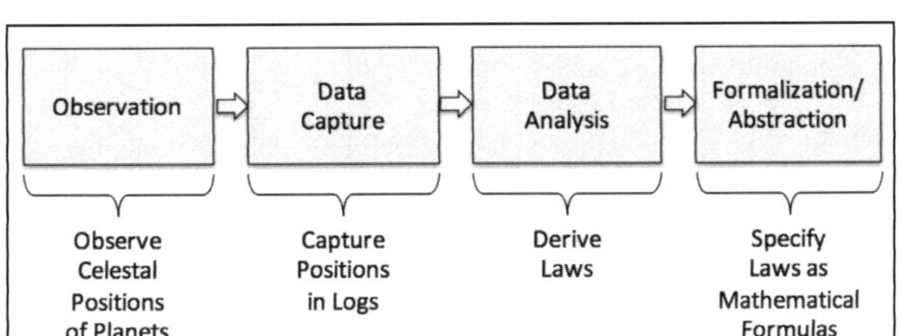

Figure 3. Principle Proceeding in Deriving Kepler's Laws

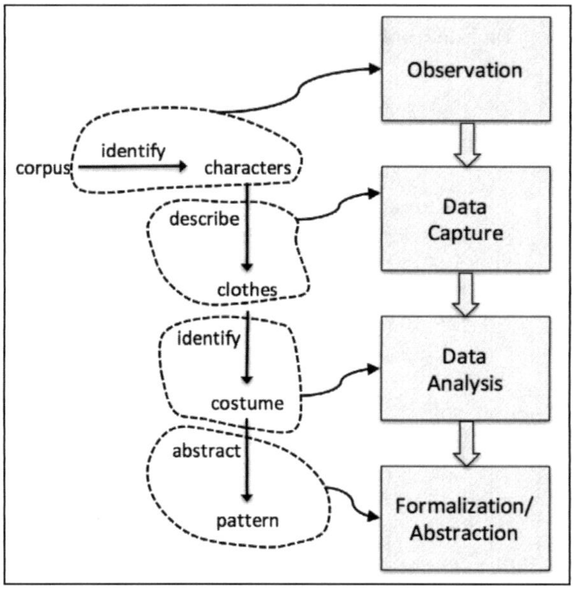

Figure 4. The MUSE Method as Scientific Method

An overall software system that supports the MUSE method has been build, and that system is applied in the domain of film studies in the humanities [13]. In particular, the discovery of costume languages is supported. This system allows to describe films, their characters and the cloths of the characters via a graphical user interface and stores this data in a database. The structure of this database as well as the domains of its central attributes are modeled by taxonomies and ontologies [12][14]. The analysis of the data is supported by means of data warehouse and OLAP (Online Analytical Processing) technologies [15], as well as by means data mining technologies [16]. The representation of the abstracted patterns and their relations (i.e., the resulting pattern language) is stored in a pattern repository [13].

The software system can be used to verify research results, thus, contributing to objectivity: Everybody can browse the captured data to assess its quality; the captured data can be analyzed over and over again to confirm the discovered regularities within the cloths of the films; the patterns reference the costumes they have been abstracted from, which support to track the abstraction of similar cloths to costume patterns. The latter, by the way, does also contribute to solvability: a pattern does not only describe abstractly the structure of a certain costume but also provides a set of concrete cloths to realize this costume.

Formalization in MUSE goes even beyond describing research results as patterns. Cloths themselves as well as their constituents are considered as words of formal languages [12]. This allows, for example, to check whether newly discovered cloths are in an already established tradition.

IV. Conclusion and Outlook

This brief contribution argued in favor of applying the scientific method in the humanities. In doing so, repeatability of research results – especially the facets of objectivity and solvability – will be emphasized. Patterns have been presented as an analogon to formulas as an integral part of the scientific method.

It has been shown how the scientific method has been applied in the film studies. The scientific method in general, and the MUSE method in particular is currently being applied in musicology [17] - in an effort called MUSE4Music.

There are important implications of applying the scientific method to domains or in ways it has not been established for, and these implications are independent from the fact whether the scientific method is applied in the humanities or in natural sciences. In order to ensure repeatability, the data as well as the algorithms used to analyze this data to achieve the results must be published [18]. This is by far not yet widely accepted because the data and algorithms are often considered proprietary or a "production secrete" for achieving research results. This is an obstruction that has to be overcome.

Note

This paper has been pre-published as a technical report of University Stuttgart no. 2016/01.

References

[1] A. Burdik, J. Drucker, P. Lunenfeld, T. Presner, and J. Schnapp, "Digital_Humanities" Cambridge/London: The MIT PRESS, 2012.

[2] C. Alexander, "The Timeless Way of Building," New York: Oxford University Press, 1979.

[3] G. Hohpe and B. Woolf, "Enterprise Integration Patterns," Addison-Wesley, 2004.

[4] C. Fehling, F. Leymann, R. Retter, W. Schupeckand, and P. Arbitter, "Cloud Computing Patterns," Wien: Springer, 2014.

[5] D. Dixon, "Analysis Tool or Research Methodology: Is There An Epistemology for Patterns?" in D. Berry (ed.): Understanding Digital Humanities, Pilgrave Macmillan 2012, pp. 191-209.

[6] Available from: http://www.iaas.uni-stuttgart.de/forschung/projects/MUSE/indexE.php

[7] S. Charey, "A Beginners Guide to Scientific Method" (4th Edition) Boston: Wadsworth, 2011.

[8] T. Hey, S. Tansley, and K. Tolle (Ed.), "The Fourth Paradigm: Data-Intensive Scientific Discovery" Microsoft Research 2009.

[9] F. Hund, "Geschichte der physikalischen Begriffe (engl. History of physical terms)," Mannheim: Bibliographisches Institut, 1972.

[10] M. Schneider, "Himmelsmechanik (engl. Celestial Mechanics)," Mannheim: Bibliographisches Institut, 1981.

[11] D. Schumm, J. Barzen, F. Leymann, and L. Ellrich, "A Pattern Language for Costumes in Films" Proceedings of the 17th European Conference on Pattern Languages of Programs (EuroPLoP), pp. C4-1–C4-30, 2012. Available from: http://www.europlop.net/sites/default/files/files/proceedings/EuroPLoP2012_companion_proceedings.pdf 2017.01.28

[12] J. Barzen and F. Leymann, "Costume Languages As Pattern Languages" in Proceedings of Pursuit of Pattern Languages for Societal Change (PURPLSOC) - Preparatory Workshop, Krems: epubli GmbH, pp. 88-117, 2014.

[13] C. Fehling, J. Barzen, M. Falkenthal, and F. Leymann, "PatternPedia - Collaborative Pattern Identification and Authoring" in Proceedings of Pursuit of Pattern Languages for Societal Change (PURPLSOC) - Preparatory Workshop, Krems: epubli GmbH, pp. 252-305, 2014.

[14] J. Barzen, "Taxonomien kostümrelevanter Parameter: Annäherung an eine Ontologisierung der Domäne des Filmkostüms (engl. Taxonomies of costume relevant parameters: approaching an ontology of the domain of the film costume)," University Stuttgart, Technical Report 2013/04, 2013. Available from: ftp://ftp.informatik.uni-stuttgart.de/pub/library/ncstrl.ustuttgart_fi/TR-2013-04/TR-2013-04.pdf 2017.01.28

[15] M. Falkenthal et al, "Datenanalyse in den Digital Humanities – Eine Annäherung an Kostümmuster mittels OLAP Cubes (engl. Data analysis in Digital Humanities - an approach to costume patterns using OLAP Cubes)," in Proceedings Datenbanksysteme für Business, Technologie und Web (BTW 2015), Bonn: Lecture Notes in Informatics, pp.663-666, 2015.

[16] M. Falkenthal et al, "Pattern Research in the Digital Humanities: How Data Mining Techniques Support the Identification of Costume Patterns" Computer Science - Research and Development, Vol. 22 (74), Heidelberg: Springer, 2016, DOI 10.1007/s00450-016-0331-6.

[17] J. Barzen et al., "The vision for MUSE4Music. Applying the MUSE method in musicology", Computer Science - Research and Development, Vol. 22 (74), Heidelberg: Springer, 2016, DOI 10.1007/s00450-016-0336-1.

[18] F. Leymann, "Linked Compute Units and Linked Experiments: Using Topology and Orchestration Technology for Flexible Support of Scientific Applications" Software Service and Application Engineering – LNCS7365, Springer, pp. 71-80, 2012.

Declarative vs. Imperative: Two Modeling Patterns for the Automated Deployment of Applications

Christian Endres[1], Uwe Breitenbücher[1], Michael Falkenthal[1], Oliver Kopp[2], Frank Leymann[1], and Johannes Wettinger[1]
[1]IAAS, [2]IPVS, University of Stuttgart, Stuttgart, Germany
Email:{lastname}@iaas.uni-stuttgart.de

Abstract—**In the field of cloud computing, the automated deployment of applications is of vital importance and supported by diverse management technologies. However, currently there is no systematic knowledge collection that points out commonalities, capabilities, and differences of these approaches. This paper aims at identifying common modeling principles employed by technologies to create automatically executable models that describe the deployment of applications. We discuss two fundamental approaches for modeling the automated deployment of applications: imperative procedural models and declarative models. For these two approaches, we identified (i) basic pattern primitives and (ii) documented these approaches as patterns that point out frequently occurring problems in certain contexts including proven modeling solutions. The introduced patterns foster the understanding of common application deployment concepts, are validated regarding their occurrence in established state-of-the-art technologies, and enable the transfer of that knowledge.**

Keywords–Modeling Patterns; Application Deployment and Management; Automation; Cloud Computing.

I. INTRODUCTION

Many cloud service offerings, for example, Infrastructure as a Service (IaaS) and Platform as a Service (PaaS) offerings, and established management technologies, such as *IBM Bluemix* [1], *Chef* [2], and *Juju* [3], support the automated deployment of applications. There are also standards, for example, the *Topology and Orchestration Specification for Cloud Applications* (TOSCA) [4]. All promise high automation, reusability, and easy usage in order to operate business functionality. Contrary, using the aforementioned technologies requires that the customer describes the deployment of the application according to the languages, capabilities, and requirements of the used technology. But, all have in common that they support the same deployment automation principles that can be divided into two major modeling approaches: the *declarative* and the *imperative* deployment modeling approach.

The declarative approach uses structural models that describe the desired application structure and state, which are interpreted by a deployment engine to enforce this state. The imperative approach uses procedural models that explicitly specify a process to be executed [5][6]. These imperative process models define explicitly all activities that have to be executed, their execution order, and the data flow between these activities. Such imperative process models are executed in an automated manner by a process engine. Using the imperative approach, the customer can customize arbitrarily the deployment but typically requires considerably more expertise, for example, if multiple different cloud provider application programming interfaces (APIs) have to be invoked [5][7].

However, technologies following these approaches significantly differ in the employed domain-specific modeling languages and concepts. Whilst all technologies advertise the revolution of deploying and managing business functionality in the Cloud, up to now, there is no systematic knowledge collection that guides in choosing the right technology. As a result, for evaluating which technology fits best the customer's needs, at the moment, one has to be an expert of each considered technology for choosing the most appropriate one.

In this paper, we tackle these issues by investigating the capabilities of established deployment technologies in order to document their commonalities in the form of patterns. In particular, we investigate (i) the Cloud standard *TOSCA*, (ii) the technologies *IBM Bluemix*, (iii) *Chef*, (iv) *Juju*, and (v) *OpenTOSCA* [8], (vi) the implementations of the most downloaded artifacts in the official repositories of Chef [9] and Juju [10], and (vii) scientific publications. The chosen technologies are among the most utilized and established ones that enable application deployment in modern cloud environments that inherently require a high degree of automation. However, we do not claim that this list of analyzed technologies is complete, but nevertheless, it provides an appropriate starting point for finding new patterns that possibly occur within other approaches, standards, and technologies as well.

To overcome the problem of modeling application deployment and evaluating the best fitting technology at the same time, we first introduce pattern primitives to establish a common wording. Then, we describe the underlying deployment modeling concepts supported by the analyzed artifacts, management technologies, and scientific publications in form of the *Imperative Deployment Model* pattern and the *Declarative Deployment Model* pattern. To validate our findings, we apply Coplien's *Rule of Three* that dictates a pattern to exist in at least "*three insightfully different implementations*" [11]. Thus, we state how and where to find the pattern's implementation to prove the "Rule of Three". Using these patterns, the knowledge about application deployment principles can be transferred, e.g., , for choosing the most appropriate technology.

The remainder of this paper is structured as follows: In Section II, we define pattern primitives with which we establish a common wording for describing application deployment technologies. In Section III, we introduce the Imperative Deployment Model pattern and the Declarative Deployment Model pattern and point to their occurrences. In Section IV, we discuss the background of the paper and the related work of the pattern community and cloud computing community. In Section V, we validate our patterns. Finally, in Section VI, we conclude the results of this paper and outline future work.

II. Pattern Primitives

In this section, we define *pattern primitives* that are identified as atomic parts in the domain of application deployment. Similar to Zdun et al. [12] and Fehling et al. [13], we use the concept of pattern primitives to describe certain elements inside patterns that have specific names and characteristics. These elements are known to domain experts and may exist in other domains under different names. Thus, this section aims to establish a common wording for a precise communication and to describe the patterns we introduce in the next section.

Application: An *application* comprises software that implements a certain business functionality. Applications typically consist of multiple *software components* that are working together to realize the desired functionality. The interplay of the components may be locally or realized via network, i.e., the collaboration of components can be arbitrarily complex.

Software component: A *software component* is a part of an application that may be reused within the same application, other applications, or other companies. Components can be divided into either *application-specific software components* and *general-purpose software components*, see next.

Application-specific software component: An *application-specific software component* is a piece of software that implements a certain piece of the business functionality of an application. Such a component is highly adapted for and integrated into a certain application and implements specific functionality. Thus, application-specific components often cannot be reused within other applications due to their specialization. One example for such components are customized enterprise resource planning software components.

General-purpose software component: A *general-purpose software component* is a piece of software that implements a functionality that can be reused by many different applications for general purposes. Thus, they are explicitly made for reuse and provide common functionality that is independent of a certain business logic. Examples for such components are web servers or database management systems.

Application environment: The term *application environment* comprises all running software and hardware components of one concrete deployment of the application on all layers, i.e., physical servers, virtual machines running on these servers, operating systems, installed web servers, etc. Thus, if a certain application is deployed multiple times in different clouds, each of these deployments forms one application environment.

Management environment: In contrast to the application environment, in which an application is running in, the term *management environment* comprises all physical components, such as servers and software components, that are employed for running *deployment & management systems*, see next.

Deployment & management system: A *deployment & management system* provides the functionality for deploying, operating, and managing applications in an automated fashion, e.g., to install, configure, or terminate applications or an application's components. Deployment & management systems are running in management environments and, therefore, are typically running and operated independently from applications. There are many different flavors of deployment & management systems: Some interpret declarative models that define the structure of the desired application deployment, others are based on imperative process models that define each step that has to be executed to realize a certain deployment task, e.g., to install the entire application. We detail these two flavors in the following sections in the form of the patterns we present.

Deployment logic: The *deployment logic* describes all steps that have to be executed to deploy all components of an application. To implement the deployment logic, different levels of abstractions can be differentiated depending on the chosen form of implementation. For example, a workflow may be created that specifies a set of *deployment tasks* and their execution order while *deployment operations* implement these deployment tasks. We detail this in the following primitives.

Deployment task: A *deployment task* denotes the task of deploying a certain software component, for example, installing and configuring an Apache web server on a running Ubuntu virtual machine. To implement a deployment task in a way that enables its automated execution, typically multiple *deployment operations* have to be executed, see next.

Deployment operation: A *deployment operation* is an automatically executable piece of software that implements a certain deployment functionality, for example, to install a software package on an operating system or to configure the HTTP-port. Thus, typically multiple deployment operations are required to execute a deployment task. Deployment operations can be implemented using various kinds of technologies, for example, in the form of scripts that are executed in the application environment to install a web server on a running virtual machine or as Java programs that are executed in the management environment to orchestrate a set of API calls.

III. Patterns for Modeling the Automated Deployment of Applications

In this section, we introduce the *Imperative Deployment Model* pattern and the *Declarative Deployment Model* pattern that describe two different flavors for modeling the deployment of applications. The main purpose of applying these *modeling patterns* is to create models that can be executed automatically to deploy a certain application. Thus, the introduced patterns help to avoid manual steps executed by humans, which is mandatorily required in the domain of cloud computing, where rapid application deployment is of vital importance.

The patterns are structured to comprise information that are derived from best practices in the pattern community [11][14]-[19]: Each pattern has a *name* and a catchy *icon* to foster memorability. The *problem* statement defines the obstacle to overcome. The *context* describes the circumstances under which the problem occurs. Subsequent, the *forces* describe why the problem is not trivial to solve and why basic approaches might fail. The *solution* describes the approach of how to solve the problem. The solution is accompanied by a *solution sketch* that depicts the solution. The *results* outline the outcomes of applying an implementation of the pattern. Proven occurrences of the pattern are referenced in the *know uses*. Therefore, we show that the patterns presented in this section satisfy the *Rule of Three* [11] that instructs that at least three independent implementations of the concepts described by the pattern have to be found, cf. Section VI.

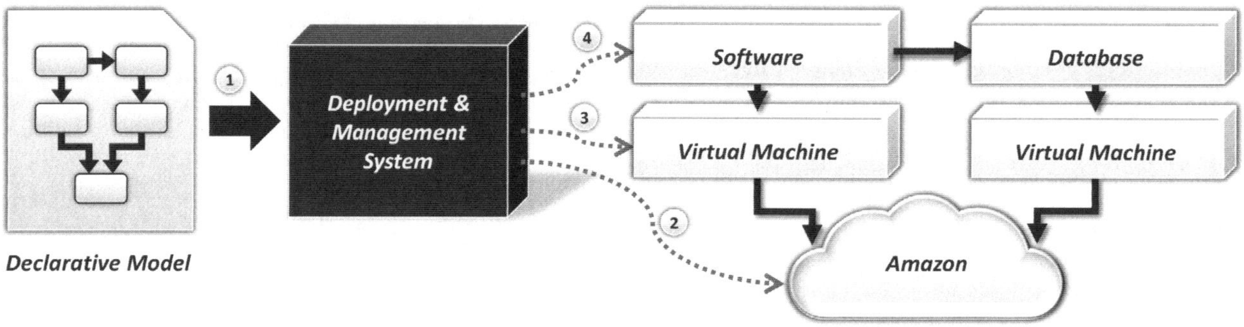

FIGURE 1. SOLUTION SKETCH FOR THE DECLARATIVE DEPLOYMENT MODEL PATTERN: A DECLARATIVE MODEL IS INTERPRETED FOR DEPLOYING A SOFTWARE IN THE AMAZON CLOUD, I.E., PROVISIONING A VM, INSTALLING SOFTWARE, AND WIRING THAT SOFTWARE WITH A RUNNING DATABASE.

A. *Declarative Deployment Model Pattern*

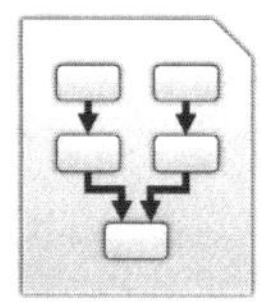

Problem: How to model the deployment of a simple application that requires only few or no individual customization in a way that enables its automated execution?

Context: Automate the deployment of an application.

Forces: Typically, applications comprise well-known, general-purpose software components, e.g., virtual machines running a Ubuntu, a Tomcat application server, or a MySQL server, for realizing common functionality. Such components are heavily used in industry, so they are often integrated and, as a result, it is well-known how to use them. However, a manual installation and configuration of such components is error-prone, time-consuming, and costly [7]. Thus, this is not appropriate in scenarios requiring the rapid deployment of applications and their components—especially if multiple instances of the application need to be deployed, which is a common requirement in the domain of cloud computing.

To automate this, imperative process execution technologies, such as scripts or the workflow technology [20], can be used. However, manually creating executable process models that automatically deploy the entire application is also complex and time-consuming [5]. Thus, for simple scenarios that employ common, reusable components, such as a Linux; Apache web server; MySQL database management server; or PHP, and that follow well-known application structures, spending this effort is very hard to argue and should be avoided.

Solution: Create a *declarative deployment model* that describes the structure of the application that shall be deployed, i.e., all the components as well as their dependencies and interplay. Subsequent, use a deployment & management system that understands this model and that automatically executes all required steps to deploy the application as described by the model. Declarative deployment models also specify necessary software implementations, e.g., the user interface implementation of a web application to be deployed. By modeling the deployment this way, the desired state of the application is defined, which provides the basis for the deployment & management system to automatically derive the necessary deployment tasks and operations to be executed. Thus, the system derives and executes the deployment logic automatically from the declarative model without involving the user. Systems that support this pattern are, e.g., Chef and Juju.

Figure 1 depicts the pattern's solution sketch. The declarative deployment model specifies the application structure, its components, and their interplay. The model (1) is passed to the deployment & management system that derives the required deployment logic from this model and executes all required tasks and operations. In this example, it (2) invokes the API of Amazon to create a virtual machine (VM), (3) accesses the VM to install required software packages, and (4) configures the software to connect to the installed database. Thus, the system creates the prescriptively modeled application in reality.

Results: Applying the pattern eases application deployment as no manual deployment steps are required and only a model has to be created. Moreover, the required technical skills are limited to the modeling of the declarative model. Since the pattern is primarily applicable to deployments that mainly comprise general-purpose components, which are well-known to deployment & management systems, the usage of these components is efficient and not costly as they only must be specified in the model. Moreover, by providing implementations for interfaces defined by the deployment & management system, also application-specific software components can be deployed automatically, for example, by referencing an script that installs a custom application-specific software component.

Known Uses: In Bluemix, an *App* can be described declaratively in the *manifest.yml* file containing information about the used *build pack*, amount of the App instances, and with which other *services* the App shall be bound [21]. Bluemix *boilerplates* are predefined application containers that consist of runtime environments and predefined services for a distinct purpose that can be adapted with various options, e.g., the database size [22]. Chef enables to model declaratively *cookbooks*, defining the structure by importing other cookbooks, adapting by specifying *attributes*, letting *chef-client* compile the *run-list*—the sequences of operations to execute—, and gather further requirements, e.g., other cookbooks, files, or attributes. Subsequent, the chef-client configures the virtual machine according the run-list [23]. Juju supports *bundles* describing services, their interplay, and configuration that can be provisioned without defining the distinct provisioning [24]. TOSCA enables modeling declaratively the application's structure with *Topology Templates* [4], [6]. Out of these declarative models, the imperative provisioning logic is generated [5]. The scientific deployment prototype *Engage* also enables to describe application structures for automated deployment [25].

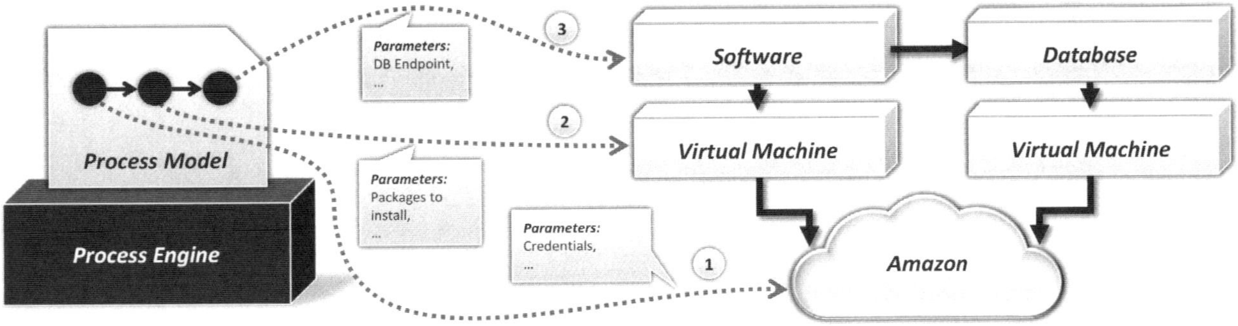

FIGURE 2. SOLUTION SKETCH FOR THE IMPERATIVE DEPLOYMENT MODEL PATTERN: A PROCESS MODEL IS EXECUTED FOR DEPLOYING A SOFTWARE IN THE AMAZON CLOUD, I.E., PROVISIONING A VM, INSTALLING SOFTWARE, AND WIRING THAT SOFTWARE WITH A RUNNING DATABASE.

B. Imperative Deployment Model Pattern

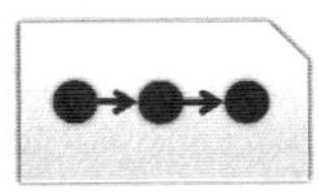

Problem: How to model the deployment of a complex application that requires application-specific customization in a way that enables its automated execution?

Context: Automate the deployment of an application.

Forces: The deployment of complex business applications that consist of various application-specific software components with complex dependencies and configurations is a serious challenge: Multiple experts have to cooperate as a significant amount of technical expertise is required and typically multiple different deployment & management systems need to be combined [7]. Thus, if an application needs to be deployed multiple times, a manual process is not possible.

Using the Declarative Deployment Model pattern is appropriate for modeling the deployment of simple applications that mainly employ general-purpose components. However, for such complex applications as described above, this pattern cannot be applied as the interpretation of declarative models in deployment & management systems cannot be influenced and customized arbitrarily [5]. Especially, when multiple deployment & management systems need to be combined, a single declarative deployment model is not possible.

Solution: Create an *imperative deployment model* that describes (i) all activities to be executed, (ii) the control flow, i.e., their execution order, and (iii) the data flow between them. Each activity implements a certain deployment task or invokes a deployment operation, e.g., an activity invokes the API of a cloud provider to provision a new virtual machine and subsequent activities copy and execute installation scripts onto this VM. Afterwards, use a *process engine* to execute the model automatically without involving the user. One robust technology for creating and executing processes is, e.g., the workflow technology [20] and standards, such as BPEL [26].

Figure 2 depicts the pattern's solution sketch. The process model is deployed on an appropriate process engine and (1) invokes the API of Amazon to create a virtual machine, (2) accesses it, e.g., via SSH, to install software packages, and (3) configures the installed software to connect to a running database that is also hosted on Amazon. Thus, if customization is required, any activity can be arbitrarily customized to invoke suitable deployment operations or other implementations.

Results: By using imperative deployment models, i.e., process models, the deployment can be modeled arbitrarily as each step to execute is specified explicitly. Thus, the model is not interpreted as in the Declarative Deployment Model pattern but executed following the model. This enables deploying general-purpose components as well as arbitrary application-specific components that require complex configurations and wirings with other components. Thus, this approach is capable of handling the complexity of arbitrary application deployments. Contrary, the deployment of such complex applications often cannot be modeled declaratively at all due to application-specific details that cannot be reflected in declarative models.

Especially the workflow technology is suited for creating complex process models as also the modeling of compensation logic is possible [27], [20]. For example, if a deployment process provisions multiple virtual machines and a failure occurs, simply stopping the process requires a manual deletion of the created VMs. By using compensation and failure handling, such cases can be explicitly considered in the process model. However, the modeling of imperative deployment logic is typically more complex for the user: With the Imperative Deployment Model pattern, a process model has to be created that explicitly defines each deployment operation to be invoked and, thus, required deep technical knowledge about the invocation and orchestration of management technologies [7]. However, this is addressed by approaches for generating such process models [5][7][28]-[31]. Moreover, there are workflow languages, such as BPMN4TOSCA [32][33], that were developed explicitly for modeling such processes.

Known Uses: For provisioning a service with Bluemix, imperative scripts can invoke depoyment tasks using the command line interface *cf* [34]. Chef-client executes the imperative *run-list* that, usually, is generated [35]. But if necessary, the run-list can be customized, e.g., by adding additional *recipes* whose actions implement deployment tasks [36]. Juju implements *hooks* that represent executable deployment tasks and are invoked in case of *events* [37]. For more direct interaction, *Actions* can be invoked with parameters to execute deployment operations [38]. TOSCA enables explicitly imperative provisioning: workflow models can be attached to services that implement the provisioning imperatively [4], [6]. The TOSCA runtime environment OpenTOSCA contains a generator for BPEL workflows that allows to generate provisioning plans that can be customized individually for certain needs [5][39].

IV. Related Work and Management Technologies

In 1979, Alexander et al. started to publish their idea to describe solutions for reoccurring problems in the domain of building architecture as patterns [15][40]. Since then, this approach has been heavily used, refined, and also been applied to the domain of IT. For example, for software developers, the principles of good object-oriented software design is captured as the patterns of the Gang of Four [16]. To foster the pattern paradigm for computer science, Buschmann et al. advanced patterns by finding patterns in the domain of IT as well as publishing their lessons learned about patterns and pattern languages [14][17]. Coplien contributed by delimiting patterns from mere copies. His *Rule of Three* states that a solution has to be implemented independently at least three times for being able to provide a base for a pattern [11].

To establish a better association between the abstract patterns and concrete pattern implementations, Falkenthal et al. introduces *Solution Implementations* that help to aggregate pattern appliances for problems that need applying multiple patterns [41][42]. Thus, these works can be used to efficiently reuse proven (declarative or imperative) deployment models as Solution Implementations of the introduced patterns.

Fehling et al. introduced patterns about how to automate certain deployment tasks in cloud computing, e.g., how to realize an elastic application [43]. Also, Fehling et al. captured reoccurring problems of migrating services to the cloud as patterns the same way [44]. The patterns' solutions are documented in the form of abstract process models that can be refined for concrete use cases. Using this approach, also proven deployment processes could be documented in an abstract manner as patterns, which are then instances of the Imperative Deployment Model pattern presented in this paper.

The methods used for findings the patterns introduced in this paper are based on the iterative approaches of how to find and author concrete patterns, introduced by Fehling et al. [13] and Reiners [18]. Wellhausen et al. introduced a concrete pattern structure, described in detail the interrelation of the pattern structure's distinct sections, and provided a step-by-step guide for improving the formulation of patterns and helping first-time authors to concisely express their patterns [19].

In 2013, the *Topology and Orchestration Specification for Cloud Applications* (TOSCA) was published in version 1.0 [4]. TOSCA explicitly supports both deployment flavors by allowing modeling application topologies and specifying workflow models for deployment. Thus, the academic open-source prototype OpenTOSCA implements the TOSCA standard and, therefore, supports both patterns [39][8]. Since years, there are established technologies as well as recently emerging ones that help putting business functionality into the cloud. For example, there are IBM Bluemix [1], Chef [2], and Juju [3] that all support declarative as well as imperative mechanisms at different points in application deployment.

V. Validation

In this paper, we discussed pattern primitives in the domain of cloud application deployment and introduced two patterns describing fundamental principles of modeling the automated deployment of applications. In this section, we discuss the process of how we found the patterns and their validity.

Table I. Occurrence of the patterns in the technologies [45]

Occurrence	Imperative Deployment Model	Declarative Deployment Model
Bluemix	✓	✓
Chef	✓	✓
Juju	✓	✓
OpenTOSCA	✓	✓
Others	✓	✓

Usually in the pattern community, experts of a domain search for pattern candidates, discuss, and dismiss and refine them until only patterns are left. This process is very costly in time and effort. Therefore, an alternative approach distills pattern candidates and patterns from artifacts, e.g., documentation [13]. These resources can be treated as the documentation of expertise of developers and scientists. Thus, we selected a variety of application deployment approaches and technologies that are omnipresent in industry and science, their documentations, implementations of the most downloaded artifacts in their official repositories, and scientific publications as a basis for our knowledge collection. Based on the found commonalities, we elaborated the patterns iteratively according to [13]. The proposed patterns are validated regarding their occurrence. In Table I, we marked found evidences for each pattern with a ✓symbol. The row *Others* encompasses scientific publications and their prototypes. The enumeration of evidences bases partly on [45]. The concrete references to the evidences can be found in the *known uses* paragraph of the respective pattern. The *Rule of Three* states the condition of three independent occurrences of the pattern in the real world [11]. Both the Declarative Deployment Model pattern and the Imperative Deployment Model pattern fulfill this condition.

VI. Conclusion and Future Work

In this paper, we presented two modeling patterns that describe principles of modeling the deployment of applications and provide a deeper understanding of the declarative and imperative approaches. By stating details of the analyzed technologies, the patterns also foster the understanding of the analyzed standard and technologies. We proved that the documented patterns occur in many state-of-the-art deployment technologies, especially, the TOSCA standard explicitly supports both patterns. We validated the patterns by stating (i) in which artifact, documentation, standard, and technology an individual implementation of the pattern can be found and (ii) that the common pattern metric *Rule of Three* [11] is met. Thus, the defined pattern primitives and found patterns provide a means for communicating the principles in general.

The proposed Declarative Deployment Model pattern and Imperative Deployment Model pattern are the beginning of a catalog of patterns. Thus, more patterns in the domain of application deployment can be found, for example, to document proven solutions for creating imperative deployment process models. Further, the catalog can be elaborated to a full pattern language that will be addressed in our upcoming research steps. We also plan to author another kind of related patterns for the domain of application management.

Acknowledgments

This work is partially funded by the BMWi projects *NEMAR* (03ET4018B) and *SePiA.Pro* (01MD16013F).

REFERENCES

[1] "IBM Bluemix – Cloud infrastructure, platform services, Watson, & more PaaS solutions," 2017, URL: https://www.ibm.com/cloud-computing/bluemix/ [accessed: 2017-02-02].

[2] "Chef – Embrace DevOps | Chef," 2017, URL: https://www.chef.io/ [accessed: 2017-02-02].

[3] "Jujucharms | Juju," 2017, URL: https://jujucharms.com/ [accessed: 2017-02-02].

[4] OASIS, Topology and Orchestration Specification for Cloud Applications (TOSCA) Version 1.0, Organization for the Advancement of Structured Information Standards (OASIS), 2013.

[5] U. Breitenbücher et al., "Combining Declarative and Imperative Cloud Application Provisioning based on TOSCA," in International Conference on Cloud Engineering (IC2E 2014). IEEE, 2014, pp. 87–96.

[6] OASIS, Topology and Orchestration Specification for Cloud Applications (TOSCA) Primer Version 1.0, Organization for the Advancement of Structured Information Standards (OASIS), 2013.

[7] U. Breitenbücher, T. Binz, O. Kopp, F. Leymann, and J. Wettinger, "Integrated Cloud Application Provisioning: Interconnecting Service-Centric and Script-Centric Management Technologies," in On the Move to Meaningful Internet Systems: OTM 2013 Conferences (CoopIS 2013). Springer, 2013, pp. 130–148.

[8] "OpenTOSCA Ecosystem," 2017, URL: http://www.opentosca.org/ [accessed: 2017-02-02].

[9] "Welcome – The resource for Chef cookbooks – Chef Supermarket," 2017, URL: https://supermarket.chef.io/ [accessed: 2017-02-02].

[10] "Store | Juju," 2017, URL: https://jujucharms.com/store/ [accessed: 2017-02-02].

[11] J. O. Coplien, Software Patterns. SIGS Books & Multimedia, 1996.

[12] U. Zdun and P. Avgeriou, "A catalog of architectural primitives for modeling architectural patterns," Information and Software Technology, vol. 50, no. 9, 2008, pp. 1003–1034.

[13] C. Fehling, J. Barzen, U. Breitenbücher, and F. Leymann, "A Process for Pattern Identification, Authoring, and Application," in Proceedings of the 19th European Conference on Pattern Languages of Programs (EuroPLoP 2014). ACM, 2014.

[14] F. Buschmann, K. Henney, and D. Schimdt, Pattern-Oriented Software Architecture, Volume 5: On Patterns and Pattern Languages. Wiley, 2007.

[15] C. Alexander, S. Ishikawa, and M. Silverstein, A Pattern Language: Towns, Buildings, Construction. Oxford University Press, 1977.

[16] E. Gamma, R. Helm, R. Johnson, and J. Vlissides, Design Patterns: Elements of Reusable Object-oriented Software. Addison-Wesley, 1994.

[17] F. Buschmann, R. Meunier, H. Rohnert, P. Sommerlad, and M. Stal, Pattern-Oriented Software Architecture, Volume 1: A System of Patterns. Wiley, 1996.

[18] R. Reiners, "An Evolving Pattern Library for Collaborative Project Documentation," Ph.D. dissertation, RWTH Aachen University, 2013.

[19] T. Wellhausen and A. Fiesser, "How to Write a Pattern?: A Rough Guide for First-time Pattern Authors," in Proceedings of the 16th European Conference on Pattern Languages of Programs (EuroPLoP 2011). ACM, 2012.

[20] F. Leymann and D. Roller, Production Workflow: Concepts and Techniques. Prentice Hall PTR, 2000.

[21] "Deploying apps," 2017, URL: https://www.ng.bluemix.net/docs/manageapps/depapps.html [accessed: 2017-02-02].

[22] "Boilerplates," 2017, URL: https://www.ng.bluemix.net/docs/cfapps/boilerplates.html [accessed: 2017-02-02].

[23] "About Nodes – Chef Docs," 2017, URL: https://docs.chef.io/nodes.html [accessed: 2017-02-02].

[24] "Using and Creating Bundles | Documentation | Juju," 2017, URL: https://jujucharms.com/docs/stable/charms-bundles [accessed: 2017-02-02].

[25] J. Fischer, R. Majumdar, and S. Esmaeilsabzali, "Engage: A Deployment Management System," in ACM SIGPLAN Notices. ACM, 2012, pp. 263–274.

[26] OASIS, Web Services Business Process Execution Language (WS-BPEL) Version 2.0, Organization for the Advancement of Structured Information Standards (OASIS), 2007.

[27] F. Leymann and D. Roller, "Building A Robust Workflow Management System With Persistent Queues and Stored Procedures," in Proceedings of the Fourteenth International Conference on Data Engineering (ICDE). IEEE, 1998, pp. 254–258.

[28] U. Breitenbücher, T. Binz, O. Kopp, and F. Leymann, "Pattern-based Runtime Management of Composite Cloud Applications," in Proceedings of the 3rd International Conference on Cloud Computing and Services Science (CLOSER 2013). SciTePress, 2013, pp. 475–482.

[29] T. Eilam, M. Elder, A. V. Konstantinou, and E. Snible, "Pattern-based Composite Application Deployment," in Proceedings of the 12th IFIP/IEEE International Symposium on Integrated Network Management (IM 2011). IEEE, 2011, pp. 217–224.

[30] K. El Maghraoui, A. Meghranjani, T. Eilam, M. Kalantar, and A. Konstantinou, "Model Driven Provisioning: Bridging the Gap Between Declarative Object Models and Procedural Provisioning Tools," in Proceedings of the 7th International Middleware Conference (Middleware 2006). Springer, 2006, pp. 404–423.

[31] R. Mietzner, "A Method and Implementation to Define and Provision Variable Composite Applications, and its Usage in Cloud Computing," Ph.D. dissertation, Universitt Stuttgart, Fakultät Informatik, Elektrotechnik und Informationstechnik, 2010.

[32] O. Kopp, T. Binz, U. Breitenbücher, and F. Leymann, "BPMN4TOSCA: A Domain-Specific Language to Model Management Plans for Composite Applications," in Proceedings of the 4th International Workshop on the Business Process Model and Notation. Springer, 2012, pp. 38–52.

[33] O. Kopp, T. Binz, U. Breitenbücher, F. Leymann, and T. Michelbach, "A Domain-Specific Modeling Tool to Model Management Plans for Composite Applications," in Proceedings of the 7th Central European Workshop on Services and their Composition, ZEUS 2015. CEUR Workshop Proceedings, 2015, pp. 51–54.

[34] "CLI- und Dev-Tools," 2017, URL: https://console.ng.bluemix.net/docs/cli/index.html#cli [accessed: 2017-02-02].

[35] "About Run-lists – Chef Docs," 2017, URL: https://docs.chef.io/run_lists.html [accessed: 2017-02-02].

[36] "About Recipes – Chef Docs," 2017, URL: https://docs.chef.io/recipes.html [accessed: 2017-02-02].

[37] "Charm hooks | Documentation | Juju," 2017, URL: https://jujucharms.com/docs/stable/authors-charm-hooks [accessed: 2017-02-02].

[38] "Implementing actions in Juju charms | Documentation | Juju," 2017, URL: https://jujucharms.com/docs/stable/authors-charm-actions [accessed: 2017-02-02].

[39] T. Binz et al., "OpenTOSCA – A Runtime for TOSCA-based Cloud Applications," in Proceedings of the 11th International Conference on Service-Oriented Computing (ICSOC 2013). Springer, 2013, pp. 692–695.

[40] C. Alexander, The Timeless Way of Building. Oxford University Press, 1979.

[41] M. Falkenthal, J. Barzen, U. Breitenbücher, C. Fehling, and F. Leymann, "From Pattern Languages to Solution Implementations," in Proceedings of the Sixth International Conferences on Pervasive Patterns and Applications (PATTERNS 2014). Xpert Publishing Services, 2014, pp. 710–726.

[42] ——, "Efficient Pattern Application: Validating the Concept of Solution Implementations in Different Domains," International Journal On Advances in Software, vol. 7, no. 3&4, 2014, pp. 710–726.

[43] C. Fehling, F. Leymann, J. Rütschlin, and D. Schumm, "Pattern-Based Development and Management of Cloud Applications," Future Internet, vol. 4, no. 1, 2012, pp. 110–141.

[44] C. Fehling, F. Leymann, S. T. Ruehl, M. Rudek, and S. Verclas, "Service Migration Patterns – Decision Support and Best Practices for the Migration of Existing Service-based Applications to Cloud Environments," in Proceedings of the 6th IEEE International Conference on Service Oriented Computing and Applications (SOCA 2013). IEEE, 2013, pp. 9–16.

[45] C. Endres, "A Pattern Language for Modelling the Provisioning of Applications," Master's thesis, University of Stuttgart, 2015.

Towards Scenario-based Discovery of Domain-Specific Patterns: a Case Study

Philips Huysmans

Antwerp Management School
Antwerp, Belgium
Email: philip.huysmans@ams.ac.be

Jan Verelst and Gilles Oorts

Normalized Systems Institute
University of Antwerp, Belgium
Email: {jan.verelst,gilles.oorts}@uantwerp.be

Abstract—**The lack and need of prescriptive design knowledge in enterprise architectures is well documented. While knowledge of various disciplines that are part of enterprise architectures is captured in principles or patterns, no integration of this knowledge is available. In order to work towards such knowledge documentation, we propose an inductive documentation of domain-specific patterns. These patterns can be observed by analyzing different design alternatives, and evaluating them against qualitative criteria, such as evolvability. In this paper, we present a method to systematically analyze and document design alternatives in a domain, building on scenario-based architecture evaluation methods. A case study is presented in which the proposed method is applied. Based on the findings of this method, domain-specific enterprise architecture patterns can be proposed in future research.**

Keywords–Modularity; Patterns; Design Structure Matrices.

I. INTRODUCTION

It has been argued that the wealth of nations relates with their ability to deal with economic complexity [1]. In this perspective, the best performing countries are not the countries with the highest qualities of inputs, but those which use the recombinational potential of already available inputs to create more diverse and complex products. Growth predictions are based on the ability to create different outputs by adding a few inputs to the current production capabilities, rather than the more classical focus of measuring how much value is added to raw materials or intermediate products. As an example, agricultural efforts in a developed versus a developing country can be differentiated based on the ability to integrate with a logistics network, a supply network, a knowledge network, a financial network, etc.

This promise of exponential growth by leveraging the recombination potential is well described by combinatorics theory. In practice however, the drawbacks of combinatorics are more easily observable than its advantages. Changes to any artefact result in ripple effects, causing more changes than anticipated. As a result, change becomes complex and expensive. In dynamic markets, change requirements occur at a frequency which prevents organizations to consider change as an adaption of a steady state, but necessitates the application of changes at a constant pace. As a result, products and services, and their combinations, increase in complexity, which again limits the possibility to reap the benefits of the recombination potential because of the ripple effects.

Prescriptive solutions which prevent these ripple effects are available in various disciplines. The idea of applying patterns to codify design knowledge is widespread in software architecture. In business process modeling, modularization patterns are described by e.g., [2]. On the management level, modularity and coupling are studied as well [3], and certain patterns are described there as well [4]. In practice however, organizations have to design artifacts in each of these disciplines (i.e., an organizational structure performing certain processes which are supported by software systems). Put differently, the design knowledge of these different disciplines needs to be combined and integrated. The field of enterprise architecture has these disciplines in scope. However, the lack of deterministic design in each of these separate disciplines demonstrates the difficulty and complexity of performing such a design in an integrated way. Unsurprisingly, few patterns are known in the field of enterprise architecture.

Rather than attempting to solve the integration of design knowledge of different disciplines in general, we believe a more feasible approach is to start with the documentation of domain-specific patterns. A domain has its key challenges, similar artifacts, and similar integration issues. This limitation of scope can make the documentation of design knowledge more focused, and hence, more feasible in the short term.

In this paper, we therefore present a method which was used to systematically research couplings between artifacts on the organizational, process and Information Technology (IT) level of different organizations in a certain domain. This method is based on scenario-based analysis methods. These methods propose to compare different architectures by evaluating how well they support certain scenarios. By documenting relevant domain-specific changes as scenarios, we can systematically research which designs are susceptible to ripple effects in various change scenarios. We use design structure matrices to document the modular couplings (which cause ripple effects) between artifacts. Different design alternatives can then be documented and, if sufficient scenarios are tested, be proposed as design patterns for that specific domain.

In Section II, we introduce the building blocks of the method. In Section III, we present the designed method. Section IV demonstrates the method by applying it to three different organizations in the hospital sector. Finally, we discuss our findings in Section V.

II. METHOD BUILDING BLOCKS

A. Scenario-based methods

In order to compare and gain insight in different architectural solutions, a scenario-based approach for decision making can be adopted [5]. The Software Architecture Analysis Method (SAAM) enables the usage of scenarios on a software level [6]. Various approaches have already elaborated on SAAM, such as the Architecture Tradeoff Analysis Method (ATAM) [7] and the Architecture-Level Modifiability Analysis (ALMA) [8]. SAAM is the simplest of the software evaluation methods. While various methods extended SAAM with other elements, these additions clearly focused on the evaluation of software architectures. The basic structure of SAAM is sufficient for our approach. SAAM itself enables the expression of different quality claims of software architectures such as, amongst others, modifiability, exibility, and maintainability. The realization of these quality claims in a certain software architecture is then evaluated using scenarios. SAAM consists of six main steps, which are generally preceded by an overview of the business context and the functional requirements of the system.

We are not the first to adopt SAAM in a context that is different from software. For example, in the paper "Characterization of Enterprise Architecture Quality Attributes" [9], the authors clearly state the use of the work of Bass et al [10] regarding software architectures, software quality attributes and scenarios as a basis. Moreover, it has been argued that scenario-based methods can be applied in any field where modifiability is a concern [11][12].

B. Enterprise Architecture

Enterprise architectures present an overview of strategic goals and organizational and technical artifacts of an organization, in order to manage the challenges of change and complexity. Enterprise architects mainly aim to reduce the complexity by creating abstractions from real-world artifacts by creating models [13]. These models are grouped in architectural levels or layers. Different enterprise architecture frameworks propose different layers, or require that organizations define their own sets of layers [14][15][16]. It has been argued that most publications on enterprise architectures report on contributions which can be located on a single layer, while few authors address integrating multiple layers [17]. A modeling approach for documenting coupling across different layers is usually not proposed in the various frameworks. As such, a complementary documentation model for these cross-layer couplings needs to be adopted.

C. Design Structure Matrices

The modularity paradigm provides tools and models which allow an explicit focus on modular dependencies. Recently, organizational modularity has gained much attention in research and practice [3]. In this paradigm, it is argued that product, processes and organizational structures can be regarded as modular structures. Moreover, certain authors claim that modularization on, for example, the product level drives modularization on other levels as well. This is referred to as the mirroring hypothesis [18]. While we do not explicitly use this hypothesis, it indicates how modularity can be used as a way to analyze the integration of different architectural layers. By adhering to the modularity paradigm, we can use theories and tools which apply modularity in our proposed method.

More specifically, we will adopt Design Structure Matrices (DSM), which were heavily used by Baldwin and Clark. DSMs provide an accepted and well-defined notation to represent architectural components and interfaces [19][20]. They are used in traditional modularity approaches (e.g., product modularity) to visualize dependencies between and within modules. A modular dependency occurs when a change to an aspect of a module could require changes to other aspects, within that module or in other modules.

III. Resulting Method

The six steps of SAAM will be used as the general outline of our method. The first step (i.e., develop scenarios) is identical to the original method, with the exception of the different nature of the selected scenarios (i.e., on the enterprise architecture level instead of on the software level). A scenario can be viewed as a brief description of a stakeholder's interaction with the system [6].

For the second step (i.e., describe the architecture), we propose the use of a design structure matrix (DSM). The different architectural layers (e.g., organizational, process and IT layers) can be conceptualized as different modular structures, and coupling between modules of different layers can be documented as modular dependencies.

In the third step, SAAM advises to classify and prioritize the scenarios. For each scenario, it needs to be determined on which layer of the DSM (as constructed in step 2) it requires a direct functional change. The scenario will then be positioned as a design element in one of the modules. For example, a scenario indicating a technological change should be placed in the IT module. In contrast, a scenario indicating a reorganization should be placed on the organization module.

In the fourth step, SAAM advises to individually evaluate the indirect scenarios. However, ripple effects can be present in direct scenarios as well. The presence of a ripple effect in a direct scenario would mean that while the architecture supports the scenario in its current form, it could require increasing adaptations once the organization needs to scale. Therefore, an architecture which does not contain ripple effects for direct scenarios will be preferable to an architecture which does contain ripple effects for direct scenarios. Consequently, we advise to include an evaluation of the direct scenarios as well. For each of the scenarios, any design parameter which will be affected by the implementation of the scenario needs to be considered. These design parameters are then added to the DSM. It should be noted that these design parameters can be positioned on other layers than the original scenario. This step already creates awareness for the analyst to take all organizational aspects into account when evaluating scenarios. An "x" should be added in the intersection of the column of the scenario and the row of the design parameters that this scenario affects.

In the fifth step, SAAM advises to assess the scenario interaction. In our approach, this requires the completion of the DSM. For every intersection, a possible dependency needs to be evaluated. Newly found dependencies should be indicated with an "x". This allows for a detailed and systematic evaluation of interactions between previously unknown scenarios or design parameters. However, the DSM can become too complex to be used as a basis to communicate. Especially the identification of chained dependencies can become complicated.

In the sixth step, SAAM advises to perform an overall evaluation. Using the dependency chains identified in step five, insight in architectural issues can be communicated easily to involved stakeholders. The developed artifact can contribute to a systematic approach to identify, communicate, and create awareness concerning design choices. A comparison of different design alternatives can create pattern candidates, which can be further evaluated qualitatively.

IV. Case Study: Application to the Hospital Domain

For this demonstration, the hospital sector was selected. The selection was motivated by the dynamic nature of the sector, and the similarity of organizational size of the prominent players. Large variations in size could have an impact on preference for certain architectural characteristics. Overall, three cases were conducted, which consisted of at least two in-depth interviews and additional review questions through email. The case participants were selected based on business experience and knowledge regarding the high-level IT architecture.

1) Step 1: Identify scenarios: The first step was performed by organizing brainstorm sessions. After an initial draft of the scenarios, their relevance was checked by discussing them with stakeholders from the other cases. The respondents agreed that the resulting set of scenarios either (1) were likely to occur in the near future, or (2) had an important impact on their organization in the past.

- Scenario 1: **Changing risiv code**: the risiv code is an identification number for a governmental entity related to sick leave and invalidity insurance. Each investigation or procedure performed in a hospital needs to append such an identification number to determine the reimbursement level of medical costs to the patient. Changes in legislation can change which code needs to be attributed to a certain procedure, or can change the coding scheme as a whole.
- Scenario 2: **New medical cabinet supplier**: In most hospitals, a decentralized supply of medicines is used. The medical cabinets are managed using an IT system which is integrated with the purchasing system. Moreover, the medicine usage of every patient is registered and charged individually. Consequently, no medicine may be retrieved without patient identification.
- Scenario 3: **Introduction of a new medical specialization**: Especially in academic hospitals, new research can result in improved methods or even new specializations. In order to support these activities, integration with existing systems and procedures need to be constructed, as well as new artifacts specific to the new medical activities.
- Scenario 4: **Changes in the patient registration process**: During emergencies, regular registration or consultation, patients need to register before being treated. A file is kept for each patient to be able to consult previous procedures or treatments. During registration, data from identification cards (regular id or medical id) needs to be extracted.
- Scenario 5: **Changes in the patient classification system**: Patients are classified for various purposes. In many hospitals, the type of registration impacts the invoicing and reimbursement procedures.
- Scenario 6: **Changes in the procedure classification system**: In most hospitals, a wide variety of clinical procedures (1000+) can be performed. The classification code for a procedure is used during communication with, for example, the sterilization department, which prepares the correct set of tools and delivers them to the operation room. However, this classification is also used in other contexts, such as communication in professional journals, which uses a possibly different and international classification scheme. Especially in academic hospitals, much discussion regarding the selection of a certain classification system are reported.
- Scenario 7: **Opening a new site**: The final scenario attempts to reflect on the scalability of the current architectures. While no functional changes to existing systems are required, duplication of existing systems, information and positions greatly increase the complexity of the organization as a whole. Nevertheless, the current mergers and push towards centralization in the sector resulted in an agreement on the importance of this scenario by all participants.

2) Step 2: Describe the architecture: Currently, none of the organizations has a documentation of their architecture. One organization has started an enterprise architecture program based on the lack of flexibility and presence of integration issues. After educating several employees, it was concluded that the required documentation and formalization, combined with the changes which require an effort to keep the models up-to-date, resulted in too much effort. Moreover, management was not convinced of the relevance of the resulting documentation.

All three organizations have two main organizational entities: an administrative and a medical entity. Both entities have separate staff and separate IT systems. A distinction between the organizations can be made based on the academic or general nature of the organization. Moreover, a distinctive characteristic is the mode of employment: medical staff can be directly employed by the hospital, or operate independently. Beyond administrative differences, this distinction impacts the sharing of information and the preference for the selection of software packages.

3) Step 3: Classify and prioritize scenarios: In this step, the scenarios need to be classified in the different architectural layers. Scenarios 2 (new medical cabinet supplier - stakeholder management), 3 (introduction of a new medical specialization - business model), and 7 (opening a new site - value clusters) are strategic in nature and can therefore be positioned in the organizational layer. Scenarios 1 (changing risiv code), 5 (changes in the patient classification system), and 6 (changes in the procedure classification system) reflected mainly organizational changes as well, and are therefore classified as such. Scenario 4 (changes in the patient registration process) is considered as mainly a process change.

When asked to position the scenarios as direct or indirect, our respondents indicated that only the scenario 1 (changing the risiv code) could be considered a direct scenario. For the other changes, changes to the current architecture would be required. The prioritization of scenarios was not elaborated upon, since this would only impact the selection of a pattern. Currently, this research focuses on the identification of modular couplings to motivate the selection of certain design alternatives. The formulation of actual patterns is too ambitious for the current cases.

4) Step 4: Evaluate the scenarios: In this step, the scenarios are evaluated. During this step, the DSM should be filled. An example DSM for this case in presented in Figure 1.

a) Scenario 1: Changing risiv code: Only a single hospital claimed that this scenario could be supported directly, because the risiv codes are linked to the procedures by a centralized invoicing department. The doctors of various departments do not need to be involved with changes or new legal requirements. The other hospitals employed both directly employed and independent doctors. As a result, multiple applications were needed to register billable activities. For certain departments, activities are registered and managed by an invoicing department, while other departments interface directly with the invoicing application. A change in risiv code can therefore affect one, two, or many applications, based on the design alternative employed.

b) Scenario 2: New medical cabinet supplier: The systems supporting medical cabinets from different suppliers use various patient identification codes. In the first case hospital, a different (internal) patient identification code syntax was used, and personnel had to convert the code formats manually. In order to remedy this situation in the future, the hospital will include its own patient identification code syntax as a requirement during cabinet acquisition. A new medical cabinet supplier would then result in the integration of a new external application in the application landscape, but have no impact on the manual (and time-consuming) processes. As such, a design rule for this dependency will be created.

In the second case hospital, a supplier switch was made recently. The design rule for the patient identification code syntax was imposed here as well. Moreover, the external software provided an application programming interface, which allowed integration with the pharmacy order administration and patient administration. A specialized message bus (HL7) was used to make this integration.

In the third case hospital, no experience with this change was present, and no design rules have been formulated to guide a future acquisition process.

c) Scenario 3: Introduction of a new medical specialization: Our respondents indicated that the most impactful change for incorporating a new medical specialization is the development and integration of new software applications. The organizational impacts of adding new processes and assigning locations are well-known. In contrast, previous integration experiences have caused several maintenance issues. In the first and second case hospitals, this has led to the use of a middleware bus (HL7). In the second case hospital, no architectural solution for integrating new applications is present.

d) Scenario 4: Changes in the patient registration process: The increased adoption of electronic IDs has resulted in registration process improvements. However, the effort required to implement these improvements varied across the hospitals.

In the first case hospital, the registration procedure is mainly centralized. Three different registration desks are available, which each handle the same registrations and use the same processes. They are responsible for all registrations.

In contrast, the second case hospital has a combination of centralized and decentralized registration desks. Changes to the procedures followed by registration desks need to be implemented in many different places. An example is the introduction of regional hubs: each hospital will need to integrate with such a hub, so doctors with a therapeutic relationship with the patients have a central repository. Since information from all registration desks will need to be included, every desk is impacted.

In the third case hospital, a combination of centralized and decentralized registration desks is used as well. The resulting complexity has led to a specific organizational role which is created to manage the process of distributing work across registration desks.

e) Scenario 5: Changes in the patient classification system: In the second case hospital, patients are categorized in a classification system during registration. This classification is the input for the invoicing process. Because of evolving structure of the classification structure, a re-ordering effort took place to simplify the structure. However, this initiative was halted since the changes to the invoicing applications proved to be too complex. The third case hospital reported similar issues, and noted that the impacts of changing their classification system would impact additional processes and applications.

In contrast, the first case hospital did not use a patient classification scheme, because the invoicing department bases its processing on the raw data of the procedures performed and medicines used. As such, the invoicing process has less dependencies on derived data.

f) Scenario 6: Changes in the procedure classification system: The third case hospital reports a vast impact of changes in procedure classifications. Soon, a new version of the official classification scheme is expected. This scheme describes the treatments, diagnoses and procedures performed which need to be reported to the government. Currently, a team of 10 employees has the full-time job of determining correct classification codes based on the data of the medical file and the lab results. Changes to the reporting scheme are expected to result in retraining and data changes.

As an example of the impact, we mention the interface between the surgical and sterilization departments. The surgical department needs to communicate its need for sterilization of tools. In the fist case hospital, a classification for the tools is known in the surgical department, and is linked to the procedure classification scheme. In the second case hospital, instead of using tools classification to communicate, the procedure classification scheme is used.

This distinction shows the difference in impact of scenario 6: based on the way of communicating, different departments will be impacted. In general, three possibilities are observed for mapping data between the classification schemes: performed by the surgical department (case 1), in the sterilization department (case 3), or shared on the HL7 bus (case 2). It should be noted that the mapping of data on the HL7 bus introduces business knowledge on the integration bus.

g) scenario 7: Opening a new site: The scenario of opening an extra site allows to reflect of the scalability of the organization as a whole. It does not require new module types, only additional instances of existing ones. Nevertheless, much of the infrastructure is currently not designed to handle such scaling: for example, the data structure of the reference lists of patients of a certain hospital service would have to be redesigned, since only patients from that service on the current site should be included. Moreover, handling of permissions to applications and data would need to include awareness of the different sites. In the third case hospital, this scenario was compared to the future merger with another hospital. Currently, efforts to standardize patient administration processes and employee relations are in progress, in order to bring the merger closer to the scenario of opening a new site. However, the impact on governance structures and organizational culture demonstrate that the impact of these changes is outside the scope of the current approach.

5) Step 5: Assess scenario interaction: In discussion with the respondents, additional dependencies not directly related to scenario interactions were analyzed next, and added to the DSM in Figure 1. This information is crucial to estimate the size of ripple effects, since this documents knowledge which is distributed in the organization. For example, the applications dependent of the syntax of patient identification needed to be gathered from the different application owners, since no centralized knowledge regarding this impact was present. The interviews show that the scheduling application was impacted in case 1, the invoicing application was impacted in all cases, the operation management application was impacted in case 2, and the integration on the HL7 bus was impacted in cases 2 and 3. Moreover, dependencies between scenarios, such as changing the patient classification system and changing the enrollment process can be identified. These dependencies are crucial for detecting chained dependencies. The resulting complexity of the model can be addressed by generating dependency chains that only focus on design parameters relevant during a certain analysis.

6) Step 6: Perform overall evaluation: In order to propose domain-specific patterns based on the (absence of) identified couplings, a comparison of the change impacts in the different designs needs to be made.

As a first observation, the centralization of registration desks increases the flexibility of the first case hospital. Changes in patient registration procedures can be implemented in one or a few desks, without integration issues with other desks.

A second example where centralization benefits the flexibility is scenario 1. In both the first and third case hospital, the procedures of all doctors are administered in the invoicing system directly. In the second case hospitals, doctors use multiple systems. As a result, changes in for example the risiv codes need to be applied in 1 (case 1 and 3) or n (case 2) applications.

Another observation is the application of design rules. In cases one and two, a design rule for the patient identification code syntax is created, which enables better functional integrations.

In contrast, certain design choices only shift the responsibility for handling a certain change. In scenario 6, it was discussed how the interface between surgical and sterilization departments requires either one or the other department to implement a change in the procedure classification system.

Finally, a remarkable difference was observed in relation to scenario 5 (changes in the patient classification system). In the second and third case hospital, the invoicing process is based on the patient classification, which can be considered as derived data: the classification combines different patient characteristics which result in a similar invoicing category at a certain point in time. However, changes in how certain procedures need to be invoiced will not always be distinguishable in the category classification. This issue has already resulted in manual data tracking. In contrast, the first case hospital bases its invoicing process on raw data. As a result, a direct traceability exists between the invoiced amount and the billable items.

V. Conclusion

The discussion above demonstrates that general engineering insights can be applied directly to a set of relevant domain changes. As such, the generalization of design solutions for domain-specific artefacts which adhere to certain quality characteristic, such as flexibility, should be pursued. While we do not argue that the number of modular dependencies should be considered as a hard quantitative metric, the absence of dependencies, combined with the prioritization of scenarios, enables a rational argument for a certain design to be proposed as a pattern.

While the current research does not yet propose concrete patterns, several contributions to the applied methods can be claimed. A set of open issues in the SAAM method has been identified by [21]. Amongst others, it is argued that SAAM lacks a clear quality metric for architectural attributes, that architecture descriptions are fuzzy notions without a standardized notation, and that SAAM limits itself to the listing of the different steps, omitting to provide techniques to actually perform the steps. Some of these remarks are addressed in this project. For the enterprise architecture field, a clear lack of prescriptive solution has been reported [22]. The elimination of modular couplings in the DSM could lead to such a set of domain-specific principles.

The current state of this research contains various limitations, which align well with the limitations of other scenario-based methods discussed by [8]. First, they argued that the information needed to make fundamental modifiability-related decisions is not necessarily available in documentation. We acknowledge that the determination of, for example, the attributes in the DSM remains largely dependent on the knowledge and experience of the stakeholders. Second, Lassing et al. argue that the actual evolution of a system remains to a large extent unpredictable. As a result, one cannot expect that the list of scenarios is complete, or that every scenario will be implemented. This remains true in our approach. However, the scenarios are first and foremost the means to an end: namely to provide a starting point to discover modular dependencies Third, architectural changes often concern complex components, and this complexity might not be known at the architecture level. In our approach, the granularity of the modules is very coarse. Capturing all complexities and interactions would require a very large DSM. Different techniques might need to be explored to fulfill this role.

References

[1] R. Hausmann, C. A. Hidalgo, S. Bustos, M. Coscia, A. Simoes, and M. A. Yldrm, The Atlas of Economic Complexity: Mapping Paths to Prosperity. MIT Press, 2013.

[2] A. Jalali, "Aspect-oriented business process management," Ph.D. dissertation, Stockholm University, 2016. [Online]. Available: https://su.diva-portal.org/smash/get/diva2:1044437/FULLTEXT01.pdf

	New medical cabinet supplier (S)	**Introduction new medical specialization (S)**	**Opening a new site (S)**	**Changing risiv code (S)**	Education personnel	Amount of experts needed for integration	**Changes in the patient classification system (S)**	**Changes in the procedure classification system (S)**	Tool classification	Flexibility personnel	Amount of registration desks	**Changes in the patient registration process (S)**	Amount of versions patient identification process	Patient identification process	Application choise	Patient identification data	Amount of applications	Integration application and HL7 bus	Amount of applications involved in integration process	Invoicing module	Integration operation room and sterilization	Operation room system	Appointment system	Sterilization system	Extra data entity 'site'	Permissions
New medical cabinet supplier (S)																										
Introduction new medical specialization (S)																										
Opening extra site (S)																										
Changing risiv code (S)																										
Education personnel							1,2					1,2,3		1,2,3	1,2,3											
Amount of experts needed for integration																			1,2							
Changes in the patient classification system (S)											1,2															
Changes in the procedure classification system (S)																										
Tool classification																										
Flexibility personnel													1,2,3				1,2,3									
Amount of registration desks		1,2																								
Changes in the patient registration process (S)											1,2,3					1,2,3										
Amount of versions patient identification process															1,2,3											
Patient identification process																1,2,3										
Application choise	1,2,3	1,2																								
Patient identification data															1,2,3											
Amount of applications																										
Integration application and HL7 bus															1,2	1,2										
Amount of applications involved in integration process																										
Invoicing module							1,2									1,2,3										
Integration operation room and sterilization								1	3																	
Operation room system								1								1										
Appointment system								3								3										
Sterilization system									3																	
Extra data entity 'site'		3	1,3																							
Permissions		2	2																							

Figure 1. Cross-Case Design Structure Matrix.

[3] D. Campagnolo and A. Camuffo, "The concept of modularity in management studies: A literature review," International Journal of Management Reviews, vol. 12, no. 3, September 2010, pp. 259–283.

[4] R. Silvestro and P. Lustrato, "Exploring the "mid office" concept as an enabler of mass customization in services," International Journal of Operations & Production Management, vol. 35, no. 6, 2015, pp. 866–894.

[5] A. Lindstrom, "On the syntax and semantics of architectural principles," in Proceedings of the 39th Annual Hawaii International Conference on System Sciences (HICSS2006), vol. 8, 2006, pp. 178b–178b.

[6] R. Kazman, L. Bass, M. Webb, and G. Abowd, "Saam: A method for analyzing the properties of software architectures," in Proceedings of the 16th International Conference on Software Engineering, ser. ICSE '94. Los Alamitos, CA, USA: IEEE Computer Society Press, 1994, pp. 81–90.

[7] R. Kazman, M. Klein, M. Barbacci, T. Longstaff, H. Lipson, and S. Carriere, "The architecture tradeoff analysis method," Software Engineering Institute, Carnegie Mellon University, Pittsburgh, PA, Tech. Rep. CMU/SEI-98-TR-008, 1998.

[8] N. Lassing, P. Bengtsson, H. van Vliet, and J. Bosch, "Experiences with alma: Architecture-level modifiability analysis," J. Syst. Softw., vol. 61, no. 1, Mar. 2002, pp. 47–57.

[9] M. R. Davoudi and F. S. Aliee, "Characterization of enterprise architecture quality attributes." in EDOCW. IEEE Computer Society, 2009, pp. 131–137.

[10] L. Bass, P. Clements, and R. Kazman, Software Architecture in Practice, 3rd ed. Addison-Wesley Professional, 1998.

[11] P. Clements, R. Kazman, and M. Klein, Evaluating Software Architectures: Methods and Case Studies. Boston, MA, USA: Addison-Wesley Longman Publishing Co., Inc., 2002.

[12] P. Johnson, E. Johansson, T. Sommestad, and J. Ullberg, "A tool for enterprise architecture analysis," in 11th IEEE International Enterprise Distributed Object Computing Conference (EDOC 2007), Oct 2007, pp. 142–142.

[13] J. W. Ross, P. Weill, and D. C. Robertson., Enterprise Architecture as Strategy – Creating a Foundation for Business Execution. Harvard Business School Press, Boston, MA, 2006.

[14] J. A. Zachman, "A framework for information systems architecture," IBM Systems Journal, vol. 26, no. 3, 1987, pp. 276–292.

[15] The Open Group, "The open group architecture framework (togaf) version 9," 2009. [Online]. Available: http://www.opengroup.org/togaf/ [Accessed: 31-01-2017]

[16] O. Noran, Handbook on Enterprise Architecture. Springer-Verlag, 2003, ch. A mapping of individual architecture frameworks (GRAI, PERA, C4ISR, CIMOSA, Zachman, ARIS) onto GERAM, pp. 65–210.

[17] M. Schenherr, "Towards a common terminology in the discipline of enterprise architecture." in ICSOC Workshops'08, 2008, pp. 400–413.

[18] A. Cabigiosu and A. Camuffo, "Beyond the "mirroring" hypothesis: Product modularity and interorganizational relations in the air conditioning industry," Organization Science, vol. 23, no. 3, May/June 2012, pp. 686–703.

[19] O. Becker, J. Ben-Asher, and I. Ackerman, "A method for system interface reduction using n^2 charts," Systems Engineering, vol. 3, 2000, pp. 27–37.

[20] C. Y. Baldwin and K. B. Clark, Design Rules, Volume 1: The Power of Modularity, ser. MIT Press Books. The MIT Press, January 2000.

[21] M. T. Ionita, D. K. Hammer, and H. Obbink, "Scenario-based software architecture evaluation methods: An overview," in Workshop on methods and techniques for software architecture review and assessment at the international conference on software engineering, 2002.

[22] T. Tamm, P. B. Seddon, G. Shanks, and P. Reynolds, "How does enterprise architecture add value to organisations?" Communications of the Association for Information Systems, vol. 28, no. 1, 2011, pp. 141–168.

Toward Evolvable Document Management for Study Programs Based on Modular Aggregation Patterns

Gilles Oorts and Herwig Mannaert

Normalized Systems Institute
University of Antwerp
Antwerp, Belgium
Email: gilles.oorts,herwig.mannaert@uantwerp.be

Ilke Franquet

Unit for Innovation and Quality Assurance in Education
Faculty of Applied Economics
University of Antwerp, Belgium
Email: ilke.franquet@uantwerp.be

Abstract—**Despite technological and operational business advances over the past decades, organizations are still required to draft and manage documents. Although a lot of these documents have taken an electronic form, their structure is in essence still the same as their analogue and physical predecessors. In this paper, we present a different view of documents as we imagine them as modular structures. Based on the patterns of the artifacts they describe, documents can be modularized and decomposed into fine-grained text modules. This leads to easier maintenance of the text modules as they offer a clear aggregate structure and any information is stored in only one text module. This enables re-usability and allows for a greater versatility of the information stored in the text modules. One can generate several new types of documents with different purposes as to the ones imaginable at this moment. All of this enables the creation of truly evolvable documents according to the Normalized Systems theory.**

Keywords–Normalized Systems theory; Modularity; Document Management; Prototype; Evolvable Documents; Modular Documents; Text Modules.

I. Introduction

Despite technological and operational business advances over the past decades, organizations are still required to draft and manage documents. These documents can take a plethora of forms, such as books, spreadsheets, slide decks, manuals, legal contracts, emails, reports, etcetera. Although a lot of these documents have taken an electronic form, their structure is in essence still the same as their analogue and physical predecessors. Invoices are often just printed and sent by mail, after which they are opened and scanned by the receiving organization. Or instead of printing and handing out new operational procedures, they are often just exported as a pdf-file and saved on a server.

Despite the endless opportunities the revolution in Information Technologies (IT) brought along, most efforts in document management were limited to just digitizing documents, i.e., transforming them from analogue to digital form as monolithic blocks. In this paper, we show how this view of static documents that are a mere representation of their analogue predecessors is out-of-date. Instead, we will present a view of multidimensional and ever-changing documents, based on the insights from modularity and Normalized Systems reasoning. The practical implications of this view will be discussed based on a case study of a document management system for study program documentation.

In Section II, we will first demonstrate the need for variability and evolvability in documents. Next, we will show how to achieve these document characteristics using the principles of modularity and evolvability based on Normalized Systems theory in Section III. To illustrate this approach we first introduce the case of study programs in Section IV before discussing a prototype of such a document system in Section V.

II. The Need for Evolvability and Variability of Documents

Documents are rarely invariant artifacts. In todays competitive business environment, companies need to be able to adapt to changing requirements of customers, government, competitors, suppliers, substitute products or services, and newcomers to the market [1]. These changes also require adaptations to the documents used in the organization. As these documents are managed in a digital way and can be easily edited by multiple people throughout time, they are changed more frequently and have several concurrent variants. In terms of *change* over time, consider for instance the following change events:

- a new legislation may require companies to add additional safety measures to their operational guidelines in order to avoid oil leaks on drill platforms;
- a software or product manual may need to be updated because a new version with added functionality or fixed bugs was designed and is put into production;
- an audit report may need to be updated with new information about the audited objects or new auditing criteria;

These are just a few examples of business changes that require adaptations of documentation. Enumerating a full list of change events that require documentation changes in contemporary businesses is impossible, as they are countless. For this reason, documents need to be designed to be changed with ease -to be *evolvable*- from the start. This will be discussed in the next sections of this paper.

The continuous change of documents also contributes to the creation of *variability* in documents. Adaptations in documents do not necessarily lead to the deletion of the previous document, as both versions might need to exist. Consider for instance the following possible variants [2]:

- a similar slide deck on a subject may be created for a one day seminar to a management audience, a one week course for developers, a full-fledged course for undergraduate students;
- a product manual may be drafted in different languages, several product variants (standard – professional – deluxe) may contain a partly overlapping set of production parts requiring similar yet different manuals, etcetera;
- similar, but slightly different, legal documents (contracts) may be drafted for different clients purchasing the same service (based on the same contract template), etcetera;

These are of course just a few examples of how different versions of a document can arise. To manage the concurrent and consequential document variants, most companies use so-called Document Management Systems (DMS). To the best of our knowledge, these systems store the documents at the "document" level. As we will discuss in this paper, we propose a solution to store and manage documents at more fine-grained modular levels, enabling the creation of evolvable and reusable documents.

III. Modular and Evolvable Documents

The concept of modularity has proven to be a very successful as a design principle in various settings. It has been cited to be very useful in product, system and organizational design [3][4].

Based on these insights, it was demonstrated how systems such as accountancy, business processes and enterprises can be regarded as modular systems in previous work [5][6][7]. This research shows that applying the modularity principle to systems entails benefits in the design, maintenance and support to the system.

We are convinced that documents can be considered to be clear examples of modular structures. Take for instance these examples [2] :

- A book or a report typically consists of a set of *chapters*. Each of these chapters will contain a set of *sections*, subsections, subsubsections, and so on. Each of these (sub)sections can then contain *paragraphs* with the actual text, tables and/or figures;
- A product manual will contain guidance *sections* regarding the different product parts and/or functionalities;
- A legal document may contain different *parts*, within each part different *clauses*, and each clause may contain different *paragraphs*.

All of these document parts can be considered to be modules. In our approach, we define a module as a part of the system that is used or activated separately. Once a part of the system cannot be used or activated as such, it is considered to be on a sub-modular level.

Modularity is however but a prerequisite in obtaining adaptive documents. For documents to easily assimilate changes over time, they need to exhibit evolvability. Based on the modularity concept, *Normalized Systems (NS) theory* was proposed to achieve such modular evolvability. Although originally defined for software architectures, its applicability and value in other domains (e.g., organizational design, business processes, accountancy) quickly became clear [5][6][7].

To obtain flexible systems that can easily evolvable over time, NS theory states that so-called *combinatorial effects* should be eliminated. These effects occur when changes to a modular structure are dependent on the size of the system they are applied to [8]. This means the impact of the change does not solely depend on the nature of change itself. Assuming systems become more complex over time, combinatorial effects would therefore become ever bigger barriers to change. As such, it is clear how combinatorial effects should be avoided if systems need to be changed easily (i.e., be evolvable).

To obtain evolvability, NS theory proposes four *theorems*, two of which are of importance in this paper [8]:

- *Separation of Concerns*, stating that each change driver (concern) should be separated from other concerns. This closely relates to the concept of cohesion;
- *Version Transparency*, stating that modules should be updatable without impacting any linked modules;

In practice, the consistent application of these theorems results in a very fine-grained modular structure.

The theory also defines *cross-cutting concerns*. This concept is often used in information technology and refers to functionality or concerns that cut right across the functional structure of a system. These cross-cutting concerns should also be encapsulated to exhibit any form of evolvability. As we will illustrate in this paper, this is not self-evident as the functionality of these concerns are embedded deep down within systems.

An important cross-cutting concern in documents is a mechanism for "relative" embedding of text parts in the hierarchical structure of overarching documents. This means one should be able to include a text module on several hierarchical levels in a document without this inclusion causing any changes in the text module. As such, a text module can be variably used as a chapter, section, subsection, etc. without any changes to the module. Preliminary research shows there are several other cross-cutting concerns for documents, such as for example typesetting (layout), language, target audience, etc.

Besides the cross-cutting concerns resulting form the nature of documents, there are also concerns specific to the underlying artifact(s) described in the document. These are mostly cross-cutting concerns that stem from content or descriptions of the artifact(s). Take for example technical documents describing the machines used in the production process of a manufacturer. These documents will contain machine specifications, operating instructions, power requirements, maintenance instructions, etc. This are necessary subjects needed in the description of every machine and can as such be defined as cross-cutting concerns according to the previous stated definition.

Based on these concepts of modularity and evolvability based on Normalized Systems Theory, a prototype was built to manage the documents of the study programs at the faculty of Applied Economics at the University of Antwerp.

IV. Study Program Design at the Faculty of Applied Economics

Before we can study program documentation, we first need to take a look at the underlying artifacts. The study programs at the Faculty of Applied Economics at the University of Antwerp were recently redesigned to be modular and evolvable. Naturally, an evolvable study program design enables all related documents to be adaptable as well. Furthermore, the well-defined modular structure of the study programs allows for new possibilities in generating related supporting documents.

The new study program design was formulated to include learning-teaching tracks and sub-tracks. As such, additional levels of modularity were added to the existing 258 courses offered in five distinct bachelor study programs and seven study programs at a master level. As proposed in previous work [9], this leads to the study program design shown in Table I. Each of the 258 courses belongs to one main (sub)track, but can be connected to other (sub)tracks as it may contain subject matters belonging to several (sub)tracks.

Besides the addition of two new modular levels in the study program design, considerable efforts were put into defining cross-cutting concerns that manifest themselves in the courses taught in the faculty. In total, 10 cross-cutting concerns were identified specific to the studied artifacts (i.e., study programs). These concerns are a short content description, regular content description, internationalization, blended learning, assignments, ethical awareness, sustainability, social impact, learning outcomes and teaching method(s). These cross-cutting concerns represent important aspects of a study programs, and therefore its underlying learning-teaching tracks and courses. In Figure 1, some of these cross-cutting concerns are presented on the vertical axis. On the horizontal axis, the learning-teaching tracks and sub-tracks are listed, each with the included courses. Besides allowing to check the presence of certain concerns in courses and learning-teaching tracks, this matrix shows the extensive modular design of documents describing the courses and learning-teaching tracks. How we design and generate documents to support this modular and evolvable study program design will be discussed in the next section.

TABLE I. OVERVIEW OF THE LEARNING-TEACHING TRACKS AND SUB-TRACKS

Learning-teaching track	**Sub-track**
General economics	Fundamentals
	Policy
Business economics	Accountancy
	European and international business
	Finance
	Marketing
	Strategy and organization
	Transport and logistics
Engineering	Fundamentals
	Sustainable technology
	Supply chains and operations
Information systems	Fundamentals
	Engineering and architecture
	Governance and audit
Quantitative methods	Mathematics
	Statistics
Practice	Apprenticeship and internship
	Summer school
Broadening areas of study	Social sciences
	Jurisprudence
Business communication	English
	French
	German
	Spanish
Projects and dissertations	Bachelor project
	Master dissertation
	Master integration project

V. A Prototype for Generating Study Program Documents

A. Decomposing Documents into Text Modules

The new modular and evolvable design of the study programs allowed for a similar redesign of documents describing the study programs. Therefore the existing content describing the courses was looked at and modularized to allow the generation of different kind of documents. Previously, most content on study programs was contained in course descriptions that were published on the faculty's website. From this descriptions, text modules with similar content were identified. In total, 10 types of text modules were recognized. These are the content cross-cutting concerns mentioned in the previous section and include for example a short content description, internationalization, etcetera. Combined, these 10 types of text modules allow for a complete representation of the courses. And as learning-teaching tracks and study programs are considered to be mere compositions of courses according to modularity reasoning, the text modules can be used to represent these parent artifacts as well. Taking into account the total number of 258 courses and 10 content cross-cutting concerns, the modularization of the course descriptions resulted in a total of $258 * 10 = 2580$ text modules. These represent all aspects of the courses, learning-teaching tacks and study programs of the faculty.

Although this amount of text modules seems cumbersome to achieve and maintain, this fine-grained decomposition actually simplifies several aspects of document management. First, this imposed separation of concerns creates structure across all course descriptions. This gives professors (who are responsible for the content of the text modules) something to hold on to in describing their courses. Furthermore it is easier to retrieve certain information, as the text modules are in separate files. This also allows for easier maintenance of the information. But by far the biggest advantage of the decomposition is the endless possible document types that can be generated with the decomposed course descriptions. The information included in the decomposed text modules allows for the generation of a vast variety of documents with different purposes. This system for example allows one to generate documents containing a short description of all courses in a study program. But the system can also generate a document listing all courses or learning-teaching tracks using a specific teaching method. Furthermore, if students were to be added, the system would allow to generate a document detailing all sustainability or social impact aspects a student has encountered in his study program. Or how much hands-on experience he has gained due to assignments or case studies. As such, it allows to draw up student-specific diploma's with one click of a button. In general, the decomposition thus allows for a versatile use of document modules and allows the definition of new types of documents with new purposes.

B. Relative Sectioning

As mentioned before, an important aspect of allowing text modules to be re-usable is to implement relative sectioning.

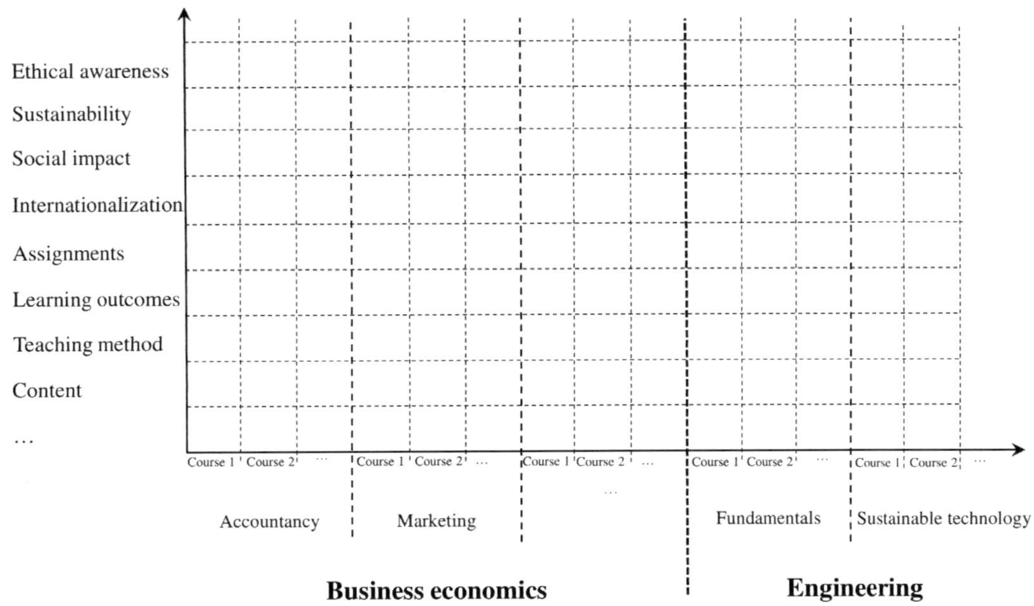

Figure 1. The cross-cutting concern presence in learning-teaching tracks and courses

To implement this prototype, the LaTeX document preparation system was used. This was done because it allows the hierarchical inclusion of sub-files (i.e., text modules) and allows the layout cross-cutting concern to be handled in a separate layout file. LaTeX however does not provide a system for relative sectioning out of the box. The hierarchical structure of sections (i.e., whether something is a chapter, section, subsection, subsubsection, etcetera) should be hard coded within .tex files and therefore limits the potential for text modules to be freely combined into final documents which might use the same text excerpts at different levels within their own document hierarchy. To overcome this problem, a LaTeX style file needed to be used that provided the functionality of relative sectioning [10]. This allows the prototype to generate a LaTeX structure file, of which the first part is shown in Figure 2. In this file, text modules are imported via the `\input{}` command. The names included in this command are the files that should be part of the generated document. More importantly, the `\leveldown` and `\levelup` commands are automatically added by the prototype whenever the next text module of the document should be added on a lower or higher level. As such, the basic text modules exist of solely a title (included within the `\dynsection{}` that is provided by the custom style file) and the content of the module.

C. Practical implementation

The practical implementation of the prototype was done in Java. A graphical user interface (GUI) was developed that allows documents to be developed as easily and efficiently as possible. The result of this effort is shown in Figure 3. In this screen, the user can enter the document title (which will also be the file name) and create up to three document levels. This is done by first selecting the content of a level, which can be cross-cutting concerns, learning-teaching tracks, sub-tracks or courses. When this selection is made, the user must specify

```
\input{input/"Content description"}
\leveldown
\input{input/"Business Economics"}
\leveldown
\input{input/"Business Economics_Accountancy_content "}
\input{input/"Business Economics_European and International Law_content "}
\input{input/"Business Economics_Finance_content "}
\input{input/"Business Economics_Marketing_content "}
\input{input/"Business Economics_Strategy and Organisation_content "}
\input{input/"Business Economics_Transport and Logistics_content "}
\levelup
\levelup
\input{input/"Assignments"}
\leveldown
\input{input/"Business Economics"}
\leveldown
\input{input/"Business Economics_Accountancy_assignments"}
\input{input/"Business Economics_European and International Law_assignments "}
\input{input/"Business Economics_Finance_assignments "}
\input{input/"Business Economics_Marketing_assignments "}
\input{input/"Business Economics_Strategy and Organisation_assignments "}
\input{input/"Business Economics_Transport and Logistics_assignments "}
\levelup
\levelup
...
```

Figure 2. The LaTeX Structure File generated by the prototype

whether he wants one single instance of content on that level, multiple instances or all of them (by using the "Select all" button). In this way, one or multiple levels can be defined.

Once the user made his selection, he can press the "Generate" button to start the process of generating the document he specified. At this point, the system will generate two LaTeX files. First, a "Structure" file is created, which is partially shown in Figure 2. This file is procedurally generated based on the selections the user made. It takes into account the amount of document levels and amount of instance selections on each level.

Next, a "Generator" file is created by the system, of which an example is shown in Figure 4. This file contains code needed for LaTeX to generate a PDF version of the designed

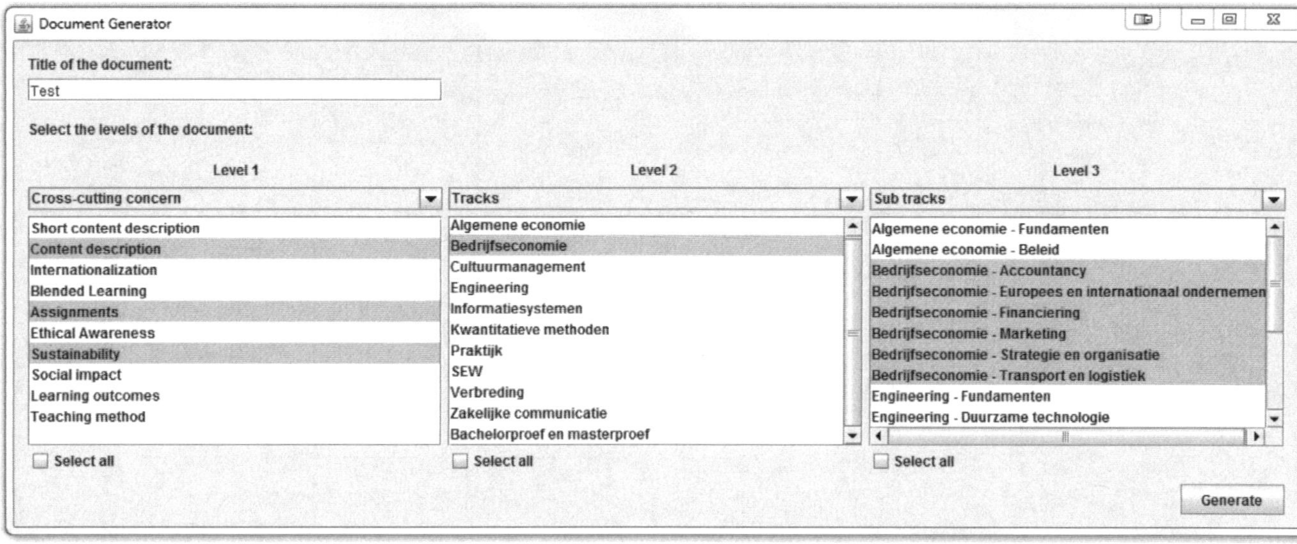

Figure 3. The Graphical Interface of the Prototype

```
\documentclass[a4paper]{report}

\usepackage{blindtext}
\makeatletter
\newif\ifusedot
\usedottrue

\usepackage{relsec}
\setcounter{secnumdepth}{3}
\setcounter{tocdepth}{3}

\title{Test}
\makeatother

\begin{document}
\maketitle'
\usedotfalse

\include{Test_StructureFile}

\end{document}
```

Figure 4. The LaTeX Generator File generated by the prototype

document. Apart from the LaTeX -specific code, this file simply contains the `\include{}` command to refer to the structure file and as such the structure and text modules defined in that file. This shows how the structure of the document is also clearly separated from the generation implementation, according to the separation of concerns principle.

Once these two files have been created, the system simply uses the LaTeX document generation functionality to generate a PDF file of the document.

D. Document Versatility, Variability, and Evolvability

Having described the prototype, we can now illustrate the possibilities of *document versatility* this system provides. Let's explain this in numbers. As mentioned previously, the faculty offers 12 study programs (5 Bachelor and 7 Master programs). For each study program, one can generate a document containing three document levels. Abstracting from the courses to make things easier, there are 3 possible selections for the first document level (i.e., cross-cutting concerns, learning-teaching tracks and sub-tracks). This means there are only two possible selections for the second level (the two remaining ones), and two possible selection for the final level (i.e., either choosing the remaining selection or not including a third level). This totals up to 12 possible selections for the document levels. Considering either including or not including the 10 cross-cutting concerns, the amount of combinations adds up to $2^{10} = 1024$ possibilities. Multiplying the 12 study programs, 12 possible document level selections and 1024 possible combinations of 10 cross-cutting concerns inclusions gives us a total of 147,456 possible document combinations that can be generated based on the 2,580 defined text modules.

If the approximate 3,000 students of the faculty were to be included in the system, the document versatility would increase exponentially. Let's assume of all students, there are 1,000 unique versions of study programs, which is a cautious estimate considering the amount of courses students can choose in some study programs. Substituting the 12 study programs by 1,000 study program versions in the previous multiplication results in 12,288,000 possible document combinations. This example clearly shows the combination potential of decomposing course descriptions into fine-grained text modules.

The decomposition in text modules also allows more fine-grained version control to manage the *variability* in all types of documents that can be generated. If version control is managed on a text module level, changes can be tracked more specifically. Each version of a text module can be archived based on their moment of change, allowing the generation of documents according to specific time specifications. One important application of this version control system is for example the re-generation of a student diploma after it has been lost. It may have been a few years since the student graduated, so courses and study programs will have changed. Yet it is important for a university to be able to generate the diploma with the correct descriptions of the version of the courses the student took. This example shows the importance of tracking changes on a fine-grained modular level.

The implementation of modular text modules also shows the importance of eliminating combinatorial effects to achieve *evolvability*. A change in the description of a course needs to be made in only one of the 2580 files/text modules. By creating a script that regenerates all documents in which this module is included, this change is easily applied to all documents it is included in. As such, combinatorial effects are avoided and the system generates evolvable documents.

VI. Conclusion

In this paper, we presented an alternative to the view of static and monolithic documents. By applying the concept of modularity and decomposing documents into text modules, several advantages can be achieved. First, modularity leads to easier to maintain text modules. This because the modules show a clear structure and specific information is stored in only one module that is easily recognized. Second, the text modules enable a greater versatility: new types of documents can be composed by combining text modules in new ways. As such new types of documents can be created with new goals and purposes. This is shown in the paper by calculating the number of possible document combinations. And finally, the systematic decomposition of modules allows for the elimination of combinatorial effects to create evolvable documents. These advantages of modular document design are clarified in the paper by the description of system to generate documents containing study program information.

In future research, other cases will be studied to corroborate the findings of the case discussed in this paper. Furthermore, the theoretical basis of modularity and evolvability of documents will be solidified.

References

[1] M. E. Porter, "Strategy and the Internet." Harvard Business Review, vol. 79, no. 3, 2001, pp. 62–78, 164.

[2] H. Mannaert, J. Verelst, and P. De Bruyn, Normalized Systems Theory: From Foundations for Evolvable Software Toward a General Theory for Evolvable design. Koppa, 2016.

[3] C. Y. Baldwin and K. B. Clark, Design Rules: The Power of Modularity Volume 1. Cambridge, MA, USA: MIT Press, 1999.

[4] D. Campagnolo and A. Camuffo, "The Concept of Modularity in Management Studies: A Literature Review." International Journal of Management Reviews, vol. 12, no. 3, 2010, pp. 259–283.

[5] D. Van Nuffel, "Towards Designing Modular and Evolvable Business Processes," Ph.D. dissertation, University of Antwerp, 2011.

[6] P. Huysmans, "On the Feasibility of Normalized Enterprises: Applying Normalized Systems Theory to the High-Level Design of Enterprises," Ph.D. dissertation, University of Antwerp, 2011.

[7] E. Vanhoof, P. Huysmans, W. Aerts, and J. Verelst, Advances in Enterprise Engineering VIII: EEWC 2014. Springer International Publishing, 2014, ch. Evaluating, pp. 76–90.

[8] H. Mannaert, J. Verelst, and K. Ven, "Towards evolvable software architectures based on systems theoretic stability," Software: Practice and Experience, vol. 42, no. 1, 2012, pp. 89–116.

[9] G. Oorts, H. Mannaert, P. De Bruyn, and I. Franquet, On the evolvable and traceable design of (under)graduate education programs. Springer International Publishing, 2016, vol. 252.

[10] C. Leichsenring, "Relsec style file," 2013. [Online]. Available: https://github.com/mudd1/relsec/blob/master/relsec.sty [Accessed: 31-01-2017]

On the Modular Structure and Evolvability of Architectural Patterns for Housing Utilities

Peter De Bruyn
Normalized Systems Institute
University of Antwerp, Belgium
Email:peter.debruyn@uantwerp.be

Jeroen Faes, Tom Vermeire and Jasper Bosmans
Department of Management Information Systems
University of Antwerp, Belgium
Email:{jeroen.faes,tom.vermeire,jasper.bosmans}@student.uantwerp.be

***Abstract*—Modularity is considered a powerful concept within many domains. While modular artifacts are believed to have the potential to exhibit several beneficial characteristics such as evolvability, the actual realization of this evolvability or flexibility remains challenging. This paper considers houses as modular structures and employs the combinatorics underlying Normalized Systems Theory, as well as the integration patterns it proposes, to analyze design alternatives for the incorporation of electricity and heating utilities within houses. The paper demonstrates that the integration patterns can be applied at several modular granularity levels. An analysis is presented regarding which integration patterns are currently most frequently used at which levels, and which patterns should deserve additional exploration. The adopted approach to analyze the modular design alternatives for housing utilities is believed to be applicable within other domains as well.**

Keywords–Modularity; Housing; Evolvability; Normalized Systems; Architectural Patterns.

I. Introduction

Modularity has proven to be a powerful concept in many domains such as computer science, product engineering, organizational sciences, and so on. The concept generally refers to the fact that a system is subdivided into a set of interacting subsystems. Modular artifacts are deemed interesting due to several potential benefits which are attributed to it. For instance, designing a product in a modular way is expected to lower the complexity as the design can be decomposed into a set of smaller (less complex) problems [1]. Another major benefit expected from modularity is increased flexibility or evolvability. In a modular artifact, one particular part (module) of the system can be substituted for another version of it, without having to build up the artifact again from scratch. This kind of plug-and-play behavior allows for variation (using the same set of available module versions, different aggregations or variants can be made available) and evolvability (over time, an artifact can evolve from one variant to another).

Nevertheless, achieving these modular benefits is very difficult. It is generally accepted that the coupling (dependencies and interactions) between the modules in a system should be studied and minimized [1][2][3]. How this should be realized in specific situations is often unclear. In particular, several features in modular structures are cross-cutting (e.g., security in a software application) in the sense that they are required across the whole modular structure (e.g., every data entity should be securely stored) and adaptations in such cross-cutting concerns can create large ripple-effects in the system (i.e., a change in one module implies a change in another module and so on), hampering the evolvability aimed for.

This paper focuses on the design of modular structures of houses and their evolvability. It is clear that houses are modular structures at several abstraction levels (e.g., houses consisting of rooms and built by bricks) and could benefit from evolvability (e.g., connecting an additional room to an existing house). Moreover, houses often lack this evolvability (e.g., the need to drill into existing walls or even tear down walls to be able to provide an additional room with water because the connecting old walls did not provide any connection). More specifically, we study the implications of different design alternatives for utilities (and in particular electricity and heating) within a housing context. We argue that such utilities can be considered as cross-cutting concerns. Our design alternatives will be based on the modular integration patterns for cross-cutting concerns as suggested by the combinatorics underlying Normalized Systems Theory (NST) [4]. The theory is suitable for this purpose as it aims to provide prescriptive guidance on how to design evolvable modular systems.

It is important to mention upfront that none of the authors of this paper are experts within the domain of housing architecture. Therefore, the intention of the paper is not the prescribe in detail how housing architectures should be improved in the future. Rather, we intend to show that it makes sense to apply the modularity reasoning presented within NST (which originated at the software level) to other domains in which modularity plays a prominent role. In Section II, we provide a brief overview of the integration patterns for modular structures as presented within NST. We then apply these patterns for the concerns electricity (Section III) and heating (Section IV). Finally, we offer our reflections and conclusions in Sections V and VI, respectively.

II. NST Integration Patterns

A. NST and combinatorics

The origins of NST are situated in the formulation of a set of design theorems for the creation of evolvable software systems. Here, evolvability is operationalized by demanding Bounded Input Bound Output (BIBO) stability on ever growing systems. The theory proves that the isolation of all change drivers in separate constructs (Separation of Concerns), the stateful calling of processing functions (Separation of States) and the ability to update data structures or processing functions without impacting other data structures or processing functions (Version Transparency) are necessary conditions in order to obtain stability [5]. It has been shown that these theorems can actually be formulated in more general terms for modular systems [6] and seem to appeal to the basic combinatorics regarding modularity [4]. More specifically, the promise of modularity is that maintaining a particular amount of versions of modular building blocks will result in an exponential amount of available system variants. However, in case a modular system is not well designed (e.g., by not adhering to the theorems), a change in one particular version of one particular module may have an impact (ripple effects) on other (versions of) modules. This number of impacts will typically grow (in an exponential way) with the size of the system and its dependencies.

B. Patterns for cross-cutting concern integration

Adhering to the NST design theorems is difficult as they demand a very strict and fine-grained design of a system, and every violation will result in a limitation of the evolvability of the system. Research on the realization of such systems has shown that their design becomes much more realistic in case a set of design patterns (so-called "elements") are employed [4]. Each individual element is a generic modular structure for a basic functionality for the type of system at hand and can be parametrized (and if necessary, customized) over and over again when an actual system is built. For instance, in the case of software systems, a general structure for data, task, flow, connector and trigger elements was provided [4]. Stated otherwise, the set of modules constituting an element becomes a reusable module at a higher abstraction (or granularity) level. In essence, each element provides a core functionality (e.g., representing data) as well as an incorporated integration with the relevant cross-cutting concerns in the domain (e.g., security and persistency for data). In order to maximize the envisioned evolvability, it is important that these cross-cutting concerns are integrated at the most fine-grained level possible (such as these elements) and that the parts in the elements connecting or dealing with the cross-cutting concerns are properly separated in distinct modules which are version transparent.

More generally, we differentiate between the following integration patterns of cross-cutting concerns. As a first category of integration patterns, we consider cross-cutting concern modules added to the main modules wherein each cross-cutting concern modules handles the full functionality of that cross-cutting concern itself. We call this the *embedded integration pattern* and refer to it as *configuration 1*. This embedded module can be dedicated (in case the module was specifically designed for the system at hand) or standardized (in case a standardized module is employed to handle the concern). We refer to the first variant as *configuration 1A* and the second as *configuration 1B*. For modules in the context of a software system, think of a separate module added to a data entity taking care of the persistency of that data entity in a custom designed way (1A) or by using a standard module (1B) for this purpose.

As a second category of integration patterns, we consider cross-cutting concern modules added to the main modules wherein the cross-cutting concern modules are merely connections ("relay modules") to a more elaborate (external) implementation framework of the cross-cutting concern and which actually perform the needed functionality. We call this the *relay integration pattern* and refer to it as *configuration 2*. Such relay modules can connect to a dedicated framework (in case the framework was specifically designed for the system at hand) or standardized framework (in case the framework is standardized and, for instance, publicly available). We refer to the first variant as *configuration 2A* and the second as *configuration 2B*. For modules in the context of software system, think of a separate module added to a data entity serving as a proxy to a persistency framework which was specifically designed for its own system (2A) or to an available standard solution such as JPA (2B). Finally, we mention the option to let the relay modules connect to another module (i.e., a *framework gateway*) and in which only this framework gateway directly connects to the external implementation framework. We refer to this third variant as *configuration 2C*. For modules in the context of a software system, think of a dedicated gateway module which connects to the JPA framework but allows all relay modules to be technologically independent of this framework by calling the gateway in a JPA agnostic way.

III. Electricity Patterns

In this section, we consider the electricity utility within houses as a cross-cutting concern. We consider the integration architectures as proposed in Section II at the modular granularity level of a city or community, house, room and device. Afterwards, we consider some advanced issues and reflections.

A. City or community level

Most cities and communities of developed countries need electricity, so it can be considered as a cross-cutting concern. Here, we consider how a city or community can power its electrical grid as a whole (the distribution of electricity to individual buildings is discussed later on).

A first option could be to have all cities/communities have there own electricity generation (configuration 1). In primitive communities, custom built solutions might be considered (1A), but typically the use of standard solutions (1B) would be more realistic (e.g., the reproduction of a typical power plant by means of nuclear reactions, coal, etc.). However, this often lacks economies of scale (it is more efficient to have large power plants producing energy for more than 1 city or community) so typically a city's electricity grid is connected to a national electricity grid with one or more electricity plants dividing the electricity over a large set of cities and communities (configuration 2). Each country might create its own specifically designed grid connecting with the multiple cities and communities (2A) or make use of a standardized electrical power distribution network between cities (2B).

While this latter solution is most frequently opted for, it also has some drawbacks in terms of dependencies. For instance, if the central grid goes down, all connected cities and communities are lacking electricity. Therefore, in reality, most electrical grids are divided into several isolated areas avoiding a problem in a particular part of the grid to get escalated into the complete (national) electricity grid. Moreover, changes in the standardized network still have their impact on the relay modules (which should nevertheless be encapsulated within the cross-cutting concern handling relay module and not in the core module itself). For instance, a change in the voltage of the network or from alternating current (AC) to direct current (DC). In fact, the limitations (at that time) for distributing DC over long distances (in order to be able to adopt integration pattern 2B), was one of the main reasons for the general prevalence of AC in the so-called "War of the Currents". One could even imagine the situation in which all cities plug their individual grids into a centralized relay module (power supply) which is tapping into the global electricity grid (2C), shielding the individual cities and communities from changes in the standardized framework used.

B. House level

Within every city, community or electricity grid area, electricity typically has to be available within every house. Therefore, it constitutes a cross-cutting concern at this level as well. Sometimes, individual houses have the possibility to generate their own electricity by using, for instance, a fuel based electricity generator, based on solar panels, heat pumps, etc. Furthermore, new technological developments have allowed the creation of home based batteries with large storage capacities, even allowing to store electrical power for a whole house for a considerable amount of time. As this provides a significant amount of independence and sometimes budget friendly solutions, this integration pattern can be interesting in certain situations. Moreover, a certain amount of flexibility is enabled as each individual house can choose for that particular type of energy which is most suitable in their case (e.g., those areas with a high exposure to sun light might opt for solar panels instead of a wind mill). In that case (except when they want to transmit the overcapacity to the central electricity distribution network), no distribution framework (see previous subsection) is required and the generators and batteries support the modules for the adoption of integration pattern 1 (typically 1B).

Most people, however, do not opt for the duplication of power generators and batteries in each and every individual house and choose for the option of a connection module plugging into the publicly available electrical power distribution network (typically standardized, so 2B). Similar as stated above, dependencies regarding the availability of the distribution network as well as changes in the power distribution network affecting all connection modules of houses, remain possible disadvantages of this integration pattern.

C. Room level

Within every house or building, most if not all rooms require electricity in terms of a set of available sockets where individual devices (cfr. infra) can plug into. Therefore, it constitutes a cross-cutting concern at this level as well. Based on the integration patterns we summarized in Section II-B and similar to our reasoning expressed above, it would be theoretically possible for each room in a house to generate the electricity required (configuration 1A if custom designed, 1B if a standard solution is opted for). Nevertheless, individual heat pumps, electricity generators, etc. for individual rooms are —to the best of our knowledge— typically not applied. Therefore, configuration 2 (typically 2B) is applied by having sockets plugging, into the grid network of the house. In certain situations, configuration 2C might be relevant as well. For instance, houses which employ a combination of electrical sources (tapping from the publicly available grid, as well as producing a portion of energy themselves by solar panels) could benefit from having the possibility of shifting between them (e.g., using the solar energy when electricity is being generated or available on the local battery and the public grid in all other cases). By having the relay modules (sockets) connecting to a gateway switching module (connecting to the solar panels and public grid), only one electricity grid for such house should be created.

D. Device level

Ultimately, electrical power should be made available to individual devices for which it is required in order to work properly. One possibility to obtain this power is by having a built-in generator or battery in a device. While the generator variant hardly exists in practice, batteries within devices are common practice. Such batteries exist in both custom built variants (integration pattern 1A) or by the use of general purpose variants (integration pattern 1B). A configuration like this obviously provides the device a certain degree of autonomy (i.e., the device can operate on its own) and absence of specific dependencies in this respect. However, incorporating batteries in every device might be a significant engineering challenge (sometimes even simply impossible) and requires the duplication of a battery in each device. Therefore, in many cases a centralized configuration will be adopted in which the device is connected to a custom developed (configuration 2A) or, typically, a standardized electrical grid (configuration 2B).

Recall that we noted in Section III-A that historically, AC was chosen above DC at the level of cities and communities due to (among other things) its possibility to transport electrical current along larger distances. The consequences of this choice ripple down to the lower modularity granularity levels, such as the level of the devices, which then have to deal with electricity delivered at AC. However, most electrical devices need DC to function properly. As stated above, it is the relay module which should encapsulate these kind of dependencies regarding the external framework and ensure conversions for mutual compatibility if required. Therefore, an adapter (typically with a device specific connection) is often included at the level of the cross-cutting connecting module (i.e., between the device and the electrical grid) in order to convert AC (coming in from the plug) to DC at the right voltage (depending on the efficiency of the adapter typically also resulting in a certain degree of loss of electrical power converted into heat). *This clearly shows the duplication of the AC to DC conversion functionality present within all relay modules (here: adapters).* Moreover, in terms of flexibility and adaptability, the situation nicely illustrates that changes in the external framework (e.g., a conversion of AC to DC within the public electrical grid) would impact all relay modules. In case the AC/DC conversion would not be separated in a distinct module (e.g., the conversion would be performed in the devices themselves instead of via a separately in/unpluggable adapter), the impact would even be more profound as the devices themselves should be adapted. Based on our analysis of the different modular granularity levels, one could argue for the investigation of the option to have the conversion of AC to DC to happen at the house level instead of the device level. This way, the duplication of adapters for each separate device could be eliminated and the dependence on DC would be avoided. More specifically, such situation would correspond to the cross-cutting concern integration pattern 2C where the main modules are the devices, the sockets are the relay modules (no need for adapters anymore) and the centralized AC to DC converter would fulfill the role of the gateway module. In fact, recent initiatives regarding new possible electricity (micro)grid configurations seem to suggest these type of integration patterns [7].

E. Overview and advanced issues

Table I provides an overview of the granularity-integration pattern combinations for the electricity provisioning of houses. We can observe that, at most modularity levels, a standardized integration pattern (i.e., 1B and 2B) is opted for. This tends to indicate a certain maturity within the respective domain, which is in accordance with our expectations. While dependence on the external framework is an important limitation regarding integration pattern 2B, we identify that an interesting research avenue regarding integration pattern 2C at the device level. Further, the table illustrates that, when aiming for maximum flexibility, the integration of concerns tends to be solved at more fine-grained levels (going downwards in Table I) and in a more standardized externally enabled way (going to the right in Table I) in the long run.

TABLE I. OVERVIEW OF THE DIFFERENT GRANULARITY-INTEGRATION PATTERN COMBINATIONS REGARDING ELECTRICITY.

	1A	1B	2A	2B	2C
city/community				•	
house		•		•	
room				•	•
device	•	•		•	○

•: currently employed, ○: to be explored

Further, the electricity cross-cutting concern might be enriched with additional features for which our proposed granularity levels and integration patterns might prove useful during the analysis of their realization options. Consider for instance on/off switching. Many devices (such as light bulbs) using electricity to function need to be able to switched on (i.e., emit light) and off (i.e., dim the light). Typical approaches consist out of a switch attached to the lamp itself (required in case of configuration 1) or a separate switch integrated into the electrical grid of the house itself (the integration structure of the external framework in case of configuration 2). While this approach has worked well for many years it still requires manual intervention at the location of the switch and, in the latter case, requires the reconfiguration and integration of the switches when a lamp would be relocated within the house. During the last decade, attention has grown for more advanced home domotics in which switches can be managed by software (e.g., allowing to automatically switch devices on at a predefined time slot) and in a remote way. Again, this could be done by placing individual sensors/programmable controllers with individual remote controllers (configuration 1B, if standardized equipment is used). Alternatively, a network of sensors/programmable controllers could be used having one central management and remote control (configuration 2B, if standardized equipment is used), which manages all connected switches. This would also allow the use of aggregated actions, such as switching on or off all light bulbs at once at a predefined time slot, and enable parameter reconfiguration in a centralized way. Integration configuration 2C could even be opted for when, for instance, all sensors/programmable controllers connect to one central connection module which allows to be manipulated by means of multiple remote controllers and protocols (e.g., a traditional remote, smartphone, etc.).

IV. Heating Patterns

In this section, we consider the heating utility within houses as a cross-cutting concern. We consider the integration architectures as proposed in Section II at the modular granularity level of a house, room and brick. Afterwards, we consider some advanced issues and reflections.

A. House level

As all households need heating, a source of heat should be transported to or being generated within every house. Therefore, it represents a genuine cross-cutting concern. Today, most houses provide for their own heat generation: a house typically has a central heating system meaning that a central heating boiler uses electricity (cfr. supra) or petroleum to generate heat and convert cold into warm water. Another option could be to use heat pumps. This water will then be distributed along the different rooms in the house later on (cfr. infra). Considering the granularity level of a house, this therefore means that typically integration pattern 1 is opted for (and more specifically 1B, as most households use a standardized heat generator for this purpose). This way of working clearly implies certain benefits such as independence from external heat generation providers. However, one might might wonder whether this is always the most efficient or environment friendly way of working. It is interesting to see that certain initiatives are being taken into the exploration of other integration patterns, such as the so-called heat distribution networks. Here, heated water is produced in a central location for multiple houses and then distributed among them. This allows for optimizations in terms of efficiency or simply the recovery of "lost heat" produced by for instance nearby factories or (nuclear) plants. While this warmed water is generally too cold to be useful for industrial purposes, it might still suffice to provide the heating for (a large amount of) houses. Therefore, integration architecture 2A (as the solution is typically not yet highly standardized) is opted for in this case.

B. Room level

While a garage or cellar might not be in need of explicit heating, most other rooms within a house (such as the living room or bathroom) are. As a consequence, it can be considered as a relevant cross-cutting concern at this level as well. As mentioned before, most houses today employ a central heating system in which heated water is produced at one centralized place in the house and then transported via water pipes to the required rooms in which a heating element/radiator is present. The warm water causes the element to warm up and release its heat into the room, after which the water (which partly cooled down) returns to the central heating system. As these systems and their pipe networks are highly standardized and commonplace, integration architecture 2B is typically applied. This allows an efficient generation of heat but also clearly entails a dependency of all rooms on this central heating system: in case it would fail or be replaced in such way that the old pipe network no long suffices, all rooms would be heavily affected. Using a framework gateway which decouples the pipe network from the boiler might prevent this and would even allow to switch between different sources of heat (electrically generated, via a heat pump or via the heat distribution network), which would correspond to integration architecture 2C. In case of absence of a central heating system, integration architecture 1 might still be used. For instance, some houses (although a minority) still use systems in which radiators are placed within rooms which use the plug to tap electricity and generate heat at their own spot (representing configuration 1B). The use of a fireplace corresponds to the same architecture as well (or configuration 1A in case it concerns a custom designed fireplace). And theoretically speaking, one might also think of situations in which each room is equipped with things such as its own heat pump, although such solutions —at this point in time— are very expensive and inefficient.

C. Brick level

Finally, in order to have more homogeneous heat dispersion in rooms, heating elements incorporated in the floor are sometimes adopted. In such design, the heating pipes are traditionally also connected with a central heating boiler, representing integration architecture 2. Nevertheless, such design is typically not really scalable or flexible as changes (for example, extensions of the heating system to other or larger rooms) might require to break up the floor as a whole. In addition, designing standardized solutions might be more difficult as many rooms take on different shapes and sizes. As a purely speculative and thought provoking alternative, we therefore envision the integration of the heating cross-cutting concern at the level of an individual brick as represented in Figure 1 [4]. In every such element, standardized transport pipes would be embedded for the transportation of hot water, nicely fitting onto the pipes of every similar adjoining brick. This would provide a remarkable degree of scalability when compared to traditional floor heating: as different rooms are built or expanded throughout time, additional bricks (with integrated pipes) could be used, enlarging the area which can be heated. Clearly, just as it was the case for the device level for the electricity concern, the brick level seems to represent the most fine-grained modularity level at which the heating cross-cutting concern can be meaningfully integrated.

D. Overview and advanced issues

Table II provides an overview of the granularity-integration pattern combinations for the heating of houses. We can observe that, at most modularity levels, a standardized integration pattern (i.e., 1B and 2B) is opted for. Again, this tends to indicate a certain maturity within the respective domain, which is in accordance with our expectations. While dependence on the external framework is an important limitation regarding integration pattern 2B, we identify that an interesting research avenue regarding integration pattern 2C at the room level. Additionally, we propose to consider the integration of the cross-cutting concern at an even more fine-grained level (i.e., a brick) in the future. Further, the table illustrates that, when aiming for maximum flexibility, the integration of concerns tends to be solved at more fine-grained levels in a more standardized externally enabled way (stated otherwise: evolving towards the right lower corner in Table II).

Further, it should be clear that the heating cross-cutting concern is highly related to the preservation of heat by, for example, isolation. Also here, the different modular aggregation levels of the house (e.g., an isolating roof), the room (e.g., a well-closing door or isolation which is put behind a wall)

TABLE II. OVERVIEW OF THE DIFFERENT GRANULARITY-INTEGRATION PATTERN COMBINATIONS REGARDING HEATING.

	1A	*1B*	*2A*	*2B*	*2C*
house		•	○		
room		•		•	○
brick				○	

•: currently employed, ○: to be explored

and the brick (e.g., isolation incorporated in every individual brick) might be relevant. And similar to the on/off switching of electricity consuming devices, heat distribution throughout a house might benefit from more specific, remote and/or automated management (of its subparts). For instance, in order to allow certain rooms in the house (e.g., the living rooms) to be heated and others (e.g., the garage) not for a certain period of time, an operating panel may be provided for every radiator turning it on and off or even measuring the current temperature and matching it with a predefined temperature goal. In more advanced settings, a central management unit at the level of the house could be provided in which a goal temperature for multiple zones could be specified after which heat is released by those radiators which are standing in zones in which the temperature is lower than specified.

V. REFLECTIONS

Sections III and IV showed that the integration of the cross-cutting concerns heating and electricity can and have to be dealt with at several modular granularity levels and can be solved in multiple ways. During the drawing of a building plan, an experienced architect will take into account these cross-cutting concerns in advance: the wires for the electricity and water pipes for the water distribution will be provided, space for central heating boiler will be assured, and so on. And although some heuristics and best practices exist, this still means that the integration problem of these concerns has to be dealt with by every architect again, every time a house is constructed. As mentioned in Section II, NST was inspired by the need for adaptability and flexibility. In the context of a house, this would for instance mean the addition of an additional room, or another provider for a particular cross-cutting concern (e.g., switching from tapping electricity from the public distribution network to self-generated solar energy). However, it is generally known that the distribution of housing cross-cutting concerns —such as the ones we considered in this paper— may cause significant problems during such house extensions or adaptations. Many times, this leads to unforeseen ripple effects, including the drilling into walls and floors, and even tearing down (parts of) walls. As we explained in Section II, NST therefore proposes to use a set of predefined design patterns (called "elements") which already solve this integration problem for a particular functionality of a modular system and can then be used over and over again.

In the context of housing and their cross-cutting concerns, we would envision an elementary construction element as such fine-grained element [4] and represented in Figure 1. We already suggested such a brick for heating, but it is clear that a construction element might provide the integration of more than one cross-cutting concern (e.g., water supply, electricity, support, etc.). Different types of such building blocks might exist, such as for inner or outer walls, for floors and ceilings, with and without certain utilities, etc. The adaptation problems and their associated ripple-effects would be less frequent by the use of such building blocks as it is often the set of cross-cutting concerns which causes these invasive drilling and tearing down activities and these would then already be integrated in the most elementary building block of a house. As they are used, the construction elements would provide the cross-cutting concerns and integrate fluently with the other previously installed building blocks. Moreover, an architect designing a new house would have to spend less effort into the integration issues regarding the cross-cutting concern as the elements already deal with it. As we are no domain experts, we are not in a position to elaborate in detail how these building blocks should actually look like. However, we do think that it would be worthwhile for such building blocks to be subject to intensive research and development, which might for instance result in connections and isolations of fluid conduits and electrical conductors that are superior with respect to handcrafted plumbing. As these building blocks would be rather general and used over and over again, the resources invested would have a significant pay off due to the high-quality re-used solution.

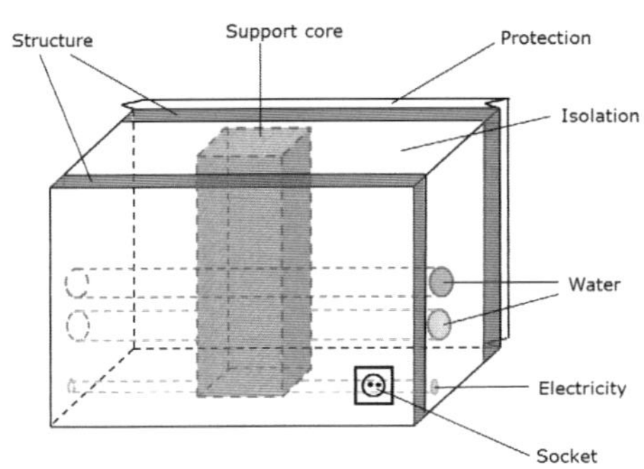

Figure 1. A construction element integration cross-cutting concerns [4].

So while in most cases, architects take the house as the main level of modular granularity, it is interesting to see that some initiatives have been taken to adopt the individual rooms of a house as a modular unit and which have even proposed some kind of elements for it (e.g., the Hivehaus "modular living space" initiative [8]. Here, houses are assembled as aggregations of prefabricated (e.g., hexagonal) modular parts, wherein the distribution of auxiliary facilities has been integrated upfront. Clearly, the design freedom concerning the house is then limited to an aggregation of these modular building blocks. This is due to the phenomenon we mentioned in Section II: the cross-cutting concerns should be integrated at the most fine-grained modular level as possible, as this determines the flexibility of the resulting artifacts. It is for this reason that we encourage the exploration of a construction element which would integrate several cross-cutting concerns as discussed above.

Note that very similar conclusions or analyses can be made for other utility concerns within houses such as water distribution or air conditioning. We anticipate that the bottom line of such analysis will be highly similar: first, the distribution of the cross-cutting concern should be considered at different modular aggregation levels. At each level, centralized (integration pattern 1) or non-centralized (integration pattern 2) integration patterns can be chosen, each in a non-standarized (A) or standardized (B) way. Whereas the decentralized version offers benefits in terms of freedom of choice, the centralized alternative might typically generate other benefits such as economies of scale. A centralized version then has to deal with the fact that all modules plugging in into the external framework are dependent on that framework unless a gateway module assuring version transparency (2C) is used.

VI. Conclusions

This paper presented an overview of the different possible integration patterns (with their associated benefits and drawbacks) for the cross-cutting concerns of electricity and heat distribution utilities in a housing context. It is important to stress that none of the authors claim to be housing electricity or heating experts. Instead, the analysis was based on general knowledge within this domain. Our actual contribution is situated elsewhere and is twofold. First, our goal was to show that the cross-cutting integration patterns for modular structures as proposed in [4] (and illustrated within the domain of software systems) are, at first sight, indeed relevant and applicable in a domain outside software as well. Given our non-expert status in the housing industry, we encourage actual domain experts to scrutinize and validate or refine our initial analyses. Second, we proposed and illustrated an approach to analyze and report on the different modular integration patterns within a domain. That is, is seems valuable to start with describing certain specifics and challenges in the domain at hand. Next, the different (hierarchical) granularity levels in the domain as well as the relevant cross-cutting concerns could be listed. For each cross-cutting concern, all possible combinations between the granularity levels and the five cross-cutting concern integration patterns can be considered and analyzed in terms of benefits and drawbacks. Some of these configurations might already exist, others might prove to be interesting avenues for future developments and still others might be purely theoretical considerations. Therefore, we hope that this paper might incite researchers and experts within other domains (e.g., logistics, manufacturing) to perform similar analyses within their respective areas of expertise.

References

[1] H. Simon, The Sciences of the Artificial. MIT Press, 1996.

[2] D. Parnas, "On the criteria to be used in decomposing systems into modules," Communications of the ACM, vol. 15, no. 12, 1972, pp. 1053–1058.

[3] C. Y. Baldwin and K. B. Clark, Design Rules: The Power of Modularity. Cambridge, MA, USA: MIT Press, 2000.

[4] H. Mannaert, J. Verelst, and P. De Bruyn, Normalized Systems Theory: From Foundations for Evolvable Software Toward a General Theory for Evolvable Design. Koppa, 2016.

[5] H. Mannaert, J. Verelst, and K. Ven, "The transformation of requirements into software primitives: Studying evolvability based on systems theoretic stability," Science of Computer Programming, vol. 76, no. 12, 2011, pp. 1210–1222, special Issue on Software Evolution, Adaptability and Variability.

[6] P. De Bruyn, "Generalizing normalized systems theory : towards a foundational theory for enterprise engineering," Ph.D. dissertation, University of Antwerp, 2014.

[7] Emerge Alliance, http://www.emergealliance.org/, Last accessed on February 4th, 2017.

[8] Hivehaus, http://hivehaus.co.uk/, Last accessed on February 4th, 2017.

Exploring Evolvable Modular Patterns for Transportation Vehicles and Logistics Architectures

Peter De Bruyn and Herwig Mannaert

Normalized Systems Institute
University of Antwerp, Belgium
Email:{peter.debruyn, herwig.mannaert}@uantwerp.be

Philip Huysmans

Antwerp Management School, Belgium
Email:philip.huysmans@ams.ac.be

***Abstract*—Many domains employ the concept of modularity as a key aspect during their design. While the use of modularity characteristics is believed to enable several beneficial effects, such as evolvability, the actual realization of this evolvability or flexibility remains difficult. This paper analyzes a set of modular structures which can be identified within transportation vehicles and logistic systems. We employ Normalized Systems Theory (NST), a theory on how to create evolvable modular structures, as our theoretical basis to analyze these transportation and logistic structures in terms of the flexibility and adaptability they do (not) enable. For these structures, multiple design alternatives exist of which the theory can clearly highlight the respective benefits and drawbacks. The paper demonstrates that NST is useful to analyze transport related modular structures at different levels of granularity. Additionally, we reflect upon the modularity characteristics of a recent logistics initiative called "The Physical Internet".**

Keywords–Modularity; Transportation; Logistics; Evolvability; Patterns; Physical Internet.

I. Introduction

In many domains including computer science, product engineering, and organizational sciences, modularity has proven to be a powerful concept. A modular system is typically considered as a system which is subdivided into a set of interacting subsystems. Several potential benefits are attributed to modular artifacts. Amongst other things, designing a product while using a set of modules is associated with a lower amount of complexity as the design is broken up into a set of smaller (less complex) problems [1]. Also, flexibility or evolvability are deemed to be improved in this way. Indeed, it allows one module of the system to be swapped for another version of it, without having to redesign the artifact from scratch. This allows some kind of plug-and-play behavior enabling variation (different aggregations based on the same set of modular building blocks can be formed) and evolvability (an artifact can evolve from one variant to another over time) and is deemed very powerful.

Achieving these benefits in reality is however quite challenging. Often, coupling (dependencies and interactions) between the modules in the system exist, which should be minimized [1][2][3]. However, specific ways on how this should precisely be done are often absent or ambiguous. For instance, some concerns in a modular system are cross-cutting (e.g., security in a software application) in the sense that their functionality is required throughout the entire system (e.g., every data entity should be securely stored). Adapting certain aspects of such cross-cutting concerns is often problematic as it typically creates profound ripple-effects throughout the system (i.e., a change in one module triggers a change in several other modules), which is clearly contradictory which the purpose of evolvability.

This paper focuses on the design of modular structures for transportation vehicles and logistics systems. It is clear that transportation vehicles (such as cars, trucks, boats, airplanes, trains) are modular structures at several abstraction levels (a car consisting out of a trunk, chassis, of which the latter consists out of several cylinders etc.) and could benefit from evolvability (e.g., replacing or upgrading particular parts or even extending the vehicle with additional seating places or engines). Also, the concept of cross-cutting concerns seems relevant within this context. That is, transportation artifacts need multiple auxiliary facilities in their design such as electricity and communication, which are needed in most of their components. More specifically, several of these auxiliary facilities within the modular design of physical artifacts (such as the different design options to distribute heating) were already discussed from a NST perspective in another publication [4] in a housing context. Analogous conclusions for these facilities can be drawn in the context of transportation artifacts. What differentiates transportation artifacts from other types of artifacts, is the presence of the additional and crucial concern of *propulsion*. Every transportation mechanism should, somehow, provide the ability for its cargo to be transported to another location. This propulsion can be realized by means of different driving mechanisms and different integration architectures, which will be the main focus of our exploratory analysis in this paper. However, most transportation vehicles are designed in such way that they lack true evolvability at several aspects (e.g., extending the seating capacity of a car or adding additional cylinders in the engine is typically impossible). This paper studies the implications of different design alternatives for transportation vehicles and logistics systems in terms of their evolvability. The considered design alternatives are based on the modular integration patterns as suggested by Normalized Systems Theory (NST)[5]. The theory is relevant in this context as it studies in-depth the necessary conditions in order to design evolvable modular systems.

It is important to mention upfront that none of the authors of this paper are experts within the domain of transportation or logistics. Therefore, the intention of this paper is not the prescribe in detail how architectures within this industry should be improved in the future. Rather, we intend to show that it makes sense to apply the modularity reasoning presented within NST (which originated at the software level) to this other domain in which we believe modularity is playing an important role. In Section II, we provide a brief overview of NST and the ways it describes to integrate the different modules within a system. We then apply these patterns to the analysis of transportation vehicles (e.g., cars, airplanes) in Section III. In Section IV, we ponder on some new initiatives and trends present within the logistics industry which seem to exhibit certain similarities with NST's (more general) modularity approach. Finally, we offer our conclusions in Section V.

II. MODULARITY AND NST INTEGRATION PATTERNS

A. NST and combinatorics

NST is a theory providing the formulation of design theorems which are proven to be necessary for obtaining an evolvable software system [5]. The authors operationalize evolvability by demanding Bounded Input Bound Output (BIBO) stability, even for systems which are growing in an unlimited way. The theorems prescribe all change drivers to be separated in distinct constructs (Separation of Concerns), processing functions to be called statefully (Separation of States) and data structures or processing functions to be updatable without impacting other data structures or processing functions (Version Transparency) [6]. Further, these theorems can actually be formulated for modular systems in general [7] and related to basic combinatorics [5]. More specifically, it is illustrated that modularity suggests that maintaining a particular amount of versions of modular building blocks should allow for an exponential amount of available system variants. However, when modularity is applied arbitrarily (e.g., by not adhering to the theorems), changing one particular version of one particular module may result into ripple effects to other (versions of) modules. This number of impacts can exponentially grow with the size of the system, which is clearly harmful for the evolvability of a (software) system.

B. Patterns for cross-cutting concern integration

Adherence to the NST theorems results in a system which is very fine-grained. This fine-grained design should be established very meticulously as every violation of every design theorem is proven to result eventually into ripple effects due to change. This is very hard to achieve and therefore, "elements" (i.e., modular design patterns) are proposed to enable the construction of such systems in a realistic setting [5]. Each of these elements provides a generically reusable modular structure for a basic functionality of the type of system one is creating. To fit the specific situation at hand, they can be parametrized and, if necessary, customized. A system is then created as being a set of parametrized instantiations of these generic modular elements. For software systems, data, task, flow, connector and trigger elements were defined as generic modular structures providing the basic functionalities of most information systems [5]. One can therefore conclude that the modules which form an element become (as a whole) a reusable module at a higher level of abstraction. Internally, every element takes care of a core functionality (e.g., the representation of data), and provides integration with some relevant cross-cutting concerns for that system (e.g., data security and persistency). To maximally enable evolvability, these cross-cutting concerns need to be integrated at the lowest modular granularity level which is possible (forming elements). The parts in the elements which connect or deal with the cross-cutting concerns need to be properly isolated in separate modules which are version transparent.

In general, different integration patterns for dealing with cross-cutting concerns can be distinguished. One possibility is to add cross-cutting concern modules directly to the main modules. Each cross-cutting concern module will then, by itself, handle the full functionality of that cross-cutting concern. We call integrations of this type the *embedded integration pattern* and will refer to it as *configuration 1*. More specifically, such embedded module can either be dedicated (i.e., the module was specifically designed for the considered system) or standardized (i.e., a standardized module for handling the cross-cutting concern is chosen). The first option is referred to as *configuration 1A*, while the latter one will be referenced as *configuration 1B*. In the context of software systems, imagine for instance a separate module added to a data entity to take care of data persistency in a custom designed way (1A) or by adopting a standard module (1B) for the same goal.

Another possibility is to add the cross-cutting concern modules to the main modules in such way that the cross-cutting concern modules only act as connections (or "relay modules") to an (external) framework, which implements the cross-cutting concern more elaborately and will therefore actually perform the needed functionality. We call integrations of this type the *relay integration pattern* and will refer to it as *configuration 2*. More specifically, a relay module can link to a framework which is dedicated (i.e., the framework was specifically designed for the considered system) or standardized (possibly even publicly available). The first option is referred to as *configuration 2A* while the latter one will be referenced as *configuration 2B*. In the context of a software system, imagine for instance a separate module added to a data entity which acts as a proxy to a specifically designed persistency framework (2A) or to a standard solution which is widely used, such as Java Persistence API (2B). Finally, it is also possible to have a relay module connecting to a *framework gateway* module. Here, it is only the framework gateway which connects directly to the external framework. This third variant is referred to as *configuration 2C*. In the context of a software system, imagine for instance a dedicated gateway module which connects to the JPA framework allowing all cross-cutting concern relay modules to call the gateway without being dependent on JPA themselves.

III. TRANSPORTATION VEHICLE PATTERNS

The identification of modules within a system is often a recursive issue [1]: at different levels of granularity, parts and subparts can be discerned. Therefore, when studying modularity within the domain of transportation, we propose to focus on the modular structure and its integration patterns at different levels: the vehicle, cargo and vehicle component levels.

A. The vehicle level

Regarding transportation, it is clear that most types of vehicles (such as cars, trucks, airplanes) provide their own propulsion mechanism, both in terms of power storage (e.g., fuel) and energy generation (typically by means of an engine). Since in most cases extensively tested and highly standardized modules are used for this purpose, this clearly aligns with integration pattern 1B as explained in Section II. This has benefits in terms of flexibility: different types of vehicles might use different types of power source (e.g., diesel, gas, electricity) or have different power needs (e.g., related to the cargo capacity). It also provides a high amount of independence and autonomy. A downside of such an architecture is clearly that the propulsion mechanism needs to be, by definition, embedded within every individual transport vehicle and that for instance technological advancements are not automatically dispersed over all available vehicles unless each of their mechanisms (e.g., engines) are individually updated or replaced. Another drawback is the fact this does not allow to realize any possible economies of scale which might arise from producing energy on a larger scale (i.e., for many vehicles at once).

While the other integration architectures are used less frequently, they are not completely inconceivable for transportation vehicles. Consider for instance an electrical train. While the propulsion forces are generated internally using electrical engines, the electrical power which is used for this purpose is generated externally. This electrical power is tapped from an externally available framework or, in this case, the electrical distribution network available along the train tracks. Therefore, one could argue that —to a certain extent— this aligns already to some extent with integration pattern 2B. One could even go one step further. Consider for instance the case of the Transrapid magnetic levitation train, or the recently proposed Hyperloop. In these types of transportation, the vehicles are propelled by the propulsion forces generated in or around the vehicle tracks. This would even more narrowly fit into the mentioned integration pattern 2B. While such centralized architectures introduce a dependency on the external framework which is employed (e.g., if the energy distribution network is down, no vehicle will be able to advance), they have clear benefits as well. For instance, they would be able to benefit from economies of scale regarding efficiency, or flexibility with respect to the introduction of (for instance) more environmentally friendly techniques for power generation.

Returning to the design of cars, it is clear that such mechanisms (i.e., as described in integration pattern 2) would only be possible in case the roads contain propulsion mechanisms or conduct power. As this is currently not the case, the electrical power for electrical cars can only be stored internally in batteries (but generated externally) and therefore stick to integration pattern 1B. Specifically focusing our attention on airplane vehicles, one can note that aircrafts require large amounts of propulsion power, which would make the use of an architecture in which the aircraft taps into an externally available standardized framework via a relay module (i.e., integration pattern 2B) extremely tempting. Nevertheless, the intertwining of propulsion and lift (which is specific for aircrafts) would make this design very difficult, and the notion seems to be completely incompatible with the current degrees of freedom airplanes enjoy to use the airspace. Indeed, such an architecture would entail the need for some kind of tubes encompassing the vehicles, which could in their turn remove the need for lifting forces. In other words, such an architecture would probably cease to be genuine air transport.

Nevertheless, as this configuration has been realized for certain transportation vehicles and offers potential for others (e.g., cars) in the future, we believe that the exploration of (the feasibility) of technologies enabling these kind of integration architectures would be very worthwhile.

B. The cargo level

It is interesting to note that the transportation industry has already, rather explicitly, adopted a high degree of modularity standardization at the level of their cargo. This can be found in the context of today's logistics landscape, in which it is important to be able to transport goods by means of cross-mode transportation. That means that, in order to go from point A to B, multiple vehicles of often different nature are employed. A laptop which is for instance ordered in the USA to be delivered in Antwerp, might travel by a combination of airplane and/or boat, train, truck and car. In order to facilitate such logistic routes, a large part of the way of how the cargoes (i.e., the goods to be transported) are packaged, is standardized by means of *containerized freight*. That is, while for some type of goods customized transportation mechanisms still exist (e.g., for the transportation of steel coils, roll-on roll-off (RoRo) goods, bulk goods, etc.), the majority of non-bulk goods is transported by means of containers. Such containers can clearly be considered as standardized cargo modules in terms of properties such as their dimensions (height, length, depth), securing mechanisms, maximum load, etc.

From a modularity point of view, one can see that in such case various sound design principles are applied, implying a set of accompanying important benefits. First, this existing containerized modular freight architecture enables the decoupling or encapsulating the cargo from the transport vehicle (cf. infra). This decoupling allows to freely combine both decoupled parts (here: cargo and transport vehicle) without having to adapt one or the other for this purpose. Stated otherwise: substitution of the modular parts is made easy. Indeed, the standardization of freight containers in terms of dimensions and securing mechanisms allows the recombination of goods on different transportation modes at the level of the individual containers. As long as goods can be securely stowed within these standardized containers, thousands of them can be loaded by cranes on sea-going cargo ships, be switched to barges in batches of tens or maybe hundred containers, routed individually within a harbor, and further shipped towards customers via trains (in a set up to 20) and/or trucks (mostly individually). Similarly, as most transportation vehicles are designed in correspondence with the standardized dimensions of the freight containers, they can transport all types of goods and do not need to undergo specific changes when, for instance, a truck has to transport couches instead of laptops. Second, the modular architecture of the cargo makes it possible to upscale or downscale the total cargo on one vehicle within certain limits. For instance, as long as a ship is large enough, one can extend the overall cargo by simply increasing the number of containers. Or, as long the traction of a locomotive is powerful enough, additional containers can be added to a transportation train. We therefore conclude that already an important amount of flexibility is achieved in terms of the type of cargo as well as the transportation mode and scale.

Interpreting the situation sketched above in terms of our

modular integration architectures as described in Section II, this means that integration architecture 2C is applied. That is, it is clear that no embedded architecture is present as the container itself has no propulsion mechanisms incorporated into it. Instead, the container has standardized connections to connect into different types of vehicles (see Section III-A) which, at their turn, have the capacity to provide the required propulsion for one or several containers. As these connections are version transparent in terms of a large set of different vehicles (truck, train and even boat), no dependency regarding a specific type of external network is present and therefore we would be inclined to categorize it within architecture 2C.

Further, in terms of this containerized freight, it is important to mention that, conceptually speaking, the idea of containerization should not necessarily limited to freight alone. For instance, one can easily imagine that similar cargo modules could be made for humans as well, although such containers would clearly have to be made more human-friendly, and the practicality and added value might —at this point in time— be questionable.

Finally, it is interesting to note that certain players in the industry are still looking for additional ways to modularize freight in a more efficient way. For instance, Airbus was only recently —in late 2015— granted a patent for a modular removable aircraft cabin, in which the whole cabin (i.e., the space for all passengers) can be substituted by another cabin [8]. The fact that major industry players are working on these kinds of ideas, seems to support the fact that such ideas on modularization in (air) transportation should definitely not be considered ludicrous nor obvious.

C. The vehicle components level

In order to further explore the modular integration for transportation vehicles, it is interesting to ponder on the decoupling or encapsulation of the various concerns at the level of the vehicle, such as a car. Here, relevant concerns could be the passenger cabine (providing a comfortable place for passengers to sit), the trunk (providing storage space for luggage), the chassis (protecting the car from the outside world) or the engine (generating the propulsion force). It is remarkable to note that, in many cases, the compatibility of these modular components of transportation vehicles seems restricted to vehicles of one particular model or, in some cases, multiple models of one manufacturer. This means that, again considering a car, most passenger cabines, trunks, chassis parts, etc. can only be replaced by their exact copies. Stated otherwise, a trunk which was designed for car model A is typically not able to be used for a car model B as it would simply not fit due to size limitations, aerodynamic constraints, weight, etc. This is due to a high degree of coupling between the individual components we consider and their model or manufacturer specifications. It would certainly provide some added value to customers, if the modules implementing these major concerns would be decoupled, encapsulated, and standardized in accordance with integration architecture 1B of Section II, allowing plug and play behavior. For instance, in such case, consumers would be able —for a certain car size category— to purchase the chassis, the engine, the passenger cabine, the trunk, etc. all independently from different vendors.

Moreover, each of these modules could then be replaced or upgraded independently as well. For example, the engine could be replaced when it breaks down, but could also be upgraded in order to have a more powerful, modern, or environmentally cleaner engine. One could even imagine to introduce an electrical engine in a car which was originally equipped with as gas or diesel engine. Of course, we mention once again that we are no experts in car manufacturing and do not elaborate on the specific manufacturing details of each aspect of the design. Moreover, we are aware of the fact that it would not be straightforward to keep the decoupling or encapsulation of the various modules intact throughout the course of significant technological evolutions in time. Nevertheless, the advantages of such design from a sustainability viewpoint would obviously be significant: cars could become more efficient and cleaner without ending up in a junkyard after a limited amount of years.

Some indications exist which suggest that the amount of coupling between vehicle components or between the vehicle and its components is not equally large among different industries. For instance, the airplane industry seems to succeed in having a better decoupling and encapsulation of certain parts of an airplane. For example, manufacturers of jet engines and the aircraft are typically different firms. In order to remain viable as an industry, this implies (and necessitates) that the engine and the rest of the vehicle should, at least to some extent, be decoupled. However, though an engine can be replaced, aircrafts are clearly designed for a certain type and amount of engines.

Considering the components of transportation vehicles at a still more fine-grained modular level, one could imagine an even more fine-grained modular structure for, for instance, car engines where cylinders could be replaced, upgraded, or simply added in order to increase the engine power. Again, in order to enable these possibilities, the modules at this very fine-grained level should be designed in such a way that they are clearly decoupled, encapsulated and standardized, corresponding to integration architecture 1B.

D. Overview and advanced issues

Table I provides an overview of the granularity-integration pattern combinations for the case of transportation vehicles. We can observe that an interesting and advanced modular architecture seems already be in place at the cargo level. This tends to indicate that the industry has reached a rather high maturity level regarding this issue. As far as the vehicle and vehicle component modularity levels are concerned, interested avenues for a further exploration of the modular integration architecture can be remarked. Certainly for the case of vehicle components, where the design of fully decoupled and encapsulated modular parts seems still to be in-progress. The table further illustrates that, when aiming for maximum flexibility, the integration of concerns tends to be solved at more fine-grained levels (going downwards in Table I) and in a more standardized way enabled by an external framework (going to the right in Table I) in the long run.

Furthermore, it is interesting to make the mental exercise to apply NST reasoning in a more complete way and adopt the notion of NST elements, which we introduced in Section II. When employing such elements to build a system, a large set of very integrated small and fine-grained modules are used to form the aggregated system (instead of one monolithic and non-scalable building block). Translating this idea to the

TABLE I. OVERVIEW OF THE DIFFERENT GRANULARITY-INTEGRATION PATTERN COMBINATIONS REGARDING TRANSPORTATION VEHICLES

	1A	*1B*	*2A*	*2B*	*2C*
vehicle		•		○	
cargo					•
vehicle components		○			

•: currently employed, ○: to be explored

components of an engine, one could imagine an engine as an aggregation of smaller integrated engines (with all required subcomponents for a small engine) delivering propulsion forces. This would theoretically mean that the propulsion power could be increased by adding more engines, and that the various small engines could be replaced and upgraded independently, even combining combustion engines and electrical engines. Once again, this could have significant benefits from a sustainability point of view. Also, this would partly solve some of the scalability issues we mentioned in Section III-A, for instance in case carrying additional cargo within a particular vehicle would be restrained due to limitations in the capacity of the vehicle's engine.

Going one step further, elements might be conceivable at a higher granularity level as well. That is, elements might be designed which also provide the integration of these small engines with non-propulsion concerns. Suppose for instance one-person transport modules or vehicles that can be aggregated or combined at any time into more-person modules. Assume further that these one-person modules have their own propulsion mechanisms and storage spaces, which are automatically combined when several modules are aggregated. This would mean that the propulsion power and the storage room would be proportional to the size of the vehicle, which would be proportional to the number of passengers. And one could further imagine that each one of those units could be enabled to tap into external propulsion power if available, while producing its own propulsion power otherwise.

One could even explore what this could possibly mean for air transportation. When considering the design of airplane artifacts, one can note that they differentiate themselves from ground transportation artifacts by the fact that another concern next to propulsion becomes apparent: the need to obtain lift. Adding this concern to the design is obviously not trivial. Indeed, both concerns —propulsion and lift— are even tightly coupled in current airplanes: the lift force is based on the velocity and therefore on the propulsion of the vehicle. This actually represents an omnipresent risk in airplanes: without propulsion, there is no lift anymore. Nevertheless, we do think that a similar reasoning based on elements is valid for air transportation. For instance, one could imagine small integrated transport modules or vehicles for a few persons, that can be aggregated or combined at any time into larger airplane modules. From an energy or sustainability point of view, it would clearly be very appealing to be able to adapt the size and propulsion power of the airplanes to the number of registered passengers.

As we are no domain experts, we are clearly not entitled to discuss the outlook of modular structures for transport propulsion in depth or judge on their practical feasibility. We also do not have any intention to oversimplify the difficulties and complexities one would be confronted with during the design of such elements. For example, the design of such modular architectures obviously does not liberate the designer from the laws of physics which need to be obeyed at all times: when considering the elements for air transportation, the relationship between the weight of the vehicle and the wing surface creating the lift, should result in the required equilibrium at the cruising speed, both for the singular and aggregated vehicles. However, instead of making such architectures impossible, these physical constraints could serve as boundary conditions to solve the design equations. So, instead of elaborating in detail on the actual design of such modular building blocks (such as the elements), our main goal is to illustrate the relevance of our modularity approach for the design of transportation vehicles and show what kind of possibilities normalized evolvable transport architectures could unleash. For instance, the scalability issue mentioned in Section III-A, would probably be largely solved if the industry would manage to realized such elements.

IV. Logistics Architectures

Modularization is not necessarily limited to the analysis of the vehicles and their load, but can also be applied at a higher conceptual level such as the logistics supply chain. For instance, triggered by the current inefficiencies of most logistics networks (e.g., use of partly empty trucks, suboptimal routes, traffic jams, overusage of highly polluting transportation modes) the *Physical Internet (PI) Initiative* aims to design "an open global logistics system founded on physical, digital and operational interconnectivity through encapsulation, interfaces and protocols" [9, p. 152]. In order to achieve this goal, they propose to design a global logistics system based on the basic architectural principles adopted by the Internet for the distribution of digital information. This means that cargo is transported as a set of (smaller) packages, will reach its destination by traveling via a set of connecting nodes, may follow different routes (possibly upfront undetermined) and employs an open infrastructure (public stock facilities or transportation providers) to this end. Related to our focus, it is interesting to observe that the initiators of the project explicitly coin the importance of well-designed modular structures in logistics and the problems originated by the opposite situation: "Innovation is bottlenecked, notably by lack of generic standards and protocols, transparency, modularity and systemic open infrastructure" [10, p. 5].

Whereas space limitations do not allow us to analyze all listed characteristics for this new logistics system, some of them can easily be related to our integration pattern analysis presented above. First, regarding the cargo level, it is remarkable that the current freight containers are considered useful, but too coarse-grained. Instead, they propose a set of unitary and composite π-containers as world-standard, smart, green and modular containers. They would differ from the currently used containers by being smaller (causing less "empty space" in containers), (de)composable (allowing to attach or disconnect multiple containers to each other), having advanced securing and sealing possibilities, being equipped with smart sensors and controllers, have conditioning capabilities if required, etc. Stated otherwise, the authors of the initiative argue that one large cargo container is not sufficient and should be considered as a modular system on its own. Of course, the decoupling between cargo and vehicle should be attained as it was the case for current containers. Therefore, at the vehicle level, vehicles should be manufactured adhering to this new π-container standard. Further, a global PI could spur the development of vehicles optimized (e.g., using the most adequate integration patterns) for the trajectory which they are required to serve (i.e., in some trajectories external propulsion mechanisms may be present, in others not).

Moreover, the vision of the physical internet refers to the logistics network as an additional aggregation level, which supersedes transportation vehicles (i.e., the aggregation level upon which this paper elaborates) and which needs to be redesigned adhering to modularity guidelines. For example, [10, p. 10] states that logistics networks need to "evolve from point-to-point hub-and-spoke transport to distributed multi-segment intermodal transport". The current logistics networks allow a certain level of intermodal transport, as discussed in Section III-B. For example, a container can be use multiple modes of transport such as trains, ships, and trucks, without the freight itself being handled. However, the smaller granularity of the cargo as proposed by the physical internet will encourage smaller segments and more advanced optimization of the different segments. Once routing decisions can be optimized for a single package, as opposed to an aggregation of packages in a container, advanced algorithms based on the routing algorithms of the digital internet can be leveraged. This vision is in line with our observations based on modularity reasoning on other abstraction levels, but needs to confront the same practical challenges discussed earlier. For example, this vision requires the development of nodes which are highly optimized for load breaking: disassembling aggregations of cargo into individual constituents, calculating the optimal route for each individual π-container, and reassembling new aggregations. As such, these nodes will need to be technologically more advanced than the current logistics hubs.

Many node-to-node segments will still be operated by traditional transportation vehicles, because of the economies of scale of these vehicles. However, because of the small granularity of a single segment and the load breaking capabilities of the nodes, the optimal transportation vehicle can be re-evaluated for each individual segment. Consider the final segment an individual package has to travel to an individual customer. In certain instances, individual air transport using a drone could be the fastest way to fulfill such a segment. Organizations such as Amazon are already experimenting with this technology, albeit within very strict limitations: the final delivery needs to be very close to an Amazon depot (a traditional hub), and strict weight limitations are enforced. This last limitation relates to the lift concern of air transportation vehicles discussed earlier. Current research demonstrates how this concern can be made scalable without introducing couplings with other concerns, such as drone control [11]. This research shows how cargo can be attached to multiple supporting drones, which, based on force sensing, follow the movement of one primary controlled drone. The primary drone can now be controlled as if it was the sole transport vehicle, albeit with a scalable propulsion concern. This can be considered as an illustration of how state-of-the-art research is able to make advancement towards NST integration patterns previously considered practically impossible. Indeed, NST prescribes that the integration of concerns needs to be solved at the most fine-grained levels, for which several practical obstacles have been identified in the past for air transportation vehicles (cf. supra). The research of [11] demonstrates the practical feasibility of adhering to this principle: a scalable integration of the lift concern at the level of an individual π-container. As such, we believe that further research elaborating on the use of NST as a theoretical underpinning for R&D in the logistics domain would be highly valuable.

V. Conclusion

This paper presented an overview of different modular structures which could be identified within transportation vehicles, as well as the different integration patterns in this respect (with their associated benefits and drawbacks), using NST as the theoretical basis. It is important to stress that none of the authors claim to be transportation or logistics experts. Instead, generally available knowledge within the domain was used as the primary source for the analysis. The main contribution is situated in the fact that we show the applicability and relevance of NST in a context (i.e., transportation and logistics) outside the original application domain of the theory (i.e., software systems). To this end, we identified modular structures at different granularity levels and discussed the benefits and drawbacks of the different modular integration patterns proposed by NST. Next, we also interpreted upcoming trends and initiatives in the field, such as the Physical Internet, with respect of their modularity characteristics. Given our non-expert status in the transportation and logistics domain, we encourage actual experts to scrutinize and validate or refine our initial analyses provided. Additionally, future research could be directed towards the application of a similar analysis regarding the integration of cross-cutting concerns into (physical) artifacts within a particular domain outside the transportation industry.

References

[1] H. Simon, The Sciences of the Artificial. MIT Press, 1996.

[2] D. Parnas, "On the criteria to be used in decomposing systems into modules," Communications of the ACM, vol. 15, no. 12, 1972, pp. 1053–1058.

[3] C. Y. Baldwin and K. B. Clark, Design Rules: The Power of Modularity. Cambridge, MA, USA: MIT Press, 2000.

[4] P. De Bruyn, J. Faes, T. Vermeire, and J. Bosmans, "On the modular structure and evolvability of architectural patterns for housing utilities," in Proceedings of The Ninth International Conferences on Pervasive Patterns and Applications, 2017.

[5] H. Mannaert, J. Verelst, and P. De Bruyn, Normalized Systems Theory: From Foundations for Evolvable Software Toward a General Theory for Evolvable Design. Koppa, 2016.

[6] H. Mannaert, J. Verelst, and K. Ven, "The transformation of requirements into software primitives: Studying evolvability based on systems theoretic stability," Science of Computer Programming, vol. 76, no. 12, 2011, pp. 1210–1222, special Issue on Software Evolution, Adaptability and Variability.

[7] P. De Bruyn, "Generalizing normalized systems theory : towards a foundational theory for enterprise engineering," Ph.D. dissertation, University of Antwerp, 2014.

[8] U.S. Patent US 9,193,460 B2, 2015.

[9] B. Montreuil, R. D. Meller, and E. Ballot, Physical Internet Foundations. Berlin, Heidelberg: Springer Berlin Heidelberg, 2013, pp. 151–166.

[10] B. Montreuil, "Toward a physical internet: meeting the global logistics sustainability grand challenge," Logistics Research, vol. 3, no. 2, 2011, pp. 71–87.

[11] A. Tagliabue, M. Kamel, S. Verling, R. Siegwart, and J. Nieto, "Collaborative Object Transportation Using MAVs via Passive Force Control," ArXiv e-prints, Dec. 2016.

The Social Picture

Sebastiano Battiato*, Giovanni M. Farinella*, Filippo L.M. Milotta*, Alessandro Ortis*,
Luca Addesso†, Antonino Casella†, Valeria D'Amico†, Giovanni Torrisi†
*Universitá degli Studi di Catania, Viale A. Doria 6, 95125 - Catania, Italy
Email: {battiato, gfarinella, milotta, ortis}@dmi.unict.it
†Telecom Italia, Viale A. Doria 6, 95125 - Catania, Italy
Email: {luca.addesso, antonino.casella, valeria1.damico, giovanni.torrisi}@telecomitalia.it

***Abstract*—We present *The Social Picture*, a framework to collect and explore huge amount of crowdsourced social images about public events, cultural heritage sites and other customized private events. The collections can be explored through a number of advanced Computer Vision and Machine Learning algorithms, able to capture the visual content of images in order to organize them in a semantic way. The interfaces of *The Social Picture* allow the users to create customized collections by exploiting semantic filters based on visual features, social network tags, geolocation, and other information related to the images.**

***Keywords*–Social Media; Crowdsourcing; Multimedia; Image Collections; Image Understanding.**

I. Introduction

Nowadays, the diffusion of social networks plays a crucial role in collecting information about people opinion and trends. In social events (e.g., concerts), the audience typically produces and share a lot of multimedia data with mobile devices (e.g., images, videos, geolocation, tags, etc.) related to what has captured their interest. The redundancy in these data can be exploited to infer social information about the attitude of the attending people by means of Machine Learning (ML) and Computer Vision (CV) algorithms. In [1] we introduced a framework called *The Social Picture* (TSP) to collect, analyze and organize huge flows of visual data, and to allow users the navigation of image collections generated by the community.

In this demo, we present some additional features that extend the work done in [1]: design of a new t-SNE (t-distributed Stochastic Neighbor Embedding) exploration tool suitable for very large collections, 3D reconstruction of heritage sites by means of the attending people's photos, more advanced statistics provided to event organizers, creation of private events collections and temporal extension of collection analysis. The rest of this paper is organized as follows. Section II describes the aims and the features of the framework presented in [1]. Section III describes some issues related to the first prototype of the framework, and presents the implemented improvements, as well as the new developed features. The acknowledgement closes the article.

II. Overview

TSP is a social framework populated by images uploaded by users or collected from other social media (Figure 1). Anyone registered to TSP can become an event manager and start a social collection accordingly to the "prosumer" paradigm, where the users are both producers and consumers of a service. Indeed, each collection has two kind of users: the event organizer and the event participant. Imagine an art-gallery manager who leases a famous Picasso's painting with the aim to include it in a event exhibition, together with other famous and expensive artworks. How does he know he did a good investment? Which was the more attractive artwork? The collection of the uploaded images of an event, gives the sources analysed in TSP to answer the aforementioned questions. The obtained information can be then exploited by the event organizers for the event evaluation and further planning. These information could be exploited, for example, to perform aimed investments. The system can suggest what is the better subject to use for the advertising campaign of the event, or which of the attractions it worth to mainly reproduce in the souvenir shop products, to support merchandising strategies. Feedback about what is the most interesting part (i.e., the most photo captured) of a landmark building can help on taking decisions about renovating some parts rather than others as first investment. Users can add an image to a collection by using either a mobile application and a website interface. Furthermore, an event collection can be populated by selecting images from the most common social networks for images (e.g., Flickr, Panoramio, Instagram). Once an image is uploaded, it is analysed by a set of CV and ML algorithms. The web interface exhibits a range of filtering tools to better explore the huge amount of data. When an event manager creates a new collection, he is allowed to specify several options to customize the image gathering, the social analysis to be performed, and the visualization tools to be shown for the users of that collection. The event manager is also allowed to set a range of statistics, which will be available after the analysis of the collected images. The several exploration tools are based on both visual and textual information, such as EXIF (Exchangeable Image File Format) data and a number of ad-hoc extracted visual features. The visual analysis module of the system feds all the images into two different CNNs (Convolutional Neural Networks), *AlexNet* [2] and *Places205-*

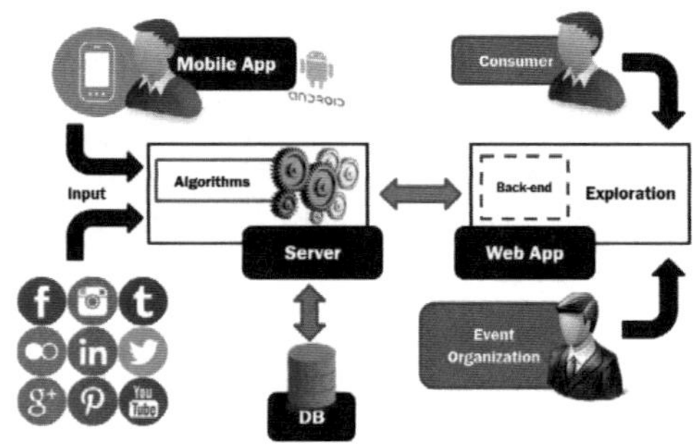

Figure 1. The Social Picture's architecture.

AlexNet [3], in order to extract the classification labels and image representations. Furthermore, the system is able to distinguish pictures depicting food, and pictures captured in indoor/outdoor environments by exploiting visual features. The system provides different exploration tools, detailed in the followings. A demonstrative video is available at the following link: http://iplab.dmi.unict.it/TSP

A. Advanced Tools in The Social Picture

Among the tools included in TSP, there is the one useful to generate automatic subsets of images from a specific photo collection. This tool allows the user to set the number of images to obtain as output for a collection in TSP, and automatically generates the subset of images taking into account visual features as well as EXIF information related to the images composing the photo collection. In this way, the user is provided by a number of representative image prototypes related to the collection, which can be used for different purposes (e.g., printing the most significative pictures of paintings of a museum for a specific social group). For this tool, CNN representation used in [3] is employed.

In [1], we exploited the *fc7* feature extracted with the *AlexNet* architecture [2] for each image and exploited the t-SNE embedding algorithm [4] to compute a 2D embedding that respects the pairwise distances between visual features.

The landmark heatmap is a visualization tool used to depict the intensity of images at spatial points. The heatmap consists of a colored overlay applied to the original image of a specific landmark building or area of interest. Areas of higher intensity will be colored red, and areas of lower intensity will appear blue. The intensity of the heatmap is related to the number of collected pictures that contain that visual area. By clicking on a point of the heatmap, the user can retrieve and visualize the images that contribuited to generate the map intensity at that point.

Finally, the automatic image captioning, as described in [5], is another feature included in TSP. With the aim to help the user to include a description to an uploaded image, *The Social Picture* automatically generates and suggests a description to the user that can then refine it. The descriptions of images can be used for text based query performed by the user.

III. Platform Improvements

A. Hierarchical t-SNE

The first implementation of the t-SNE exploration tool in TSP was unable to scale with the number of the collections' images. The new tool presented in this demo implements an hierarchical version of the t-SNE embedding which allows to explore picture collections without limits on the amount of processed pictures. This helps the user to better explore the image distribution in a custom level of detail. Furthermore, the user can choose a subset of images and compute the t-SNE embedding of them directly on the browser. As the number of pictures of a collection is unpredictable, the computation of the t-SNE coordinates could be very expensive. Besides the t-SNE computation, which needs to be executed only one time per dataset, a huge number of pictures can affect the browser efficiency for the visualization of the 2D embedding. We organize the entire collection of pictures in a hierarchical structure. After the collection is analysed (i.e., the *fc7* features have been computed for all the images) the system performs a hierarchical k-means clustering of the image features. The algorithm divides the dataset recursively into k clusters, for each computation the k centroids are used as elements of a *k-tree* and removed from the set. When this new version of the t-SNE tool (hierarchical t-SNE) is executed, it shows to the user the t-SNE embedding computed only for the elements in the root of the *k-tree* (i.e., the picture centroids of the first *k-means* computation). When the user selects one of these pictures, the system computes the t-SNE of the pictures included in the child node corresponding to the selected picture element. This hierarchical exploration can be continued by selecting one of the shown pictures and computing the t-SNE embedding for its sub-elements in the hierarchy.

B. 3D Reconstruction

Starting from VSFM (Visual Structure From Motion) [6], we are able to compute a 3D sparse reconstruction of large photos collections. The models are augmented with colors for vertices, related to the frequency of been acquired in a photo, colors for cameras, related to the number of visual features acquired by each photo, and with a plane which show the spatial density of contributing users. We embedded in TSP the models through a 3D web viewer based on Threejs, allowing the users to browse the 3D sparse reconstructed models gaining a cue about what are the points of view and the subjects preferred by users when take photos. Moreover, the models in the 3D web viewer can also be browsed through Leap Motion system, an intuitive and fast interactive system.

C. Private Events

Private collections can be created in TSP: the private collections con be accessed only by the owner and the invited users. Owner invites users to contribute adding new photos to the collection, while users receive the invitation through an e-mail.

D. Temporal Update

We developed a temporal uddate for collection: owners of collections can launch collection update request to server. It is possible to check if new photos have been added since at most 1 year from the time of creation or last update of the collection. Once the window for update is set, server quiries social networks for new photos and add them to the collection.

Acknowledgments

The authors would like to thank Marco Cavallo and Michele Bellocchi for helping in the implementation of the web framework.

References

[1] S. Battiato et al., "The social picture," in Proceedings of the 2016 ACM on International Conference on Multimedia Retrieval. ACM, 2016, pp. 397–400.

[2] A. Krizhevsky, I. Sutskever, and G. E. Hinton, "Imagenet classification with deep convolutional neural networks," in Advances in neural information processing systems, 2012, pp. 1097–1105.

[3] B. Zhou, A. Lapedriza, J. Xiao, A. Torralba, and A. Oliva, "Learning deep features for scene recognition using places database," in Advances in Neural Information Processing Systems, 2014, pp. 487–495.

[4] L. Van der Maaten and G. Hinton, "Visualizing data using t-sne," Journal of Machine Learning Research, vol. 9, no. 2579-2605, 2008, p. 85.

[5] A. Karpathy and L. Fei-Fei, "Deep visual-semantic alignment for generating image descriptions," in Computer Vision and Pattern Recognition, 2015.

[6] C. Wu, "Towards linear-time incremental structure from motion," in 3D Vision-3DV 2013, 2013 International Conference on. IEEE, 2013, pp. 127–134.

Mass Events Monitoring Through Crowdsourced Media Analysis

Marco Cavallo, Ermanno Guardo and Alessandro Ortis

Universitá degli Studi di Catania
Viale A. Doria 6, 95125
Catania, Italy
Email: marco.cavallo@dieei.unict.it,
ermanno.guardo@unict.it,
ortis@dmi.unict.it

Marco Sapienza and Giuseppe La Torre

Telecom Italia
Viale A. Doria 6, 95125
Catania, Italy
Email: marco1.sapienza@telecomitalia.it,
giuseppe.latorre@telecomitalia.it

***Abstract*—In the context of Smart Cities, the crowdsourced approach provides huge amount of information that can be exploited for the detection and monitoring of critical events. To this aim, a framework to collect and analyze a multitude of crowdsourced data is described in this paper. The proposed system exploits the existing Radio Access Network (RAN) to collect profiled users' contributes within a specific area of interest, which are properly analyzed. The results of such processing are made available to the service that required the monitoring. This supports the decision making process devoted to the critical event response.**

***Index Terms*—Crowdsourcing; Data Monitoring; Mobile Edge Computing; Multimedia Analysis.**

I. Introduction

Nowadays, the pace of urbanization is exponentially increasing, with a multitude of information sources such as wireless sensor networks, cameras, smartphones, wearable devices and social networks. Such a huge amount and variety of data provide new technological assets to deal with unprecedented challenges in the context of smart cities.

In this scenario, the occurrence of critical events, such as fires, heartquakes or explosions, needs to be quickly noticed in order to safeguard the nearby citizens, who are often unaware about accidents and risk their safety or hinder the emergency operations. In this context, transports and ICT play a crucial role in disaster response and management based on information collected from smart heterogeneous entities such as personal devices, cameras, connected vehicles, forming the recent emerging Internet of Things (IoT) paradigm [1]. IoT aims to have more pervasive connected objects which provide heterogeneous information useful for future Smart Cities. The Smart City aims to have a distributed, shared, horizontal and social intelligence, which encourages the participation of citizens and the organization of the city in a perspective of optimizing resources and results [2].

The management of the aforementioned critical events, in a Smart City context, requires two main actions: event detection and monitoring. The first aims to detect signal anomalies, such as anomaly values on mass movements, pollution data, etc. The detection phase is devoted to a continuous observation of a number of predefined data and the design of statistical models of these observations in a normal context. When a critical event occurs, the system detects an anomalous data pattern with respect to ordinary conditions. This kind of analysis aims to promptly understand what it is happening and how the event is evolving, in order to support the decision making process. Although the detection can be easily obtained by the continuous observation of signals over a specific geographical region, the monitoring of an event could require the collection of live customized data in not observable areas. As an example, an anomaly detection system could spot unusual behavior, such as the presence of mass of people who are moving towards an area due an accident. To quickly understand what is happening in that specific area, a monitoring system needs to collect more specific data related to the involved region. In this context, it could be optimal to have a video stream from cameras which observe that region. However, there is no guarantee of the presence of such devices. One solution could be to ask nearby people to contribute on collecting specific data through their personal devices, exploiting a crowdsourced approach.

In this work, we propose a framework able to correlate user data such as video, images and text, exploiting this information in order to detect and monitor critical events and rapidly notify the citizens. To this aim, the proposed framework exploits the existing Radio Access Network (RAN), which also provides computational capabilities defined by the Mobile Edge Computing (MEC) paradigm [3]. Such a computing paradigm allows the allocation of MEC IT application servers that can be directly integrated on the LTE access nodes in order to provide low latency and location awareness for real time services, allowing the pre-processing of the data provided by the users located within the range of the specific Base Transceiver Station (BTS) [4].

The rest of this paper is structured as follows: Section II describes some background information on detection of critical events and how the crowdsourced approach can facilitate a disaster management. Section III presents an overview of the reference scenario. Section IV describes the architecture and a typical execution flow of the proposed framework. Finally in the last Section, some consideration and future work have been presented.

II. Related Work

Many approaches have been proposed to automatically detect patterns such as accidents (e.g., stampedes, fire) but also busy roads and traffic jam. In [5], authors proposed an automatic event detection technique for camera anomaly based on image analysis. Starting from a procedure that extracts reduced-reference features from multiple regions in the surveillance images, this technique detects anomaly events by analyzing variation of features when image quality decreases and field of view changes. In [6], it is presented a solution to detect anomaly specifically designed for traffic cameras. This work introduced a new state transition system that involves the outcomes of image quality assessment and mixture of optical flow histogram analyzing. A two-stage scheme was proposed to reduce the computational complexity in order to meet the real-time requirements of large-scale monitoring system. This method can be used for traffic camera only. The work proposed in [7] demonstrates how crowdsourcing can be facilitated in the contexts of smart buildings and cities in order to support a more effective and efficient integrated disaster management approach. In this scenario, is explained how various participant users including critical infrastructures, cars, buildings, and humans could be connected via sensors and mobile APIs in order to acquire data from surrounding environment.

In order to monitor abnormal events, the proposed approach acquires data related to the environment by exploiting personal devices, video surveillance systems deployed in the city and wireless air quality sensor systems. These information can be analyzed with proper techniques of pattern recognition and data analysis, enabling the distribution of computation on the smart cities with Mobile Edge Computing, exploiting a crowdsourced approach.

III. Scenario

Over the last few years, with considerable complicity of social networks, we have discovered the enormous value that people can bring to different areas by means the information they produce. Common users have become prosumer (producer-consumer) of original contents.

The scenario considered in this paper regards the detection and the monitoring of abnormal events in a city with the help of its citizens. The main strength of a crowdsourced approach is the pervasiveness of the people, who can be considered as "mobile sensors". A similar pervasiveness is hard to achieve using an infrastructure of real sensors (eg. cameras) mainly to their costs in terms of hardware, installation and management. People are instead inclined to share information and multimedia contents about their activities and the environment around them. Each user can be considered as a source of information and can contribute to improve the knowledge on the area where it is located and about a possible occurring event. The contributions from many different users can be combined to obtain an overall view of the area of interest. The proposed scenario exploits a crowdsourced approach to determine the type of event that occurs in a specific area and monitor how the situation evolves.

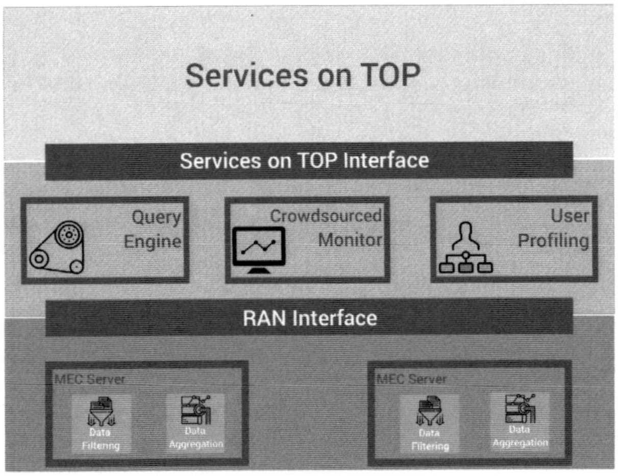

Fig. 1. Proposed Framework

After an event detection notification, due to the observation of abnormal signals, the proposed framework receives the geographic information of the involved area. This information is exploited to make a request to a proper MEC application, which handles the communication between the involved users and the framework. The system empowers the BTS to broadcast a "fast query" to the users within the interested area.

IV. Proposed Framework

This section describes the proposed framework in order to achieve a quick and efficient monitoring and being also able to identify the specific critical event, warn citizens and call the rescue services.

Initially, the event detection is carried out evaluating the sudden movement of a large mass of people, through the sensors on the personal devices, such as: accelerometer, gyroscope, proximity sensor and GPS position, enabling an implicit crowdsourcing.

The main components of the framework, shown in Figure 1, are the following:

- Service Interface: this component provides the access API to the framework's capabilities, which can be properly exploited by an external service;
- Query Engine: this module is devoted to the definition of fast queries used to interact with users, in a simple and immediate way, with the aim of acquiring general information about the status of a specific area affected by an event. Moreover this module is also responsible for generating multimedia contribution request to improve the awareness about the area of interest.
- Crowdsourced Monitor: this module includes a set of algorithms devoted to perform analysis and the inference on the user gathered contents. The obtained results are provided to the services on TOP and affect the user profiling.
- User Profiling: this component collects historical data about users interactions and performs a profiling based

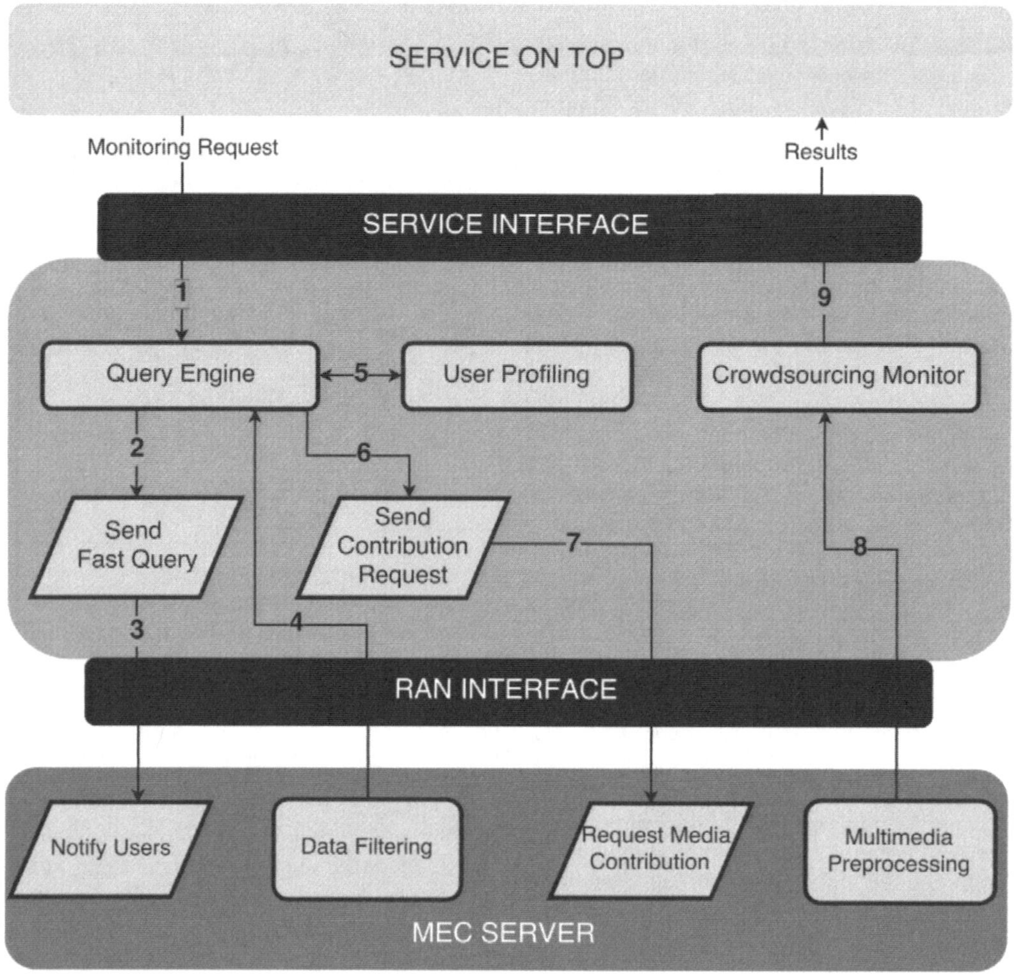

Fig. 2. A flow diagram that describes the step-by-step interactions among the different modules of the proposed framework

on the quality of the obtained information and the used devices.

- RAN Interface: this module allows the interaction between the proposed framework and the RAN by means a proper API.

In Figure 2, the details of the monitoring process are shown. The monitoring process may be triggered by an automatic system of event detection or by an operator to gain awareness of what is happening in the affected area and acquire additional details about the event in progress. The numbered arrows describe a typical execution flow. Here follows a step-by-step description of the actions taken by the system to serve the request:

1) The framework receives through the *Service On Top Interface* a monitoring request for a specific area.
2) The *Query Engine* processes the received request and prepare a set of fast queries to send to the users located in the area of interest.
3) The *RAN Interface* forwards the query messages to the specific BTS, which covers the area and sends broadcast text messages, containing the short questions.
4) The MEC Application deployed on the *MEC Server* analyzes the users' answers and filters them according to the information accuracy (e.g., event awareness).
5) The *Query Engine* combines the acquired information with the historical users' profile data (e.g., trusted users, device model).
6) The *Query Engine* exploits this information to define the suitable contribution request.
7) The *RAN Interface* sends the contribution request to the specific BTS which forwards it to the users demanding multimedia contribution (e.g., video stream, pictures).
8) In this step, the MEC Application performs some pre-processing on the multimedia contributes. For instance, if the number of provided video streams is high, they can be filtered considering several quality factors (e.g., video resolution, frame rate, stability). This prevents the system to elaborate noisy information, and the reduction

of the amount of the data to process.

9) The *Crowdsourcing Monitor* performs the analysis of the acquired data. These analysis depend on the kind of the required data and the aim of the analysis. For instance, if the system requires to perform the visual monitoring of the area of interest, the video streams provided by the users can be clustered according to the visual content with the aim to understand what is the most viewed scene [8].

The whole above described process is made transparent to the user by means of both the mentioned interfaces. The system only requires the area of interest to be monitored.

V. CONCLUSION

This work presents a framework able to provide a quickly monitoring of critical events, obtained by exploiting a crowdsourcing approach and Mobile Edge Computing paradigm. Upon receiving a monitoring request, the system defines a process that allows to collect, analyze and make proper inferences on crowdsourced data, with the aim to provide useful results to the service. The contributes of the users are selected considering several factors including user proximity, quality of the provided information, user profiling, as well as the user answer to a fast query. The collected data are then aggregated and analyzed. Examples of contributes aggregation analysis are visual clustering and saliency of video streams. The analysis results are then provided to the Service On Top and exploited to update the users' profiles.

In the next steps of this work in progress project, we are building up an actual prototype of the proposed framework with the aim to achieve experimental results and assess the effectiveness of the method described in this paper.

In the last few years, emerging technologies have been leading toward the realization of efficient cities, where technology will be applied to improve and support citizens' daily living in a realistic Smart City scenario in which the proposed framework is fully integrated.

REFERENCES

[1] Z. Alazawi, O. Alani, M. B. Abdljabar, S. Altowaijri, and R. Mehmood, "A smart disaster management system for future cities," in Proceedings of the 2014 ACM international workshop on Wireless and mobile technologies for smart cities. ACM, 2014, pp. 1–10.

[2] H. Schaffers et al., "Smart cities and the future internet: Towards cooperation frameworks for open innovation," in The Future Internet Assembly. Springer, 2011, pp. 431–446.

[3] M. Patel et al., "Mobile-edge computing introductory technical white paper," White Paper, Mobile-edge Computing (MEC) industry initiative, 2014.

[4] M. Sapienza et al., "Solving critical events through mobile edge computing: an approach for smart cities," in Smart Computing (SMARTCOMP), 2016 IEEE International Conference on. IEEE, 2016, pp. 1–5.

[5] E. Asimakopoulou and N. Bessis, "Buildings and crowds: Forming smart cities for more effective disaster management," in Innovative Mobile and Internet Services in Ubiquitous Computing (IMIS), 2011 Fifth International Conference on. IEEE, 2011, pp. 229–234.

[6] Y.-K. Wang, C.-T. Fan, K.-Y. Cheng, and P. S. Deng, "Real-time camera anomaly detection for real-world video surveillance," in Machine Learning and Cybernetics (ICMLC), 2011 International Conference on, vol. 4. IEEE, 2011, pp. 1520–1525.

[7] Y.-K. Wang, C.-T. Fan, and J.-F. Chen, "Traffic camera anomaly detection." in ICPR, 2014, pp. 4642–4647.

[8] A. Ortis et al., "Recfusion: Automatic video curation driven by visual content popularity," in Proceedings of the 23rd ACM international conference on Multimedia. ACM, 2015, pp. 1179–1182.

Easing Pattern Application by Means of Solution Languages

Michael Falkenthal and Frank Leymann

Institute of Architecture of Application Systems
University of Stuttgart
Stuttgart, Germany
Email: {lastname}@iaas.uni-stuttgart.de

***Abstract*—Patterns and pattern languages are a pervasive means to capture proven solutions for frequently recurring problems. They capture the expertise of domain specialists, as well as the essence of concrete solutions in an abstract and generic manner. These characteristics guarantee that patterns and pattern languages are applicable for many concrete use cases. However, due to this nature the knowledge about applying them to concrete problems at hand is lost during the authoring process. The lack of guidance on how to implement a pattern in a specific technical or environmental context leads to immense manual efforts and unnecessary reimplementations of already existing solutions. In our previous work, we presented the concept of linking concrete solutions to patterns in order to ease the pattern application. In this work, we extend this concept and present an approach to organize concrete solutions into Solution Languages, which are means to structure the solution space of a pattern language. We show how Solution Languages can be used to systematically collect specific implementation knowledge to purposefully navigate through a set of concrete solutions to ease and guide the realization of patterns. We validate the approach of Solution Languages in the domain of cloud application architecture and illustrate its technical feasibility by a wiki-based prototype.**

***Keywords*–Pattern Language; Solution Language; Pattern Application; Solution Selection.**

I. Introduction

In many domains, expertise and proven knowledge about how to solve frequently recurring problems are captured into patterns. Originated by Alexander et al. [1] in the domain of building architecture, the pattern concept was also heavily applied in many disciplines in computer science. Patterns were authored, e.g., to support object-oriented design [2], for designing software architectures [3], for human-computer interaction [4], to integrate enterprise applications [5], for documenting collaborative projects [6], or to foster the understanding of new emerging fields like the Internet of Things [7]. Triggered by the successful application of the pattern concept in computer science, it is also gaining momentum in the humanities, especially as a result of collaborative endeavors and research in the field of the *digital humanities* [8].

In general, patterns segment domain knowledge into *nuggets of advice*, which can be easily read and understood. They are interrelated with each other to form pattern languages, which ease and guide the navigation through the domain knowledge. This is often supported by links between patterns, which carry specific semantics that help to find relevant other patterns based on a currently selected one [9]. In previous work, we showed that this principle can be leveraged to organize patterns on different levels of abstraction into pattern languages [10]. *Refinement links* can be used to establish navigation paths through a set of patterns, which lead a user from abstract and generic patterns to more specific ones that, e.g., provide technology-specific implementation details about the problem – often presented as implementation examples. We further showed that also concrete solutions, i.e., concrete artifacts that implement a solution described by a pattern, can be stored in a solution repository and linked to patterns [11] [12]. Thus, we were able to show that pattern-based problem solving is not only limited to the conceptual level, but rather can be guided via pattern refinement towards technology-specific designs and, finally, the selection and reuse of concrete solutions.

However, this approach still lacks guidance for navigation through the set of concrete solutions. Navigation is only enabled on the level of pattern languages, while it is not possible to navigate from one concrete solution to others, due to missing navigation structures. This hinders the reuse of available concrete solutions especially in situations when many different and technology-specific concrete implementations of patters are available. As a result, it is neither easily understandable which concrete solutions can be combined to realize an aggregated solution, nor which working steps actually have to be done to conduct an aggregation. Thus, an approach is missing that allows to systematically document such knowledge in an easily accessible, structured and human-readable way.

Therefore, we present the concept of Solution Languages, which introduces navigable semantic links between concrete solutions. A Solution Language organizes concrete solution artifacts analogously to pattern languages organize patterns. Their purpose is to ease and guide the navigation through the set of concrete solutions linked to patterns of a pattern language. Thereby, knowledge about how to aggregate two concrete solutions is documented on the semantic link connecting them.

The remainder of this paper is structured as following: we provide background information and give a more detailed motivation in Section II. Then, we introduce the concept of Solution Languages and a means to add knowledge about solution aggregation in Section III. We validate our approach by a case study and discuss how presented concept can be applied in domains besides information technology (IT) in Section IV. We show the technical feasibility of Solution Languages by a prototype based on wiki-technology and by implementing the presented case study in Section V. We discuss related work in Section VI and, finally, conclude this work in Section VII by a summary of the paper and an outlook to future work.

II. Background and Motivation

Patterns document proven solutions for recurring problems. They are human-readable documentations of domain expertise. Thereby, their main purpose is to make knowledge about how to effectively solve problems easily accessible to readers. According to Meszaros and Doble [13], they are typically written and structured using a common format that predefines sections such as the *Problem*, which is solved by a pattern, the *Context* in which a pattern can be applied, the *Forces* that affect the elaboration of concrete solutions, the *Solution*, which is a description of how to solve the exposed problem, and a *Name* capturing the essence of a pattern's solution.

Patterns are typically not isolated from each other, but they are linked with each other to enable the navigation from one pattern to other ones, which are getting relevant once it is applied. In this manner, a navigable network of patterns is established – a pattern language. Often, a pattern language is established by referring other patterns in the running text of a pattern by mentioning them. This applies, especially, to pattern languages that are published as a monograph. Using wikis as platforms for authoring and laying out a library of patterns has further enabled to establish semantic links between patterns [6] [14]. This allows to enrich a pattern language to clearly indicate different navigation possibilities by different link types. Such link types can, e.g., state *AND*, *OR*, and *XOR* semantics, describing that after the application of a pattern more than one other patterns are typically also applied, that there is a number of further patterns, which can be alternatively applied, or that there is an exclusive choice of further patterns that can be applied afterwards, respectively [6]. Further, they can tell a reader, e.g., that a pattern is dealing with the equivalent problem of another pattern, but gives solution advice on a more fine-grained level in terms of additional implementation- and technology-specific knowledge [10]. Thus, the navigation through a pattern language can be eased significantly.

Since patterns and pattern languages capture the essence and expertise from many concrete solutions of recurring problems, implementation details, such as technology-specific or environmental constraints, which affect the actual application of a pattern for specific problems at hand, are abstracted away during the pattern authoring process [15] [16]. As a result, this abstraction ensures that the conceptual core ideas of how to solve a problem in a context are captured into a pattern, which makes a pattern applicable for many concrete use cases that may occur. In the course of this, the application of patterns for specific use cases is getting harder because concrete solutions, i.e., implementations of a pattern, are lost during the authoring process. Thus, we showed that connecting concrete solutions to patterns in order to make them reusable when a pattern has to be applied is a valuable concept to save time consuming efforts [11] [12]. This concept is depicted in Fig. 1, where a pattern language is illustrated as a graph of connected patterns at the top. Based on the conceptual solution knowledge, the pattern language opens a solution space, illustrated as an ellipse below the pattern language, which is the space of all possible implementations of the pattern language. Concrete solutions that implement individual patterns of the pattern language are, consequently, located in the solution space and are illustrated as circles. They are related to the pattern they implement, which enables to directly reuse them once a pattern is selected from the pattern language in order to be applied.

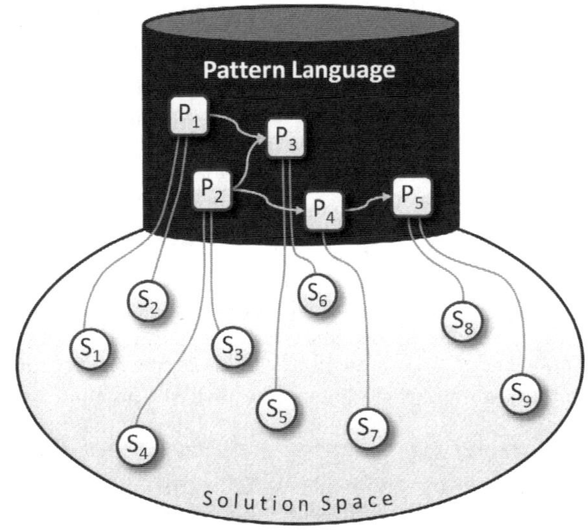

Figure 1. Missing Navigation Support through the Space of Concrete Solutions connected to a Pattern Language

However, while navigation through conceptual solutions is provided by pattern languages in terms of links between patterns, such navigation capabilities are currently not present on the level of concrete solutions, due to the absence of links between the concrete solutions. Thus, if a concrete solution is selected, there is no guidance to navigate through the set of all available and further relevant concrete solutions. Navigation is only possible via the conceptual level of patterns by navigation structures of the pattern language. This is time consuming if experts have their conceptual solution already in mind and want to quickly traverse through available concrete solutions in order to examine if they can reuse some of them for implementing their use case at hand. Further, if a set of concrete solutions is already present that provides implementation building blocks for, e.g., a specific technology, it is often necessary to quickly navigate between them in order to understand their dependencies for reusing them. This is specifically the case, if concrete solutions cannot be reused directly, but need to be adapted to a specific use case. Then, they still can provide a valuable basis for starting adaptions instead of recreating a concrete solution from scratch. Finally, if some concrete solutions have proven to be typically used in combination it is valuable to document this information to ease their reuse. While this could be done on the level of a pattern language, we argue that this is bad practice because implementation details would mix up with the conceptual character of the pattern language. This would require to update a pattern language whenever implementation insights have to be documented. This can get cumbersome, if concrete solutions are collected over a long period of time and technology shifts lead to new implementations and approaches on how to aggregate them, while the more general pattern language stays the same.

Therefore, to summarize the above discussed deficits, there is (i) a lack of organization and structuring at the level of concrete solutions, which (ii) leads to time consuming efforts for traversing concrete solutions, and that (iii) prevents the documentation of proven combinations of concrete solutions.

III. Solution Languages: Means to Structure and Organize Concrete Solutions

To overcome the presented deficits, we introduce the concept of *Solution Languages*. The core idea of Solution Languages is to transfer the capabilities of a pattern language to the level of concrete solutions having the goal of easing and guiding the application of patterns via reusing concrete solutions in mind. Specifically, the following capabilities have to be enabled on the level of concrete solutions: (i) navigation between concrete solutions, (ii) navigation guidance to find relevant further concrete solutions, and (iii) documentation capabilities for managing knowledge about dependencies between concrete solutions, e.g., how to aggregate different concrete solutions to elaborate comprehensive solutions based on multiple patterns.

A. Ease and Guide Traversing of Concrete Solutions

To realize the requirements (i) and (ii), a Solution Language establishes links between concrete solutions, which are annotated by specific semantics that support a user to decide if a further concrete solution is relevant to solve his or her problem at hand. Thereby, the semantics of a link can indicate that concrete solutions connected to different patterns *can be aggregated* with each other, that individual concrete solutions are *variants* that implement the same pattern, or if exactly one of more *alternative* concrete solutions can be used in combination with another one. Depending on the needs of users, also additional link semantics can be added to a Solution Language. To give one example, semantic links can be introduced that specifically indicate that selected concrete solutions *must not be aggregated*. This is useful in cases, when concrete solutions can be technically aggregated on the one hand, but, on the other hand, they implement non-functional attributes that prevent to create a proper aggregated solution. Such situations might occur, e.g., in the field of cloud computing, where applications can be distributed across different cloud providers around the world. Then, this is also implemented by the concrete solutions that are building blocks of such applications. Different concrete solutions can force that individual parts of an application are deployed in different regions of the world. In some cases, law, local regulations, or compliance policies of a company can restrict the distribution of components of an application to specific countries [17]. In such situations, it is very valuable to document these restrictions on the level of concrete solutions via the latter mentioned link type. This can prevent users from unnecessarily navigating to concrete solutions that are irrelevant in such use cases. Nevertheless, the concrete solutions that are not allowed to be used in a specific scenario can be kept in a Solution Language, e.g., for later reuse if preventing factors change or as a basis for adaptions that make them compliant.

While (i) and (ii) can be realized by means of semantically typed links between concrete solutions as introduced above, (iii) requires to introduce the concept of a *Concrete Solution Aggregation Descriptor (CSAD)*. A CSAD allows to annotate a link between concrete solutions by additional documentation that describes the dependency of concrete solutions in a human-readable way. This can, e.g., be a specific description of the working steps required to aggregate the concrete solutions connected by the annotated link. Beyond that, a CSAD can also contain any additionally feasible documentation, such as a sketch of the artifact resulting from the aggregation, which supports a user. The actual content of a CSAD is highly specific

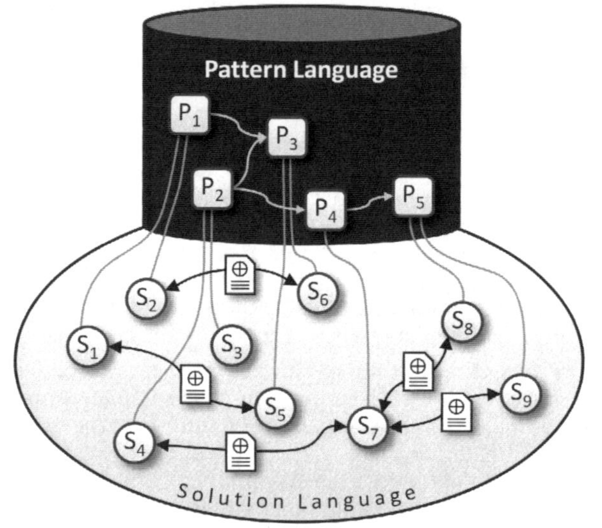

Figure 2. A Solution Language Structures the Solution Space of a Pattern Language and Enables Navigation through Relevant Concrete Solutions

for the domain of the concrete solutions. The aggregation of concrete solutions that are programming code can, e.g., often be described by adjustments of configurations, by manual steps to be performed in a specific integrated development environment (IDE), or by means of additional code snippets required for the aggregation. In other domains, such as the non-technical domain of costumes in films, the required documentation to aggregate concrete solutions looks quite different and can, e.g., be a manual about how to combine different pieces of clothing, which in this case are concrete solutions, in order to achieve a desired impression of a character in a movie. So, a CSAD can be leveraged to systematically document concrete implementation knowledge about how to create aggregated overall solutions. Thus, CSADs are the means to add arbitrary documentation about how to aggregate concrete solutions to a Solution Language. Hence, a Solution Language can be iteratively extended over time to preserve the expert knowledge of a domain on the implementation level, the same way as pattern languages do on the conceptual level. Especially in situations, when technologies are getting outdated and experts, which are required to maintain systems implemented in such technologies are getting only scarcely available, Solution Languages can be valuable instruments that preserve technology-specific implementation expertise and documentation. Since concrete solutions are also connected to patterns, which they implement, conceptual, as well as implementation knowledge can be kept easily accessible and inherently connected.

The overall concept of a Solution Language is illustrated in Fig. 2. There, concrete solutions are linked to the patterns they implement. This enables a user to navigate from patterns to concrete implementations that can be reused, as described in our earlier work [11] [12]. Additionally, the concrete solutions are also linked with each other in order to allow navigation on the level of concrete solutions. For the sake of simplicity and clarity, Fig. 2 focusses on links that represent *can be aggregated with* semantics, thus, we omitted other link types. Nevertheless, the relations between the concrete solutions can capture arbitrary semantics, such as those presented above. The semantic links between concrete solutions and the fact that they are also linked to the patterns, which they implement, enables to enter the Solution Language at a certain concrete solution and allows to navigate among only the relevant concrete solutions that are of interest for a concrete use case at hand. For example, if concrete solutions are available that implement patterns in different technologies, then they typically cannot be aggregated. Thus, entering the Solution language at a certain concrete solution and then navigating among only those concrete solutions that are implemented using the same technology, using semantic links indicating this coherence (e.g., *can be aggregated with*), can reduce the effort to elaborate an overall solution significantly. Finally, Fig. 2 depicts CSADs attached to links between concrete solutions in the form of documents. These enrich the semantic links and provide additional arbitrary documentation on how to aggregate the linked concrete solutions.

This way, a Solution Language delegates the principles of pattern languages to the level of concrete solutions, which helps to structure and organize the set of available concrete solutions. While a pattern language guides a user through a set of abstract and conceptual solutions in the form of patterns, a Solution Language provides similar guidance for combining concrete solutions to overall artifacts, all provided by semantic links between concrete solutions and additional documentation about how to aggregate them. Navigation support between concrete implementations of patterns cannot be given by a pattern language itself, because one pattern can be implemented in many different technologies, even in ones that did not exist at the time of authoring the pattern language. Thus, the elucidated guidance is required on the solution level due to the fact that a multitude of different and technology-specific concrete solutions can implement the concepts provided by a pattern language.

B. Mapping Solution Paths from Pattern Languages to Solution Languages

Since pattern languages organize and structure patterns to a navigable network, they can be used to select several patterns to solve a concrete problem at hand by providing conceptual solutions. A user typically tries to find a proper entry point to the pattern language by selecting a pattern that solves his or her problem at least partially. Starting from this pattern, he or she navigates to further patterns in order to select a complete set of patterns that solve the entire problem at hand in combination. This way, several patterns are selected along paths through the pattern language. Thus, the selected patterns are also called a *solution path* through the pattern language [10] [18]. Fig. 3 shows such a solution path by the selected patterns P_2, P_4, and P_5. If several solution paths proof to be successful for recurring use cases, this can be documented into the pattern language to present stories that provide use case-specific entry points to the pattern language [19]. Further, if several concrete solutions are often aggregated by means of the same CSAD, then this can reveal that there might be a candidate of a composite pattern that can be added to the pattern language by abstracting the underlying solution principles, which might be supported and automated by data mining techniques in specific domains [20].

Due to the fact that concrete solutions are linked with the patterns they implement, solution paths through a pattern language can support to find suitable entry points to the corresponding Solution Language. Accordingly, a user can navigate from P_2 to the concrete solution S_4. From there, the Solution Language provides navigation support to find further concrete solutions that can be aggregated with S_4. If concrete solutions are available for all patterns contained in the solution path, and if these can be aggregated with each other, then the solution path can be mapped to the Solution Language. This is illustrated in Fig. 3 by the highlighted path from S_4 via S_7 to S_9 through the Solution Language. This allows to translate design decisions that are taken on the conceptual level of the pattern language to reusable concrete solutions that are organized into the Solution Language. The mapping of the solution path to a corresponding set of concrete solutions of the Solution Language can, consequently, provide knowledge about how to elaborate an aggregated solution of the selected patterns by CSADs of the Solution Language, which can significantly speed up the elaboration of an overall concrete solution.

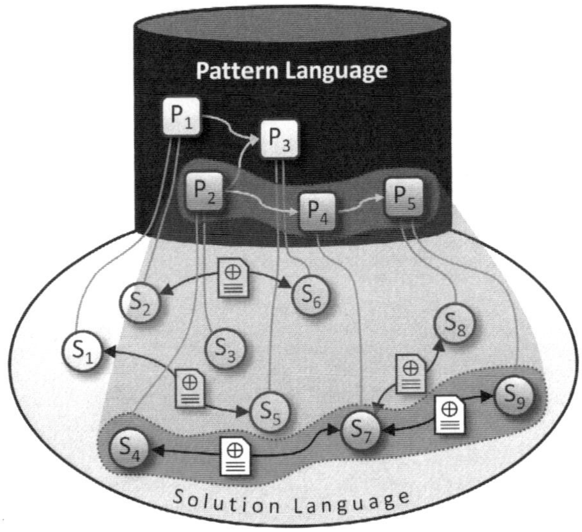

Figure 3. Solution Path from a Pattern Language projected to a Solution Language

IV. Application in the Domain of Cloud Computing

The pattern language of Fehling et al. [21] provides knowledge about tailoring applications to leverage the capabilities of cloud environments, such as Amazon Web Services (AWS) [22]. One important capability in terms of cloud computing is the automatic and elastic scaling of compute resources. To enable this, the pattern language provides the patterns *Elastic Load Balancer (ELB)* and *Stateless Component (SC)*. ELB describes, how workloads of an application can be distributed among multiple instances of the application. If workload increases, additional instances are added to keep the application responsive. Once, workload decreases, no longer required instances are decommissioned, i.e., to save processing power and expenses. The ELB pattern links to the SC pattern, which describes how components that contain the business logic of an application can manage their state externally, e.g., in an additional database. These patterns are depicted at the top of Fig. 4.

Realizations of these patterns can be connected to them, as depicted in the figure by S_1 and S_2. These concrete solutions implement the patterns by means of AWS CloudFormation [23]

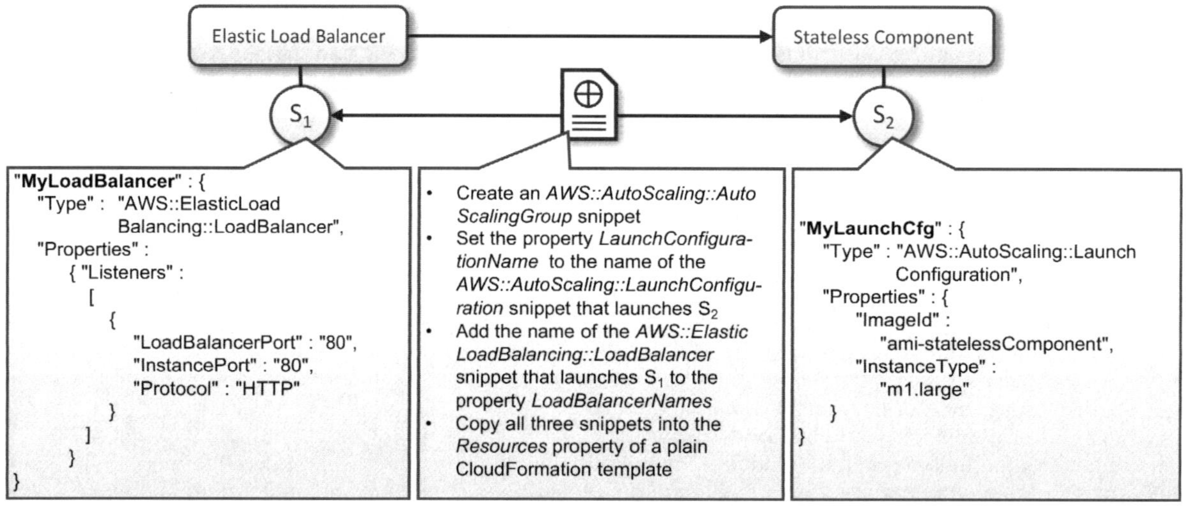

Figure 4. Concrete Solution Aggregation Descriptor Documenting how to Aggregate Concrete Solutions in the Form of two CloudFormation snippets

snippets, which allows to describe collections of AWS-resources by means of a java script object notation (JSON)-based configuration language. Such configurations can be uploaded to AWS CloudFormation, which then automatically provisions new instances of the described resources. An excerpt of the CloudFormation snippet that describes a load balancer is shown on the left of Fig. 4. The *MyLoadBalancer* configuration defines properties of the load balancer, which are required to receive and forward workload. The corresponding CloudFormation snippet, which implements the concrete solution S_2 is shown on the right. So-called *Amazon Machine Images (AMI)* allow to package all information required to create and start virtual servers in the AWS cloud. Therefore, the *MyLaunchCfg* snippet of S_2 contains a reference to the AMI *ami-statelessComponent*, which is able to create and start a new virtual server that hosts an instance of a stateless component. The link between S_1 and S_2 illustrates that they *can be aggregated* in order to obtain an overall solution, which results in a complete configuration that allows the load balancer instance to distribute workload over instances of virtual servers hosting the stateless component.

If a user wants to aggregate both snippets, he or she can study the CSAD attached to the link between both concrete solutions, which is outlined in the middle of the figure. It provides detailed information about the actual working steps that have to be executed in order to bring both CloudFormation snippets together. Therefore, the CSAD describes that both snippets have to be aggregated via a so-called *AutoScalingGroup*, which is itself also a CloudFormation snippet. The AutoScalingGroup references both, the *MyLoadBalancer* and the *MyLaunchCfg* snippets via the properties *LaunchConfigurationName* and *LoadBalancerNames*. Finally, all three snippets have to be integrated into the property *Resources* of a plain CloudFormation template. By documenting all this information into the Solution Language, (i) the link from concrete solutions in form of CloudFormation snippets to the patterns they implement, (ii) the semantic link between these concrete solutions indicating that they *can be aggregated*, and (iii) the detailed documentation about how to perform the aggregation, can significantly ease the application of the ELB and SC pattern in combination.

Besides the domain of IT, which deals with concrete solutions that are intangible in the sense that they are often programming code or other forms of digital artifacts, there are also domains, exemplarily the domains of building architecture [1] or costumes in films [24], which deal with concrete solutions that are tangible artifacts. While the aggregation of intangible solutions can often be automated [12], e.g., by merging code snippets to an aggregated solution, the aggregation of tangible solutions, such as concrete construction plans of buildings or costumes in a wardrobe, has to be done manually. Especially, in the latter case of tangible solutions, the concept of Solution Languages can be used for documenting knowledge about how to combine concrete solutions. Such knowledge is typically not systematically captured, because of a missing methodical approach. *CSADs* can be used to overcome this problem by documenting procedures and manuals describing the working steps to combine tangible solutions. For the case of costumes in films [15], a Solution Language can be authored that allows to reuse already present costumes for dressing actors. A *CSAD* then can describe, e.g., how roles have to be dressed in a specific scene of a film in order to create the intended expression of how these roles relate to each other to create a perfect immersion.

V. PROTOTYPE

To proof the technical feasibility of the presented approach of Solution Languages, we implemented a prototype on the basis of PatternPedia [14]. PatternPedia is a wiki that is built upon the MediaWiki [25] technology and the Semantic MediaWiki extensions [26]. We implemented the case study presented in the previous section. Therefore, we captured the cloud computing patterns in form of wiki pages into PatternPedia and added links between them accordingly to the pattern language of Fehling et al. [21]. We also added the concrete solutions in the form of AWS CloudFormation snippets to PatternPedia so that each AWS CloudFormation snippet is represented by a separate wiki page that references a file containing the corresponding JSON-code. Then, we linked the wiki pages of the concrete solutions with wiki pages representing the patterns they implement to enable the navigation from abstract solution principles captured in patterns to technology-specific implementations in the form of concrete solutions. So, we were able to navigate from patterns to concrete solutions and select them for reuse once a pattern has to be applied. To establish a Solution Language we declared a new property *can be aggregated with* using the Semantic MediaWiki extensions. Properties can be used to define arbitrary semantics, which can be added to wiki pages. The defined property accepts one parameter as a value, which we used to reference wiki pages that represent concrete solutions. This way, concrete solutions can be semantically linked with each other by adding the property into the markdown of their wiki pages and providing the link to the wiki page of the concrete solution, which the *can be aggregated with* semantics holds.

To annotate the link between two specific concrete solutions with information required for their aggregation, we added a CSAD as a separate wiki page containing a detailed description of the working steps required for aggregating them. Finally, we used the query functionality of the Semantic MediaWiki extensions to attach the CSAD to the semantic link between two concrete solutions. We utilized the parser function *#ask* of the Semantic MediaWiki extensions to query the two concrete solutions that are semantically linked with each other via the *can be aggregated with* property. This allowed us to also navigate from one concrete solution to other relevant concrete solutions based on the information of the semantic links, by also providing information about how to aggregate both concrete solutions to an overall one in a human-readable way.

VI. Related Work

The term pattern language was introduced by Alexander et al. [1]. They use this term metaphorically to express that design patterns are typically not just isolated junks of knowledge, but are rather used and valuable in combination. At this, the metaphor implies that patterns are related to each other like words in sentences. While each word does only sparsely provide any information only the combination to whole sentences creates an overall statement. So, also patterns only unfold their generative power once they are applied in combination, while they are structured and organized into pattern languages in order to reveal their combinability to human readers.

Mullet [9] discusses how pattern catalogues in the field of human-computer interaction design can be enhanced to pattern languages to ease the application of patterns in combination. He reveals the qualities of pattern languages by discussing structuring elements in the form of different semantics of pattern relations. Further, the possibility to connect artifacts to patterns, such as detailed implementation documentation or also concrete implementations is identified as future research.

Zdun [18] formalizes pattern language in the form of pattern language grammars. Using this approach, he tackles the problem of selecting patterns from a pattern language. He reflects design decisions by annotating effects on quality attributes to a pattern language grammar. Relationships between patterns express semantics, e.g., that a pattern *requires* another pattern, a pattern is an *alternative* to another one, or that a pattern is a *variant* of another pattern. Thus, he describes concepts of pattern languages, which are transferred in this work to the level of concrete solutions and Solution Languages.

Reiners et al. [27] present a requirements catalogue to support the collaborative formulation of patterns. These requirements can be used as a basis to implement pattern repositories. While the requirements mainly address the authoring and structuring of pattern languages, they can also be used as a basis to detail the discussion about how to design and implement repositories to author Solution Languages. Pattern Repositories [6] [14] [28] have proven to support the authoring of patterns. They enable to navigate through pattern languages by linking patterns with each other. Some (c.f. [6] [14]) also enable to enrich links between patterns by semantics in order to further ease the navigation. Also, conceptual approaches exist that allow to connect a pattern repository with a solution repository, which can be the foundation to implement the concepts introduces in this work. These concepts and repository prototypes can be combined with our approach to develop sophisticated solution repositories.

Barzen and Leymann [15] present a general approach to support the identification and authoring of patterns based on concrete solutions. Their approach is based on research in the domain of costumes in films, where they formalize costume languages as pattern languages. Costumes are concrete solutions that solve specific design problems of costume designers. They enable to hark back to concrete solutions a pattern is evolved from by keeping them connected. They also introduce the terminus Solution Language as an ontology that describes types of clothes and their relations in the form of metadata, as well as instances of these types. This completely differs from the concept of a Solution Language as described in this work.

Fehling et al. [16] present a method for identifying, authoring and applying patterns. The method is decomposed into three phases, whereby, in the pattern application phase, they describe how abstract solutions of patterns can be refined towards concrete implementations. To reduce the efforts to spend for implementing patterns, they apply the concept of concrete solutions by means of code repositories that contain reference implementations of patterns. While our approach is designed and detailed for organizing concrete solutions the argumentation in their work is mainly driven by considerations about patterns and pattern languages. Thus, the method does not introduce how to systematically combine semantics and documentation in order to organize concrete solutions for reuse, which is the principal contribution of our work.

VII. Conclusion and Future Work

In this work, we presented the concept of Solution Languages that allows to structure and organize concrete solutions, which are implementations of patterns. We showed how Solution Languages can be created and how they can support the navigation through the solution space of pattern languages based on semantic links, all targeting to ease and guide pattern application. We further presented the concept of Concrete Solution Aggregation Descriptors, which allows to add arbitrary human-readable documentation to links between concrete solutions.

In future work, we are going to conduct research on how to analyze Solution Languages in order to derive new pattern candidates based on Concrete Solution Aggregation Descriptors annotated to links between concrete solutions, but also on the question if a Solution Language can indicate new patterns in a pattern language, for instance, in the case if links between concrete solutions are missing or if aggregation documentation cannot be clearly authored. We are also going to apply the concept of Solution Languages to domains besides cloud computing, e.g., to the emerging field of the Internet of Things.

ACKNOWLEDGMENT

This work is partially funded by the BMWi project SePiA.Pro (01MD16013F) as part of the Smart Service World.

REFERENCES

[1] C. Alexander, S. Ishikawa, and M. Silverstein, A pattern language: towns, buildings, construction. New York: Oxford University Press, 1977.

[2] E. Gamma, R. Helm, R. Johnson, and J. Vlissides, "Design Patterns: Abstraction and reuse of objectoriented design," in European Conference on Object-Oriented Programming, 1993, pp. 406–431.

[3] F. Buschmann, R. Meunier, H. Rohnert, P. Sommerlad, and P. Stal, Pattern-oriented software architecture: A system of patterns, 1996, vol. 1.

[4] M. van Welie and G. C. van der Veer, "Pattern Languages in Interaction Design : Structure and Organization," in Human-Computer Interaction '03: IFIP TC13 International Conference on Human-Computer Interaction. IOS Press, 2003, pp. 527–534.

[5] G. Hohpe and B. Woolf, Enterprise Integration Patterns: Designing, Building, And Deploying Messaging Systems. Addison-Wesley, 2004.

[6] R. Reiners, "An Evolving Pattern Library for Collaborative Project Documentation," PhD Thesis, RWTH Aachen University, 2013.

[7] L. Reinurt, U. Breitenbücher, M. Falkenthal, F. Leymann, and A. Riegg, "Internet of things patterns," in Proceedings of the 21th European Conference on Pattern Languages of Programs, 2016.

[8] J. Barzen et al., "The vision for MUSE4Music," Computer Science - Research and Development, vol. 22, no. 74, 2016, pp. 1–6.

[9] K. Mullet, "Structuring pattern languages to facilitate design. chi2002 patterns in practice: A workshop for ui designers," 2002. [Online]. Available: https://www.semanticscholar.org/paper/Structuring-Pattern-Languages-to-Facilitate-Design-Mullet/2fa5e4c25eea30687605115649191cd009a8f33c

[10] M. Falkenthal et al., "Leveraging pattern application via pattern refinement," in Proceedings of the International Conference on Pursuit of Pattern Languages for Societal Change, in press.

[11] M. Falkenthal, J. Barzen, U. Breitenbuecher, C. Fehling, and F. Leymann, "From Pattern Languages to Solution Implementations," in Proceedings of the 6th International Conferences on Pervasive Patterns and Applications, 2014, pp. 12–21.

[12] M. Falkenthal, J. Barzen, U. Breitenbücher, C. Fehling, and F. Leymann, "Efficient Pattern Application : Validating the Concept of Solution Implementations in Different Domains," International Journal On Advances in Software, vol. 7, no. 3&4, 2014, pp. 710–726.

[13] G. Meszaros and J. Doble, "A Pattern Language for Pattern Writing," in Pattern Languages of Program Design 3. Addison-Wesley, 1997, ch. A Pattern Language for Pattern Writing, pp. 529–574.

[14] C. Fehling, J. Barzen, M. Falkenthal, and F. Leymann, "PatternPedia Collaborative Pattern Identification and Authoring," in Pursuit of Pattern Languages for Societal Change - The Workshop 2014: Designing Lively Scenarios With the Pattern Approach of Christopher Alexander. epubli GmbH, 2015, pp. 252–284.

[15] J. Barzen and F. Leymann, "Costume Languages as Pattern Languages," in Pursuit of Pattern Languages for Societal Change - The Workshop 2014: Designing Lively Scenarios With the Pattern Approach of Christopher Alexander, 2015, pp. 88–117.

[16] C. Fehling, J. Barzen, U. Breitenbücher, and F. Leymann, "A Process for Pattern Identification, Authoring, and Application," in Proceedings of the 19th European Conference on Pattern Languages of Programs, 2015, article no. 4.

[17] U. Breitenbücher et al., "Policy-Aware Provisioning and Management of Cloud Applications," International Journal On Advances in Security, vol. 7, no. 1 & 2, 2014, pp. 15–36.

[18] U. Zdun, "Systematic pattern selection using pattern language grammars and design space analysis," Software: Practice and Experience, vol. 37, no. 9, jul 2007, pp. 983–1016.

[19] F. Buschmann, K. Henney, and D. C. Schmidt, Pattern-Oriented Software Architecture: On Patterns and Pattern Languages. Wiley & Sons, 2007, vol. 5.

[20] M. Falkenthal et al., "Pattern research in the digital humanities: how data mining techniques support the identification of costume patterns," Computer Science - Research and Development, vol. 22, no. 74, 2016.

[21] C. Fehling, F. Leymann, R. Retter, W. Schupeck, and P. Arbitter, Cloud Computing Patterns: Fundamentals to Design, Build, and Manage Cloud Applications. Springer, 2014.

[22] Amazon, "Amazon Web Services," 2017. [Online]. Available: http://aws.amazon.com/

[23] ——, "Amazon Cloud Formation," 2017. [Online]. Available: https://aws.amazon.com/cloudformation/

[24] D. Schumm, J. Barzen, F. Leymann, and L. Ellrich, "A Pattern Language for Costumes in Films," in Proceedings of the 17th European Conference on Pattern Languages of Programs, 2012, article no. 7.

[25] Wikimedia Foundation, "MediaWiki," 2017. [Online]. Available: https://www.mediawiki.org/

[26] M. Krötzsch, "Semantic MediaWiki," 2017. [Online]. Available: https://www.semantic-mediawiki.org/

[27] R. Reiners, M. Falkenthal, D. Jugel, and A. Zimmermann, "Requirements for a Collaborative Formulation Process of Evolutionary Patterns," in Proceedings of the 18th European Conference on Pattern Languages of Programs, Irsee, 2013, article no. 16.

[28] U. van Heesch, "Open Pattern Repository," 2009. [Online]. Available: http://www.cs.rug.nl/search/ArchPatn/OpenPatternRepository

All links were last accessed on 14.01.2017

(Don't) Join the Dark Side

An Initial Analysis and Classification of Regular, Anti-, and Dark Patterns

Alexander G. Mirnig and Manfred Tscheligi
Center for Human-Computer Interaction & Department of Computer Sciences
University of Salzburg, Salzburg, Austria
Email: firstname.lastname@sbg.ac.at

Abstract— **Patterns describe proven solutions to reoccurring problems. Anti-patterns describe solutions, which are proven not to work for solving reoccurring problems. Both concepts are well understood, documented, and employed in several different disciplines. Another, more obscure pattern concept, is that of "dark patterns". Dark patterns describe solutions used to trick users and are often considered to be anti-patterns. In this paper, we show that dark patterns have a different status and focus. Depending on the circumstances, a dark pattern can either be a regular pattern or an anti-pattern. Treating and documenting a dark pattern in the same way as a regular or anti-pattern could result in making malicious solutions easy to access and reproduce. We provide a review and delineation criteria for regular patterns, anti-patterns, and dark patterns in Human-Computer Interaction (HCI). This enables a more reflected knowledge transfer via patterns and protection of users from malicious designs.**

Keywords-basics on patterns; design patterns; anti-patterns; dark patterns.

I. INTRODUCTION

Design is usually not a blind, directionless activity, but happens with a certain focus. In HCI, 'design' is most often encountered in regards to user interface (UI) design. A good or well-designed UI should be readable and understandable for the intended user group, provide quick access to the most often used commands and functions, not obstruct the view onto other parts of the program that are not part of the UI, as well as satisfy the user depending on the specific application and context. As can be expected, there is no "one size fits all" solution to good UI design. General guidelines and knowledge on what constitutes sensible UI design do exist, but these require the hand of an experienced designer when it comes to covering specific cases and contexts, where tweaks and modifications in even the smallest details are often necessary – details, which general guidelines do not cover [1][2].

A pattern or design pattern is a documentation of a working solution to a particular (design) problem, embedded in its context and with concrete implementation examples. In contrast to patterns, an anti-pattern (sometimes also written 'antipattern') presents a solution that is proven not to work for solving a particular problem. A dark pattern describes a design solution intended to trick or otherwise deceive the user.

Both, regular and anti-patterns, are aimed at carefully documenting the solutions contained within them and are tied to approaches and structures that support this aim. With dark patterns, however, such an approach would arguably defeat the purpose behind naming and describing patterns, namely making the described solutions easy to access and reproduce. A specific level of information is certainly necessary, but if one wants to protect users from harmful designs, is providing step-by-step instructions on how to easily reproduce such designs really the right way or rather even counterproductive? This is the reason why a more detailed analysis of dark patterns and their relation to regular and anti-patterns is important.

In this paper, we provide such an analysis. We explore patterns, anti-patterns, and dark-patterns and the concepts behind them. We reflect on available literature in order to extract the basic characteristics of each type of pattern. We provide a minimal definition for each type of pattern and discuss these. As we will eventually discover, dark patterns carry their name only in the very loosest sense of the word, due to the lack of focus on reproducibility of the described solutions and other factors. In Section II, we provide a brief overview on related work to patterns, anti-patterns, and dark patterns. In Section III, we take a look at common definitions, structures, and examples for each pattern type, in order to extract the minimal requirements for a good or successful pattern of each of these types. The overall aim of the paper is to show the potential dangers of not clearly separating patterns, anti-patterns, and dark patterns and provide usable classification for all three pattern types to avoid these dangers. The paper concludes with a discussion of the results and future work in section IV, and an overall summary in Section V.

II. RELATED WORK

The term 'pattern' in this context was first coined by Christopher Alexander [3] to document techniques and solutions in architecture. His idea was to develop these small, standalone solutions with the eventual goal of making buildings by "stringing together patterns" [4]. Nowadays, the term generally refers to documented proven solutions to reoccurring problems in specific fields and contexts. Various pattern approaches exist and are applied in different disciplines, interaction design and software engineering being the most prominent among these [5][6].

In HCI, patterns have been adopted for capturing UI design solutions in several domains, such as web design [7], contextual User Experience design [8], or the automotive domain [9]. In this paper, we shall mostly focus on UI design patterns as they are used in the HCI community, in order to keep the analysis and discussion condensed, though the eventual results should be expandable into other domains.

Providing solutions to problems and giving guidance to novices and experts was traditionally done via guidelines. Using guidelines is subject to a number of problems [1][2]. They are often too simplistic or too abstract, they can be difficult to interpret by the designer, or they can even be conflicting with other guidelines, due to their general nature and the many different application contexts. Due to this same general nature, it can be difficult to identify which concrete problem(s) a guideline actually addresses. One particularity of patterns is that they are always focused on a certain problem. Where a guideline would give an overall answer to a question of the form "How do I do x?" a pattern would answer "How do I solve x?".

Patterns are less holistic but more specific, with a focus on providing a completely retraceable solution to a specific problem. According to Van Welie and van der Weer [6], this makes them even potentially better tools than guidelines. Patterns usually contain more specific knowledge than guidelines, but with a much narrower thematic focus. Depending on the abstraction level of a pattern [10], it can contain little to no guidance towards any greater overall task the problem might be a part of. Patterns can thus be seen as complementing guidelines and other means of general guidance. It is also possible for a pattern to contain information from several guidelines, but only the parts pertaining to a particular situation or problem [11].

Pattern creation or "mining", as it is often called (e.g., [5][17]), is a lengthy and structured process, requiring designers who were actually able to solve a certain problem to retrace their steps and carefully document how they arrived at their solution in several iterations. The goal is to fully document the solution finding and implementation process embedded in its context, so that the solution can be faithfully reapplied in a similar or even different context, if possible. Contemporary pattern approaches still follow Alexander's general intention of individual patterns working together as solution elements to larger problems. Patterns are, therefore, rarely standalone, but are collected in collections or repositories, which are either published as paper volumes or online.

Where patterns describe working solutions to reoccurring problems, anti-patterns do the opposite; they describe solutions to reoccurring problems that are proven to not work. The basic idea is the same as with regular patterns – carefully document the solution process as well as its embedded context. The overall goal, however, is to *avoid* the solution the anti pattern describes rather than its implementation. Appleton [12] describes anti-patterns as descriptions of lessons learned instead of the best practices described by regular patterns.

A third type of patterns, although not as well documented as the former two, is that of dark patterns. Brignull [13] defines dark patterns as descriptions of design solutions, which "*appear[s] to have been carefully crafted to trick users into doing things [...] and they do not have the user's interests in mind.*" What might be desirable and good design in one instance could very well be a dark pattern in another – otherwise, e.g., spoofing would not work as well as it (sadly) often does.

So the distinction between regular and dark patterns is not as clear-cut, as it might seem at first glance. Similarly, it is sensible to expect a dark pattern solution to work at least moderately well for its envisioned purpose or it would not warrant the attention. In this case, however, it would be incorrect to label it an anti-pattern, as anti-patterns document solutions that do *not* work well in the first place. This somewhat muddy situation is reflected in the literature. To provide an example, in their 2014 DIS Paper, Greenberg et al. [15] define dark patterns as anti-patterns in a wider sense, whereas darkpatterns.org [14], a website dedicated to expose deception and malicious design practices, explicitly separates dark patterns from anti-patterns as their own pattern category.

III. Analysis

In the following three sections, we provide common concepts, structure templates (where available), and examples of patterns (also referred to as 'regular patterns' in order to not confuse them with the latter two types), anti-patterns, and dark patterns. We then use these to derive commonalities for each pattern type. At the end of each subsection, we transform these commonalities into a brief list of minimal requirements for each pattern type. The analysis is a high-level one, with focus on common concepts. It is not intended to be an encompassing and detailed meta-analysis of all available pattern literature.

A. *Regular Patterns*

Since a pattern describes a proven solution to reoccurring problems, this means that each pattern starts from a problem, which requires a solution. The solution described in a pattern needs to be a reliable and proven one. If it worked only once, then it is not a good solution for a pattern. The general rule for what constitutes a solution as proven is commonly known as the *rule of three* [5]. If a solution has worked to solve the problem in at least three cases, then it is considered a working solution. This is not a hard rule, but it has generally been accepted in most pattern approaches.

As mentioned previously, one of the main ideas behind pattern approaches in general is to describe only that single solution instead of giving general guidance. At the beginning of the pattern mining process, the pattern writer retraces each step that leads to the eventual solution until s/he has a complete description of every single step, which led to the solution, including the exact context the solution was embedded in, as well as contextual forces and other variables. The term 'writer' might suggest only one individual, but it is not unusual for several individuals to be involved in a pattern mining and writing process.

In order to ensure a good end product of such an involved process, a successful pattern should usually satisfy a number of requirements in order to be considered of sufficient quality. In a meta-study on pattern requirements and guidelines, Wurhofer et al. [8] defined the following requirements for patterns, based on the work of Niebuhr et al. [18], McGee [19], Khazanchi et al. [20], Borchers [10], and Dearden et al. [21]:

a) Findability: A pattern needs to be easily findable within a pattern collection or language. If it already requires considerable effort to find a pattern in the first place, then that defeats the aim of patterns to provide easier access to specific information.

b) Understandability: The described solution must be understood by its users. A solution, which is not understood, can hardly be implemented correctly (or at all).

c) Helpfulness: The described solution must be feasibly realizable within the reader's available resources. It must furthermore contain enough information, so that the reader can realize the solution in practice.

d) Empirical Verification: The pattern solution should be supported by empirical data. A solution supported by empirical data is of higher quality than one, which is based only on individual experiences and/or observations.

e) Overall acceptability: This is an additional criterion to capture the subjective component of whether or not a reader agrees with a pattern solution or not, regardless of the presence or absence of deficiencies in any of the other quality requirement categories.

To ensure that a pattern satisfies these and similar quality criteria, they are often written according to predefined structures or templates. Such templates contain fields for all the essential information for a successful pattern in a certain domain. Gamma et al. [5] proposed a detailed structure in their influential work about design patterns, which consists of 13 fields, tailored towards documenting object oriented software solutions. Tidwell [7] proposes a slightly simpler and more generally suited structure, which consists of the fields *Name*, *Examples*, *Context*, *Problem*, *Forces*, *Solution*, *Resulting Context*, and additional *Notes*.

In another pattern collection, Tidwell [22] even proposes a rather minimalistic pattern structure containing only the four categories *What*, *How*, *Why*, and *When*. This structure expresses the minimal requirements of a pattern, in that it needs to address a problem via its solution (the *What*), describe the solution and the steps that need to be taken (the *How*), a justification and explanation of why the solution works as it does (the *Why*), and an explanation of the context and conditions for successful reapplication (the *When*).

Mirnig et al. [11] propose a general pattern structure intended for use across disciplines. This pattern structure is very similar to Tidwell's and consists of only five mandatory elements: *Name*, *Problem Description*, *Context* and/or *Forces*, *Solution*, and *Examples*.

B. *Minimal Regular Pattern Requirements*

Based on these observations, we can conclude that a successful pattern should at least contain the following elements:

a) Means of reference: Name, Type, Keywords, and similar elements serve to distinguish a solution description from others, help build references between solutions, which are dependent on other solutions or problems, and aid in finding or re-finding the particular solution in a collection or database containing several patterns. Corresponds to the criterion of findability. At least one such means of finding and reference should be contained in every pattern.

b) Problem description: Patterns are not general guidance documents but always targeted at a specific problem. This problem must be described or explicitly mentioned at least briefly, to let the reader decide whether the pattern is of use in the particular case or not.

c) Context description: Since patterns provide solutions for very concrete problems, these problems need to be described in the context the solution occurred in. Depending on the context, some solutions are not feasible or have different effects than they would have in other contexts. Ideally, this context description includes a detailed listing of the forces influencing the solution, but not necessarily. The basic requirement is a description detailed enough to let the reader decide whether the solution can be applied in the particular context or not.

d) Solution description: The solution is arguably the most important part of a pattern. It must be described, not merely mentioned, ideally from the identification to the problem to the fully working implementation of the solution in a step-by-step manner.

e) At least one example: In order to satisfy the general requirement of giving practical guidance, the pattern should contain at least a description of one case of a successful solution implementation.

It should be noted that none of the examined templates and structures contained written documentation of the solution status as "proven" as a requirement. Corresponding to the criterion of empirical verification by Wurhofer et al. [8], the assumption is that a pattern ideally contains more than one example in order to show that it worked in more than one case. However, the rule of three or other potential standards in this regard are rarely explicitly mentioned or enforced in pattern templates or structures. For this reason, the status as proven or the number of successful solution applications is also not included in the list of minimal pattern requirements above.

C. *Anti-Patterns*

If patterns are the "Dos", then anti-patterns are the "Don'ts". Anti-patterns are documentations of bad or nonworking solutions to problems. Appleton [12] distinguishes between two kinds of anti-patterns:

Type 1: Those that describe a bad solution to a problem, which resulted in a bad situation.

Type 2: Those that describe how to get out of a bad situation and how to proceed from there to a good solution.

The second type of anti-pattern is also known as an "Amelioration Pattern" [17]. Type 2 or amelioration patterns skirt the boundaries between pattern types and are – depending on their level of detail – more of a combination of a type 1 anti-pattern (description of the bad solution) and a corresponding regular pattern (description of the working solution). Anti-patterns are not as widely used as regular patterns, although they are arguably just as useful as regular patterns, in that they document solutions that, according to Coplien [24], might "look like a good idea, but which backfire badly when applied." Like regular patterns, the negative nature of the anti-pattern's solution might not be obvious, and the anti-pattern serves to make this fact explicit.

Despite this, anti-patterns are not always documented in the same level of detail as regular patterns are. For example, Github's list of anti-patterns [23] consists of only five elements, each one to two lines long, with only two of them containing actual reasons for why the solution is considered an anti-pattern.

The Portland Pattern Repository Wiki [17], on the other hand, provides a detailed template very similar to that of a regular pattern, outlining the components a well-written anti-pattern should feature. The structure proposed by this template is very similar to that of most regular pattern approaches. The main differences are references to other anti-patterns and positive patterns (in case it is a Type 2 or amelioration pattern), together with two context sections.

In this paper, we want to understand anti-patterns as more than a simple listing of things not to do, since a simple listing does not ensure understandability, non-reproducibility, verification, and other factors tied to the concepts the term 'patterns' carries. We shall call those, which satisfy these factors *genuine* anti-patterns, and those, which do not (i.e., simple listings or incomplete anti-patterns) *nongenuine* anti-patterns.

D. *Minimal Anti-Pattern Requirements*

Keeping in line with regular pattern requirements and quality criteria, the following would be sensible high-level expectations from any (genuine) anti-pattern: (1) ensure (non-)reproducibility of the solution; (2) foster understanding why the solution does not work as intended; (3) provide distinction between the desired and actual outcome; (4) make the description accessible to experts and novices. Taking these into consideration and by matching them to the discussed anti-pattern approaches, we can conclude that a successful anti-pattern should at least contain the following elements:

a) Means of reference: An anti-pattern needs to be easily found and be able to be referenced, so the same standards as for regular patterns apply.

b) Problem description: An anti-pattern provides a solution to a problem, just like a regular pattern does. Since the distinction lies in the (in-)appropriateness of the solution and since the reader needs to be able to decide whether the anti-pattern is relevant for him/her, the same standards as for regular patterns apply.

c) Context description: Just like in a regular pattern, whether or not a solution works or can be considered "good", depends on the application context and influencing factors. Therefore, the same standards as for regular patterns apply.

d) Solution description: Unlike solution descriptions in regular patterns, the focus in not on reproducibility of the described solution. However, anti-patterns can describe well-intentioned bad solutions, so the instructions should be detailed enough, so that the individual steps can be retraced. This way, it is easier to pinpoint where the solution went wrong (start, middle, end). Therefore, similar standards as for regular patterns apply here as well.

e) Result description: An anti-pattern describes a solution, which does not work well or which does not work as intended. In order to adequately do this, the pattern needs to contain a description of the result of applying the pattern solution in the particular context(s), in order to allow the reader to compare the desired with the actual result.

f) At least one example: Similar to regular patterns, the anti-pattern should contain at least one example case. In an anti-pattern, however, the focus is not on reproducing the solution. Therefore, the example should serve to justify the implicit or explicit assumption that the solution described by the anti-pattern leads to the described result.

E. *Dark Patterns*

A dark pattern describes a design solution, which "*appear[s] to have been carefully crafted to trick users into doing things ... and they do not have the user's interests in mind.*" [13]. Unlike anti-patterns, this definition by Brignull et al. does not leave room for well-intentioned solutions, which did not work out as intended. The definition found on darkpatterns.org, an adaptation of the previous definition, makes this even more explicit: "*Dark Patterns ... are not mistakes, they are carefully crafted with a solid understanding of human psychology, and they do not have the user's interests in mind.*" [14]

Where a pattern describes a well-working solution and an anti-pattern describes one, which does not work well (or as well as it was intended to work), a dark pattern describes a solution, where the *intention* behind it is a negative one. Documenting a solution as a dark pattern is a way of exposing often well-hidden malicious practices (e.g., hidden costs in "free" services or disguised advertisements). There is no direct requirement of the solution having to work well (pattern) or not (anti-pattern). Greenberg et al. [15] and Zagal et al. [16] also highlight the intentionality of a dark pattern as the main distinguishing characteristic from an anti-pattern. Nonetheless, they combine both dark patterns and anti-patterns in a broader sense in their work.

However, it would be reasonable to expect a dark pattern to be more important or more dangerous, if the solution it describes worked well rather than the opposite. After all, if a design intended to trick the user does not work very well as per its intended use, then that solution is less dangerous than one, which works very well in tricking users.

So in a way, it would seem more sensible to consider dark patterns to be closer to regular patterns instead of anti-patterns. Taking the proposed minimal recommendations we found for regular patterns and applying them to dark patterns would also be misguided, however, as the focus of regular patterns lies in their reapplicability – the exact opposite of dark pattern solutions, which should *not* be reproduced [13]-[16].

As we can see, the distinguishing characteristic of a dark pattern is not the quality of its solution, and neither is it the level of detail of its solution description. It is rather the *intention* behind the design solution and its status of undesirability, which makes a particular solution a dark pattern solution. Dark patterns are, much like shallow anti-patterns, often simply documented as brief statements of the solution implementation, followed by a list of examples. The focus is more on warning the user and exposing malpractices.

F. Minimal Dark Pattern Requirements

Considering that a dark pattern is not about reproducing a solution, but a statement as to how and why a particular solution is malicious and should be avoided, we arrive at the following minimal requirements to satisfy these aspects:

a) Means of reference: If a dark pattern should carry the name 'pattern' for a reason, then it should also satisfy the general pattern requirement of being easily referenceable, in order to build a pattern collection or language. Therefore, similar standards as for regular and anti-patterns apply.

b) Solution description: Just like a regular pattern or an anti-pattern, a dark pattern is about a particular solution implementation. This solution needs to be described in enough detail, so that the reader can recognize it.

c) Solution goal or intention: The focal points of dark pattern solutions are the malicious intentions behind the solution implementation. While the intention in regular or anti-patterns is, in most cases, simply the intention of solving the problem, malicious goals can be manifold and not always known to the reader (phishing, spoofing, credit card fraud, etc.). Therefore, the intention needs to be made explicit in dark patterns.

d) Undesirability statement: The fact that the solution with its respective goal is an undesirable one might not be obvious to every reader, depending on his or her background, experience or legal knowledge. A dark pattern should, therefore, contain a statement about the undesirability of the solution. This also clearly demarcates it as a dark pattern.

e) Undesirability justification: More important than the undesirability statement itself is an appropriate justification as to why the intention behind the described solution is undesired in a particular context (or all of them). This justification might often be obvious or already implicitly contained in the solution description, but it is nevertheless very important for three intuitively plausible reasons. First, a dark pattern should expose practices that skirt or cross legal and/or moral boundaries. They should not be based on one's subjective sensibilities regarding aesthetics or other nonrelevant factors. Second, moral codes are still subjective in a wider sense and not uniform across societies, so an intersubjectively traceable reference should be provided. Third, legal constraints are similarly not uniform across nations, so an adequate reference or justification should be provided.

f) At least one example: Similar in form to regular patterns and anti-patterns, examples have an entirely different function for dark patterns. They should warn users from interacting with the designs presented in the examples section. The focus should be on quantity over quality, since the designs need not be reproduced.

To sum up, a regular pattern provides the reader with clear reasoning and context as to why and how a certain solution solved a particular problem. In the same spirit, a dark pattern provides the reader with a clear reasoning and context as to why and how a certain solution is undesirable from a legal and/or moral standpoint.

TABLE I. MINIMAL REQUIREMENTS PER PATTERN TYPE

Requirement	Patterns	Anti-Patterns	Dark Patterns
Reference means	X	X	X
Problem	X	X	
Context	X	X	
Solution	X	X	X
Goal/Intention			X
Result		X	
Undesirability statement			X
Undesirability justification			X
Example(s)	X	X	X

G. Minimal Requirements - Summary

When comparing the minimal requirements for the three pattern types we can see that, the only requirements all three have in common are reference means, solution description, and examples. Problem statement and context description are only relevant for regular patterns and anti-patterns. Anti-patterns require an additional result description, in order to show how the solution does not work well or as well as intended. Dark Patterns, having a different focus, require an additional statement about the solution intention, the undesirability of it, and a justification for said undesirability. Since they do not focus on reproducibility of the solution, problem statement and context description are not required for dark patterns. An overview of the minimal requirements for each pattern Type is provided in Table 1.

IV. SUMMARY AND DISCUSSION

From this preceding analysis, we derive that there are two dimensions, which govern the separation between regular patterns, anti-patterns, and dark patterns. These two levels are **completeness** and **focus**.

The *completeness* of a pattern determines whether it is genuine or non-genuine. Since completeness means fulfilling the minimum requirements outlined above, it is reasonable to state that only genuine patterns could be considered good or high quality patterns. There is no guarantee, however, that a genuine pattern is automatically of high quality, as its content may still be lacking. This depends on the pattern mining and writing processes and cannot be dictated by structural requirements alone.

The *focus* of a pattern finally decides whether the solution is a dark pattern solution or not. For the distinction between anti-patterns and regular patterns, the intentions behind the solution are irrelevant. Anti-patterns can be well intentioned with unintended side effects or misguided from the start, whereas regular patterns do not infer any legally or ethically relevant intentions beyond simply wanting to solve the particular problem. Thus, patterns and anti-patterns are focused on the solution and how well it works. We call these **solution-centered patterns**. Dark patterns are focused on the intentions behind a pattern solution. We call these **intention-centered patterns**. In their genuine form, patterns, anti-patterns and dark patterns are separate, non-overlapping categories. Only in their non-genuine form there is an (potential) overlap between anti-patterns and dark patterns. Regular patterns and anti-patterns share their status as solution-centered patterns. Only dark patterns are in the separate category of intention-centered patterns.

A. Intentions Matter

As we have learned, requirements for genuine dark patterns are different from both pattern and anti-pattern requirements. Furthermore, reproducibility is not a factor, and viability of the solution is a secondary rather than a primary factor. The solution might be easy or difficult to reproduce. It might be a solution that works well, moderately well, or not even all that well. But this does not really matter as to whether the solution description constitutes a dark pattern. What matters is the intention behind a problem solution. Consider phishing emails as an example case. There are more and less convincing phishing attempts – the more convincing ones are usually grammatically well written and spoof domain names, as well as corporate designs in some cases. Whether they are well done or not, the intention behind them is still a malicious one – be it obtaining personal information without a user's consent, stealing passwords, committing monetary fraud, or a combination of these.

The deciding factor in whether a solution is a dark pattern solution or not, is the intention with which it is implemented. This can mean that a dark pattern solution is newly developed for a certain nefarious purpose, or that a well-working and proven solution is appropriated and reused with malicious intent. This also serves as another clear delineation criterion from anti-patterns, as it might well be that an anti-pattern solution might lead to private date being made public with all its negative consequences (identity theft, credit card fraud, public shaming, etc.). If the intention behind the solution was, however, a positive one and the solution simply misguided for whatever reason, then the pattern is clearly an anti-pattern and not a dark pattern.

B. What is a Pattern?

This brings us to the issue of whether a dark pattern justifiably carries the term 'pattern' in its name at all. Describing a dark pattern solution at the same level of detail as a regular pattern or anti-pattern can lead to the opposite of what a dark pattern should do. A dark pattern should warn both users and designers from malicious solutions. They should not encourage such designs. If a dark pattern describes the malicious solution in great detail, however, then it does just that by making it more accessible and easier to (re-)implement. In order to be protected from a dark pattern solution, one needs to know what it looks like, what the intentions behind it are, and where it is or can be encountered. Knowing how to reproduce the malicious solution is hardly relevant at all in this context.

The only time in which it seems appropriate to conflate dark patterns and anti-patterns is when we talk about non-genuine patterns. Non-genuine patterns are patterns only in a wider sense, as they are problem solution descriptions of some sort, but without the level of detail, reproducibility focus and accessibility of genuine patterns. So if it is only appropriate to conflate dark patterns with other pattern types when they are incomplete, which essentially lowers their quality potential, there is little reason for dark patterns carrying 'pattern' in their name. However, it seems inappropriate to police the use of the term 'dark pattern' too strictly, as it is already widely used and usually understood in a somewhat consistent way. But we want to stress that dark patterns should not be considered patterns in the same way that regular patterns and anti-patterns are. The focus and purpose of dark patterns are decidedly different, and the 'pattern' in 'dark patterns' should be used with care.

C. A View Ahead and the Dangers of Knowing Too Much

Informing user-centered design solutions and protecting the user from malicious intentions is often a difficult balancing act. Knowledge transfer is important, as is design, which caters to individual user needs and requirements. Well-documented and well-working solutions – especially those focused on trustworthiness, acceptance, and similar factors – are in constant danger of being "hijacked" by those with sinister intents. We cannot realistically expect to come up with user-centered designs, which are completely safe from being used with malicious intent. Neither can we expect phishing, scamming, spoofing, and other forms of cyber crime to disappear anytime soon.

What we can do, then, is to be more careful when collecting, summarizing, and editing information. This keeps the knowledge transfer more focused by including necessary and omitting unnecessary information. Treating regular patterns, anti-patterns, and dark patterns as complex concepts with concrete purposes and requirements lessens the danger of a dark pattern containing instructions on how to easily reproduce its solution. Similarly, it lessens the chance of a regular pattern solution being used with malicious intent without anybody noticing. While it is probably true for dark pattern solutions that knowing too much can be bad, the opposite can be said to be true for knowledge *about* dark patterns. By knowing exactly what the purpose and requirements of a particular pattern type are, the patterns themselves can be more easily molded to fit that, and only that, particular purpose. This, in turn, raises their effectiveness, while at the same time reducing the potential of misuse, misdocumentation, or over documentation. Thus, preserving knowledge and protecting the user need not always be at odds.

V. CONCLUSION

Dark patterns are different from both regular patterns and anti-patterns due to their focus. Dark patterns are not patterns in the sense that they describe solutions embedded in their context with a focus on (non-)reproducibility, but serve more as warnings. They, therefore carry the name 'patterns' only in a very loose sense of the word. In order to satisfy quality requirements, which are often associated with patterns in the tradition of Alexander [3][4], Gamma et al. [5], and others, we provided a minimal definition for genuine dark patterns, thus bridging the gap between dark patterns and other pattern types as much as possible. A fundamental difference in focus and requirements between the pattern types still remains and the 'pattern' in 'dark patterns' should be used with care.

Future work will focus on refining dark pattern structures and centralization of information collection about malicious practices for use both within and outside of HCI. The definitions provided in this paper should serve to structure pattern approaches within and outside of HCI, especially regarding the sometimes neglected concepts of anti-patterns and dark patterns, as well as inspire more careful and focused handling of user-centered design knowledge.

ACKNOWLEDGMENT

The financial support by the Austrian Science Fund (FWF): I 2126-N15 is gratefully acknowledged.

REFERENCES

[1] A. Dix, G. Abowd, R. Beale, and J. Finlay, "Human-Computer Interaction," Prentice Hall, Europe, 1998.

[2] M. J. Mahemoff and L. J. Johnston, "Principles for a Usability-Oriented Pattern Language," In Proc. Australian Computer Human Interaction Conference OZCHI'98, IEEE Computer Society, 1998, pp. 132–139.

[3] C. Alexander, "A Pattern Language: Towns, Buildings, Construction," Oxford University Press, New York, USA, 1997.

[4] C. Alexander, "The Timeless Way of Building," Oxford University Press, New York, USA, 1979.

[5] E. Gamma, R. Helm, R. Johnson, and J. Vlissides, "Design Patterns: Elements of Reusable Object-Oriented Software." Pearson, 1994.

[6] M. Van Velie and G. C. van der Veer, "Pattern Languages in Interaction Design: Structure and Organisation," In Proc. Ninth Int. Conf. on Human-Computer Interaction, IOS Press, 2003, pp. 527-534.

[7] J. Tidwell, "Common Ground: A Pattern Language for Human-Computer Interface Design," http://www.mit.edu/~jtidwell/interaction_patterns.html, retrieved: January 2017.

[8] D. Wurhofer, M. Obrist, E. Beck, and M. Tscheligi, "A Quality Criteria Framework for Pattern Validation," International Journal on Advances in Software 3, no. 1&2, IARIA, 2010, pp. 252-264.

[9] T. Kaiser, A. G. Mirnig, N. Perterer, A. Meschtscherjakov, and M. Tscheligi, "Car User Experience Patterns: A Pattern Collection in Progress," In Proc. Eighth International Conference on Pervasive Patterns and Applications (PATTERNS 2016), IARIA, 2006, pp. 9-16.

[10] J. Borchers, "A Pattern Approach to Interaction Design," AI & Society 12, Springer, 2001, pp. 359-376.

[11] A. G. Mirnig et al., "User experience patterns from scientific and industry knowledge: An inclusive pattern approach, International Journal On Advances in Life Sciences 7, no. 3&4, IARIA, 2015, pp. 200-215.

[12] B. Appleton, "Patterns and Software: Essential Concepts and Terminology," http://www.bradapp.com/docs/patterns-intro.html, retrieved: January 2017.

[13] H. Brignull, "Dark Patterns: Deception vs. Honesty in UI Design," http://alistapart.com/article/dark-patterns-deception-vs.-honesty-in-ui-design, 2011, retrieved: January 2017.

[14] H. Brignull, M. Miquel, and J. Rosenberg, Dark Patterns Library. http://darkpatterns.org, retrieved: January 2017.

[15] S. Greenberg, S. Boring, J. Vermeulen, and J. Dostal, "Dark Patterns in Proxemic Interactions: A Critical Perspective," In Proc. 2014 conference on Designing interactive systems (DIS '14), ACM (2014), pp. 523-532.

[16] J. Zagal, S. Bjork, and C. Lewis, "Dark Patterns in the Design of Games," In Proc. Foundation of Digital Games, 2013. http://www.fdg2013.org/program/papers.html, retrieved: January 2017.

[17] The Portland Pattern Repository Wiki. http://c2.com/cgi/wiki, retrieved: January 2017.

[18] S. Niebuhr, K. Kohler, and C. Graf, "Engaging patterns: Challenges and means shown by an example," Engineering Interactive Systems, Springer, 2008, pp. 586–600.

[19] K. McGee, "Patterns and Computer Game Design Innovation," In Proc. 4th Australasian conference on Interactive entertainment, RMIT University, 2007, pp. 1–8.

[20] D. Khazanchi, J. Murphy, and S. Petter, "Guidelines for Evaluating Patterns in the IS Domain," In Proc. MWAIS, AISeL, 2008, paper 24.

[21] A. Dearden and J. Finlay, "Pattern Languages in HCI: A Critical Review," Human-Computer Interaction 1, Lawrence Erlbaum Associates Inc., 2006, pp. 49–102.

[22] J. Tidwell, "Designing Interfaces," 2nd Edition, O'Reilly, Sebastopol, CA, USA, 2011.

[23] Anti-patterns on Github. https://github.com/angular/angular.js/wiki/Anti-Patterns, retrieved: January 2017.

[24] J. O. Coplien, "Software Patterns," SIGS Books, New York, NY, USA, 1996.

[25] W. J. Brown, R. C. Malveau, H. W. McCormick, and T. J. Mowbray, "AntiPatterns," 1998, Wiley.

An Automated Method for the Detection of Topographic Patterns at Tectonic Boundaries

Bobak Karimi
Department of Geology
Colorado College
Colorado Springs, Colorado, USA
Email: bobby.karimi@coloradocollege.edu

Hassan A. Karimi
School of Information Sciences
University of Pittsburgh
Pittsburgh, Pennsylvania, USA
Email: hkarimi@pitt.edu

***Abstract*—Detection of spatial and contextual patterns is of great importance to geoscientists interested in understanding and analyzing tectonic boundaries. To date, geoscientists have developed mostly manual detection methods and only recently has interest in the development of automated methods grown with the availability of high-resolution satellite data and the advancement of technologies such as Geographic Information Systems (GIS). Geoscientists are examining different approaches to automate the manual detection method of tectonically related phenomena, but considering the complexity, time-consumption, and assumptions usually made in the manual method, new automated detection techniques are anticipated to surface soon and will vary in implementation, accuracy, and time performance. In this paper, we present a Digital Elevation Model (DEM) based automated method for detection of spatial and contextual topographic patterns at tectonic boundaries. Our automated method was experimented and compared against recent existing methods with the same objective and the manual method, which is considered as the baseline. The results show that our automated method produces more accurate results than the existing methods.**

Keywords - Automated pattern detection; cluster analysis; lineaments; tectonics.

I. INTRODUCTION

Context plays a major role in detecting patterns and can help improve the accuracy of the automated detection methods. In particular, spatial context is necessary and imperative in detection of patterns in natural phenomena. In this paper, we discuss a new automated detection method in the context of lineaments (such as faults). We chose this context, as a representative spatial context, primarily for the reason that it is complex and involves several steps, including image processing for pixel extraction from raster datasets, conversion of extracted pixels to vector lines, and detection of line clusters based on the context.

Tectonic stresses acting upon a region can create deformation structures, such as folds, faults, and fractures. These structures act as pathways for weathering and erosion, influencing topographic pattern development in a region. Selecting lines (or lineaments) along changes in topography (ridges, valleys, etc.) is a common method in highlighting patterns of geologic structures. The scale of the lineaments often reflects the most prominent types of geologic structures [1]–[3]. Detection and selection of lineament patterns is most accurately conducted manually; however, automated methods are improving and their results are converging on the accuracy of the manually selected data. These automated methods still are prone to error, and validation of the dataset is crucial. Since large, tectonically sourced lineaments are not just expressions of a specific feature, but also a manifestation of lithospheric paleostress fields [4]–[7], errors in the orientation of lineaments can lead to incorrect interpretations of the geologic stress patterns through time [4].

The most common methods of automatically extracting lineament data is from DEMs [8], [9], or from some surface derived from a DEM [10]–[12]. Derived surfaces are created to better enhance distinct topographic changes ('edges'), and the derived surface most frequently used are hillshades [4], [11], [12]. The popularity of utilizing hillshades to select lineaments is based on how well it highlights topographic changes; however, since a hillshade is based on azimuthal direction and vertical angle of a 'sun', a single image will prominently highlight features perpendicular to the azimuthal orientation selected to make the hillshade [13]. Features not ideally oriented will be harder to select as the difference in Digital Number (DN) value across the ridge will be close to negligible. To overcome this hurdle, several hillshades with different azimuthal sun orientations can be created from the original DEM [13], [14]. Once edges have been enhanced, edge linking methods are used for automated line extraction [4], or modules such as LINE in PCI Geomatica.

The line datasets selected from the various hillshades sometimes highlight the same topographic features, and the resulting final dataset has clusters of lines representing a single feature. Manually picking lineaments from the hillshades avoids this data clustering [13]; however, these clusters are unavoidable in automatically selected lineament data based on a multiple hillshade approach, requiring a method to de-cluster or assess the data. Assessment of automatically picked lineaments has most commonly been done subjectively as a visual assessment [12], [15]. There have been several objective approaches suggested: [4] used a hierarchical clustering of different datasets based on count and statistics of orientation and length of lineaments, similarly, [16] computed statistics of count and length of lineaments to compare different datasets, [8] implemented a confusion matrix approach with the distance between lineaments, and [9] used calculated reference point data to correlate with ground truth datasets as a comparison metric. While these objective methods deploy specific metrics to assess or de-cluster data,

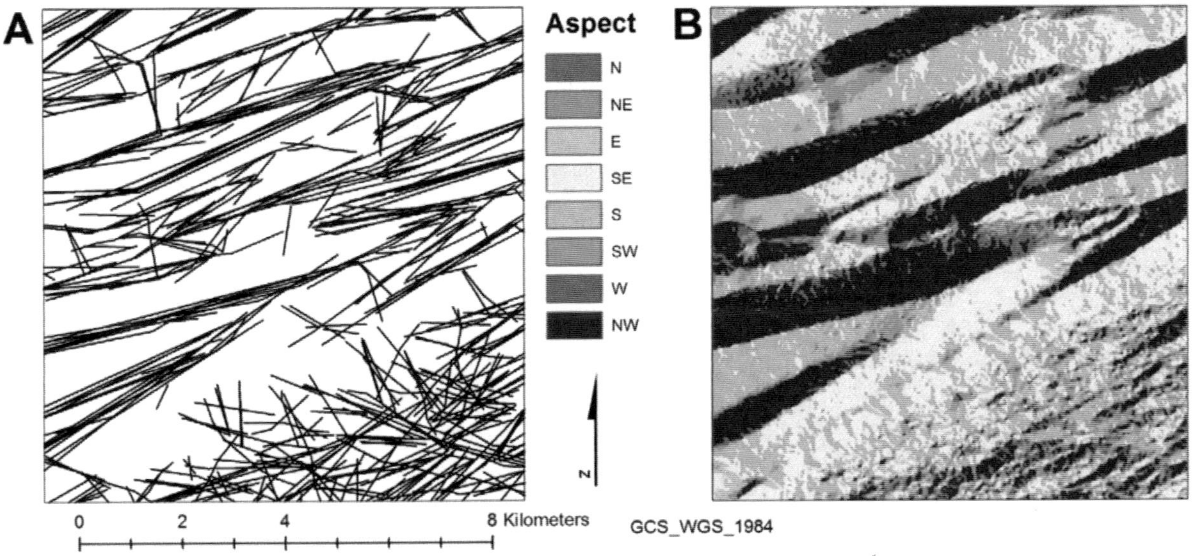

Figure 1. (a) The final dataset of all lines extracted from the multiple hillshades in PCI Geomatica with noise reduction, and (b) Aspect of the DEM.

none reference the original dataset, the DEM, to evaluate lines within a cluster as the most representative of the topographic feature they are meant to represent. Without consideration of what the lines represent, any de-clustering method or assessment allows for misoriented linear evaluations of topographic features, leading to misinterpretations of geologic stresses.

The objective of this paper is to present a new method in assessing the different datasets that result from a multiple hillshade (MH) lineament selection approach, referencing the original DEM dataset as an objective assessment of lines. Our results are to be compared to the leading DEM based lineament method by [4] and a manual method, which we consider to be the baseline. The manual method, despite being very time consuming and in some parts involving subjective assumptions, is currently the only known method that produces highly accurate results. This, coupled with the observation that the geoscience community has spent many years refining and improving the manual method, would make it suitable to be used as a baseline for comparing the accuracy of automated methods, such as the one discussed in this paper.

The rest of this paper is structured as follows. In section 2, we discuss the study area and the digital elevation model we use. Section 3 outlines our methods: automated selection of lines, derivation of metric to validate lines, and cluster analysis. Our results are presented in section 4 and discussed in section 5. Concluding remarks and future work are found in section 6.

II. Study Area and Data

The eastern margin of North America has been subjected to several mountain building (orogenic) events over the last 500 million years, the final event constructing the Appalachian Mountains. For the purposes of this study, we locate our region of interest to an approximately 9km x 9km region in central Pennsylvania within the Valley and Ridge province of the Appalachian Mountains. This area is dominated by folded beds whose preferential weathering and erosion dominate the topographic development in the area. Ridges and valleys within this particular area trend NE-SW at an azimuth of 67°. Our DEM is a 1-arc second (~30m) resolution elevation model from the Shuttle Radar Topography Mission (SRTM) V2. Within the DEM, there are two distinct topographic expressions. In the northern and western portions, there is a distinct topographic representation of the valleys and ridges associated with the province, with high topographic relief. The southeastern portion has no pronounced ridge system and the topographic relief in this region is low. It is likely that the structures expressed by topography in this region are joints (fractures).

III. Methods

Our new method discussed in this paper is similar to the Multi-Hillshade Hierarchical Clustering (MHHC) method presented in [4]. The selection of clusters follows similar steps, but our methods vary in how we process those clusters. Our method is composed of three parts: 1) automatic selection of lines in PCI Geomatica, 2) derivation of a metric to validate the best oriented lines, and 3) the cluster analysis.

A. *Automatic Selection of Lines*

The automatic selection of lines is composed of four steps: 1) creation or acquisition of a DEM, 2) derivation of hillshades from the DEM at various illumination azimuths, 3) line extraction based on edge detection, and 4) reduction of noise. The DEM can be created from vector or LIDAR data, or acquired as a subset or mosaic of existing DEMs. In our case, we utilized a subset of a DEM with coverage in central Pennsylvania. From the DEM, we derived eight hillshades at 45° illumination orientations starting with 0° (north) and ending with 315° (northwest). We selected these eight orientations to best highlight topographic changes (ridges/valleys) that may otherwise not be well-highlighted given only a single illumination orientation. For example, a ridge oriented east-west will best be highlighted with a north-south illumination and not an east-west orientation. Each image was then imported into PCI Geomatica, calling on the LINE module to extract lineaments. The LINE algorithm is comprised of three steps. The first is the edge detection operator (Canny edge detector) followed by thresholding to produce a binary edge raster [17]. This image is then processed by many substeps to extract the vector lines [4], [17]. Further, and more detailed, description of the workflow for the LINE module can be found in [17]. The LINE module requires several parameters to be input, and these parameters can impact the count, length, and spatial accuracy of the selected lines [4]. Parameter selection was based on several trials and visual assessment of the output. The parameters we selected are provided in Table 1. The values in Table 1 are expressed in pixels (px) as these are the values of inputs used by the software. A vector shapefile of automatically selected lineaments is output for each of the eight hillshade images. These shapefiles were merged into a single dataset, and each line was split at vertices. Splitting the lines increases the number of lines and the dataset size, but it also allows for interpretation of multiple structures influencing a single topographic feature. Azimuthal orientation and length of each line was calculated and added as a field to the dataset.

Noise reduction was performed using a raster approach outlined in [4]. The merged dataset was converted to a raster image using the line density tool in the computer program, ArcMap [18]. In the output raster, considering a relatively low value for search radius, clusters of lines are depicted as regions with high DN values, while solitary lines have lower DN values. Zonal statistics of the line density output raster were calculated within a 60m buffer around each line and the mean DN value was appended to the line dataset. Lines associated with low DN values were deleted from the dataset. It must be noted that, while this noise reduction decreases the total number of lines, it also may remove small, but structurally relevant data. At this stage of the research, we continued with the noise reduction, as it is what was employed by [4] in their method. As our work continues, we will need to make considerations of the validity of noise reduction in the context of geologic structural and field data. The final dataset is shown in Fig. 1A. Clusters of lines can clearly be seen that follow ridge/valley profiles.

TABLE I. TABLE OF PARAMETERS FOR LINE SELECTION IN PCI GEOMATICA.

Parameter	Value Used
Filter Radius	10 px
Edge Gradient Threshold	30 px
Curve Length Threshold	30 px
Line Fitting Error Threshold	9 px
Angular Difference Threshold	30°
Linking Distance Threshold	20 px

B. *Derivation of Metric to Validate Lines*

In deriving a metric to validate lines, special attention must be paid to what these line features represent, which, based on the MH approach, are changes in topography. Not all lines within a cluster are true representations of the topographic feature they are meant to highlight. The most accurately oriented line will have slopes oriented differently on both the right and left side of the line, as that line represents some valley or ridge. This will not hold true for lines inaccurately oriented, as the same slope orientation can exist on both sides of the line. To implement this idea and develop a metric which we refer to as the *inflection value*, we first derive an aspect image from our DEM (see Fig. 1B). This provides us with the azimuthal orientation each slope is facing within the DEM. The aspect image is converted to a point shapefile. We then create 60m left and right buffers around each line. Unfortunately, the zonal statistics tool does not take into consideration circular statistics, so we calculated the sine and cosine for the azimuth at each point and developed our own zonal statistics tool specifically for circular data. This tool uses the aspect point shapefile and the left and right buffers as input and calculates the mean of the sine and cosine within each buffer, and converts that value back to azimuthal notation. The difference between the mean aspect values in the left and right buffers of each line gives us the *inflection value*. High *inflection values* represent lines that more accurately represent the feature they are meant to highlight, since the slopes on either side of a ridge or valley should face opposite directions.

C. *Cluster Analysis*

The following workflow, adapted from [4], is applied to the line dataset to reduce clusters to one linear feature:

1) Choose the longest line in the main dataset.
2) Make a buffer around the chosen line.
3) Select all lines completely within that buffer.
4) Select lines with azimuth within 20° from the line selected in step 1.
5) Select the line with the largest inflection value, save it to a new shapefile – the final dataset - and delete all selected lines in the main dataset.
6) Repeat from step 1 until no lines remain in the main dataset.

We compare our cluster analysis with that suggested in [4], which follows a similar workflow up until step 5:

5) If the selection contains more than 4 lines, continue to step 6, otherwise save the originally selected line to a new shapefile – the final dataset – and continue to step 8.
6) Create a buffer around selected lines (=cluster) with the following attributes: count of selected lines, average length, and average azimuth.
7) Create a new line using the average length and azimuth in step 6, and save it to the final dataset shapefile.
8) Delete all selected lines from the main dataset.

9) Repeat from step 1 until no lines remain in the main dataset.

In deploying the method outlined in [4], we had to explore and make some assumptions as to the size of buffers. The buffer size in step 2 is determined by processing the dataset using the two methods using 150m, 200m, 250m, and 300m buffers. The results are visually assessed to evaluate the buffer size that best de-clusters data; where clusters are reduced to a single line and not an excess of lines are deleted. In step 6 for [4], we utilized a buffer of 60m, which was large enough to allow all buffered lines to intersect one another. Beyond these assumptions, we maintained the exact process as described in [4] to better compare the two methods and assess sources of difference. For both methods, the algorithms were written in Python in ArcGIS using the ArcPy library.

IV. Results

The results of the method by [4] using 150m, 200m, 250m, and 300m buffers at step 2 are shown in Fig. 2. Similarly, Fig. 3 shows the results using our new method. The lines in these images represent final de-clustered line datasets within the region of interest using different buffer sizes in step 2.

Both sets of results were compared to a more accurate lineament dataset manually selected using hillshades and the original DEM. Through visual assessment, we are able to identify that a 300m buffer resulted in too few lines in the final dataset in both methods. Lower buffer sizes (150m and 200m) left too many lines representing single features. A buffer size of 250m provided the best results in the case of both methods. Results of both methods compared to the manually selected lines are shown in Fig. 4. In Fig. 4, the top rose plot is of the manual data, middle rose plot is of the data from our method, and the bottom is from the method in [4].

V. Discussion

We calculate a completeness percentage of the resulting output lines from the two methods as compared to a manually selected dataset [19]. This calculation was done by buffering the lines from the two methods with a buffer size of 50m, and extracting the length of manual lines within those buffers. The percentage of the length of lines within the buffers is the completeness percentage. Our method had a 60% completeness compared to 47% that resulted from the method in [4]. Upon a visual assessment of the lines output by the two methods using a 250m buffer size in step 2 to manually selected lines (see Fig. 4), we can note that automatic lineament selection in the northern portion of the dataset was far more successful than what is seen in the southeastern region. Completeness percentages were higher with both methods in the north: 80% for the results of our method, and 68% for the method by [4]. We compared our initial total dataset before the clustering method was applied, and were able to ascertain that the cluster analysis caused the significant loss of data in the southeastern region. This leads us to believe

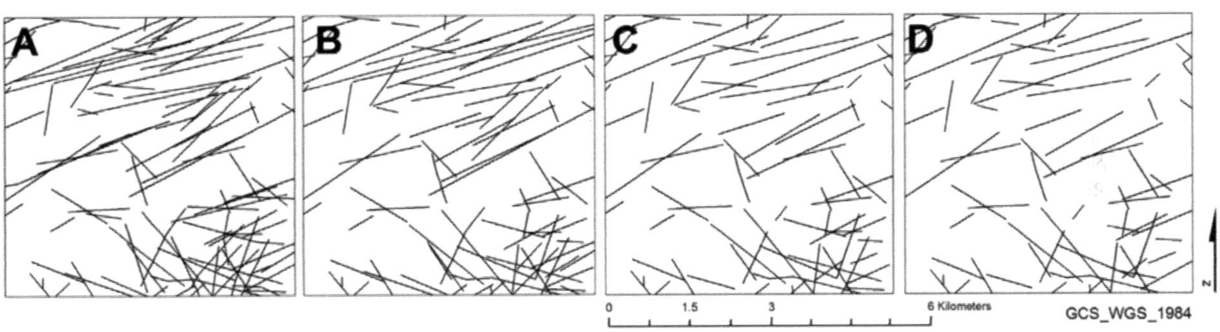

Figure 2. Results of the method in [4] at (a) 150m, (b) 200m, (c) 250m, and (d) 300 m buffers.

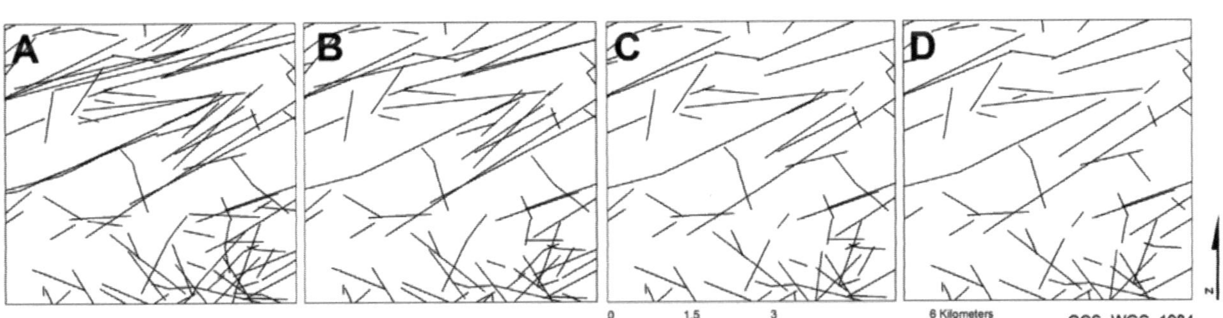

Figure 3. Results of our method at (a) 150m, (b) 200m, (c) 250m, and (d) 300 m buffers.

that subdivisions of the dataset should be made based on a first pass visual assessment of the automatically selected line dataset. These subdivisions can then be processed using different buffer sizes, or even approaches, to produce a more accurate result for that subarea. Since the southeastern portion of the area of interest has been identified as compromised, we make our assessment on the effectiveness of the two methods based on the northern portion.

In the northern region, both methods do not highlight every line, but this happens where the buffer size to select a cluster overlaps lines representing an adjacent feature with similar orientation and size. One potential way to avoid this in the future could be to remove the necessity for buffering at step 2 and only select lines that intersect the longest line. Not all lines within a cluster intersect every other line, so this could lead to additional errors. Additionally, lines in clusters near the ends of another cluster could intersect the longest line as well.

A visual assessment between the three datasets in the northern area suggests that our method more often picks lines that match in orientation with the manual dataset. By creating a metric for each line that references the original dataset, we have provided a new method in differentiating the most representative line in a cluster. Beyond quantitative and visual assessments, rose plots have been created for the three datasets (see Fig. 4). These rose plots represent the frequency of azimuthal orientations of lines in the overall dataset. The manually derived dataset has a clear east-northeast trend that is bimodal (peaks at 60° and 75°) within a range of 30°. This general trend is shared with our method, and the method from [4]; however, the bimodal characteristic with similarly oriented peaks is seen only in the rose plot of our new method.

This combination of quantitative, visual, and data trends assessment leads us to suggest that our new method is better in differentiating datasets (MH lines). Additionally, our new method highlights the importance of referencing the original DEM when validating or assessing clusters of lines. While our

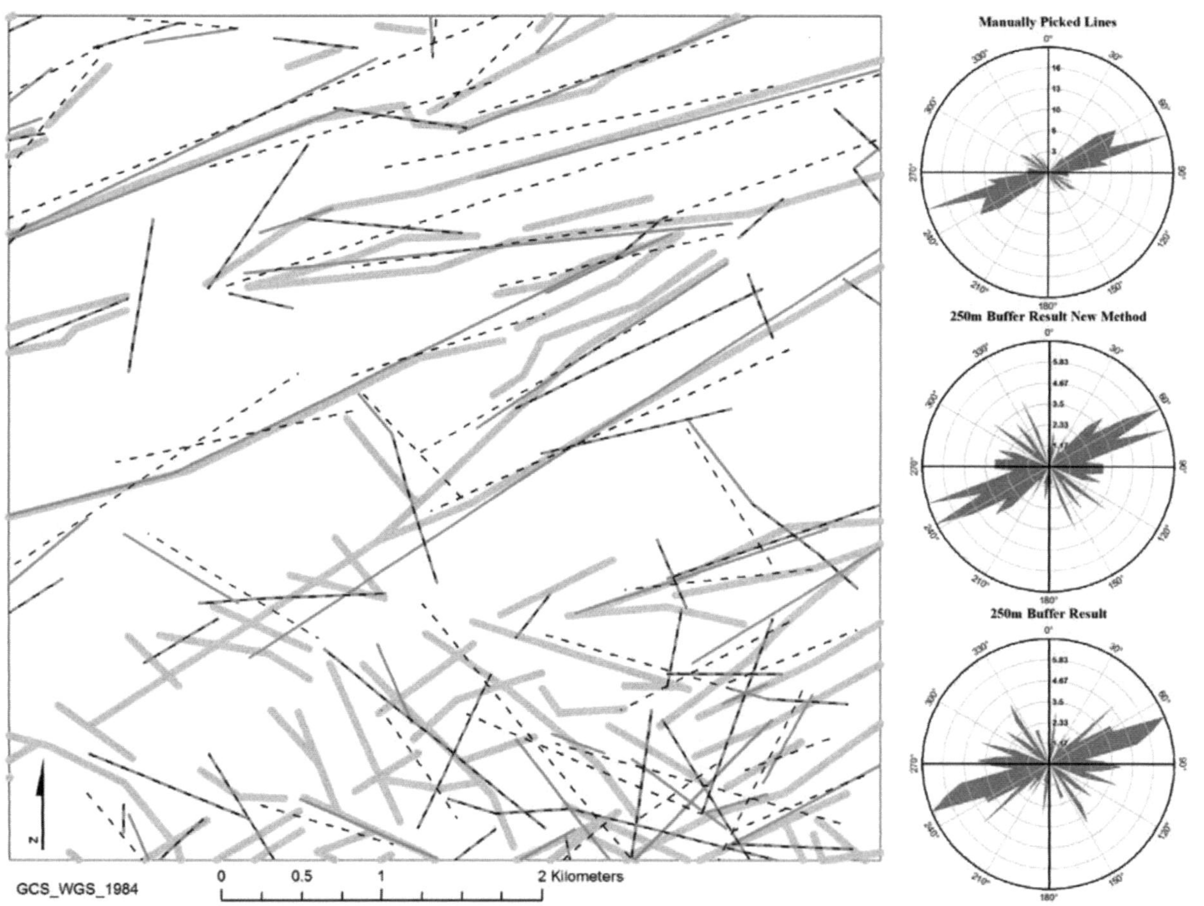

Figure 4. Comparison of the manually picked dataset (red lines) to our new method (solid grey lines) and to the results of the method in [4] (dotted black lines) using a 250m buffer. Rose diagrams are provided for each dataset.

method produces more accurate results, there are still many improvements to be considered, such as avoiding the loss of adjacent data with similar orientations and lengths. Since the algorithms for these improvements are computationally complex, processing large datasets would take an enormous amount of time. Work has to be done on creating a more time-efficient approach. Furthermore, we hope to explore more quantitative and automated methods of parameter selection where parameter selection is based on trial-and-error and subjectivity, such as the input values for the module used in PCI Geomatica (Table 1).

VI. Conclusion and Future Research

We have successfully proven that referencing the original DEM when assessing line data within clusters results in a more accurate representation of features in a region. However, our method requires adjustments to take into consideration distances between clusters, and how regions dense with data (southeastern area in our region) should be handled to avoid a significant loss of relevant data. Future work will address these issues and aim to apply our method to larger regions for geologic interpretations based on the resulting linear database. We will also improve our method by developing new algorithms (e.g., to avoid the loss of adjacent data with similar orientations and lengths). Additionally, we hope to explore more advanced quantitative methods of evaluating similarity between linear datasets by using Hausdorff distances [20]. Once these improvements are made, generalization of our method for detecting patterns in other contexts will be another future research direction.

Acknowledgment

We would like to thank Meirman Syzdykbayev at the University of Pittsburgh for assisting with development of the initial Python code and Noah Villamarin-Cutter, Matt Gottfried, and Matt Cooney at Colorado College for their help working with the ArcPy library and debugging code.

References

[1] M. J. Smith and C. D. Clark, "Methods for the visualization of digital elevation models for landform mapping," *Earth Surf. Process. Landf.*, vol. 30, no. 7, pp. 885–900, Jul. 2005.

[2] M. J. Smith and S. M. Wise, "Problems of bias in mapping linear landforms from satellite imagery," *Int. J. Appl. Earth Obs. Geoinformation*, vol. 9, no. 1, pp. 65–78, Feb. 2007.

[3] I. S. Evans, "Geomorphometry and landform mapping: What is a landform?," *Geospatial Technol. Geomorphol. Mapp. Proc. 41st Annu. Binghamt. Geomorphol. Symp.*, vol. 137, no. 1, pp. 94–106, Jan. 2012.

[4] J. Šilhavý, J. Minár, P. Mentlík, and J. Sládek, "A new artefacts resistant method for automatic lineament extraction using Multi-Hillshade Hierarchic Clustering (MHHC)," *Comput. Geosci.*, vol. 92, pp. 9–20, Jul. 2016.

[5] S. Solomon and W. Ghebreab, "Lineament characterization and their tectonic significance using Landsat TM data and field studies in the central highlands of Eritrea," *J. Afr. Earth Sci.*, vol. 46, no. 4, pp. 371–378, Nov. 2006.

[6] P. Štěpančíková, J. Stemberk, V. Vilímek, and B. Košťák, "Neotectonic development of drainage networks in the East Sudeten Mountains and monitoring of recent fault displacements (Czech Republic)," *Impact Act. Tecton. Uplift Fluv. Landsc. Drain. Dev.*, vol. 102, no. 1, pp. 68–80, Nov. 2008.

[7] A. Batayneh, H. Ghrefat, and A. Diabat, "Lineament characterization and their tectonic significance using gravity data and field studies in the Al-Jufr area, southeastern Jordan plateau," *J. Earth Sci.*, vol. 23, no. 6, pp. 873–880, 2012.

[8] D. Alegre Vaz, "Analysis of a Thaumasia Planum rift through automatic mapping and strain characterization of normal faults," *Geol. Mapp. Mars*, vol. 59, no. 11–12, pp. 1210–1221, Sep. 2011.

[9] U. Mallast, R. Gloaguen, S. Geyer, T. Rödiger, and C. Siebert, "Derivation of groundwater flow-paths based on semi-automatic extraction of lineaments from remote sensing data," *Hydrol Earth Syst Sci*, vol. 15, no. 8, pp. 2665–2678, Aug. 2011.

[10] D. Wladis, "Automatic lineament detection using digital elevation models with second derivative filters," *Photogramm. Eng. Remote Sens.*, vol. 65, pp. 453–458, 1999.

[11] A. A. Masoud and K. Koike, "Auto-detection and integration of tectonically significant lineaments from SRTM DEM and remotely-sensed geophysical data," *ISPRS J. Photogramm. Remote Sens.*, vol. 66, no. 6, pp. 818–832, Nov. 2011.

[12] G. Jordan and B. Schott, "Application of wavelet analysis to the study of spatial pattern of morphotectonic lineaments in digital terrain models. A case study," *Remote Sens. Environ.*, vol. 94, no. 1, pp. 31–38, Jan. 2005.

[13] D. U. Wise, R. Funiciello, M. Parotto, and F. Salvini, "Topographic lineament swarms: Clues to their origin from domain analysis of Italy," *Geol. Soc. Am. Bull.*, vol. 96, no. 7, pp. 952–967, Jul. 1985.

[14] B. Karimi, N. McQuarrie, J.-S. Lin, and W. Harbert, "Determining the geometry of the North Anatolian Fault East of the Marmara Sea through integrated stress modeling and remote sensing techniques," *Tectonophysics*, no. 0.

[15] Y. Kageyama and M. Nishida, "Lineament detection from land cover information in mixels using Landsat-TM data," *Electr. Eng. Jpn.*, vol. 148, no. 4, pp. 65–73, Sep. 2004.

[16] A. Abdullah, J. M. Akhir, and I. Abdullah, "Automatic mapping of lineaments using shaded relief images derived from digital elevation model (DEMs) in the Maran-Sungi Lembing area, Malaysia," *Electron. J. Geotech. Eng.*, vol. 15, pp. 1–9, 2010.

[17] P.C.I. Geomatics Enterprises, *Geomatica Help. [software help]*. Richmond Hill, Ontario, Canada, 2011.

[18] Environemental Systems Research Institute, *ArcMap*. Redlands, CA.

[19] H. Tveite, "An accuracy assessment method for geographical line data sets based on buffering," *Int. J. Geogr. Inf. Sci.*, vol. 13, no. 1, pp. 27–47, Jan. 1999.

[20] R. T. Rockafellar and R. J.-B. Wets, *Variational Analysis*. Springer Science & Business Media, 2009.

Analyzing User Generated Content on Instagram: the Case of Travel Agencies

Rony Germon*, Karina Sokolova*

*PSB Paris School of Business
Chair D^3 Digital, Data, Design,
Paris, France
email:{r.germon, k.sokolova}@psbedu.paris

Adil Bami†

†ISCAE Casablanca
Casablanca, Morocco
email:abami@groupeiscae.ma

Abstract—**Social networks can become an essential part of a brand's communication strategy; they not only assist in reaching potential customers, but also help develop an online community, where users generate content about the service themselves: User Generated Content (UGC). It is known that the actual user experience, as well as feedback on social media, can have a higher impact on customer acquisition than direct commercial offers. Social media usage is on the increase in the travel industry. Instagram - the photography-centred social network - has a high number of users generating content, and this appears to be advantageous for travel agencies. The goal of this article is to understand the use and the strategy of Instagram UGC concerning travel agencies, and to analyse the impact of UGC on the community engagement. The results are based on Instagram data collected for three online travel agencies: Very Chic, Voyage Privé and Airbnb.**

Keywords–User Generated Content; UGC; Social Media; Instagram; Travel Agency; indicators of success.

I. Introduction

Over recent decades, with the development of information and communication technology, the travel industry has become highly digitalised and now enjoys a high web profile. Most of the travel-related transactions now take place through the Internet via official websites. Moreover, customers like to share their travel experience online and often rely on previous customer's opinions to help make choices. User-generated content currently has greater impact on customer acquisition than traditional commercial offers, which are often seen as too aggressive.

Instagram - a social network based on photo-sharing with 600 million monthly active users - is rapidly growing and has already become the third most widely used social network worldwide. Travellers usually take many photographs during their multiple trips and share them online, together with their opinions. In this study we examine the hypothesis that Instagram user-generated content has an effect upon communication for travel agencies as well as upon customer acquisition strategies. Even if the electronic word of mouth (eWOM) of consumers is studied in depth, and is proven to have a positive effect on the company image, as well as an even stronger impact on user acquisition than marketing campaigns [1]–[6], only a few studies have been focused on Instagram [7][8] and on the Instagram UGC [9][10]. To our knowledge, no studies have yet been conducted on eWOM regarding online travel agencies and Instagram. The goal of this article is to offer a preliminary analysis of Instagram's communication strategies concerning online travel agencies, to measure the impact of each strategy on the community, and to identify the indicators of success.

The article is organised as follows: Section 2 presents related works. Section 3 presents the data collection process and the indicators that we chose to study in this work. Section 4 presents the results of the study in the case of three specific travel agencies. We end the article with a conclusion and suggest future work.

II. Related work

In [11], the authors reported that research on UGC, also known as electronic word-of-mouth (eWOM), works exactly like traditional word-of-mouth [12]. Online social media such as Facebook, YouTube, Twitter and Instagram are examples of places where users share UGC. As UGC is based on consumers' own experiences, it has proven to be trustworthy, useful and unbiased [13][14]. Early research focused on popular forums, such as message boards or Internet-based chat rooms [15]. It then extended to websites and blogs [16][17], and later to social media platforms such as Facebook and Twitter [18]. UGC reviews have been extensively studied, in particular in relation to decision-making. Other researchers have examined the effects and implications of UGC in the tourism sector [19]. In this paper UGC is mainly used to refer to reviews and interactions between users on travel recommendation websites, such as Instragram webpages.

Instagram offers to organizations a network of more than 600 million global accounts, with 30 billion photographs shared, and 4.2 billion daily likes (data extracted in 2017 from the official Instagram moderator blog). Instagram is the chosen social media platform for this study due to the growing popularity of the platform for marketing and branding initiatives. This social network focuses on advertising, promotion, marketing, distribution of ideas/goods, and also for providing information services fast, precisely and accurately, especially in the tourism sector.

III. Methodology

We conducted a semiotic study of photographs published on Instagram by voyageprive.com, verychic.com and airbnb.com. In this study, we chose to analyse 10 photographs for each of the travel agencies, as follows. First we collected the 50 most recent Instagram posts for each agency. Second,

TABLE I. MINIMUM, MAXIMUM AND AVERAGE VALUES OF INDICATORS OBTAINED FOR EACH TRAVEL AGENCY

	VeryChic	VoyagePrivé	AirBnb
Average #Likes	1,098	231	13,368
Maximum #Likes	2,288	375	40,545
Minimum #Likes	471	56	3,889
Average Engagement	2.2%	2.1%	1.11%
Maximum Engagement	3.9%	3.41%	3.38%
Minimum Engagement	0.8%	0.51%	0.32%
Average #Hashtags	6	27	23
Maximum #Hashtags	12	29	30
Minimum #Hashtags	4	25	1
Average #Comments	20	2	449
Maximum #Comments	98	7	1317
Minimum #Comments	2	0	29

we measured the average engagement level of the agency based on the number of likes that each photograph obtained. Finally, from the initial dataset and for qualitative analysis, we chose four photographs having the highest amount of likes, two having numbers of likes almost equal to the average engagement level of the agency, and four photographs having significantly less likes than the average.

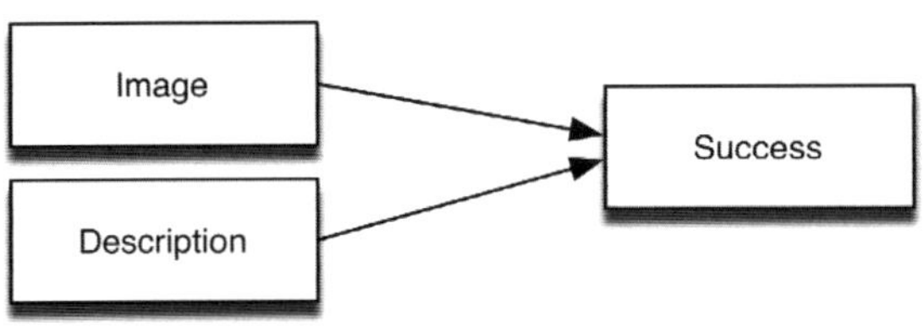

Figure 1. Methodology representation

Based on the dataset obtained, we investigated the impact of image and image description-based indicators on the indicators of success. The methodology used in this study is visually represented in Fig. 1. We established eight criteria for our study based on the image, the image description and community reactions. We obtained two image-related indicators, four description-related indicators and four indicators of success.

- Image-related indicators
  - Image family: landscape, person/selfie, activity (hotel, cooking, sport, attractions, etc.).
  - Image source: the image created by the agency; the image created by another Instagram user; the image found outside Instagram.
- Description-related indicators
  - Description type: commercial message; citation; image description; call for an action.
  - Number of hashtags used in the description.
  - Hashtags types: related to image description, related to the call for an action.
  - Geolocation type: place name or an exact location.
- Indicators of success
  - Number of likes.
  - Number of comments.
  - Engagement
  - Comment types: general interest expression, information request, friendship request, answer for a question, negative feedback.

Additionally, for simple numeric indicators, such as the number of likes, the number of hashtags and the number of comments, we defined an indicator of engagement showing how many interactions an image obtained, comparing this to the current community of the agency Instagram account. We defined the engagement on Instagram as the number of likes obtained by a photograph (denoted $likes(p)$), compared to the number of followers of the Instagram channel of the agency (denoted $followers(a)$). The engagement of a post p published by an agency p is denoted $Engagement(p, a)$ and is calculated as stated in (1).

$$Engagement(p, a) = \frac{\#likes(p)}{\#followers(a)} \quad (1)$$

The next section presents the results that were obtained.

IV. RESULTS

Table I presents the minimum, maximum and the average numbers of likes, hashtags, comments, and the engagement scores for the photographs of each online agency. We observed that AirBnB has a very large Instagram community, while the VoyagePrivé has the smallest community in terms of the maximum number of likes (40.545 and 231 respectively). However, AirBnb has a lower average engagement score (1.11%) than VoyagePrivé (2.1%) meaning that Voyage Privé has fewer but more engaged followers.

We observed that the indicators of success (the number of likes, the number of comments and engagement level) are correlated. We also observed that the number of comments increases when the number of likes is high. This suggests that most of the comments received by the travel agencies are related to positive opinions from customers rather than negative.

Considering the VeryChic photographs, the less popular images mainly send out commercial messages using slightly fewer hashtags than the more popular images. The most popular messages are all borrowed from external sources.

Surprisingly, the most popular photographs include commercial messages. We observed that 9 out of 10 images depict landscapes, suggesting a common guideline within the strategy.

VoyagePrivé was also observed to publish landscape photographs (9 out of 10). Again, the top four photographs come from bloggers outside of Instagram; the description of those photographs contains calls for an action. This suggests that a good way to engage people is not only by sharing interesting information or content, but also by engaging them in acting or reacting. Once again, we observed that the less engaging photographs are agency-owned and contain commercial messages.

AirBnB publishes diverse types of photographs, of which the most engaging depict landscapes and activities, and the less engaging show people. Most of the AirBnB photographs are not agency-owned and come from bloggers or Instagram users. The most popular image descriptions contain calls for action and the least popular posts contain simple description of the photography. Most of the AirBnB photographs are associated with precise locations, which indicate a desire to contextualise/personalise their community management (9 out of 10).

Considering the content of the comment published on Instagram posts, we do not see any negative feedback on VoyagePrive and VeryChic, and only the minority of AirBnB comments are negative. Surprisingly, only VoyagePrivé answered the questions asked by community members in Instagram comments.

We observed that the photographs published by AirBnB seem to be more professional and of a higher quality than the those published by VeryChic. The content of those of AirBnB have generally the same style and a similar colour palette, although other agencies do not define any particular publishing style. Among the most engaging photographs published by AirBnB, we mainly observed the use of blue, green and brown colours. We also observed that most of the borrowed photographs emphasise highlight the photographer in the description, and the community republish photographs that are more engaging, probably because of the popularity of the photographer. We did not observe any impact of geolocation on the success indicators, probably due to the reduced dataset.

The number of hashtags used in the description do not influence the engagement level: the most and the least engaging photographs had about the same number of hashtags. New indicators, such as types of hashtags, should be added in order to better capture the engagement level based on the usage of hashtags. We observed that AirBnB have their own agency hashtags #airbnb and #LiveThere, and the agency ask users to publish their experience through photographs using those hashtags. We also observed that AirBnB regularly republishes user-created content and obtains a high engagement level. However, VeryChic do not have any branded hashtag and VoyagePrivé never publish photographs of other Instagram users.

V. Conclusion and Future Work

This paper has described our first exploratory study on the indicators of Instagram communication success and on the role of user-generated content on community engagement. We analysed Instagram images with different engagement levels produced by online travel agencies. We observed that UGC has a higher success for the online travel agencies community than for specially created images, and that is especially the case with AirBnB. The most engaging photographs depicted landscapes and contained calls for action in the description: calls such as like, retweet or comment. The most successful content came from Instagram users or, more often, from non-Instagram bloggers sharing their experiences. Although our current dataset is limited, it already shows the importance of user-generated content in community management on Instagram.

This current study is the basis of our larger study on the indicators of Instagram communication success. We observed, for example, that the most engaging photographs had similar colours, and that high quality photographs generate more comments. These observations provide us with new indicators to be added to the research. We plan, in our research agenda, to combine new indicators and to test them on a broader dataset. We wish also to include finer indicators of UGC in order to better understand its use by the agencies.

Another potential research direction is a deeper investigation of post descriptions and hashtags via semantic analyses and text mining. The same analysis could be applied to understand what type of content provides what sort of reactions. Finally, it would be interesting to analyse the Instagram community of agencies, agency hashtags use and message propagation.

References

[1] A. Z. Bahtar and M. Muda, "The Impact of User – Generated Content (UGC) on Product Reviews towards Online Purchasing – A Conceptual Framework," *Procedia Economics and Finance*, vol. 37, pp. 337–342, 2016.

[2] H. J. Cheong and M. A. Morrison, "Consumers' Reliance on Product Information and Recommendations Found in UGC," *Journal of Interactive Advertising*, vol. 8, no. 2, pp. 38–49, 2008.

[3] C. Cox, S. Burgess, C. Sellitto, and J. Buultjens, "The Role of User-Generated Content in Tourists' Travel Planning Behavior," *Journal of Hospitality Marketing and Management*, vol. 18, no. 8, pp. 743–764, 2009.

[4] Q. Ye, R. Law, B. Gu, and W. Chen, "The influence of user-generated content on traveler behavior: An empirical investigation on the effects of e-word-of-mouth to hotel online bookings," *Computers in Human Behavior*, vol. 27, no. 2, pp. 634–639, 2011.

[5] P. O'Connor, *User-Generated Content and Travel: A Case Study on Tripadvisor.Com*. Vienna: Springer Vienna, 2008, pp. 47–58.

[6] Z. Zhang, Q. Ye, R. Law, and Y. Li, "The impact of e-word-of-mouth on the online popularity of restaurants: A comparison of consumer reviews and editor reviews," *International Journal of Hospitality Management*, vol. 29, no. 4, pp. 694–700, 2010.

[7] J. Park, G. L. Ciampaglia, and E. Ferrara, "Style in the age of instagram: Predicting success within the fashion industry using social media," in *Proceedings of the 19th ACM Conference on Computer-Supported Cooperative Work & Social Computing*, ser. CSCW '16. New York, NY, USA: ACM, 2016, pp. 64–73.

[8] E. Ferrara, R. Interdonato, and A. Tagarelli, "Online popularity and topical interests through the lens of instagram," in *Proceedings of the 25th ACM Conference on Hypertext and Social Media*, ser. HT '14. New York, NY, USA: ACM, 2014, pp. 24–34.

[9] L. Manikonda, Y. Hu, and S. Kambhampati, "Analyzing user activities, demographics, social network structure and user-generated content on instagram." *CoRR*, vol. abs/1410.8099, 2014.

[10] Y. Hu, L. Manikonda, and S. Kambhampati, *What we instagram: A first analysis of instagram photo content and user types*. The AAAI Press, 2014, pp. 595–598.

[11] C. Burmann, "A call for 'User-Generated Branding'," *Journal of Brand Management*, vol. 18, no. 1, pp. 1–4, 2010.

[12] K. Manap, "The Role of User Generated Content (UGC) in Social Media for Tourism Sector," in *The 2013 WEI International Academic Conference Proceedings*. The West East Institute, 2013, pp. 52–58.

[13] F. A. Buttle, "Word of mouth: understanding and managing referral marketing," *Journal of Strategic Marketing*, vol. 6, no. 3, pp. 241–254, 1998.

[14] Y. Verhellen, N. Dens, and P. De Pelsmacker, "Consumer responses to brands placed in youtube movies: the effect of prominence and endorser expertise," *JOURNAL OF ELECTRONIC COMMERCE RESEARCH*, vol. 14, no. 4, pp. 287–303, 2013.

[15] S. Mehdizadeh, "Self-presentation 2.0: Narcissism and self-esteem on facebook," *Cyberpsychology, Behavior, and Social Networking*, vol. 13, no. 4, pp. 357–364, 2010.

[16] E. Mazur and L. Kozarian, "Self-presentation and interaction in blogs of adolescents and young emerging adults," *Journal of Adolescent Research*, vol. 25, no. 1, pp. 124–144, 2010.

[17] N. Ellison, R. Heino, and J. Gibbs, "Managing impressions online: Self-presentation process in the online dating environment," *Journal of Computer-Mediated Communication*, vol. 11, no. 2, 2006.

[18] N. J. Hum, P. E. Chamberlin, B. L. Hambright, A. C. Portwood, A. C. Schat, and J. L. Bevan, "A picture is worth a thousand words: A content analysis of Facebook profile photographs," *Computers in Human Behavior*, 2011.

[19] J. Kristian Steen Jacobsen and A. Munar, "Tourist Information Search and Destination Choice in a Digital Age," *Tourism Management Perspectives*, vol. 1, no. 1, pp. 39–47, 2012.

Analysing Human Migrations Patterns Using Digital Social Network Analysis

Charles Perez

PSB Paris School of Business, Chair D^3 Digital, Data, Design,
Paris, France
email:c.perez@psbedu.paris

***Abstract*—The success of smartphones and digital social networks has permitted a constant increase in the mobile social networks of users in the last decades. It is now possible for anyone to share content with enriched metadata, providing user's context and, in particular, times and locations. Contextual information associated with messages' content allows for the large-scale analysis of users' spatio-temporal behaviour, affording various possible applications (e.g., geo-marketing, security, smart cities). A number of studies have focused on spatio-temporal social data analyses for event detection and the identification of region of interests. This paper proposes a methodology that relies on social network analyses to identify the migrations of users between regions of interest. The proposed methodology allows for the capture of similar events and their characterization by participants' behaviour (source location and destination, etc.). The methodology is tested on 3 millions tweets from the San Francisco Bay Area.**

Keywords–Social media, Social network analysis, Region of Interests, Migration,Spatio-temporal graphs, Twitter.

I. INTRODUCTION

The emergence of smartphones, in conjunction with the success of social platforms, has led to an increase in mobile social applications. Smartphones capture spatio-temporal traces of interactions with an internal clock and a GPS. This allows for new services to be available to users and also becomes an opportunity for research activities to understand communication and relations between humans in space and time at a large scale.

The Twitter microblogging platform is an example of a mobile application that allows the public to share contextual information. It is currently one of the top public sources of spatio-temporal data with an estimated 20% of tweets geolocated [1]. Microblogging is a type of blogging that allows for brief text updates. Due to the short length of messages, approximately half of Twitter users access the platform through a mobile application installed on their smartphones, generating large amounts of spatio-temporal data to be analysed.

It is common to represent a social network as a social graph denoted $G(N, E)$, where N represents the set of nodes and E the set of edges. Profiles are represented by nodes while edges represent relationships between profiles. These relationships illustrate any type of interaction captured online between a given pair of profiles. Social platforms compute the social graph from connections between individuals based on their inclusion in a contact list. However, other types of interactions may be retrieved and analysed. For example, two individuals communicating about the same subject may be considered connected in examining communities of interests. A diffusion graph is an another example, wherein two individuals are connected when one retweets the other. Diffusion graphs are often used for analysing virality in social networks.

This article proposes the study of two different types of relationships related to spatio-temporal data. First, spatio-temporal graphs of meetings between people capture the quality of spatio-temporal data and the number of users concerned about such types of analyses. Second, using previous observations, the study proposes computing the migration graph of regions of interest (ROI). Dynamic analyses of such a graph highlight the relationships between ROI at multiple scales. It is likely that this contribution will allow for a better understanding of human mobility patterns and could allow for the identification and qualification of ROI from a novel perspective (variety of people concerned, temporality of event, distance of people coming to the event, etc.).

The remainder of the article is organized as follows. Section II introduces the related works. Section III describes an approach to building and analyzing the spatio-temporal patterns of users. Section IV reports the results on a dataset of 3 millions tweets collected from Twitter. The article ends with a brief discussion and a conclusion.

II. RELATED WORKS

Many works have modelled and analysed human mobility patterns. While in the past, collecting such data required specific devices [2], [3], smartphones and social media have helped in overcoming this limitation.

A common method to model spatio-temporal interactions is to use temporal graphs. As defined in [4], a temporal graph is a graph observed at different times as a sequence of time windows. A temporal graph is denoted $G_t^w(t_{min}, t_{max})$, where w is the time between two snapshots, the starting time of the experiment t_{min} and the ending time t_{max}. The temporal graph is a sequence of the following graphs: $\{G_{t_{min}}, G_{t_{min+w}}, \ldots, G_{t_{max}}\}$. At each frame, one observes the relationships between actors are observed and represented as a graph.

Various, state-of-the-art approaches differ in the way that graphs are built using spatio-temporal data. The authors of [5] propose a time aggregated graph to model temporal graphs. Each relationship (i.e., edges) is represented with a series of time labels indicating the type of relationship observed in each time frame. Such an approach reduces storage and computational costs. In their work to detect malicious circles of users, the authors of [6] employed a spatio-temporal co-occurrence graph. This graph is generated from posts published on Facebook whose spatio-temporal constraints are adapted to match an original friend graph. They found that particular constraints allow for finding strong correlations between the two graphs. In [7], authors analysed data generated by smartphones using Bluetooth. They proposed a proximity network, composed of people and connections between them. Connections are established when people spend more than a certain number of minutes together. The authors of [8] propose the concept of encounter networks. Such a network is deduced from the number and duration of meetings between two individuals. Each edge is weighted using a friendship probability measure that depends on the number and duration of meetings.

In [9], the authors analysed fluctuations in the activity of mobile phone users based on the number of calls per hour and per geographical location. The approach permits the detecting of abnormal spatio-temporal patterns, such as events. The authors of [10] also present a statistical approach to detect events from mobile devices. The approach discovers the busiest locations at a city-wide scale and detects unexpectedly busy locations. In [11], the authors estimate the centres of earthquakes and the trajectories of typhoons from Twitter activity. A method for detecting ROI from Twitter network is proposed by [12]. Such geo-social event detection relies on the geographical regularities observed in user behaviour with regard to the normal level of interest from a geographical region.

Spatio-temporal considerations have also been integrated into collaborative filtering [13]. The approach relies on the calculation of user similarity, such as spatio-temporal proximity. Spatio-temporal proximity is calculated as the ratio of items that each pair of users has consumed in the same time and at the same place. The authors of [14] studied the geography of the Twitter network, finding that geographical distance, language, and country have a role in determining the creation of a connection on Twitter. In [15], the authors show that it is possible to detect the location of users depending solely on the content of their tweets and are able to estimate a Twitter user's location in a city with the technique.

The authors of [16] proposed a method to evaluate the relationship between social ties and spatio-temporal patterns. The approach divides the world into discrete cells and counts co-occurrences based on the observation of individuals in the same cell at the same time. The approach proposes a probabilistic model to infer friendship on the Flickr networks. Co-occurrences are based on the fact that two users took pictures in the same spatio-temporal frame.

In [17], authors analysed spatio-temporal data generated by smartphone users. Their analysis focuses on the contact duration and frequency between two individuals. They propose applying a community detection based on a graph weighted by contact duration. The authors of [18] propose integrating spatio-temporal considerations in multi-layer friendship modelling. This friend recommendation system takes into account the social graph layer, interests graph layer, and co-occurrence graph layer. The location metric between two users is defined as the minimum value of the update distance divided by the sum of updates times in the two locations. They show a clear correlation between such indicators and the fact to be friend or not on the mobile social network.

The mobility patterns of Foursquare users were analysed in [19]. The authors expose geo-temporal rhythms, check-in dynamics, and activity transitions to highlight possibilities of integrating spatio-temporal patterns into recommendation systems. The authors of [20] analysed the event-based social network (EBSN). The paper highlights the specificities of such networks, such as the correlations between online and offline relationships. The authors apply this cyber-physical analysis to study community detection and information diffusion. A study of 100,000 anonymous mobile phone users over a period of 6 months was conducted by the authors of [21]. The authors highlight that human trajectories have a high degree of spatio-temporal regularity. Moreover, humans tended to only move within a set of limited locations during the experiment. This observation is important as it indicates that human mobility observations follow simple, reproducible patterns.

To the best of the current study's knowledge, this article is one of the first to focus on how social users migrate between events.

III. METHODOLOGY

This section presents the general methodology for building migration networks from contextual social data. Such networks allow for connections between locations of interest (medium to large-scale events) based on the migration of Twitter users. The first subsection presents the process to identify ROI based on Twitter users meetings. The second subsection presents an algorithm for creating the migration graph. Applications of this methodology are discussed later in the paper.

A. Overview

Figure 1 displays the main steps of the methodology proposed in this paper. First, Twitter data in the San Francisco Bay Area was crawled for a period of 3 months. The crawler relies on the Twitter streaming application programming interface (API) and provides tweets belonging to the defined area (step I). More than 3 million tweets were collected during this step. From the collected tweets, spatio-temporal proximity was computed between the most active users to identify meetings between people (step II). In step III, a spatio-temporal graph of meetings is analysed. Such analysis allows for a better understanding of the physical interactions between users and provides an overview of the most active users (step IV). In step V, a migration graph is built to identify dynamic changes in ROI. Social network analysis (SNA) metrics applied in step VI aid in further understanding of the size and the characteristics of the ROI.

B. User selection and spatio-temporal meetings

Some profiles, despite geolocated tweets, are not suitable for the current spatio-temporal analysis. Two different typologies of geolocated users were observed: (1) individuals whose profiles are located and whose tweets are associated

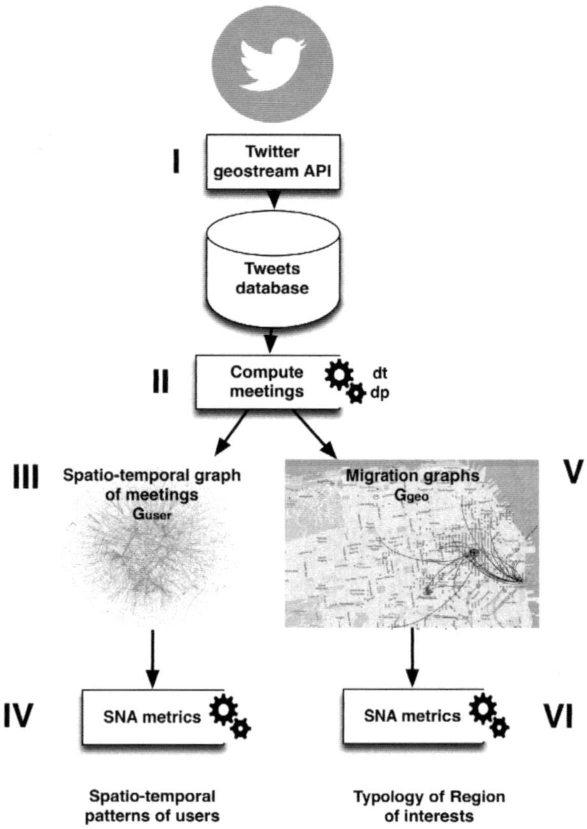

Figure 1. Methodology for analysis of migrations of Twitter users between regions of interest.

with the location of their profile; (2) profiles that share their location at the moment tweets are sent. The current study only included tweets belonging to the 2 types of profiles in this analysis. To ensure that only relevant profiles were included in the analyses, a set of locations related to users' tweets was computed and it was verified that multiple locations exist in the list. Profiles whose location remain constant were removed from the analysis. Profiles that shared less than two updates a day were also removed.

Meetings between profiles were computed as follows. If two profiles belong to the same geographic area (the raw ρ of a circle around the location of a user) at the same time (denoted δt), they are concidered *met*. The global time frame for the observation of profiles is identified by the interval $I = [0, T]$. For each observation time t_k, the function of sharing local spatio-temporal windows of dimension $\rho * \delta t$ is proposed. Given that $d(u, v)$ is a geographical distance between two profiles $(u, v) \epsilon P^2$, a spatio-temporal meeting at a given time step t_k can be identified as follows.

$$Meet_k(u, v) = \begin{cases} 1 & \text{if } v \in \{n \in P| \\ & \min_{[t_k - \delta t,\, t_k + \delta t]} d(u, v) \leq \rho\} \\ 0 & \text{otherwise} \end{cases} \tag{1}$$

Using the list of meetings, a spatio-temporal user proximity graph is computed-denoted $G_{user}(N, E)$- where N denotes profiles and E denotes meetings between them. For this purpose, a weight is attached to each edge that corresponds to the number of spatio-temporal meetings observed between these two individuals as in (2).

$$w(u, v) = \sum_{k=1}^{n} Meet_k(u, v) \tag{2}$$

When $w(u, v) = 0$, no meeting is recorded during the full time of the experiment and no connection is created between the two profiles. If $Meet_k(u, v) = 1$, at least one meeting was recorded during the time frame of the experiment. The choice of the parameters (spatio-temporal frame $\rho * \delta t$) depends on the desired level of precision. For example, analysing global spatio-temporal patterns over one year does not require strong spatio-temporal constraints. However, detecting an event at a city-scale requires strong spatio-temporal constraints. The next section presents the capture of user migration between ROI.

C. Migration graph construction

As shown in Figure 2, the given area is divided into a set of squared cells of length δz. The choice of the size depends on the level of precision required for the performance of the detection of spatial patterns and can be adapted as necessary. The aim of the current approach is to assign each cell to a geographical node and to evaluate the relationship between these nodes based on the recorded meetings of users. In the current study, two locations are connected whenever a user meeting has been detected in both distinct locations. The meetings need not to involves the same pair of individuals, but instead at least one of the two individuals is required in both locations. The edge is weighted by the number of moves made between locations to capture ROI and migrations in a unique algorithm. Note that ROI is this article are defined as relatively small geographical areas that receive a large number of users over a short period of time. This is made possible without any additional analysis due to the spatio-temporal constraints applied to meetings. Indeed, Twitter users who tweet in the same area at the same time are detected as met and this is more likely to occur during events attracting a particular density of individuals at a normal time. An individual sending a tweet without other active users in the area is not included in the analysis as they do not belong to a ROI. If a location is not associated with an edge, it is considered irrelevant and removed from the set of nodes (ROI).

Figure 3 presents the algorithm for computing the geo-spatio-temporal graph. For each time step and each couple of profiles (lines 1-2), the meet function (line 3) tests whether or not a meeting is recorded. Each meeting is tracked and associated with a timestamp and geolocation (line 4).

When all meetings are recorded, the relationships between cells of the geographical space, delimited by the A and B points, are extracted. Each cell is identified as a node with a unique identifier. The algorithm creates an edge between two cells (i.e., two locations) when an individual has *met* (as stated in equation 1) persons at least once in each location (line 10). A matching function is used to identify the cells concerning each meeting.

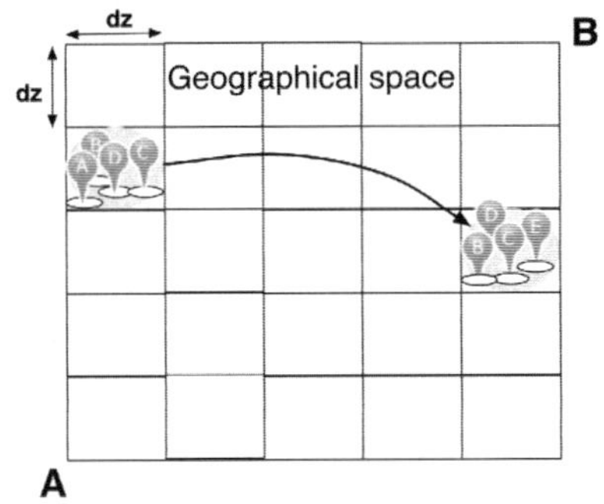

Figure 2. Construction of spatial cells and identification of meetings for building edges of $G_{geo}(N^{'}, E^{'})$.

Inputs:
Set of profiles P
Cell size δz
Spatio-temporal frame $\rho * \delta t$
Spacial borders $A(Lat_{min}, Lng_{min})$ and $B(Lat_{max}, Lng_{max})$
Time frame of observation $I = [0, T]$
Output:
$G_{geo}(N^{'}, E^{'})$ the spatio-temporal geo graph

1 foreach time step **k**
2 **foreach** $(u, v)\epsilon P^2$
3 **if** $Meet_k(u, v) = 1$ (see equation 1)
4 $Meetings$ ←Record a meeting between u and v at period k at location l
5 **endif**
6 **endforeach**
7 endforeach
8 N' ←set of squared cells of size δz delimited by A and B (see Figure 2)
9 foreach couple of cells $(c_1, c_2)\epsilon N^{'2}$
10 $e_k(c_1, c_2)$ ←Number of $Meetings$ that both belong to c_1 and c_2
11 $E' \leftarrow e(c_1, c_2)$
12 endforeach
13 return $G_{geo}(N^{'}, E^{'})$

Figure 3. Pseudo-code for computing the spatio-temporal geo graph

The resulting graph $G_{geo}(N^{'}, E^{'})$ of spatial locations reveals the frequency at which users meet at a particular place. Since meeting is directly dependent on the online activity of users online (e.g., sending messages), the graph permits to illustrating the importance of each location for user activity. In performing the algorithm, locations where individuals tend to meet can be retreived, in addition to the migration of individuals between locations.

The methodology allows for a vision of migration ROI, but further analysis can be applied to the final $G_{geo}(N^{'}, E^{'})$ graph to characterize the events. Table I presents the potential interpretations of SNA metrics on the characteristics of an event (nodes of the $G_{geo}(N^{'}, E^{'})$ graph). The unweighted indegree captures the number of locations people come from, providing an idea of the variety of individuals than an event attracts (in particular when applied worldwide). The unweighted outdegree captures the variety of locations people goes after leaving an event. The PageRank captures the importance of an event based on its ability to attract people coming from important location [22]. For example, analysing information technology-related tweets at a large spatio-temporal scale may allow for the capture of the fact that a Consumer Electronics Show (CES) event attracts many people coming from WebSummit, contributing to the importance of both events. Finally, the Hyperlink-Induced Topic Search (HITs) algorithm can provide interesting interpretations when applied to $G_{geo}(N^{'}, E^{'})$. The algorithm assumes that nodes can be ranked in terms of their ability to be good hubs and authorities [23]. In the present case, a good hub could be concidered a ROI that points to many other ROI, and a good authority would be an ROI that is linked by many different hubs. A good hubs would typically be an airport or a train station, while a good authority is an event that succeeds in attracting people from many hubs. This would be a way to capture popular events within a country, region, or city.

TABLE I. SNA METRICS APPLIED TO NODES OF $G_{geo}(N^{'}, E^{'})$ AND THEIR POTENTIAL USE FOR BETTER UNDERSTANDING OF ROI.

SNA Metric	ROI Characteristics
Unweighted Indegree	Number of ROI people comes before arriving to the event.
Unweighted Outdegree	Number of ROI people go after leaving the event.
PageRank	Importance of the ROI in terms of ability to attract people from other important ROI.
HITS	Identify ROI that are hubs and authorities.

IV. EXPERIMENT AND RESULTS

The analysis was performed on a sample of 3 millions tweets sent by 50,000 active, geolocated Twitter users in and around San Francisco. Figure 4 represents the spatio-temporal graph extracted from the footprints of users in the area over a period of 3 months. This sample is composed of 3,781 users twith dynamic, geographical data associated with their messages. The spatio-temporal constraints in the analysis are $\rho = 0.6\,miles$ and $\delta t = 1\,min$. The graph is composed of 4,720 edges which indicates the number of recorded meetings. Table II indicates the graph metrics, revealing the general activity of San Francisco users. On average, people have between 2 and 3 meetings during the observation time. The maximum observed degree is 135, which is high. Nodes with many meetings appear larger in figure 4. The modularity of the graph is high, meaning that the network tends to organize into clusters (spatio-temporal constraints tend to organize people in communities).

The degree distribution highlights that a few nodes have a high degree (10 nodes have a degree up to 50), while most nodes have a low degree. This observation suggests that some profiles have a central role in spatio-temporal meetings, meaning that they are able to be very active and are regularly observed in ROI.

TABLE II. GRAPH METRICS OF THE SPATIO-TEMPORAL USER GRAPH

Graph Metric	Value
Nodes	3781
Edges	4720
Average Path Length	5.347
Modularity	0.769
Number of Communities	241
Density	0.001
Average Degree	2.497

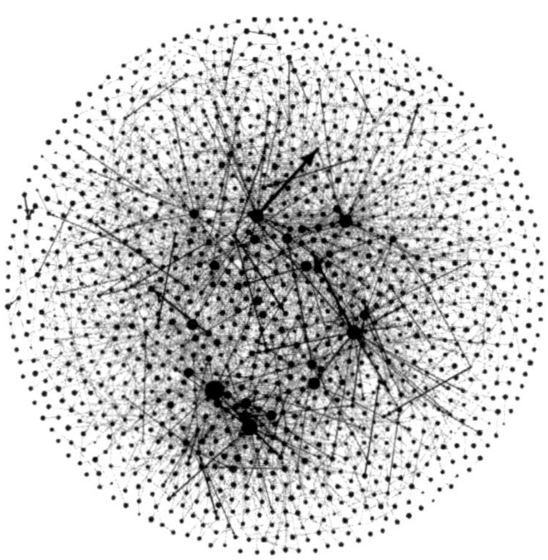

Figure 4. Aggregated spatio-temporal user graph from the full duration of the experiment.

Figure 5 illustrates the results of the algorithm for two distinct choices of δz and ρ spatial parameters. The background image illustrates the relationship between ROI regarding the meeting of users in the San Francisco Bay Area. A meeting is identified if two users have been observed in the same neighbourhood ($\rho = 0.8\,miles$) and at the same time ($\delta t = 30\,s$). Airports appear to be important ROI. Many events also occur in the city center. The foreground image illustrates the same algorithm when performed in the shortest space area and with shorter geographical cells (i.e., $\rho = 0.08\,miles$). This more precisely highlights more precise possible ROI, such as AT&T Park, Westfield San Francisco Centre, Yerba Buena Center for the Arts (YBCA), etc. The two figures illustrate the performance of the algorithm at different scales. Note that these graphs are based on all observations captured during the experiment.

Moreover, analysis of the evolution G^k_{geo} graphs allows for the discovery of particular temporal locations of interest for users. Figure 6 highlights two graphs for different intervals of time. One can observe the changes between the central locations in the graph. Centrality indicates that an event has occurred within the time interval. In other words, the location has attracted many individuals who were previously meeting in different locations.

Events can be detected by comparing the time frame degree of nodes regarding their average degree. A high variation indicates that an event likely occurs in the particular spatio-temporal context. Due to constraints, more details concerning

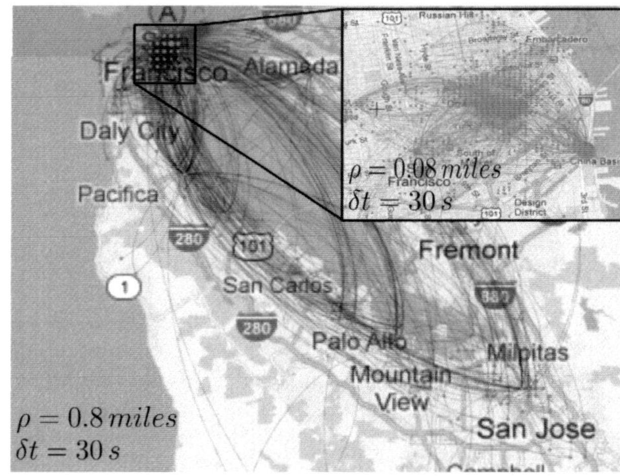

Figure 5. Example of ROIs relationships at two different spatial scales: $\rho = 0.8\,miles$ for the San Francisco Bay Area map and $\rho = 0.08\,miles$ for the San Francisco city map.

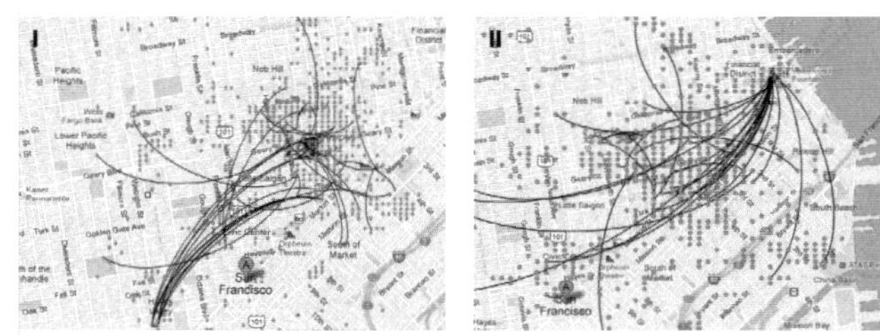

Figure 6. Samples of the spatio-temporal graphs at three different time steps, revealing multiple ROI and their relationships.

SNA metrics applied to the graph are not provided.

V. DISCUSSION

This current study has several applications and potential extensions to be discussed. For example, the study does not include content-based analysis of tweets. A potential improvement would be the automatic identification of the main discussion topic of events using content-based analysis. The current study can also be a first step in the prediction of the next location of users based on common patterns found. It is likely that the graph parameters (nodes, edges, density, degree distribution) can allow for the automatic identification of ROI. The best parameters may be found by optimizing some of the graph features, such as modularity, or by analysing the obtained degree distribution (e.g. parameters of the power law). That study relies on tweets for measuring spatio-temporal meetings provides some advantages and disadvantage. A disadvantage is the lack of a regular vision of the location of users, which complicates the detection of small-scale events. However, it is observe that people tend to tweet more when participating in events, which, by construction, allows for most of the captured meetings to be related to ROI.

VI. CONCLUSION

The success of digital, social media, combined with smartphones, contributes to an increasing amount of spatio-temporal data. Its availability for analysis can contributes to improving of multiple fields. The current paper proposes a novel approach to detecting spatio-temporal changes in crowds of Twitter users. The study shows that the relationship between locations based on the meetings of users can contribute to the detection of large-scale events. This contribution allows not only for the identification of ROI for users, but also their evolution and characterization at multiple scales. The efficiency of the methodology is shown with a sample of 3 millions tweets in the San Francisco Bay Area, analysed at different scales.

REFERENCES

[1] C. D. Weidemann, "Geosocialfootprint (2013): Social media location privacy web map," Ph.D. dissertation, University of Southern California, 2013.

[2] E. Paulos and E. Goodman, "The familiar stranger: Anxiety, comfort, and play in public places," in Proceedings of the SIGCHI Conference on Human Factors in Computing Systems, ser. CHI '04. New York, NY, USA: ACM, 2004, pp. 223–230.

[3] R. Want and O. R. Limited, "The Active badge location system," 1992.

[4] V. Kostakos, "Temporal graphs," Physica A, vol. 388, no. 6, Mar. 2009, pp. 1007–1023.

[5] B. George and S. Shekhar, "Journal on data semantics xi," S. Spaccapietra, J. Z. Pan, P. Thiran, T. Halpin, S. Staab, V. Svatek, P. Shvaiko, and J. Roddick, Eds. Berlin, Heidelberg: Springer-Verlag, 2008, ch. Time-Aggregated Graphs for Modeling Spatio-temporal Networks, pp. 191–212.

[6] Z. Halim, M. M. Gul, N. ul Hassan, R. Baig, S. Ur Rehman, and F. Naz, "Malicious users' circle detection in social network based on spatio-temporal co-occurrence."

[7] N. Eagle and A. (Sandy) Pentland, "Reality mining: Sensing complex social systems," Personal Ubiquitous Comput., vol. 10, no. 4, Mar. 2006, pp. 255–268.

[8] D. Quercia, J. Ellis, and L. Capra, "Using Mobile Phones to Nurture Social Networks," IEEE Pervasive Computing, vol. 9, no. 3, 2010, pp. 12–20.

[9] J. Candia, M. C. González, P. Wang, T. Schoenharl, G. Madey, and A.-L. Barabási, "Uncovering individual and collective human dynamics from mobile phone records," Journal of Physics A: Mathematical and Theoretical, vol. 41, no. 22, May 2008, p. 224015.

[10] M. Loecher, M. Loecher, and T. Jebara, "CitySense TM: multiscale space time clustering of GPS points and trajectories." Joint Statististical Meeting, 2009.

[11] T. Sakaki, M. Okazaki, and Y. Matsuo, "Tweet analysis for real-time event detection and earthquake reporting system development," IEEE Trans. on Knowl. and Data Eng., vol. 25, no. 4, Apr. 2013, pp. 919–931.

[12] R. Lee and K. Sumiya, "Measuring geographical regularities of crowd behaviors for Twitter-based geo-social event detection," in Proceedings of the 2nd ACM SIGSPATIAL International Workshop on Location Based Social Networks. New York, NY, USA: ACM, 2010, pp. 1–10.

[13] A. de Spindler, R. De Spindler, M. C. Norrie, M. Grossniklaus, and B. Signer, "Spatio-Temporal Proximity as a Basis for Collaborative Filtering in Mobile Environments." Ubiquitous Mobile Information and Collaboration Systems UMICS.

[14] Y. Takhteyev, A. Gruzd, and B. Wellman, "Geography of Twitter networks," Social Networks, vol. 34, no. 1, Dec. 2011, pp. 73–81.

[15] Z. Cheng, J. Caverlee, and K. Lee, "You are where you tweet: A content based approach to geo-locating twitter users," in In Proc. of the 19th ACM Int'l Conference on Information and Knowledge Management (CIKM), 2010.

[16] D. J. Crandall, L. Backstrom, D. Cosley, S. Suri, D. Huttenlocher, and J. Kleinberg, "Inferring social ties from geographic coincidences," Proceedings of the National Academy of Sciences, vol. 107, no. 52, 2010, pp. 22 436–22 441.

[17] P. Hui and J. Crowcroft, "Human mobility models and opportunistic communications system design," Philosophical Transactions of the Royal Society A: Mathematical, Physical and Engineering Sciences, vol. 366, no. 1872, 2008, pp. 2005–2016.

[18] N. Li and G. Chen, "Multi-layered friendship modeling for location-based mobile social networks," in 2009 6th Annual International Mobile and Ubiquitous Systems: Networking Services, MobiQuitous, 2009, pp. 1–10.

[19] A. Noulas, S. Scellato, C. Mascolo, and M. Pontil, "An empirical study of geographical user activity patterns in foursquare," in The International AAAI Conference on Weblogs and Social Media, pp. 570–573.

[20] X. Liu, Q. He, Y. Tian, W.-C. Lee, J. McPherson, and J. Han, "Event-based social networks: Linking the online and offline social worlds," in Proceedings of the 18th ACM SIGKDD International Conference on Knowledge Discovery and Data Mining, ser. KDD '12. New York, NY, USA: ACM, 2012, pp. 1032–1040.

[21] M. C. Gonzalez, C. A. Hidalgo, and A.-L. Barabasi, "Understanding individual human mobility patterns," Nature, vol. 453, no. 7196, June 2008, pp. 779–782.

[22] L. Page, S. Brin, R. Motwani, and T. Winograd, "The pagerank citation ranking: Bringing order to the web," in Proceedings of the 7th International World Wide Web Conference, Brisbane, Australia, 1998, pp. 161–172.

[23] J. M. Kleinberg, "Authoritative sources in a hyperlinked environment," J. ACM, vol. 46, no. 5, Sep. 1999, pp. 604–632.

Temporal Patterns: Smart-type Reasoning and Applications

Dineshen Chuckravanen
Jacqueline W. Daykin

Department of
Computer Science
Aberystwyth University
(Mauritius Branch Campus)
Mauritius
Email: dic4@aber.ac.uk
Email: jwd6@aber.ac.uk

Karen Hunsdale

Department of
Applied Management
Winchester Business School
University of Winchester
UK
Email: Karen.Hunsdale
@winchester.ac.uk

Amar Seeam

Department of
Computer Science
Middlesex University
(Mauritius Branch Campus)
Mauritius
Email: a.seeam@mdx.ac.uk

***Abstract*—Allen's interval algebra is a calculus for temporal reasoning that was introduced in 1983. Reasoning with qualitative time in Allen's full interval algebra is nondeterministic polynomial time (NP) complete. Research since 1995 identified maximal tractable subclasses of this algebra via exhaustive computer search and also other *ad-hoc* methods. In 2003, the full classification of complexity for satisfiability problems over constraints in Allen's interval algebra was established algebraically. Recent research proposed scheduling based on the Fishburn-Shepp correlation inequality for posets. We describe here three potential temporal-related application areas as candidates for scheduling using this inequality.**

Keywords–Allen's interval algebra, artificial intelligence; qualitative temporal reasoning; scheduling; smart-type reasoning.

I. Introduction

Temporal reasoning is a mature research endeavor and arises naturally in numerous diverse applications of artificial intelligence, such as: planning and scheduling [1], natural language processing [2], diagnostic expert systems [3], behavioural psychology [4], circuit design [5], software tools for comprehending the state of patients in intensive care units from their temporal information [6], business intelligence [7], and timegraphs, that is graphs partitioned into a set of chains supporting search which originated in the context of story comprehension [8].

Allen [9] introduced an algebra of binary relations on intervals (of time), for representing and reasoning about time. These binary relations, for example *before*, *during*, *meets*, describe *qualitative* temporal information which we will be concerned with here. The problem of satisfiability for a set of interval variables with specified relations between them is that of deciding whether there exists an assignment of intervals on the real line for the interval variables, such that all of the specified relations between the intervals are satisfied. When the temporal constraints are chosen from the full form of Allen's algebra, this formulation of satisfiability problem is known to be NP-complete. However, reasoning restricted to certain fragments of Allen's algebra is generally equivalent to related well-known problems such as the interval graph and interval order recognition problems [10], which in turn find application in molecular biology [11][12][13].

TABLE I. [14] THE SET $\mathbf{B}$ OF THE THIRTEEN BASIC QUALITATIVE RELATIONS DEFINED BY ALLEN.

Basic Interval Relation	Symbol	Endpoint Relations
X precedes (before) Y	p ($\prec$)	$X^+ < Y^-$
Y preceded-by (after) X	$p\smile$ ($\succ$)	
X meets Y	m	$X^+ = Y^-$
Y met-by X	$m\smile$	
X overlaps Y	o	$X^- < Y^- < X^+ < Y^+$
Y overlapped-by X	$o\smile$	
X during Y	d	$X^- > Y^-$, $X^+ < Y^+$
Y includes X	$d\smile$	
X starts Y	s	$X^- = Y^-$, $X^+ < Y^+$
Y started-by X	$s\smile$	
X finishes Y	f	$X^- > Y^-$, $X^+ = Y^+$
Y finished-by X	$f\smile$	
X equals Y	$\equiv$	$X^- = Y^-$, $X^+ = Y^+$

A. Allen's Interval Algebra

Allen's [9] calculus for reasoning about time is based on the concept of *time intervals* together with *binary relations* on them. In this approach, time is considered to be an infinite dense ordered set, such as the rationals $\mathbf{R}$, and a *time interval* X is an ordered pair of time points (X^-, X^+) such that $X^- < X^+$.

Given two time intervals, their relative positions can be described by exactly one of the members of the set $\mathbf{B}$ of 13 basic interval relations, which are depicted in Table I; note that the relations $X^- < X^+$ and $Y^- < Y^+$ are always valid, hence omitted from the table. These basic relations describe relations between *definite* intervals of time. On the other hand, *indefinite* intervals, whose exact relation may be uncertain, are described by a set of all the basic relations that may apply.

The universe of Allen's interval algebra consists of all the binary relations on time intervals which can be expressed as disjunctions of the basic interval relations. These disjunctions are written as sets of basic relations, leading to a total of $2^{13} = 8192$ binary relations, including the *null relation* $\emptyset$ (also denoted by $\perp$) and the *universal relation* $\mathbf{B}$ (also denoted by $\top$). The set of all binary relations $2^{\mathbf{B}}$ is denoted by $\mathcal{A}$; every temporal relation in $\mathcal{A}$ can be defined by a conjunction of disjunctions of endpoint relations of the form $X < Y, X = Y$ and their negations.

The operations on the relations defined in Allen's algebra

are: unary *converse* (denoted by $^\smile$), binary *intersection* (denoted by $\bigcap$) and binary *composition* (denoted by $\circ$), which are defined as follows:

$$\begin{aligned} \forall\, X,Y: \quad & Xr^\smile Y \leftrightarrow YrX \\ \forall\, X,Y: \quad & X(r\textstyle\bigcap s)Y \leftrightarrow XrY \bigwedge XsY \\ \forall\, X,Y: \quad & X(r\circ s)Y \leftrightarrow \exists Z:(XrZ \bigwedge ZsY), \end{aligned}$$

where X,Y,Z are intervals, and r,s are interval relations. Allen [9] gives a composition table for the basic relations.

Fundamental *reasoning problems* in Allen's framework have been studied by a number of authors, including Golumbic and Shamir [15] [16], Ladkin and Maddux [17], van Beek [18] and Vilain and Kautz [19].

B. Posets and the Fishburn-Shepp Inequality

We now consider novel research proposed in [20], namely to specify heuristics for scheduling based on representing a collection of intervals of time with constraints as a poset, and applying the Fishburn-Shepp inequality to guide a scheduling algorithm. In [20], applications are sought for this approach: we address this first step here by describing potential applications which are also related to smart-type reasoning. First, we commence with overviews of the scheduling problem and the Fishburn-Shepp inequality.

Generally, a *schedule* of tasks (or simply schedule) is the assignment of tasks to specific time intervals of resources, such that no two tasks occupy any resource simultaneously – additionally, a requirement can be that the capacity of resources is not exceeded by the tasks. A schedule is *optimal* if it minimizes a given optimality criterion. However, our ultimate interest is in providing an algorithm to solve, or schedule, temporal constraint satisfaction problems; since we also consider indefinite qualitative temporal information, the solution may assign events simultaneously to intervals.

Let Q be a finite *poset* (partially ordered set) with n elements and C be a chain $1 < 2 < \cdots < c$. For (Q,C), a map $\omega : Q \rightarrow C$ is *strict order-preserving* if, for all $x,y \in Q$, $x<y$ implies $\omega(x) < \omega(y)$. Let $\lambda : Q \rightarrow \{1 < 2 < \cdots < n\}$ be a *linear extension* of Q, that is, an order-preserving injection.

A poset Q is equivalently a *directed acyclic graph (DAG)*, $G=(V,E)$; for temporal reasoning, the vertices represent time intervals, and edges between vertices are labeled with relations in Allen's algebra which satisfy the partial ordering. For scheduling problems, a linear extension λ of Q (or G) can be used to schedule tasks: λ must respect interval constraints, that is relations between comparable elements. Algorithmically, a linear extension of a DAG, G, can be determined in linear time by performing a depth-first search of G; while G (Q) can be represented by an adjacency matrix.

The Fishburn-Shepp inequality [21] [22] is an inequality for the number of extensions of partial orders to linear orders, expressed as follows. Suppose that x, y and z are incomparable elements of a finite poset, then

$$P(x<y)P(x<z) < P((x<y)\wedge(x<z)) \qquad (1)$$

where P(*) is the probability that a linear extension has the property *. By re-expressing this in terms of conditional probability, $P(x<z) < P((x<z) \mid (x<y))$, we see that $P(x<z)$ strictly increases by adding the condition $x<y$. The problem posed in [20] concerns applying the Fishburn-Shepp inequality to efficiently find a favourable schedule under specified criteria, where a naive scheduling algorithm is also given together with an illustrative example. However, our focus here is in introducing application scenarios. The rest of the paper is structured as follows.

In Section II, we describe various applications in temporal reasoning that include applications in smart homes, applications in intelligent conversational agents, and also applications in exercise physiology followed by Section III which describes conclusion and future work.

II. Applications in Temporal Reasoning

A. Applications in Smart Homes

Buildings consume a considerable amount of energy. Managing that energy is challenging, though is achievable through building control and energy management systems. These systems will typically monitor, measure, manage and control services for the lighting, heating, ventilation and air conditioning (HVAC), security, and safety of the building. They also permit a degree of scheduling, albeit they are often limited by static programming and may have no awareness incorporated of external events. For example, a building's HVAC system may heat rooms that are unoccupied as the setpoint has been programmed to be a certain temperature for a specified interval of the day. Clearly this is quite inefficient, and though motion detectors can play a role in actuating lights during periods of room occupancy, maintaining a comfortable indoor climate using similar sensors to detect people cannot provide the same benefits. Furthermore, the indoor climate is impacted by outdoor thermodynamic processes, as well as internal heat gains which can be unaccountable (e.g., people, mobile equipment, etc). However, most modern non-residential building's energy management systems will be configured to turn building services on and off throughout the day using a pre-programmed schedule (e.g., a repeating daily pattern of heating use) and can also employ intelligent start-up controllers with external temperature compensation to delay the turning on of heating for example. Modern heating controllers (i.e., programmable thermostats) in homes can also have setpoints configured in a daily schedule (e.g., 6-8am: increase setpoint to 20°C, representing a waking-up phase; 9am - 4pm: heating deactivated or set to a maximum (e.g., 15°C); and from 5pm - 6pm: 21°C, representing a heating-up phase to anticipate arrival of an occupant from a workplace, and so forth).

Aside from heating control, homes can now also employ smart home systems to perform some degree of energy management and appliance automation. These systems are becoming more commonplace, particularly as the Internet of Things (IoT) paradigm is gaining more traction, whereby humans are bypassed, and machine to machine communication takes place (e.g., Smart Homes communicating with Smart Grids [23]). This gives rise to smart automation and reasoning where decision making can take place and determine when home appliances can be scheduled, particularly in the case of peak-load shaving [24] or demand response optimization [25]. In these cases, consumption patterns can be shifted to times of lower cost electricity. Appliance scheduling can be further classified by, for instance, their minimum required periods of operations, whether or not their operations can be interrupted, and if a human occupant is involved (i.e., in climate control scenarios). For instance, washing machines will have varying periods of operation depending on the program (wash, spin, dry) and cannot (typically) be interrupted if scheduled. Heating or cooling systems will have optimum start-up times to turn on in anticipation of occupants requiring the temperature of the house to be at a preset setpoint upon arrival. The Internet of Things has even enabled this particular scenario to be influenced by the distance an occupant is from the home or building, whereby the driving time is estimated via tracking of a Global Positioning System (GPS signal) [26]. In [27], driving patterns were analysed, and a programmable thermostat augmented with GPS control enabled energy savings of 7%.

The emerging Internet of Things in this respect will be responsible for huge volumes of temporal pattern data (i.e., timestamped sequences of events, be it a change in temperature, or a light being turned on and off, or the duration of activity of an entertainment system, etc), thus also incorporating quantitative temporal information. In the smart home, the ability to detect user behaviour or house activities from this kind of temporal pattern data can provide a better understanding of how to identify patterns of energy use and thus determine when or how to gain energy savings. Naturally, the accumulative savings factor is increased many-fold in the smart city concept. Temporal pattern event detection inspired by Allen's relations has proved useful in smart environments: for anomaly detection in assisted living applications [28], and in activity monitoring [29]. In these examples, intervals represent the sensed data (cooking would imply the stove being on while an inhabitant is present in the kitchen [30]). Such kinds of recognition are useful for determining normal behaviour of elderly occupants, and thus, for instance, detecting any onsets of dementia [31].

Clearly, efficient, or ideally optimized, scheduling of events can lead to enhanced savings of time and energy – it is with this goal that we propose applying the Fishburn-Shepp inequality, possibly to a specified subset of events in a larger complex system.

B. *Applications in Intelligent Conversational Agents*

Intelligent conversational agents (CA) enable natural language interaction with their human participant. Following an input string, the CA works through its knowledge-base in search of an appropriate output string. The knowledge-base consists of natural language sentences based on a specific domain. Through the use of semantic processing using a lexical database with grouped sets of cognitive synonyms, word similarity is determined, with thus the highest semantically similar ranked string returned to the user as output.

Scripts consist of contexts that relate to a specific theme or topic of conversation. Each context contains one or more rules, which possess a number of prototype natural language sentences. An example of a scripted natural language rule is shown below, where s is a natural language sentence and r is a response statement.

<Rule-01>

s: I am having problems accessing my email account.
r: I'm sorry to hear that. Have you tried contacting IT support?

One such CA, as proposed by O'Shea *et al.* ([32] [33] [34]), uses semantics as a means to measure sentence similarity. The CA is organized into contexts consisting of a number of similarly related rules. Through the use of a sentence similarity measure, a match is determined between the user's utterance and the scripted natural language sentences. Similarity ratings are measured in the range from 0 to 1, in which a value of 0 denotes no semantic similarity, and 1 denotes an identical sentence pair. The highest ranked sentence is fired and its associated response is sent as output. The following algorithm describes the application:

1. Natural language dialogue is received as input from the user.

2. Semantic-based CA receives natural language dialogue from the user which is sent to the sentence similarity measure.

3. Semantic-based CA receives natural language sentences from the scripts files which are sent to the sentence similarity measure.

4. Sentence similarity measure calculates a firing strength for each sentence pair which is returned and processed by the semantic-based CA.

5. The highest ranked sentence is fired and its associated response is sent as output.

Natural language interaction between two participants (human or otherwise) can be modeled using Allen's interval algebra: the intervals of speech could satisfy the basic relation p, if one speaks before the other, or the relation o if their speech overlaps, and so on. In terms of scheduling a set of speech events with specified relations, that is constructing a linear extension by applying the Fishburn-Shepp inequality, we envisage an application for the learning impaired which schedules the events sequentially to reduce confusion from simultaneous speech. This could then be integrated with a CA facility.

C. *Applications in Physiology*

In exercise physiology, the study of complex rhythms arising from the peripheral systems (for example, the cardiovascular system) and the central nervous system of the human body is important to optimize athletic performance while using a suitable type of pacing. Pacing plays an important part during athletic competition so that the metabolic resources are used effectively to complete the physical activity in the minimum time possible, as well as to maintain enough metabolic resources to complete that task [35]. Moreover, according to the Central Governor Model (CGM) [36], there is a central regulator that paces the peripheral systems during physical activity to reach the endpoint of that physical activity without physiological system failure. This central governor model of fatigue is a complex integrative control model which involves the continuous interaction, in a deterministic way, among all the physiological, and that of the central systems.

In this context, the decision making process involved when an athlete changes his or her pacing strategy during a particular race (and especially during endurance exercise) seems quite complex. However, the change in the decision making process could be simply explained by the basic relations in Allen's interval algebra. Consider the following scenario where an athlete or runner needs to complete a 20-km race. An experienced runner will subconsciously be aware of the amount of energy resources they will need during the race so that they can effectively complete the race without catastrophic failure. During the race, there are both exogenous and endogenous factors which will influence the optimal performance of the runner, and therefore she or he has to make important decisions as to when, or when not, change their pacing during the race so that they can complete the race in the minimum time possible.

For instance, there may be three major changes in the patterns of the running speed, power output, or pacing strategies that the runner could adopt for a long distance race such as the 20-km race [37]. Initially, on the first stage of the race, he or she will accelerate from a resting standing (or crouching) position to reach a constant optimal speed as determined by the runner's physical ability; meanwhile their heart rate (HR) will accelerate as well as their volume of oxygen consumption (VO2). In the second stage, they will maintain the same constant running speed for most of the race while their heart rate will be quite steady; moreover, the volume of oxygen consumption will be kept practically constant throughout the race. Finally, in the third stage of the race, the runner will accelerate or sprint in order to complete the race, which will at the same time, increase their heart rate as well as the rate of volume of oxygen consumption.

This represents one possible scenario that may occur during a race, which illustrates that Allen's temporal relations can be exploited to more clearly express the complex decision-making processes related to the human body during physical exertion, and hence allow for scheduling the pacing strategy adopted by a runner during a particular race. Furthermore, smart-type devices can be worn by an athlete which can also feed into the decision-making process in real time.

III. CONCLUSION AND FUTURE WORK

Previous research in temporal pattern reasoning surrounding smart homes has largely focused on activity recognition of inhabitants, and gaining an understanding from sensor data retrieved from indoor environments (such as electricity, temperature, light, or motion). The Internet of Things, however, will provide further dimensions of data from people (wearable sensors, tracking of GPS, etc.). This kind of outdoor data will provide additional context to the smart home and enable it to make better and more informed decisions as to how to actuate and control building services.

For example, returning to the case of augmented heating control using GPS - an occupant leaves the house and goes for a short jog (automatically disabling the heating as they leave) - as they run their own body temperature rises. The wearable sensors will be monitoring their temperature and their GPS coordinates. As they return and approach their home, the augmented heating control with the GPS system will turn on the heating, but will also take into account the occupant's current body temperature, and accordingly apply the appropriate heating control strategy (i.e., reducing the return-to-home setpoint from a previously higher setting and actuation time). In this case, the quantitative temporal information between arrival and heating activation will be lengthened as the temperature setpoint requirement will be reduced. This is just one of a myriad of possibilities that can be realized from the abundance of potential sensor data generated from the Internet of Things. We believe the relation between indoor and outdoor sensing (as well as any other sensing source for that matter) and reasoning strategies requires further exploration, and as part of our future research strategy we will investigate smart home event and action temporal reasoning from multiple data streams beyond enclosed indoor scenarios. In particular, smart-type scheduling is a key factor in energy-related issues.

We envisage enhanced synergy in the smart-environment by integrating intelligent conversational agents. Useful responses to even simple sentences such as *Where are my keys?* can have impact on human energy and stress levels and allow for more efficient use of time.

To date, physiological research into pacing strategies has focused on the amount of energy resources that are available for a runner to complete a long distance race. We propose that the future area in which the exercise physiology field should endeavour to concentrate more on, is the optimal time in switching between the different types of pacing strategies, so that a race is completed successfully and in the minimum time possible without homeostatic failure. In order to achieve this, the various changes in pacing, namely, increasing, constant or decreasing pace, depends on each individual's resource capacity and endurance for each type of pacing so as to achieve the target in the least possible time. Moreover, we suggest that the decision-making process underlying the choice of the various pacing strategies can be informed through the application of Allen's algebra, and the resulting scheduling can be applied to promote and improve world elite athletic performance.

REFERENCES

[1] J. F. Allen, "Temporal reasoning and planning.in j.f. allen, h.a. kautz, r.n. pelavin and j.d. tenenberg (eds.)," in Reasoning about Plans. Morgan Kaufman, 1991, pp. 1–67.

[2] F. Song and R. Cohen, "The interpretation of temporal relations in narrative," National Conference on Artificial Intelligence (AAAI-88), 1988.

[3] K. Nökel, Temporally distributed symptoms in technical diagnosis. Springer Science & Business Media, 1991, vol. 517.

[4] C. H. Coombs and J. Smith, "On the detection of structure in attitudes and developmental processes." Psychological Review, vol. 80, no. 5, 1973, p. 337.

[5] S. A. Ward and R. H. Halstead, Computation structures. MIT press, 1990.

[6] J. Juarez, M. Campos, A. Morales, J. Palma, and R. Marin, "Applications of temporal reasoning to intensive care units," Journal of Healthcare Engineering, vol. 1, no. 4, 2010, pp. 615–636.

[7] H.-U. Krieger, B. Kiefer, and T. Declerck, "A framework for temporal representation and reasoning in business intelligence applications." in AAAI Spring Symposium: AI Meets Business Rules and Process Management, 2008, pp. 59–70.

[8] A. Gerevini, L. Schubert, and S. Schaeffer, "Temporal reasoning in timegraph i–ii," ACM SIGART Bulletin, vol. 4, no. 3, 1993, pp. 21–25.

[9] J. F. Allen., "Maintaining knowledge about temporal intervals," Commun., vol. 26, no. 11, 1983, pp. 832–843.

[10] I. Pe'er and R. Shamir, "Satisfiability problems on intervals and unit intervals," Theoretical Computer Science, vol. 175, no. 2, 1997, pp. 349–372.

[11] M. C. Golumbic, H. Kaplan, and R. Shamir, "On the complexity of dna physical mapping," Advances in Applied Mathematics, vol. 15, no. 3, 1994, pp. 251–261.

[12] R. M. Karp, "Mapping the genome: some combinatorial problems arising in molecular biology," in Proceedings of the twenty-fifth annual ACM symposium on Theory of computing. ACM, 1993, pp. 278–285.

[13] I. Mandoiu and A. Zelikovsky, Bioinformatics algorithms: techniques and applications. John Wiley & Sons, 2008, vol. 3.

[14] B. Nebel and H.-J. Bürckert, "Reasoning about temporal relations: a maximal tractable subclass of allen's interval algebra," Journal of the ACM (JACM), vol. 42, no. 1, 1995, pp. 43–66.

[15] M. C. Golumbic and R. Shamir, "Algorithms and complexity for reasoning about time," in AAAI, 1992, pp. 741–747.

[16] G. Martin Charles and R. Shamir, "Complexity and algorithms for reasoning about time: A graph-theoretic approach," Journal of the ACM (JACM), vol. 40, no. 5, 1993, pp. 1108–1133.

[17] P. B. Ladkin and R. D. Maddux, On binary constraint networks. Kestrel Institute Palo Alto, CA, 1988.

[18] P. Van Beek, "Reasoning about qualitative temporal information," Artificial intelligence, vol. 58, no. 1-3, 1992, pp. 297–326.

[19] M. B. Vilain and H. A. Kautz, "Constraint propagation algorithms for temporal reasoning." in Aaai, vol. 86, 1986, pp. 377–382.

[20] J. W. Daykin, M. Miller, and J. Ryan, "Trends in temporal reasoning: Constraints, graphs and posets," in International Conference on Mathematical Aspects of Computer and Information Sciences. Springer, 2015, pp. 290–304.

[21] P. C. Fishburn, "A correlational inequality for linear extensions of a poset," Order, vol. 1, no. 2, 1984, pp. 127–137.

[22] L. A. Shepp et al., "The xyz conjecture and the fkg inequality," The Annals of Probability, vol. 10, no. 3, 1982, pp. 824–827.

[23] K. M. Tsui and S.-C. Chan, "Demand response optimization for smart home scheduling under real-time pricing," IEEE Transactions on Smart Grid, vol. 3, no. 4, 2012, pp. 1812–1821.

[24] G. T. Costanzo, J. Kheir, and G. Zhu, "Peak-load shaving in smart homes via online scheduling," in 2011 IEEE International Symposium on Industrial Electronics. IEEE, 2011, pp. 1347–1352.

[25] J. Zhu, F. Lauri, A. Koukam, and V. Hilaire, "Scheduling optimization of smart homes based on demand response," in IFIP International Conference on Artificial Intelligence Applications and Innovations. Springer, 2015, pp. 223–236.

[26] A. B. John Krumm, "Learning time-based presence probabilities," in Pervasive 2011. Springer Verlag, June 2011. [Online]. Available: https://www.microsoft.com/en-us/research/publication/learning-time-based-presence-probabilities [retrieved 2/2017].

[27] M. Gupta, S. S. Intille, and K. Larson, "Adding gps-control to traditional thermostats: An exploration of potential energy savings and design challenges," in International Conference on Pervasive Computing. Springer, 2009, pp. 95–114.

[28] V. Jakkula and D. J. Cook, "Anomaly detection using temporal data mining in a smart home environment," Methods of information in medicine, vol. 47, no. 1, 2008, pp. 70–75.

[29] J. Ullberg, A. Loutfi, and F. Pecora, "Towards continuous activity monitoring with temporal constraints," in Proc. of the 4th Workshop on Planning and Plan Execution for Real-World Systems at ICAPS09, 2009, pp. 3833–3860.

[30] F. Palumbo, J. Ullberg, A. Štimec, F. Furfari, L. Karlsson, and S. Coradeschi, "Sensor network infrastructure for a home care monitoring system," Sensors, vol. 14, no. 3, 2014, pp. 3833–3860.

[31] P. C. e. a. Roy, "A possibilistic approach for activity recognition in smart homes for cognitive assistance to alzheimers patients," in Activity Recognition in Pervasive Intelligent Environments. Springer, 2011, pp. 33–58.

[32] K. O'shea, Z. Bandar, and K. Crockett, "Towards a new generation of conversational agents using sentence similarity," in Advances in Electrical Engineering and Computational Science, L. N. in Electrical Engineering, Ed. Sio-Long Ao and Len Gelman, Ed. Netherlands: Springer, 2009, vol. 39, pp. 505–514.

[33] K. O'shea, Z. Bandar, and K. A. Crockett, "Application of a semantic-based conversational agent to student debt management," in World Congress on Computational Intelligence, I. International, Ed. Conference on Fuzzy Systems, Barcelona: 978-1-4244-6917-8, 2010, pp. 760–766.

[34] K. O'shea, "An approach to conversational agent design using sentence similarity measures," International Journal of Artificial Intelligence, 2012, pp. 558–568.

[35] H. Ulmer, "Concept of an extracellular regulation of muscular metabolic rate during heavy exercise in humans by psychophysiological feedback," Experimentia, vol. 52, 1996, pp. 416–420.

[36] E. Lambert, A. St Clair Gibson, and T. Noakes, "Complex systems model of fatigue: integrative homeostatic control of peripheral physiological systems during exercise in humans," B J Sports Med, vol. 39, 2004, pp. 52–62.

[37] D. Chuckravanen and S. Rajbhandari, "Management of metabolic resources for a 20-km cycling time-trial using different types of pacing," Journal of Human Sport and Exercise, vol. 10, no. 1, 2015, pp. 95–103.

Trie Compression for GPU Accelerated Multi-Pattern Matching

Xavier Bellekens
Division of Computing and Mathematics
Abertay University
Dundee, Scotland
Email: x.bellekens@abertay.ac.uk

Amar Seeam
Department of Computer Science
Middlesex University
Mauritius Campus
Email: a.seeam@mdx.ac.uk

Christos Tachtatzis & Robert Atkinson
EEE Department
University of Strathclyde
Glasgow, Scotland
Email: name.surname@strath.ac.uk

***Abstract*—Graphics Processing Units (GPU) allow for running massively parallel applications offloading the Central Processing Unit (CPU) from computationally intensive resources. However GPUs have a limited amount of memory. In this paper, a trie compression algorithm for massively parallel pattern matching is presented demonstrating 85% less space requirements than the original highly efficient parallel failure-less Aho-Corasick, whilst demonstrating over 22 Gbps throughput. The algorithm presented takes advantage of compressed row storage matrices as well as shared and texture memory on the GPU.**

Keywords–Pattern Matching Algorithm; Trie Compression; Searching; Data Compression; GPU

I. INTRODUCTION

Pattern matching algorithms are used in a plethora of fields, ranging from bio-medical applications to cyber-security, the internet of things (IoT), DNA sequencing and anti-virus systems. The ever growing volume of data to be analysed, often in real time, demands high computational performance.

The massively parallel capabilities of Graphical Processor Units, have recently been exploited in numerous fields such as mathematics [1], physics [2], life sciences [3], computer science [4], networking [5], and astronomy [6] to increase the throughput of sequential algorithms and reduce the processing time.

With the increasing number of patterns to search for and the scarcity of memory on Graphics Processing Units data compression is important. The massively parallel capabilities allow for increasing the processing throughput and can benefit applications using string dictionaries [7], or application requiring large trees [8].

The remainder of this paper is organised as follows: Section II describes the GPU programming model, Section III provides background on multi-pattern matching algorithms while, Section IV discusses the failure-less Aho-Corasick algorithm used within this research. Section V highlights the design and implementation of the trie compression algorithms, while Section VI provides details on the environment. The results are highlighted in Section VII and the paper finishes with the Conclusion in Section VIII.

II. BACKGROUND

A. GPU Programming Model

In this work, an Nvidia 1080 GPUs is used along with the Compute Unified Device Architecture (CUDA) programming model, allowing for a rich Software Development Kit (SDK). Using the CUDA SDK, researchers are able to communicate with GPUs using a variety of programming languages. The C language has been extended with primitives, libraries and compiler directives in order for software developers to be able to request and store data on GPUs for processing.

GPUs are composed of numerous Streaming Multiprocessors (SM) operating in a Single Instruction Multiple Thread (SIMT) fashion. SMs are themselves composed of numerous CUDA cores, also known as Streaming Processors (SP).

B. Multi-Pattern Matching

Pattern matching is the art of searching for a pattern P in a text T. Multi-pattern matching algorithms are used in a plethora of domains ranging from cyber-security to biology and engineering [9].

The Aho-Corasick algorithm is one of the most widely used algorithms [10][11]. The algorithm allows the matching of multiple patterns in a single pass over a text. This is achieved by using the failure links created during the construction phase of the algorithm.

The Aho-Corasick, however, presents a major drawback when parallelised, as some patterns may be split over two different chunks of T. Each thread is required to overlap the next chunk of data by the length of the longest pattern -1. This drawback was described in [12] and [13].

C. Parallel Failure-Less Aho-Corasick

Lin *et al.* presented an alternative method for multi-pattern matching on GPU in [14].

To overcome these problems, Lin *et al.* presented the failure-less Aho-Corasick algorithm. Each thread is assigned to a single letter in the text T. If a match is recorded, the thread continues the matching process until a mismatch. When a mismatch occurs the thread is terminated, releasing GPU

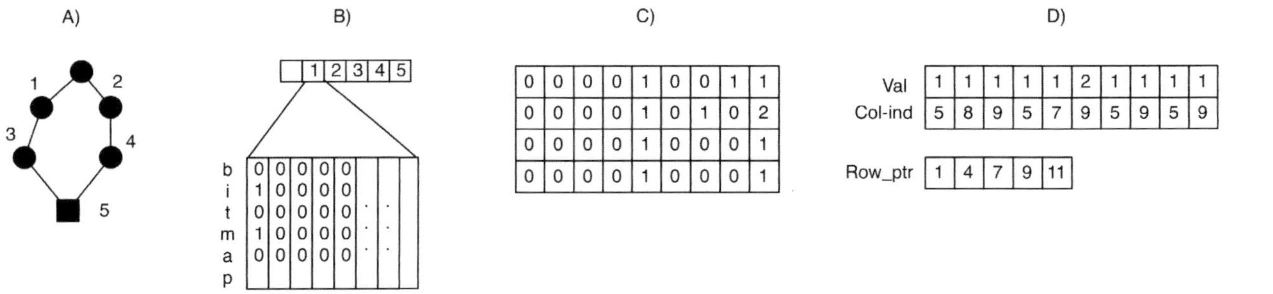

Figure 1. Memory layout transformation for a simplified transfer between the host and the device, allowing for better compression and improved throughput

resources. The algorithm also allows for coalesced memory access during the first memory transfer, and early thread termination.

III. Design and Implementation

The trie compression library presented within this section builds upon prior research presented in [15] and [16] and aims to further reduce the memory footprint of the highly-efficient parallel failure-less Aho-Corasick (HEPFAC) trie presented in [16], while improving upon the tradeoff between memory compression operation and the throughput offered by the massively parallel capabilities of GPUs.

The compressed trie presented in our prior research is created in six distinct steps. I) The trie is constructed in a breadth-first approach, level by level. II) The trie is stored in a row major ordered array. III) The trie is truncated at the appropriate level, as described in [15]. IV) Similar suffixes are merged together on the last three levels of the trie (This may vary based on the alphabet in use). V) The last nodes are merged together. VI) The row major ordering array is translated into a sparse matrix as described in [16].

In this manuscript, an additional step is added. The sparse matrix representing the trie is compressed using a Compressed Row Storage (CRS) algorithm, reducing furthermore the memory footprint of the bitmap array [17][18]. The compressed row storage also allows the array to be stored in texture memory, hence benefiting from cached data. The row pointer generated by the CRS algorithm is stored in shared memory, benefiting from both the cache and an on-chip location reducing the clock cycles when accessing data.

Figure 2 is a visual representation of steps I to V undertaken during the construction of the trie. As shown, the trie is truncated to an appropriate level. This technique was used by Vasiliadis *et al.* [19] and further studied by Bellekens *et al.* [16]. After truncation, similar suffixes within the trie are merged together and the leave nodes are replaced by a single end node.
Figure 3 shows the composition of the nodes in the trie. Each node is composed of a bitmap of 256 bits from the ASCII alphabet. The bitmap is modular and can be modified based on the trie requirements (e.g., for DNA storage). Each node also contains an offset value providing the location of the first child of the current node. Subsequent children can be located following the method described in [16].

Figure 1 depicts four different memory layouts in order to achieve better compression and increase the throughput on GPUs. Figure 1 (A) represents the trie created with a linked list. Figure 1 (B) represents the trie organised in a row major order, this allows the removal of pointers and simplifies the transition between the host and and the device memory. Figure 1 (C) represents the trie in a two dimensional array, allowing the trie to be stored in Texture memory on the GPU and annihilate the trade-off between the compression highlighted in Figure 1 A) and the throughput. Finally, Figure 1 (D) is improving upon the compression of our prior research while allowing the trie to be stored in texture memory and the row_ptr to be stored in shared memory.

The CRS compression of the non-symmetric sparse matrix A is achieved by creating three vectors. The val vector stores the values of the non-zero elements present within A, while the $col-ind$ store the indexes of the val. The storage savings for this approach is defined as $2nnz + n + 1$, where nnz represents the number of non-zero elements in the matrix and n the number of elements per side of the matrix. In the example provided in Figure 1 (C and D), the sparse matrix is

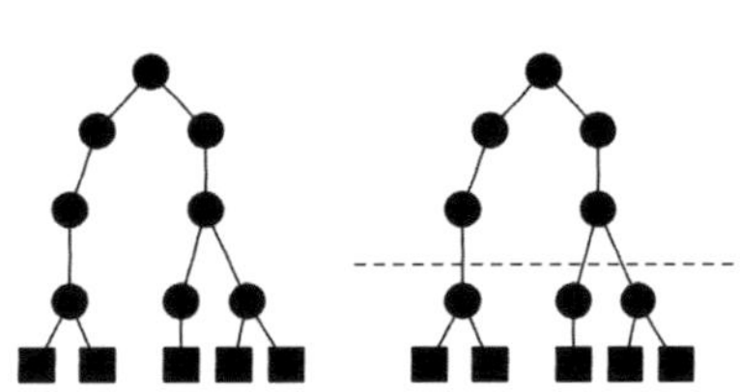

Figure 2. Trie Truncation and Node Compression

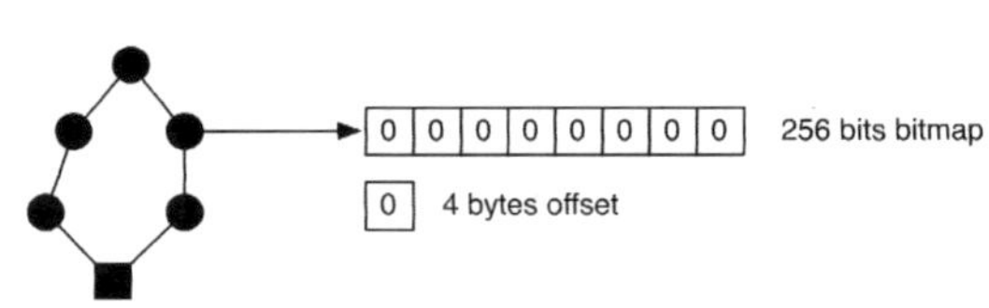

Figure 3. Bitmapped Nodes

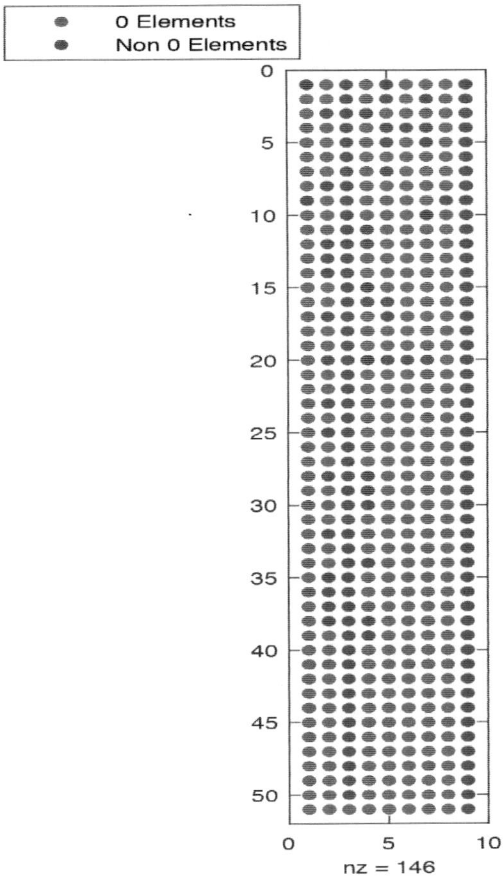

Figure 4. Sparse Matrix Representation of the a Compressed Trie Containing 10 Patterns

reduced from 36 to 24 elements.

The sparse matrix compression combined with the trie compression and the bitmap allows for storing large numbers of patters on GPUs allowing its use in big data applications, anti-virus and intrusion detection systems. Note that the CRS compression is pattern dependent, hence the compression will vary with the alphabet in use and the type of patterns being searched for.

IV. Experimental Environment

The Nvidia 1080 GPU is composed of 2560 CUDA cores divided into 20 SMs. The card also contains 8 GB of GDDR5X with a clock speed of 1733 MHz. Moreover the card possesses 96 KB shared memory and 48 KB of L1 cache, as well as 8 texture units and a GP104 PolyMorph engine used for vertex fetches for each streaming multiprocessors. The base system is composed of 2 Intel Xeon Processors with 20 cores, allowing up to 40 threads and has a total of 32GB of RAM. The server is running Ubuntu Server 14.04 with the latest version of CUDA 8.0 and C99.

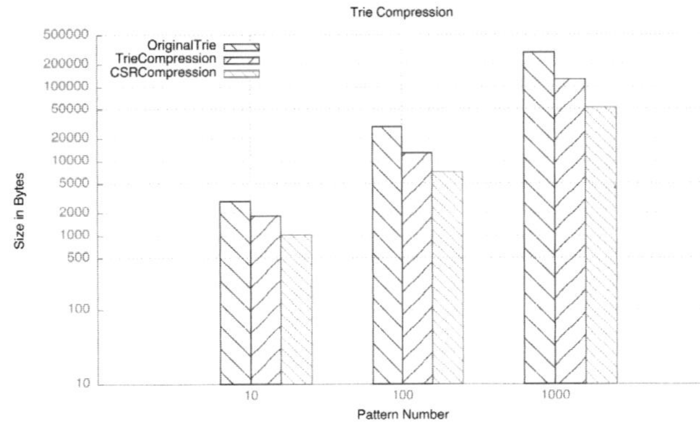

Figure 5. Comparison between the current state of the art and the CRS Trie

V. Results

The HEPFAC algorithm presented within this manuscript improves upon the state of the art compression and uses texture memory and shared memory to increase the matching throughput.

The evaluation of compression algorithm presented is made against the King James Bible. The patterns are chosen randomly within the text using the Mersenne Twister algorithm [20].

Figure 4 is a representation of the compressed trie stored in a 2D layout. The trie contains ten Patterns. The blue elements represent non-zero elements in the matrix while the red elements represent empty spaces within the matrix. The last column of the matrix only contains the offsets of each node.

Figure 5 demonstrates the compression achieved by the different compression steps aforementioned. The original trie required a total of 36 bytes for each nodes, 256 bits to represent the ASCII alphabet and four bytes for the offset. The trie compression, on the other hand requires 36 bytes for each node but reduces the size of the trie based on the

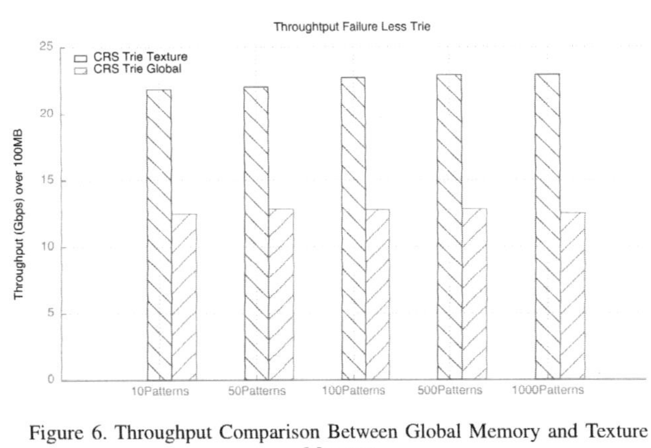

Figure 6. Throughput Comparison Between Global Memory and Texture Memory

alphabet used (in this case to eight levels), then merges similar suffixes together and merges all final nodes in a single one. Finally, the CRS compression algorithm compresses the sparse matrix representation of the trie. This technique allows an 83% space reduction in comparison to the original trie and a 56% reduction in comparison to the trie compression algorithm presented in [15].

Figure 6 depicts the throughput obtained when storing the CRS trie in global memory and in Texture memory. Global Memory does not provide access to a cache and requires up to 600 clock cycles to access data. This inherently limits the throughput of the pattern matching algorithm to 12 Gbps. When the CRS trie is stored in texture memory and the row_ptr is stored in shared memory the algorithm demonstrate 22 Gbps throughput when matching a 1000 patterns within an alphabet $\Sigma = 256$.

VI. Conclusion

In this work a trie compression algorithm is presented. The trie compression scheme improves upon the state of the art and demonstrates 83% space reduction against the original trie compression and 56% reduction over the HEPFAC algorithm. Moreover, our approach also demonstrates over 22 Gbps throughput while matching a 1000 patterns. This work highlighted the algorithm on single GPU node, however, the algorithm can be adapted to cloud computing, or on FPGAs.

References

[1] A. Nasridinov, Y. Lee, and Y.-H. Park, "Decision tree construction on gpu: ubiquitous parallel computing approach," Computing, vol. 96, no. 5, 2014, pp. 403–413.

[2] N. Nakasato, "Oct-tree method on gpu," arXiv preprint arXiv:0909.0541, 2009.

[3] S. Memeti and S. Pllana, "Combinatorial optimization of work distribution on heterogeneous systems," in 2016 45th International Conference on Parallel Processing Workshops (ICPPW), Aug 2016, pp. 151–160.

[4] D. Aparicio, P. Paredes, and P. Ribeiro, "A scalable parallel approach for subgraph census computation," in European Conference on Parallel Processing. Springer International Publishing, 2014, pp. 194–205.

[5] G. Rétvári, J. Tapolcai, A. Kőrösi, A. Majdán, and Z. Heszberger, "Compressing ip forwarding tables: towards entropy bounds and beyond," in ACM SIGCOMM Computer Communication Review, vol. 43, no. 4. ACM, 2013, pp. 111–122.

[6] J. Bédorf, E. Gaburov, and S. P. Zwart, "Bonsai: A gpu tree-code," arXiv preprint arXiv:1204.2280, 2012.

[7] M. A. Martínez-Prieto, N. Brisaboa, R. Cánovas, F. Claude, and G. Navarro, "Practical compressed string dictionaries," Information Systems, vol. 56, 2016, pp. 73–108.

[8] G. Navarro and A. O. Pereira, "Faster compressed suffix trees for repetitive collections," Journal of Experimental Algorithmics (JEA), vol. 21, no. 1, 2016, pp. 1–8.

[9] T. T. Tran, M. Giraud, and J.-S. Varré, "Bit-parallel multiple pattern matching," in International Conference on Parallel Processing and Applied Mathematics. Springer, 2011, pp. 292–301.

[10] A. V. Aho and M. J. Corasick, "Efficient string matching: An aid to bibliographic search," Commun. ACM, vol. 18, no. 6, Jun. 1975, pp. 333–340. [Online]. Available: http://doi.acm.org/10.1145/360825.360855

[11] S. Vakili, J. Langlois, B. Boughzala, and Y. Savaria, "Memory-efficient string matching for intrusion detection systems using a high-precision pattern grouping algorithm," in Proceedings of the 2016 symposium on architectures for networking and communications systems. ACM, 2016, pp. 37–42.

[12] X. Bellekens, I. Andonovic, R. Atkinson, C. Renfrew, and T. Kirkham, "Investigation of GPU-based pattern matching," in The 14th Annual Post Graduate Symposium on the Convergence of Telecommunications, Networking and Broadcasting (PGNet2013), 2013.

[13] A. Tumeo, O. Villa, and D. Sciuto, "Efficient pattern matching on gpus for intrusion detection systems," in Proceedings of the 7th ACM international conference on Computing frontiers. ACM, 2010, pp. 87–88.

[14] C.-H. Lin, S.-Y. Tsai, C.-H. Liu, S.-C. Chang, and J.-M. Shyu, "Accelerating string matching using multi-threaded algorithm on GPU," in Global Telecommunications Conference (GLOBECOM 2010), 2010 IEEE, Dec 2010, pp. 1–5.

[15] X. J. A. Bellekens, C. Tachtatzis, R. C. Atkinson, C. Renfrew, and T. Kirkham, "A highly-efficient memory-compression scheme for gpu-accelerated intrusion detection systems," in Proceedings of the 7th International Conference on Security of Information and Networks, ser. SIN '14. New York, NY, USA: ACM, 2014, pp. 302:302–302:309. [Online]. Available: http://doi.acm.org/10.1145/2659651.2659723

[16] X. J. A. Bellekens, "High performance pattern matching and data remanence on graphics processing units," Ph.D. dissertation, University of Strathclyde, 2016. [Online]. Available: http://ethos.bl.uk/OrderDetails.do?uin=uk.bl.ethos.698532

[17] K. Wu, E. J. Otoo, and A. Shoshani, "Optimizing bitmap indices with efficient compression," ACM Transactions on Database Systems (TODS), vol. 31, no. 1, 2006, pp. 1–38.

[18] H. Wang, "Sparse array representations and some selected array operations on gpus," Master's thesis, School of Computer Science University of the Witwatersrand A dissertation submitted to the Faculty of Science, University of the Witwatersrand, Johannesburg, 2014.

[19] G. Vasiliadis and S. Ioannidis, "Gravity: a massively parallel antivirus engine," in International Workshop on Recent Advances in Intrusion Detection. Springer, 2010, pp. 79–96.

[20] M. Matsumoto and T. Nishimura, "Mersenne twister: A 623-dimensionally equidistributed uniform pseudo-random number generator," ACM Trans. Model. Comput. Simul., vol. 8, no. 1, Jan. 1998, pp. 3–30. [Online]. Available: http://doi.acm.org/10.1145/272991.272995

A Data Adjustment Method of Low-priced Data-glove based on Hand Motion Pattern

Kenji Funahashi
Department of Computer Science
Nagoya Institute of Technology
Nagoya 466–8555 Japan
Email: kenji@nitech.ac.jp

Yutaro Mori[1] Hiromasa Takahashi[2]
Nagoya Institute of Technology
([1]present: NEC Solution Innovators, Ltd.)
([2]present: Chubu Electric Power Co.,Inc.)
[1]Email: moriyu@center.nitech.ac.jp
[2]Email: hiromasa@center.nitech.ac.jp

Yuji Iwahori
Department of Computer Science
Chubu University
Kasugai, Aichi 487-8501 Japan
Email: iwahori@cs.chubu.ac.jp

***Abstract*—A data glove is one of the major interfaces used in the field of virtual reality. In order to get detailed data about the finger joint angles, we must use a data glove with many sensors. However, a data glove with many sensors is expensive and a low-priced data glove does not have enough sensors to capture all the hand data correctly. In our previous work, we propose a method to obtain all finger joint angles by estimating the pattern of hand motion from the low-priced data glove sensor values. In our experiment system, we assumed some representative hand motion patterns as grasping behavior. We also assumed that other hand motions can be represented by synthetic motion of the representative patterns. In our previous work, we used the data glove with sensors covering two joints of each finger. In this paper, we estimate the finger joint angles when using the data glove whose sensors cover only the middle angle of each finger.**

***Keywords*–Data-glove; Hand motion estimation; Finger joint angles estimation.**

I. INTRODUCTION

Virtual Reality (VR) is a rapidly growing research field in recent years. VR technologies give us various advantages. There are simulators to practice an operation and to fly a plane as examples of VR technologies. These simulators enable us to avoid the risk and to save on cost. VR researches that targets to households also have been attracted. A data glove is one of the major interfaces which are used in the field of VR. It measures curvatures of fingers using bend sensors. In order to obtain accurate hand motions, it is necessary to use a data glove which has many sensors, but it is expensive. It is preferable that an interface is small scale and low cost. Various types of researches about data glove have been conducted [1][2][3]. On the other hand, there is a low cost data glove which measures an angle for each finger through one sensor. But it cannot get detailed data directly. For example, the 5DT Data Glove 5 Ultra and DG5 VHand have a single sensor on each finger, so they have five sensors in the whole hand (see Figures 1 and 2). However, there are three finger joints for each finger, a single sensor can not measure all of these three angles directly. In our laboratory, we have proposed a method to get plausible user hand motion pattern from the low-cost glove. This method estimates the kind of hand motion patterns using each relation among angles of fingers during operation. Then, it estimates all finger joint angles by estimating the types of hand motion patterns from the correlation between each finger angle in the hand motion pattern [4]. We assume some representative hand motion patterns, and consider that other hand motions can be represented as a synthetic motion of the representative hand motion patterns. In addition, we calculate the ratio of each representative motion pattern. Moreover, estimating each finger angle using the result, we express any hand motion patterns other than the representative hand motions. In our previous work, we have used 5DT Data Glove (see Figure 1) whose sensors cover two joints of each finger. Here, we estimate finger joint angles when using the data glove DG5 VHand (see Figure 2) whose sensors cover only the middle angle of each finger.

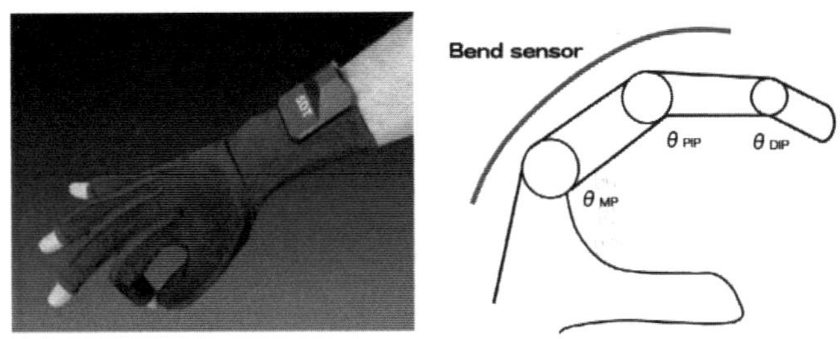

Figure 1. 5DT Data Glove 5 Ultra

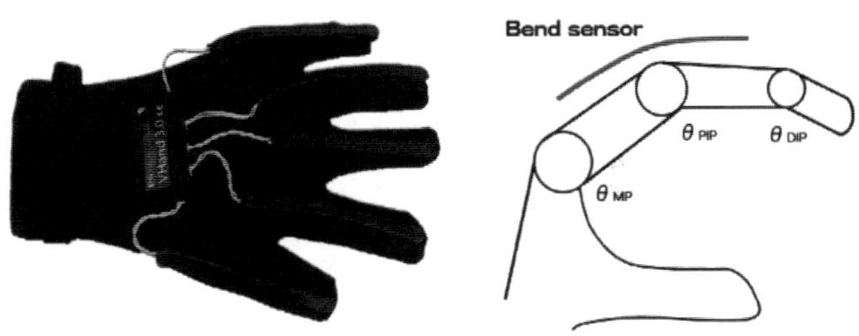

Figure 2. DG5 VHand

The rest of the paper is structured as follows. In Section II, we describe how to estimate finger joint angels. In Section III, we apply this method to the data-glove that sensor positons are limited. In Section IV, the experimental results are shown. Finally, we conclude in Section V.

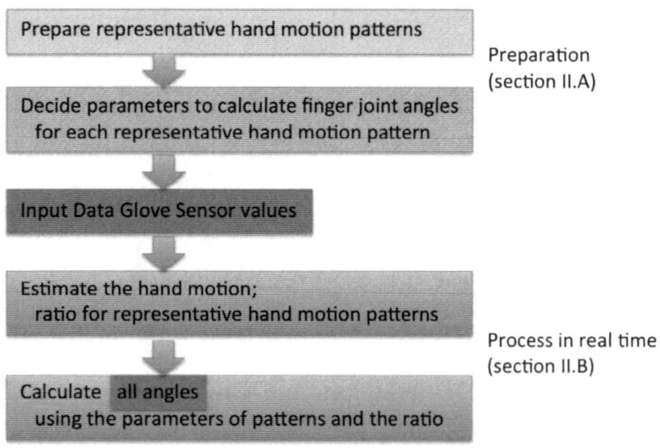

Figure 3. Overview of method

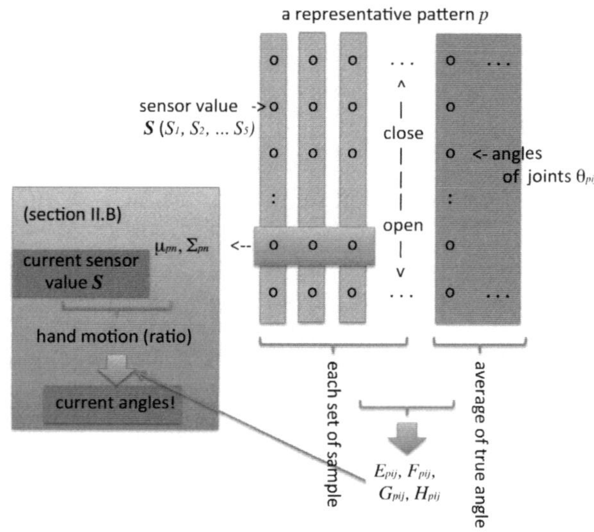

Figure 4. Detail of method

II. Estimation of Finger Joint Angles

In section II, we describe an estimation method of finger joint angles using 5DT data glove which has been developed in our laboratory (see Figure 3).

A. Representative Hand Motion Patterns

To estimate finger joint angles, this method limits user's hand motion to grasping motion. First of all, we chose four representative hand motion patterns (see Figure 5)[4] from human's grasping motion (Figure 6)[5].

Furthermore, we assume that a human's grasping motion can be represented as a synthetic motion of representative hand motion patterns. To derive three finger joint angles from a single sensor value, we use the following method (see Figure 4). We sample many sets of the sensor values with the low-priced data glove when some subjects open their hand first and then close it to each representative hand motion patterns. Also, we sample the sets of the true angles of finger joints for the same representative patterns, provided that we use true angles obtained from a data glove which has a lot of sensors. We use Immersion CyberGlove as data glove with a lot of sensors. Then, the sensor values and the true angles of finger joints at the same time are associated. We show an example of correspondence in Figure 7.

We derive the following numerical formulas using this correspondence.

$$\theta_{pi1} = \frac{2}{3}\theta_{pi2} \quad (1)$$

$$\theta_{pi2} = E_{pi2}S_i^3 + F_{pi2}S_i^2 + G_{pi2}S_i + H_{pi2} \quad (2)$$

$$\theta_{pi3} = E_{pi3}S_i^3 + F_{pi3}S_i^2 + G_{pi3}S_i + H_{pi3} \quad (3)$$

where pattern p is one of representative hand motion patterns. Angles θ_{pi1}, θ_{pi2} and θ_{pi3} express the DIP, PIP, and MP joint angle of the finger i for the pattern p. The DIP, PIP, and MP joint mean the first, second and third joint of a finger respectively. The S_i is sensor value of finger i. And E_{pij}, F_{pij}, G_{pij} and H_{pij} are constant parameters for the pattern p, finger i and joint j. These parameters, E_{pij} to H_{pij}, are calculated by pre-experiment. Besides, DIP joint angle is obtained by proportional connection with PIP joint angle (eq. 1)[6]. Joint angles of finger i of pattern p are obtained by these numerical formulas.

B. Hand Motion Estimation and Angles Estimation

To represent user's hand motion as synthetic motion of representative hand motion patterns, we need to know how similar the user's hand motion is and to which representative hand motion patterns. Then, we set the following formula based on the probability density function of the multivariate normal distribution for n points in the five dimensional feature amount space.

$$L_{pn} = exp\{-\frac{1}{2}(\boldsymbol{S} - \boldsymbol{\mu}_{pn})^T \boldsymbol{\Sigma}_{pn}^{-1}(\boldsymbol{S} - \boldsymbol{\mu}_{pn})\} \quad (4)$$

where $\boldsymbol{S}$ is the sensor value vector. And $\boldsymbol{\mu}_{pn}$ and $\boldsymbol{\Sigma}_{pn}$ represent mean vector of sensor sample values, and variance-covariance matrix of sample point n (an integer satisfying $1 \leq n \leq$ a number of samples) in representative hand motion pattern p. Besides, $\boldsymbol{\mu}_{pn}$ and $\boldsymbol{\Sigma}_{pn}$ are obtained by pre-experiment for an average user. If the sensor values are obtained actually from the glove, we select the maximum value according to the following formula.

$$L_p = \max_n\{L_{pn}(\boldsymbol{S} : \boldsymbol{\mu}_{pn}, \boldsymbol{\Sigma}_{pn})\} \quad (5)$$

Thus, we get the likelihood on representative hand motion pattern p in current sensor values. After that, we decide the ratio r_p of hand motion pattern p according to the following formula.

$$r_p = \frac{L_p}{\Sigma_{p=1}^{P} L_p} \quad (6)$$

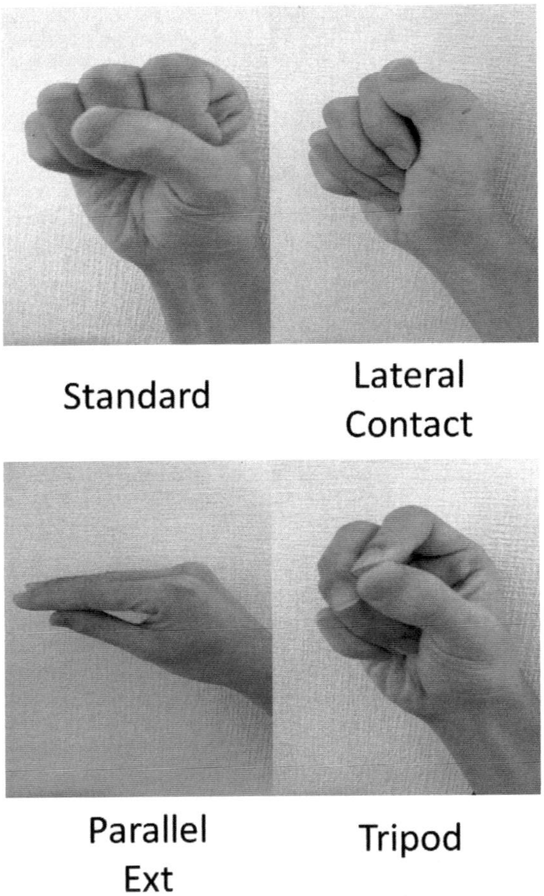

Figure 5. Representative hand motion patterns

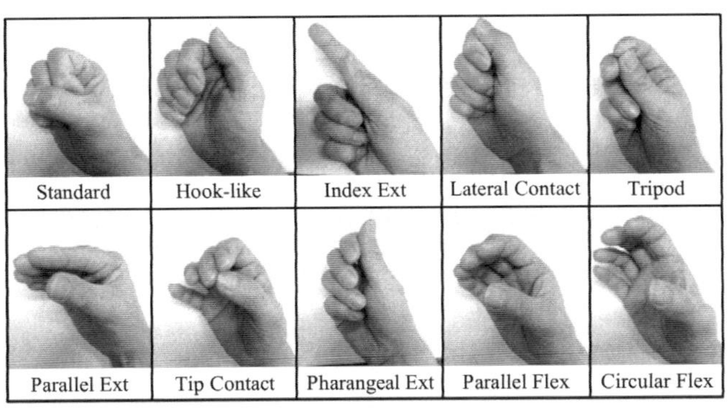

Figure 6. Candidates of representative motions

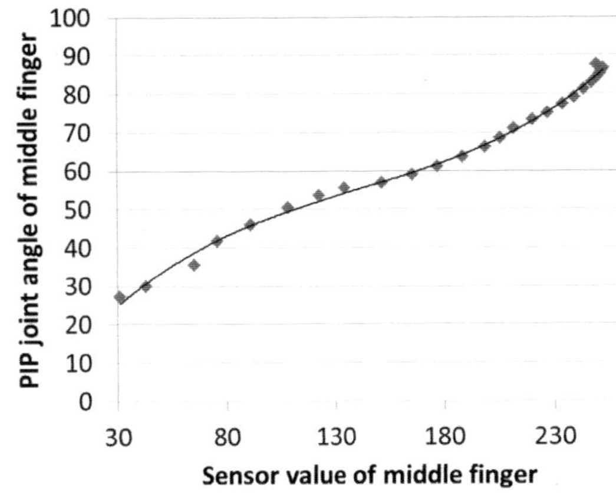

Figure 7. Example of correspondence

where P is the total number of representative hand motions, which takes the value of four. As stated above, we can obtain θ_{pij} and r_p. At last, each angle θ_{ij} of current hand posture is derived by the following formula.

$$\theta_{ij} = \sum_{p=1}^{P} r_p \cdot \theta_{pij} \tag{7}$$

III. Data-Glove that Sensor Positions are Limited

In section III, we describe an estimation method of finger joint angles using DG5 data glove whose sensor positions are limited only to PIP joints.

A. *MP Angle for Representative Hand Motion Pattern*

Although we mentioned above representative hand motion patterns are selected, the pattern Parallel Ext. is almost the motion related only to MP joints. When doing the Parallel Ext. pattern, the sensor values hardly change. We tentatively use three other patterns as representative hand motion patterns for now.

For the 5DT data glove whose sensors cover PIP and MP joints, the DIP angle is related to PIP directly, as mentioned in the previous section. It means the sensor values contain all of their information. However, using DG5 whose sensors are only on PIP, the motion of MP does not change the sensor value. Of course, we assume that the hand motion is a grasping one, so the MP angle of a finger is related to the PIP angle of the same finger. Then we can assume that the MP of a finger is related to the PIPs of all fingers.

We consider a new estimation model to obtain angles for representative hand motion patterns using multiple regression analysis. First, we make a estimation equation with explanatory variable is a set of sensor values, and response variable is each MP joint angle, as follows.

$$\theta_{pi3} = \sum_{f=1}^{5} C_{pif3} S_f + I_{pi3} \tag{8}$$

where θ_{pi3} is MP joint angle of finger i of representative pattern p, S_f is sensor value of finger f, and C_{pif3} and I_{pi3} are constant.

Now, a subject opens his hand first and then closes it to each representative pattern with DG5 data glove, the set of sensor value $S_f(time)$ of finger f at $time$ is sampled. Then, the subject moves his hand as each same pattern with CyberGlove which has many sensors, the set of angle value $\theta_{pi3}(time)$ is sampled as true one.

Here, we should get the constant C_{pif3} and I_{pi3}. The residual sum of squares Q is represented as in (9).

$$Q = \sum_{time} \left\{ \theta_{pi3}(time) - \left(\sum_{f=1}^{5} C_{pif3} S_f(time) + I_{pi3} \right) \right\}^2 \quad (9)$$

Focusing on coefficient C_{pi13} where $f = 1$;

$$\begin{aligned} Q = \sum_{time} \Bigg\{ & \left(S_1(time) C_{pi13}\right)^2 \\ & + 2 S_1(time) C_{pi13} \left(\sum_{f=2}^{5} C_{pif3} S_f(time) + I_{pi3} \right) \\ & - 2\theta_{pi3}(time) S_1(time) C_{pi13} \\ & + \left(\sum_{f=2}^{5} C_{pif3} S_f(time) + I_{pi3} \right)^2 \\ & - 2\theta_{pi3}(time) \left(\sum_{f=2}^{5} C_{pif3} S_f(time) + I_{pi3} \right) \\ & + \left(\theta_{pi3}(time)\right)^2 \Bigg\} \end{aligned} \quad (10)$$

Using the partial differentiations with C_{pi13};

$$\frac{\partial Q}{\partial C_{pi13}} = 2 \sum_{time} S_1(time) \left\{ \sum_{f=1}^{5} C_{pif3} S_f(time) + I_{pi3} - \theta_{pi3}(time) \right\} \quad (11)$$

Using the partial differentiations also with C_{pif3} and I_{pi3};

$$\frac{\partial Q}{\partial C_{pif3}} = 2 \sum_{time} S_f(time) \left\{ \sum_{f'=1}^{5} C_{pif'3} S_{f'}(time) + I_{pi3} - \theta_{pi3}(time) \right\} \quad (12)$$

$$\frac{\partial Q}{\partial I_{pi3}} = 2 \sum_{time} \left\{ I_{pi3} + \sum_{f=1}^{5} C_{pif3} S_f(time) - \theta_{pi3}(time) \right\} \quad (13)$$

The constant C_{pif3} and I_{pi3} to be obtained make Q represented as the minimum of the equation from (9). And the C_{pif3} and I_{pi3} that make Q minimum satisfy following equation.

$$\frac{\partial Q}{\partial C_{pif3}} = \frac{\partial Q}{\partial I_{pi3}} = 0 \quad (14)$$

Solving this, coefficient C_{pif3} and constant I_{pi3} are obtained to estimate MP joint angle for representative pattern with (8). The angles of PIP are obtained directly from the sensor value with (2), and the angles of DIP are also obtained only from PIP with (1).

B. Hand Motion Estimation with Pseudo-Inverse Matrix

When the variance of sensor values is zero at the sample point n of representative hand motion pattern, the variance-covariance matrix will be abnormal at the sample point n. It means the inverse matrix of variance-covariance matrix of sensor values $\boldsymbol{\Sigma}_{pn}^{-1}$ can not be obtained, and the likelihood for the sample data of representative pattern p can not be obtained with (4).

So we use Moore-Penrose pseudo-inverse matrix to solve it. The variance-covariance 5×5 matrix of sensor values $\boldsymbol{\Sigma}_{pn}^{-1}$ which is abnormal at the sample point n is represented as next equation with $5 \times r$ matrix $\boldsymbol{A}_{pn}$ and $r \times 5$ matrix $\boldsymbol{B}_{pn}$ where $\mathrm{rank}\,(\boldsymbol{\Sigma}_{pn}) = r$;

$$\boldsymbol{\Sigma}_{pn} = \boldsymbol{A}_{pn} \boldsymbol{B}_{pn} \quad (15)$$

Here the Moore-Penrose pseudo-inverse matrix $\boldsymbol{\Sigma}_{pn}^{+}$ for $\boldsymbol{\Sigma}_{pn}$ is described as:

$$\begin{aligned} \boldsymbol{\Sigma}_{pn}^{+} &= \boldsymbol{B}_{pn}^{T} \left(\boldsymbol{A}_{pn}^{T} \boldsymbol{\Sigma}_{pn} \boldsymbol{B}_{pn}^{T} \right)^{-1} \boldsymbol{A}_{pn}^{T} \\ &= \boldsymbol{B}_{pn}^{T} \left(\boldsymbol{B}_{pn} \boldsymbol{B}_{pn}^{T} \right)^{-1} \left(\boldsymbol{A}_{pn}^{T} \boldsymbol{A}_{pn} \right)^{-1} \boldsymbol{A}_{pn}^{T} \end{aligned} \quad (16)$$

Using this Moore-Penrose pseudo-inverse matrix $\boldsymbol{\Sigma}_{pn}^{+}$ for (4) instead of the inverse matrix of variance-covariance matrix of sensor values $\boldsymbol{\Sigma}_{pn}^{-1}$ at the sample point n where inverse matrix can not be defined, the likelihood is obtained and the ratio of each hand motion pattern is determined with (5) and (6), respectively. Now, we can use a low-priced data glove whose sensors cover only the middle angle of each finger to estimate all finger joint angles of current hand posture with (7).

IV. Experiment and Result

We performed an experiment to confirm the effectiveness of the method described above. The experiment system was constructed using the DG5 Data Glove whose sensor positions are limited only on middle joints. Other hand motions that were different from representative patterns were tested. The minimum of Activities of Daily Living (ADL) needs the following hand motions (see Figure 8) [7].

1) Power grasps (used in 35% ADLs)
2) Precision grasps (30% ADLs)
3) Lateral grasps (20% ADLs)
4) Extension grasps (10% ADLs),
5) Tripod grasps,
6) Index pointing, and
7) Basic gestures.

We tested five motions; 1)–5).

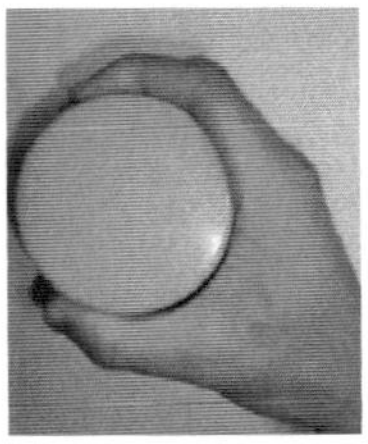

(1) Power grasp

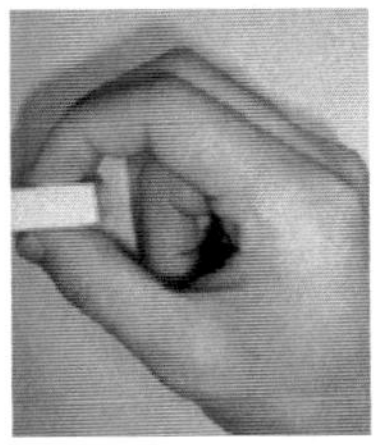

(2) Precision grasp

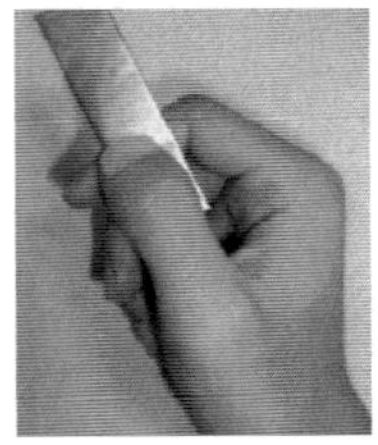

(3) Lateral grasp

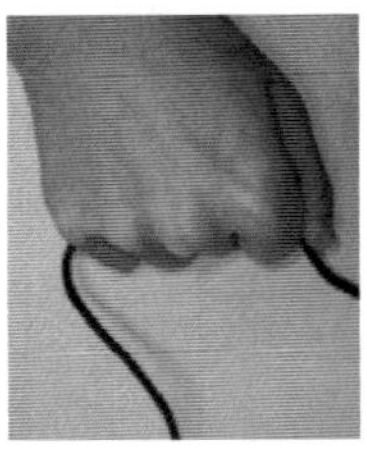

(4) Extension grasp

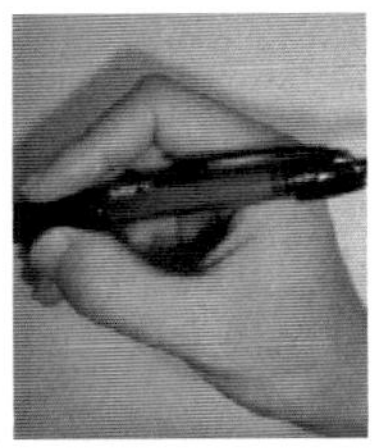

(5) Tripod grasp

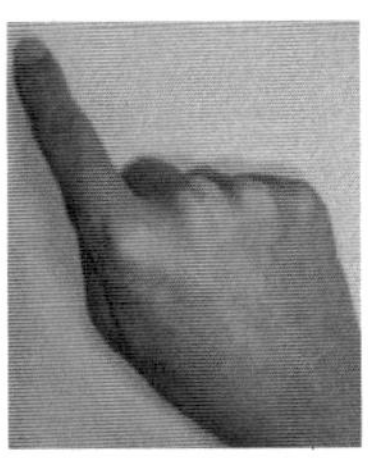

(6) Index pointing

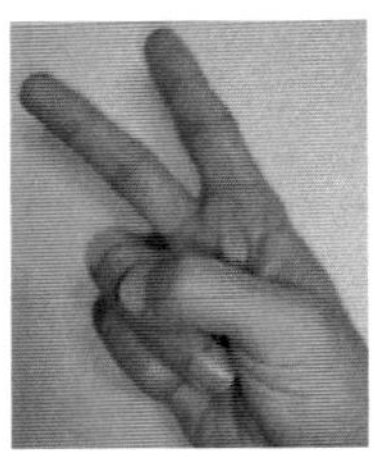

(7) Basic gestures

Figure 8. Hand motions needed for ADL

TABLE I. ERROR OF FINGER JOINT ANGLES [DEGREE]

	thumb	index	middle	ring	little	average
Power G.	7.3	12.0	10.5	12.5	10.0	10.5
Precision G.	8.1	9.2	7.2	7.0	6.8	7.7
Lateral G.	9.4	6.0	8.8	7.5	10.5	8.4
Extension G.	9.8	8.1	11.0	11.3	9.0	9.9
Tripod G.	8.5	8.5	7.2	11.6	10.9	9.3
average	8.6	8.7	8.9	10.0	9.4	9.2

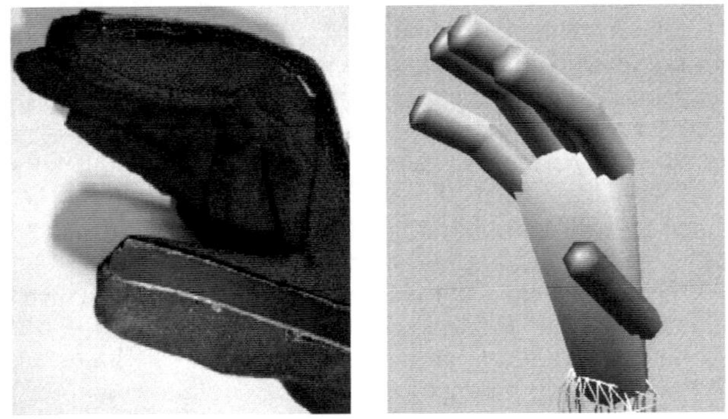

Figure 9. Result CG for Power grasp

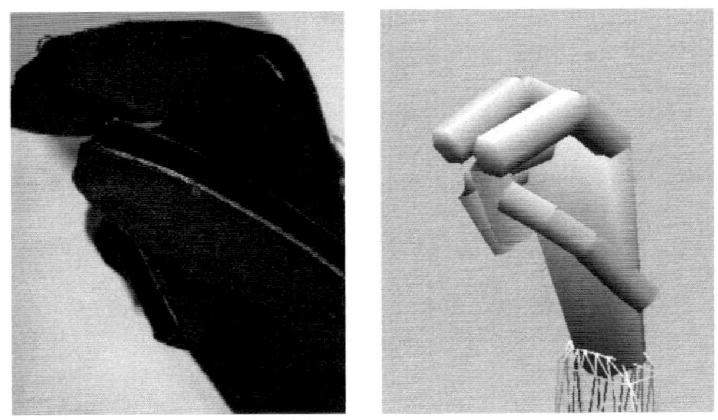

Figure 10. Result CG for Precision grasp

The subjects opened their hands and then closed them to each test pattern 1)–5) with DG5 data glove. The average of estimated joint angles were compared with the true angles obtained from CyberGlove which had many bend sensors.

Table I shows the average error of finger joint angles. Each error is around 10 degrees. The result using the 5DT data glove whose sensors cover two joints of each finger also had about 10 degrees error [4]. This means that the lower-priced data glove can obtain joint angles accurately enough.

Actual hand posture images and the CG images generated from estimated joint angles are shown in Figures 9 and 10. The MP joints that were not covered with bend sensors are estimated from the sensors on PIP joints.

V. Conclusion

In this paper, we described a useful method using a low-priced data-glove based on hand motion patterns. It estimates all finger joint angles using the data glove whose sensors cover only the middle angle of each finger. The method has been expanded from our previous method using a data-glove whose sensors cover two joints of each finger. A data glove is one of the major interfaces which are used in the field of VR. It measures curvatures of fingers using bend sensor. However, in order to obtain accurate hand motions, it is necessary to use an expensive data glove which has many sensors. On the other hand, there is a low cost data glove which measures an angle for each finger through one sensor.

It cannot get detailed data directly. Our method estimates plausible user hand motion patterns using each relation among angles of fingers during the operation of the low-cost glove first. Then, it estimates all finger joint angles by estimating the types of hand motion patterns from the correlation between each finger angle in the hand motion pattern. We assumed some representative hand motion patterns, and considered that other hand motions could be represented as synthetic motion of these. The ratio of each representative motion pattern is calculated using Moore-Penrose pseudo-inverse matrix, and all finger angles are estimated using multiple regression analysis. With the low priced data-glove being useful, it is expected that VR systems that target households will become more popular. In the future, we should reconsider the representative hand motion patterns because we removed Parallel Ext. from our previous research based on medical knowledge. We should also expand the target hand motion patterns to various ones that are not only grasping patterns.

ACKNOWLEDGMENT

The authors would like to thank our colleagues in our laboratory for useful discussions.

REFERENCES

[1] P. Temoche, E. Ramirez, and O. Rodrigues., "A Low-cost Data Glove for Virtual Reality," in *Proceedings of the XI International Congress of Numerical Methods in Engineering and Applied Sciences (CIMENICS)*, 2012, pp. TCG31–36.

[2] F. Camastra and D. Felice, "LVQ-based Hand Gesture Recognition using a Data Glove," in *Proceedings of the Neural Nets and Surroundings Smart Innovation, Systems and Technologies*, vol. 19, 2013, pp. 159–168.

[3] N. Tongrod, T. Kerdcharoen, N. Watthanawisuth, and A. Tuantranont, "A Low-Cost Data-Glove for Human Computer Interaction Based on Ink-Jet Printed Sensors and ZigBee Networks," in *Proceedings of the International Symposium on Wearable Computers (ISWC)*, 2010, pp. 1–2.

[4] H. Takahashi and K. Funahashi, "A Data Adjustment Method of Low-priced Data-glove based on Representative Hand Motion Using Medical Knowledge," in *Proceedings of the ICAT2013*, 2013, (USB Flash Drive, no page number).

[5] N. Kamakura, H. Matsuo, M. Ishii, and Y. Mitsuboshi, F. Miura, "Patterns of Static Prehension in Normal Hands," *Am J Occup Ther 34*, pp. 437–445, 1980.

[6] G. Elkoura, "Handrix: Animating the Human hand," in *Proceedings of the ACM SIGGRAPH/Eurographics Symposium on Computer Animation*, 2003, pp. 110–119.

[7] C. Capriani, "Objectives, criteria and methods for the design of the SmartHand transradial prosthesis," in *Proceedings of the Robotica 2010*, vol. 28, 2010, pp. 919–927.

Obtaining Shape from Endoscope Image Using Medical Suture with Two Light Sources

Hiroyasu Usami Yuji Iwahori

Department of Computer Science
Chubu University
Kasugai, 487-8501 Japan
Mail:usami@cvl.cs.chubu.ac.jp
Mail:iwahori@cs.chubu.ac.jp

Boonserm Kijsirikul

Dept. of Computer Engineering
Chulalongkorn University
Bangkok, 10330 Thiland
Mail:Boonserm.K@chula.ac.th

M. K. Bhuyan

Dept. of Electronics
and Electrical Engineering
Indian Institute of Technology Guwahati
Guwahati, 781039 India
Mail:mkb@iitg.ernet.in

Aili Wang

Higher Education Key Lab
Harbin University of Science and Technology
Harbin, 150080 China
Mail:aili925@hrbust.edu.cn

Kunio Kasugai

Dept. of Gastroenterology
Aichi Medical University
Nagakute, 480-1195 Japan
Mail:kuku3487@aichi-med-u.ac.jp

***Abstract*—Obtaining polyp size and shape is important for the medical diagnosis. In this paper, a 3-D shape reconstruction of computer vision technology is introduced in the medical diagnosis for this purpose. Some approaches based on Shape from Shading have been proposed for polyp in endoscope image. Previous approaches need some parameters such as depth parameter Z from endoscope lens to the surface point and reflectance parameter C. In the endoscope image, it is important to obtain these parameters for accurate polyp shape recovery. This paper proposes a new approach for obtaining parameters Z and C from one endoscope image where a medical suture is taken. A medical suture is used to estimate the horizontal plane locally and an observation model of medical suture is used with the horizontal plane. Two light sources endoscope observation system is assumed based on the actual endoscope for improving the accuracy of the polyp shape recovery. Experiments are conducted to validate the proposed approach.**

Keywords–Shape from Shading; Endoscope; Point Light Source; Perspective Projection; Camera Calibration; Reflectance Parameter.

I. Introduction

The size of a colonic polyp is a biomarker that correlates with its risk of malignancy and guides its clinical management. Given this central role of polyp size as a biomarker, the precision and accuracy of polyp measurement is an important issue [1]. In addition, advanced adenomas are those that are larger ($\geq 1cm$) or that contain appreciable villous tissue or high-grade dysplasia [2]. Therefore, obtaining polyp size and shape is important for the precise diagnosis.

For these situations, it becomes more important to develop a medical supporting application of computer vision in the medical field, where the 3-D shape reconstruction is expected to be practically used in the medical diagnosis. As a 3-D shape reconstruction technology, Shape from Shading (SFS) [3] is one valuable approach of 3-D reconstruction. SFS uses the image intensity directly to recover the surface orientation of a target object from a single image. Based on SFS, some approaches [4] [5] have been proposed to recover polyp shape from endoscope images. The paper [4] proposes a polyp recovering approach using both photometric and geometric constraints, assuming an endoscope with one light source. Another approach [5] recovers polyp shape assuming a more actual endoscope, which has two light sources, and it uses a neural network to modify the obtained surface gradients.

These polyp shape recovery approaches based on SFS assume a Lambertian image and need some parameters such as a depth parameter Z from the endoscope lens to the surface point. To obtain the depth Z, paper [6] proposes an approach using two images using a medical suture between the movement of Z direction in endoscope video under the assumption of one light source.

To relax the constraint for shape recovery, this paper proposes a novel approach for obtaining depth Z and surface reflectance parameter C from a single endoscope image of medical suture. Medical suture is used to estimate its horizontal plane locally and observation model of medical suture is used with the horizontal plane. In addition, two light source endoscope is assumed to improve the accuracy of polyp shape based on the actual endoscope.

Experiments of polyp shape recovery are conducted with the estimated parameters and it is shown that polyp shape is recovered with its absolute size.

The rest of the paper is structured as follows. In section II, the logic of the proposed approach is explained. In section III, experiments are conducted to validate the proposed approach and the conclusion of the proposed method is referred in section IV.

II. Proposed Approach

A. Procedure

The proposed approach consists of the following steps. First, camera calibration is conducted to obtain the inner parameters of the endoscope and subsequent steps are based on these obtained parameters. Second, the horizontal plane of the medical suture for the lens plane is estimated locally. Third, depth Z and the reflectance parameter C are obtained by using the estimated horizontal plane and its observation model of horizontal plane of medical suture. Finally, the polyp shape is recovered using the obtained Z and C based on two light sources photometric constraint.

Step1 Estimating inner parameters of the endoscope by conducting camera calibration.

Step2 Estimating the horizontal plane of medical suture to the lens plane locally.

Step3 Obtaining Z and C using observation model of horizontal plane of medical suture.

Step4 Recovering polyp shape using obtained depth Z and reflectance parameter C assuming two light source endoscope based on the approach [5].

B. Camera Calibration

First, the inner parameters of the endoscope are obtained by a camera calibration assuming two light source endoscope for the subsequent approaches.

1) Observation System: The observation system of endoscope is assumed to be a point light source and perspective projection. According to the actual environment of the endoscope, two light point sources are assumed to obtain the accurate results in parameter estimation and shape recovery. The observation system of two light sources endoscope is shown in Figure 1. Here, let the coordinate of the center of lens be $(0, 0, 0)$, f be the focal length, $\mathbf{S_1}$ and $\mathbf{S_1}$ be the distances from the lens to the surface point and $\mathbf{n}$ be the normal surface vector.

2) Estimating Inner Parameters of Endoscope: Estimating inner parameters of the endoscope is performed using multiple images of checker board taken by the endoscope based on the camera calibration techniques [7] [8]. An example of checker board images used in the proposed approach is shown in Figure 2.

Figure 2. Examples of Checker Board Images

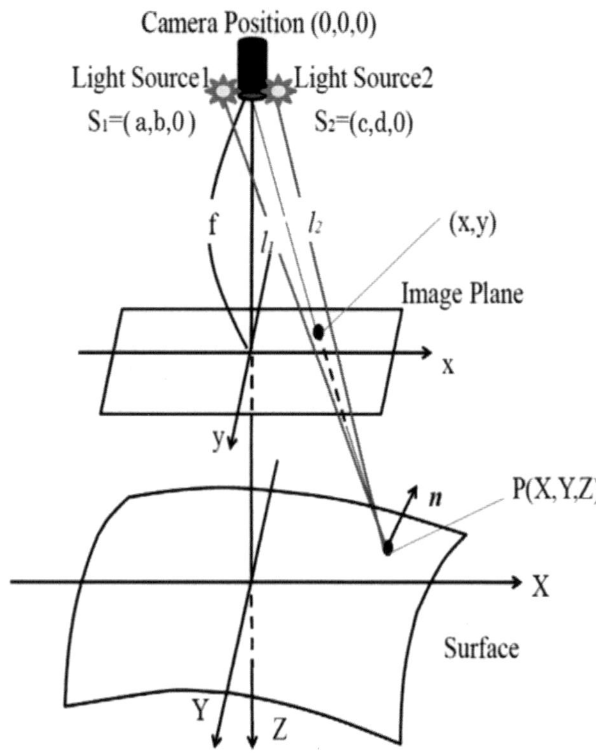

Figure 1. Observation System of Two Light Source Endoscope.

C. Estimation of Parameters Using Medical Suture

1) Estimation of Parameters: Parameters Z and C for shape recovery under SFS approach are obtained by estimating the horizontal plane of medical suture locally using its observation system. The procedures for obtaining parameters Z and C are shown in the following steps.

Step1 Estimating horizontal plane of medical suture locally from a single image.

Step2 Obtaining the depth Z using the horizontal plane of medical suture using its observation system.

Step3 Obtaining C using two light source photometric constraint.

The details of these steps are described below.

2) Estimation of Horizontal Plane: The horizontal planes of columnar forms against the lens can be obtained by considering the continuity of width from the columnar centerline to both end edges. The columnar width cut out by horizontal plane against the lens (as shown in Figure 3) continues while the cropped region is horizontal against the lens. The horizontal planes of medical suture can be obtained locally based on this property from one endoscope image.

The procedure of obtaining the horizontal plane is as follows.

Step1 Extract the medical suture region5 from original image4.

Step2 Extract the medical suture centerline by applying thinning processing as shown in Figure 6.

Step3 Extract medical suture edge using the morphology operation as shown in Figure 7.

Step4 Draw a line orthogonal to the centerline and crop the line by both end edges. Finally, extract regions where the cropped line continues the same width as shown in Figure 8.

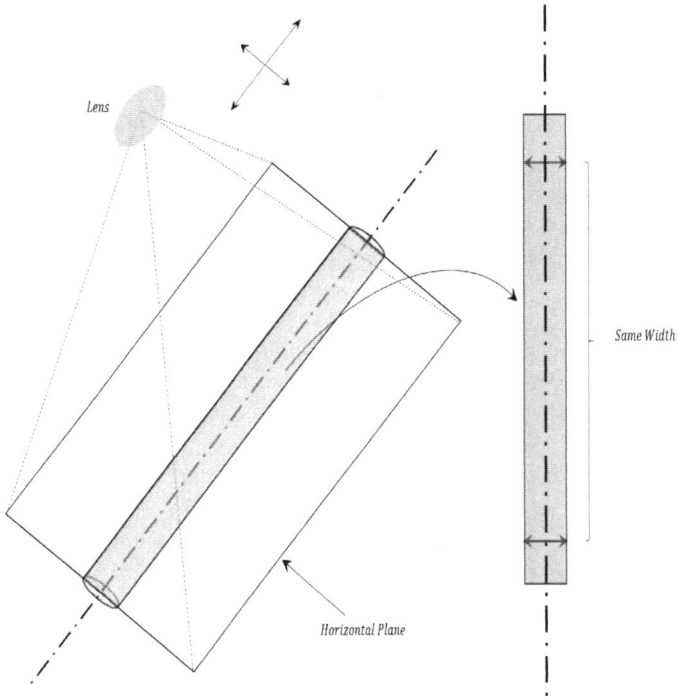

Figure 3. Horizontal Plane of Columnar against Lens

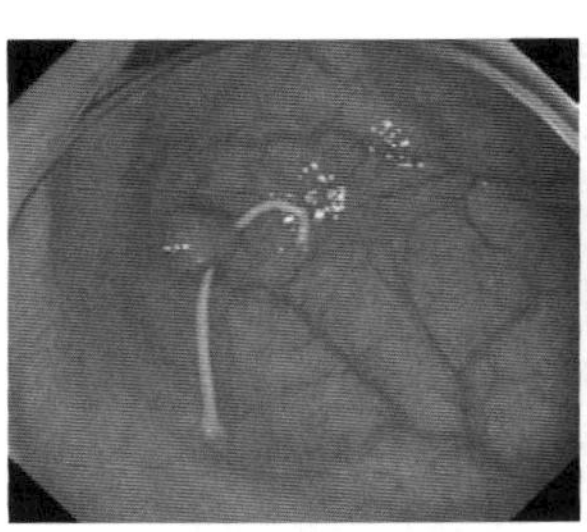

Figure 4. Original Image of Medical Suture

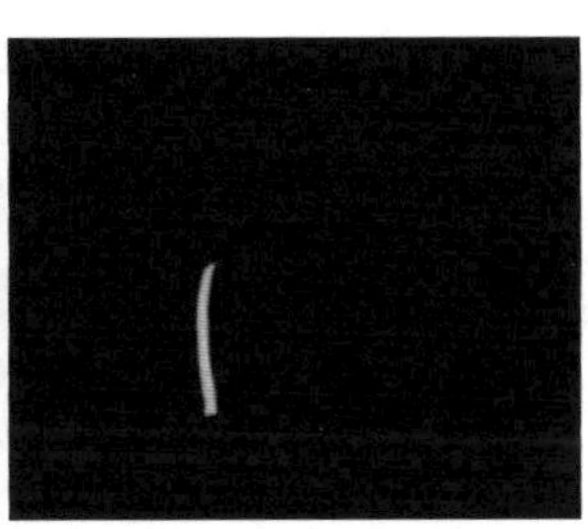

Figure 5. Example of Extracted Medical Suture Region

Figure 6. Example of Line Thinning Processing

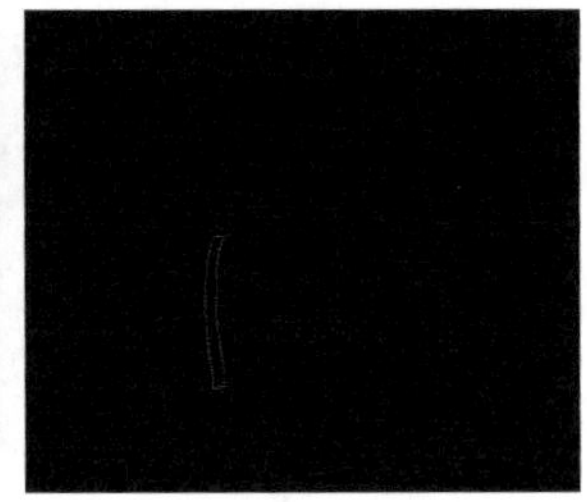

Figure 7. Example of Edge Extraction

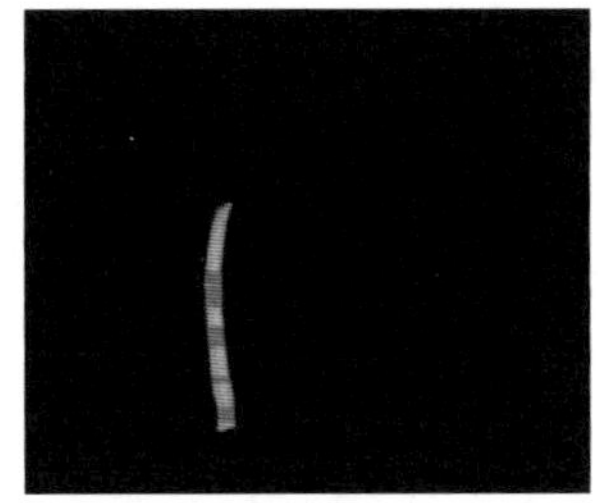

Figure 8. Example of Estimation of Horizontal Plane

3) Estimation of Depth Z: Here, an observation system of the horizontal plane of medical suture is proposed to obtain the depth parameter Z from the endoscope lens to the surface point. The observation system is shown in Figure 9.

Depth Z from the lens can be calculated using the model with respect to the estimated horizontal plane of medical suture. The procedure for calculating parameter Z is described below.

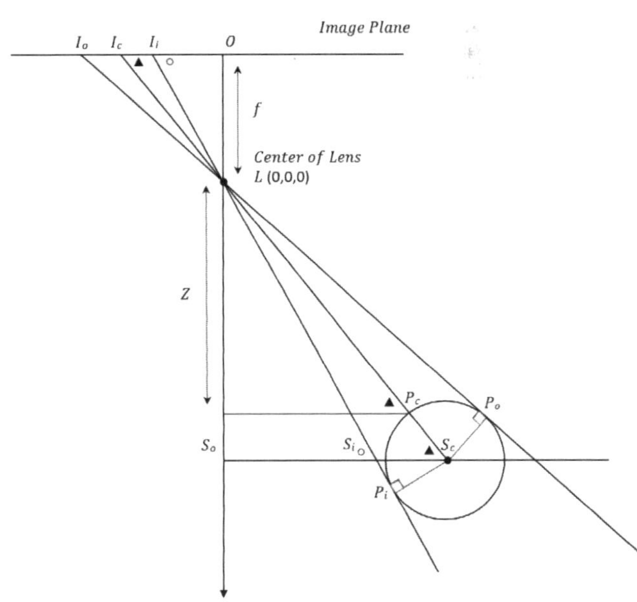

Figure 9. Observation System of Horizontal Plane

From $\triangle LOI_i \sim \triangle LS_oS_i$, $\angle LS_iS_o$ is an external angle of

$\triangle LS_oS_i$, $\angle LS_iS_c$ is obtained by Equation (1).

$$\angle LS_iS_c = \pi - \angle LI_iO \tag{1}$$

From $\triangle LOI_c \sim \triangle LS_oS_c$, $\triangle LS_cS_o$ is given by Equation (2).

$$\angle LS_cS_i = \angle LI_cO \tag{2}$$

$$\angle S_iLS_c = \pi - \angle LS_iS_c - \angle LS_cS_i \tag{3}$$

Similarly, $\angle LS_cP_i$ can be obtained from Equation (4).

$$\angle LS_cP_i = \pi - \frac{\pi}{2} - \angle S_iLS_c \tag{4}$$

Focusing on the hypotenuse from the lens L to the center of the suture center S_i in $\triangle LS_cS_i$, distance LS_c can be obtained from Equation (5). Here, distance P_cS_c is the same as the suture radius.

$$LS_c = \frac{P_iS_c}{cos\angle LS_cP_i} \tag{5}$$

The distance from the lens L to the surface of the suture P_c can be obtained from Equation (6). Here, P_cS_c is the same as the suture radius.

$$LP_c = LS_c - P_cS_c \tag{6}$$

Finally, from $\triangle LZP_c \sim \triangle LOI_c$, the depth Z can be given by Equation (7).

$$Z = LP_csin\angle LI_cO \tag{7}$$

4) Estimation of Reflectance Parameter C: The reflectance parameter C is calculated using the obtained Z and two light sources photometric constraint. Let the coordinate of the center of lens be (0,0,0) as shown in Figure 1.

The image intensity E can be expressed using the inverse square law of illuminance, as shown in Equation (8).

$$E = C(\frac{\mathbf{n}\cdot\mathbf{s_1}}{l_1^2} + \frac{\mathbf{n}\cdot\mathbf{s_2}}{l_2^2}) \tag{8}$$

Here, $\mathbf{n}$ is the normal surface vector represented using gradient parameters (p,q)=$(\partial Z/\partial X,\, \partial Z/\partial Y)$ as

$$\mathbf{n} = \frac{[p,q,-1]}{\sqrt{p^2+q^2+1}} \tag{9}$$

$\mathbf{s}_1$ and $\mathbf{s}_2$ are the light sources direction vectors for light sources 1 and 2, respectively. l_1 and l_2 are the distances from light sources 1 and 2, respectively to the surface point.

Let the light sources direction vectors be $\mathbf{s}_1$ and $\mathbf{s}_2$, and let the position of light source 1 be $(a,b,0)$, let the position of light source 2 be $(c,d,0)$. Light source direction vectors are represented by Equation (10) as unit vectors.

$$\mathbf{s}_1 = \frac{[a-x, b-y, -Z]}{\sqrt{(a-x)^2+\sqrt{(b-y)^2+Z^2}}}$$
$$\mathbf{s}_2 = \frac{[c-x, d-y, -Z]}{\sqrt{(c-x)^2+\sqrt{(d-y)^2+Z^2}}} \tag{10}$$

Distances l_1 and l_2 are represented using the coordinates of each light sources as Equation (11).

$$l_1 = \sqrt{(a-x)^2+(b-y)^2+Z^2}$$
$$l_2 = \sqrt{(c-x)^2+(d-y)^2+Z^2} \tag{11}$$

Substituting Equation (9), Equation (10) and Equation (11) into $\mathbf{s_1}$, $\mathbf{s_2}$, $\mathbf{n}$, $\mathbf{l_1}$ and $\mathbf{l_2}$ gives

$$C = E\left\{\frac{\{(a-x)^2+(b-y)^2+f^2\}^{\frac{3}{2}}Z^2\sqrt{p^2+q^2+1}}{f^2(-p(a-x)-q(b-y)+f)} + \frac{\{(c-x)^2+(d-y)^2+f^2\}^{\frac{3}{2}}Z^2\sqrt{p^2+q^2+1}}{f^2(-p(c-x)-q(d-y)+f)}\right\} \tag{12}$$

where f is the focal length.

D. Shape Recovery Using Obtained Z and C

Shape recovery is performed using the obtained Z and C based on the paper [5]. The procedure for shape recovery is as follows.

- Step1 Uniform Lambertian image is generated by the method [9] which is converted from the original RGB (red, green, and blue) color model endoscope image.
- Step2 Recover the initial depth by optimization using photometric constraints under the condition of two light sources and using obtained Z and C.
- Step3 Apply NN (Neural Network) learning using gradient parameters (p,q) of a Lambertian sphere, which is used to modify the obtained surface gradient (p,q).
- Step4 Update the depth Z using optimization by treating the obtained gradient parameters (p,q) as constants again.

III. Experiments

Experiments were performed to evaluate the proposed method using actual endoscope images. Here, a medical suture with size 1-0 silk suture and its diameter 0.33mm is used in the endoscope image.

A. Result of Camera Calibration

The result of the camera calibration is shown in Table I. The inner parameters of the endoscope are focal length, principal point and radial distortion and those parameters were obtained by the camera calibration.

Here, two parameters were obtained respectively based on the aspect ratio of image.

TABLE I. Result of Estimation

Parameter	*Result of Calibration*
Focal length (pixels)	[718.7447 + / - 0.8387, 718.3827 + / - 0.8654]
Principal point (pixels)	[879.0439 + / - 0.4669, 533.5813 + / - 0.4240]
Radial distortion	[- 0.3913 + / - 0.0010, 0.1178 + / - 0.0008]

B. Result of Estimated Depth Z

Depth Z was estimated using the obtained inner parameters of the endoscope. The results of estimating the horizontal plane of medical suture are as shown in Figures 10 to Figure 17, respectively. Here, more than 6 continuous regions with same width are adapted as the horizontal plane section in tracing the suture center line.

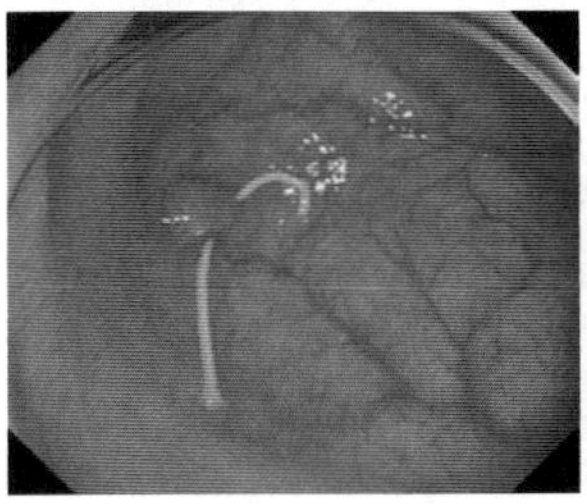

Figure 10. Scene1
Original Image

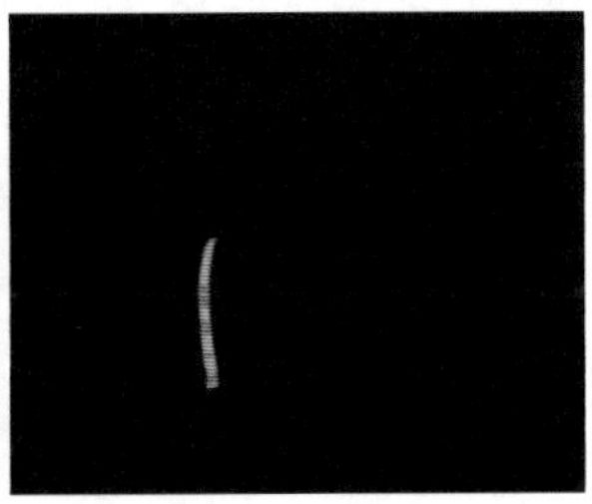

Figure 11. Scene1
Horizontal Plane

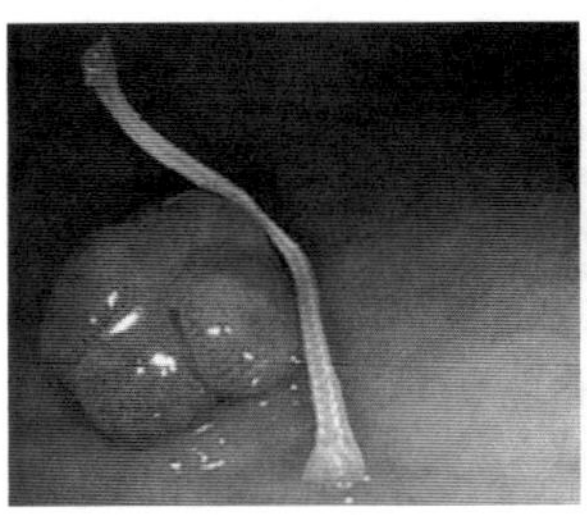

Figure 12. Scene2
Original Image

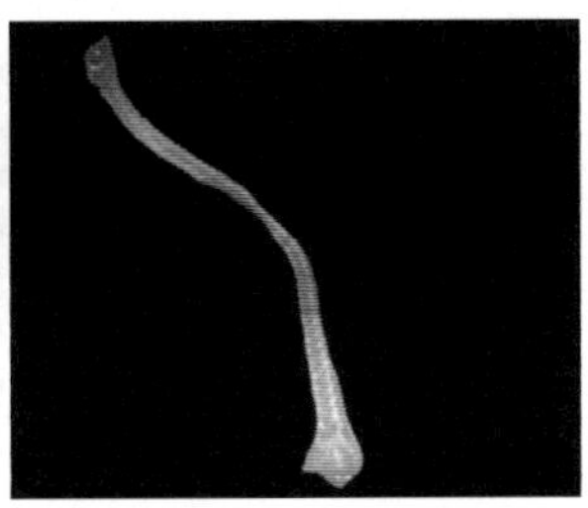

Figure 13. Scene2
Horizontal Plane

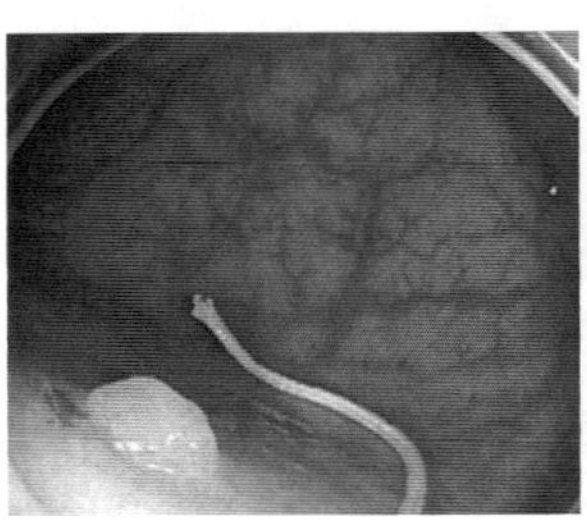

Figure 14. Scene3
Original Image

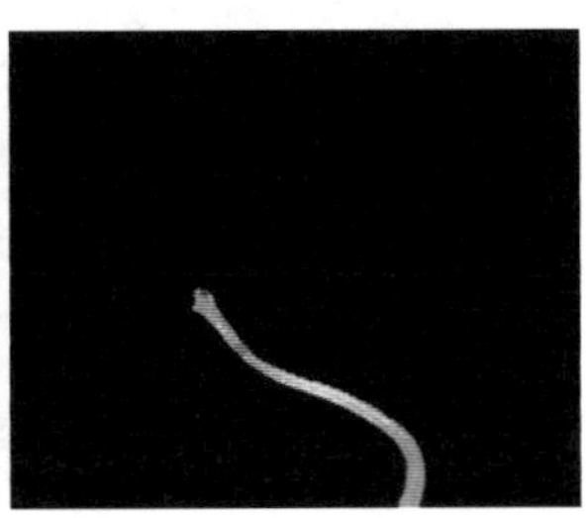

Figure 15. Scene3
Horizontal Plane

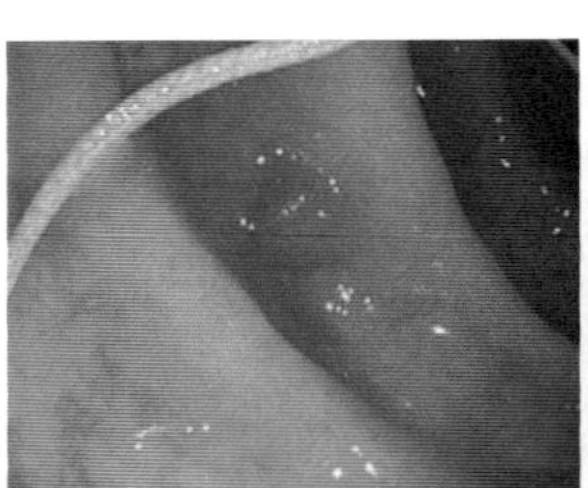

Figure 16. Scene4
Original Image

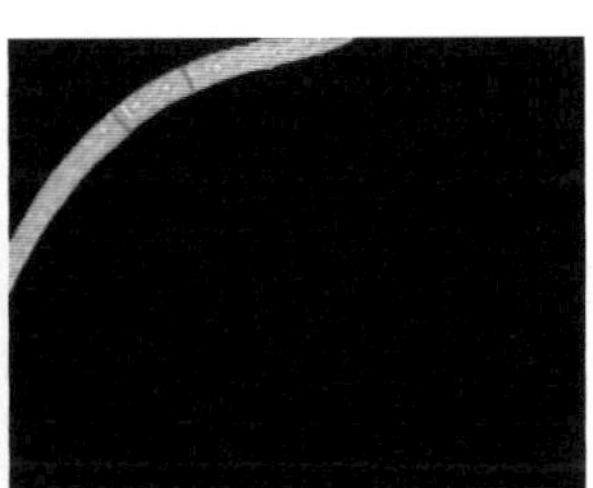

Figure 17. Scene4
Horizontal Plane

TABLE II. RESULT OF ESTIMATED Z

Scene	*Section*	*Estimated Z [mm]*	
		MEAN	STD
1	1	34.3456	0.0000
	2	34.3424	0.0044
	3	34.2384	0.0051
	4	34.1847	0.0081
	5	34.9362	0.0086
2	1	30.8150	7.7443
	2	17.0185	0.0000
3	1	34.5360	0.0028
4	1	13.9666	2.6010
	2	15.1002	0.0000

The result of depth Z estimation for each scene and estimated horizontal section are shown in Table II. From these results, the horizontal section of medical suture within $[nm]$ level variation of the depth Z could be obtained in each scene. It is shown that the horizontal plane of the medical suture and depth Z were obtained with high accuracy in each endoscope image.

C. Result of Shape Recovery

Polyp shape recovery was performed using calculated Z and C. The results of polyp shape recovery are shown in Figures 18 to 21. Here, some regions which interfere with the shape recovery such as a hood cover of the endoscope were cut out. From the recovered shapes, it is confirmed that approximate polyp shape could be recovered using the calculated parameters Z and C of the proposed approach.

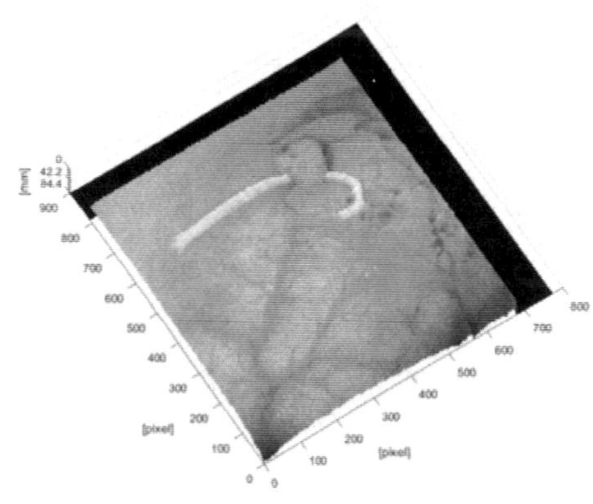

Figure 18. Recovered Shape of Scene1

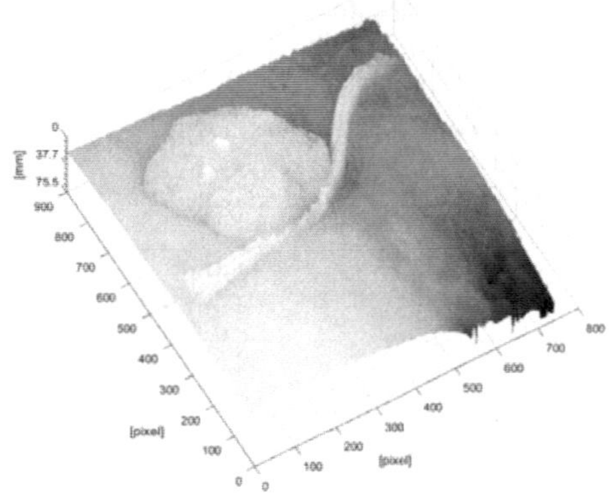

Figure 19. Recovered Shape of Scene2

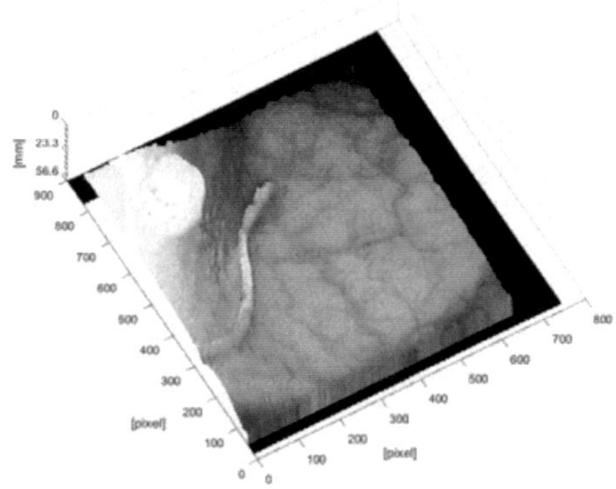

Figure 20. Recovered Shape of Scene3

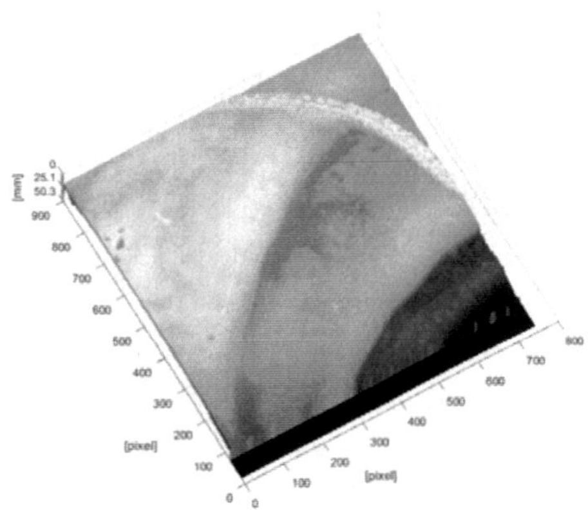

Figure 21. Recovered Shape of Scene4

IV. CONCLUSION

This paper proposed a new approach for obtaining depth parameter Z from endoscope lens to the surface point and reflectance parameter C from one endoscope image of medical suture by estimating the horizontal plane of medical suture locally and its observation model. The result shows that approximate polyp shape could be recovered using the calculated parameters Z and C. Applying this proposed method to the blood vessel for mitigating constraint conditions and improving the accuracy of shape recovery are left as future works.

ACKNOWLEDGEMENT

Iwahori's research is supported by JSPS Grant-in-Aid for Scientific Research (C)(26330210) and Chubu University Grant.

REFERENCES

[1] R. M. Summers, "Polyp size measurement at ct colonography: What do we know and what do we need to know? 1," Radiology, vol. 255, no. 3, 2010, pp. 707–720.

[2] J. H. Bond, "Polyp guideline: diagnosis, treatment, and surveillance for patients with colorectal polyps," The American journal of gastroenterology, vol. 95, no. 11, 2000, p. 3053.

[3] B. K. Horn, "Obtaining shape from shading information," in Shape from shading. MIT press, 1989, pp. 123–171.

[4] Y. Iwahori, K. Tatematsu, T. Nakamura, S. Fukui, R. J. Woodham, and K. Kasugai, "3d shape recovery from endoscope image based on both photometric and geometric constraints," in Knowledge-Based Information Systems in Practice. Springer, 2015, pp. 65–80.

[5] H. Usami, Y. Hanai, Y. Iwahori, and K. Kasugai, "3d shape recovery of polyp using two light sources endoscope," in Computer and Information Science (ICIS), 2016 IEEE/ACIS 15th International Conference on. IEEE, 2016, pp. 1–6.

[6] Y. Iwahori, Y. Daiki, T. Nakamura, K. Boonserm, B. M. K., and K. Kunio, "Estimating reflectance parameter of polyp using medical suture information in endoscope image," in ICPRAM, 2016, pp. 503–509.

[7] Z. Zhang, "A flexible new technique for camera calibration," IEEE Transactions on pattern analysis and machine intelligence, vol. 22, no. 11, 2000, pp. 1330–1334.

[8] J. Heikkila and O. Silvén, "A four-step camera calibration procedure with implicit image correction," in Computer Vision and Pattern Recognition, 1997. Proceedings., 1997 IEEE Computer Society Conference on. IEEE, 1997, pp. 1106–1112.

[9] Y. Shimasaki, Y. Iwahori, D. R. Neog, R. J. Woodham, and M. Bhuyan, "Generating lambertian image with uniform reflectance for endoscope image," in PRoceedings of the International Workshop on Advanced Image Technology (IWAIT'13), 2013, pp. 60–65.

Polyp Classification Using Multiple CNN-SVM Classifiers from Endoscope Images

Masataka Murata Hiroyasu Usami Yuji Iwahori

Department of Computer Science
Chubu University
Kasugai, 487-8501 Japan
Email: {mmurata|usami}@cvl.cs.chubu.ac.jp
Email: iwahori@cs.chubu.ac.jp

Wang Aili

Higher Education Key Lab
Harbin University of Science and Technology
Harbin, 150080 China
Email: aili925@hrbust.edu.cn

Naotaka Ogasawara Kunio Kasugai

Department of Gastroenterology
Aichi Medical University
Nagakute, 480-1195 Japan
Email: {nogasa|kuku3487}@aichi-med-u.ac.jp

***Abstract*—This paper proposes a classification approach of a malignant or bening polyp type by multiple CNN-SVM classifiers using Convolutional Neural Networks (CNN) as feature extractor and Support Vector Machine (SVM) as classifier from three kinds of endoscope images as white light image, dye image and Narrow Band Image (NBI). First, the polyp feature is extracted using CNN as feature extractor from three kinds of endoscope images using each datasets. Second, classifiers are generated as many as three kinds of combinations using SVM and each image is classified. Finally, the final classification result is judged by voting processing from the result obtained by each classifier. The effectiveness of the proposed method was confirmed through experiments in which both validity and accuracy of multiple CNN-SVM voting results were evaluated using actual malignant or benign polyp images.**

***Keywords*–Polyp Classification; Endoscope Image; Voting Processing; Pre-Trained Network; Convolutional Neural Network; Support Vector Machine.**

I. INTRODUCTION

The polyp diagnosis is conducted using the endoscope in the medical scene, according to the prevalence rate of colorectal cancer has been increasing. There are various forms of polyps, such as protuberance type, surface flat type, surface recessed type and so on. These shapes are used as a reference when judging the malignancy/benignity of polyps. However, it is difficult to judge if a polyp is benign/malignant only by its shape, in some cases, and the diagnostic result of polyp using endoscope depends on the experience of the medical doctor. There are many cases where correct diagnosis is obtained by the medical doctor as the pathological diagnosis judges correctly. Therefore, it is necessary to develop a computer-aided system with computer vision technology to eliminate the difference in the diagnosis results from the experience of the doctor and to reduce the burden of the medical provider.

As a method to judge the malignant/benign polyp from endoscope images, some methods [1][2] have been proposed. In these methods [1][2], a ultra-high magnification endoscope is used for the polyp diagnosis with high precision. The ultra-high magnification endoscope has higher magnification than regular endoscope and it enables the diagnosis at the cell level. However, it requires a lot of diagnosis time when ultrahigh magnification is used, and this would put additional burden on the patient.

Therefore, this paper proposes a method to classify malignant or benign polyp using regular endoscope images.

Actually, there are many non-polyp scenes in endoscope video of the regular endoscope, which makes it difficult to classify the malignant or benign polyp. Therefore, for our proposed method, a necessary condition is that only the polyp images be used as the target. Paper [3] and [4] were proposed for polyp detection. These papers detect polyps with the rectangles (as shown in Figure 1). There are three types of images which are taken by the regular endoscope: with white light, dye and narrow band image (NBI) in general. These three kinds of images have different characteristics and the difficulty of classification level of malignant or benign polyp depends on the condition of each image. In this paper, the polyp region is extracted with the rectangle by methods [3][4] and three types of images taken by the regular endoscope are used for the classification. Accurate classification of malignant or benign polyp are tried from each image features for supporting the medical diagnosis.

Section II introduces the proposed method. Section III gives the result of our experiment. Finally, Section IV concludes the proposed method.

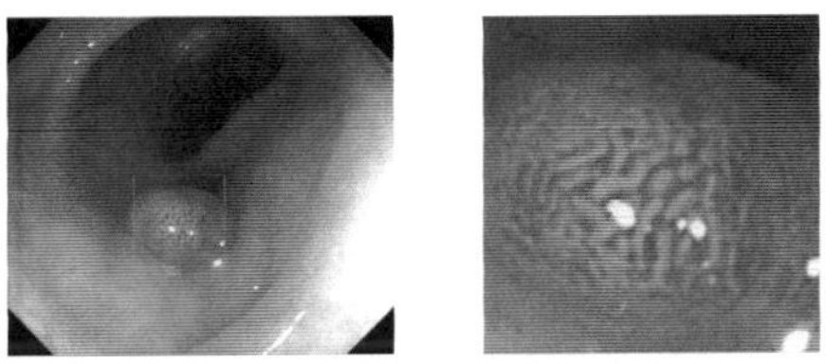

(a)Result of Detection (b)Region of Rectangle

Figure 1. Detected Polyp

II. Proposed Method

Our proposed method uses features [5][6] obtained by pre-trained network for malignant or benign polyp classification. Specifically, each feature is extracted from Convolutional Neural Network (CNN) [7] using each of three kinds of images with white light, dye and NBI, respectively. Multiple Support Vector Machine (SVM) [8] is used for the classification of diagnosis using extracted CNN features.

The procedure of the proposed method is as follows (as shown in Figure 2).

- Step 0 Assign labels to endoscope images.
- Step 1 Extract CNN features obtained from each input image of three kinds of images.
- Step 2 Construct multiple SVM classifiers using CNN features.
- Step 3 Extract features for evaluation with CNN as Step 1.
- Step 4 Classify malignant or benign polyp using multiple SVM classifiers constructed in Step 2 using features obtained in Step 3.
- Step 5 Determine the final result by a voting process using the classified result of multiple SVM classifiers.

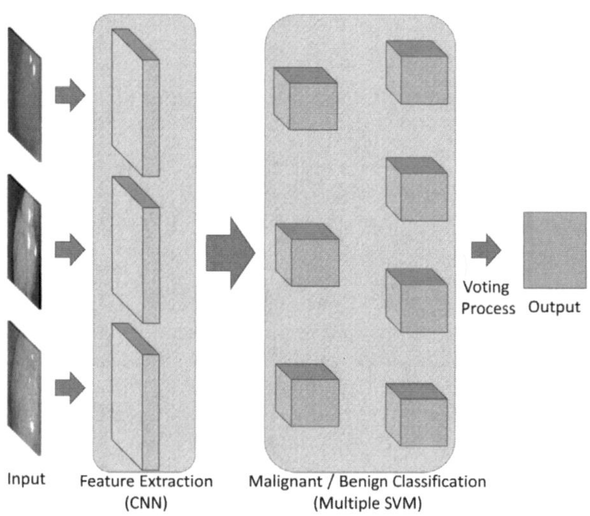

Figure 2. Flow of The Proposed Method

A. Assign Label to Endoscope Images

There are White Light (Figure 3(a)(d)), Dye (Figure 3(b)(e)) and NBI (Figure 3(c)(f)) that can be taken by the regular endoscope. These endoscope images have different characteristics and they have the following features.

- White Light: Taken in normal condition.
- Dye: Taken with indigo carmine stain solution or crystal violet stain solution sprayed on the polyp, and the irregularities of the lesion are emphasized.
- NBI: Taken in the state irradiated with light which is easily absorbed by hemoglobin in the blood different from normal light and its blood vessels and patterns are emphasized around the lesion.

Assign labels to these image as malignant polyp (Figure 3(d)(e)(f)) or benign (Figure 3(a)(b)(c)) polyp and also assign labels on the types of the above endoscope images. Six kinds of labels are attached, as shown in the Figure 3.

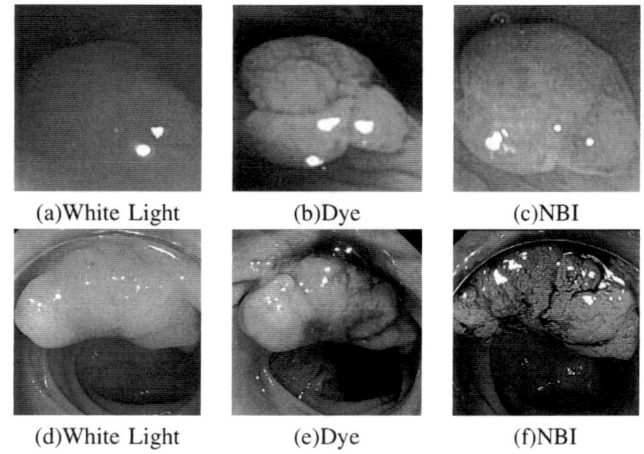

Figure 3. Endoscope Image

B. Feature Extraction Using CNN

Differences in polyp features are necessary to classify the malignancy/benignity of a polyp. However, it is difficult in general to use the empirical feature, such as Scale invariant feature transform (SIFT) [9] to classify malignancy/benignity polyp. CNN is highly evaluated as a feature extractor in recent years and the CNN feature is used for feature extraction in case of the polyp images. AlexNet [10] is used as a model of CNN for feature extraction and corresponding 4096-dimensional polyp features are extracted from each of the seventh layers among totally connected layers with input of each of three kinds of endoscopic images: white light, dye, and NBI.

1) Convolutional Neural Network: CNN is a network consisting of convolution layers that perform local feature extraction of images and pooling layers that collect extracted features where feature extraction and classification are performed in a network. Recently, it has been treated as a feature extractor by using only the feature extraction location, and it has been proved to have highly general versatility as a feature extractor.

2) AlexNet: AlexNet is a model learned for image classification using the classification task of ILSVRC 2012 and it is CNN consisting of 8 layers (as shown in Figure 4). This CNN model extracts features of 4096-dimensions for each input image and performs classification of 1000 classes. In this paper, feature extraction is obtained from the seventh layer as all connected layers of AlexNet.

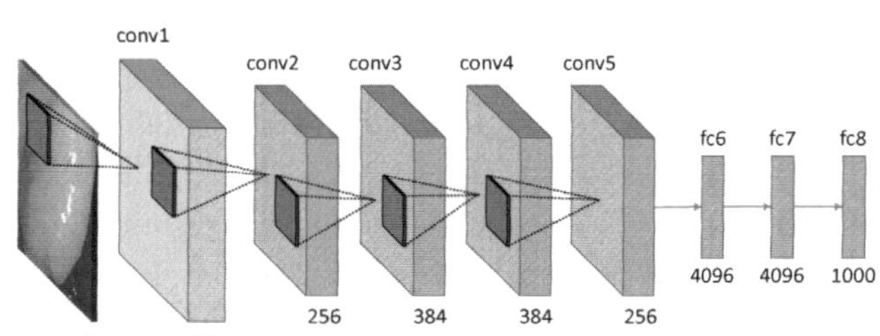

Figure 4. Alexnet layers

C. Construction of Classifiers Using Extracted Features

Classifiers of malignant or benign polyps are constructed using the extracted features described in Section II-B. SVM is used as classifier and it is constructed for three kinds of features consisting of white light, dye and NBI extracted from CNN, but the condition changes based on which image type is easy to be classified as malignant or benign polyp. Classifiers are constructed for the maximum number of combinations consisting of three kinds of features, and each classifier corresponds to each kind of image. Each classifier easily classifies malignant or benign polyp or not depending on polyp. Here, the input of each classifier is corresponding image features which were used when constructing each one. The output of each classifier is each diagnosis result of input images. Table I shows the combination type of features and the number of classifications.

TABLE I. COMBINATION

Combination of Features	*Number of Classifications*
White Light	1
Dye	1
NBI	1
White Light + Dye	2
White Light + NBI	2
Dye + NBI	2
White Light + Dye + NBI	3

D. Classification Result with Voting Processing

The result of each classifier constructed with the method from Section II-C may be different even for the same polyp depending on the kind of image. Therefore, the final result is determined by combining the results from each classifier. In the voting processing, classification score as the classification result obtained from each SVM is added to the evaluation score so that the reliability of the final score is improved rather than only handling one classification as one vote. Here, the approach handles the classification score as a weight of one vote. The calculation formula of the voting process is shown in Equation (1).

Here, "Label" represents the classification score derived from Equation (2), "Score" represents the classification score of the result classified by SVM, n represents the number of classification classes, "Decision" represens the classification result of SVM, "Benign" indicates probability of a benign polyp, "Malignant" indicates probability of a malignant polyp.

$$Label = \sum_{n=0}^{12} Score_n \tag{1}$$

$$Label = \begin{cases} Benign & (if\ Decision = Benign) \\ Malignant & (otherwise) \end{cases} \tag{2}$$

Based on the probabilities of a benign polyp and the probability of a malignant polyp calculated by Equation (1), the final result is determined by the larger value as shown in Equation (3).

Here, "result" represents the final result.

$$result = \begin{cases} Benign & (if\ Benign > Malignant) \\ Malignant & (otherwise) \end{cases} \tag{3}$$

As described above, voting processing is performed using classification scores from the results classified from seven classifiers. This solves the difficulties of classification derived from the difference of polyps. Simultaneously, the accuracy of classification becomes higher than classification by each classifier.

III. EXPERIMENT

Experiments were performed to validate the proposed method. The datasets used in the experiment were polyp images obtained as the rectangle detected by methods [3][4]. In order to increase the dataset, images were added with three types of rotation processing to the original image. In addition, since the label of the dataset of the learning image is unbalanced, undersampling on malignant/benign labels was performed in this experiment. Tables II and III show the number of the learning images and the test images, respectively.

TABLE II. TRAINIMAGE

	Malignant	*Benign*
White Light	188	380
Dye	112	408
NBI	32	140

TABLE III. TESTIMAGE

	Malignant	*Benign*
White Light	180	180
Dye	180	180
NBI	180	180

Table IV shows the kind of classifier consisting of each combination and correct/incorrect number of malignant and benign polyps with the voting processing. As evaluation of classification accuracy, each of *Sensitivity*, *Specificity*, *Accuracy*, *Positive Predictive Value* (*PPV*) and *Negative Predictive Value* (*NPV*) were calculated by the following formula.

TABLE IV. CLASSIFICATION RESULT

	Malignant		Benign	
	True	False	True	False
White Light	149	31	132	48
Dye	94	86	167	13
NBI	59	121	158	22
White Light + Dye	130	50	156	24
White Light + NBI	52	128	140	40
Dye + NBI	122	58	152	28
White Light + Dye + NBI	118	62	153	27
Poll Result	152	28	164	16

True Positive (*TP*) represents numbers that classified malignant as malignant. *False Negative* (*FN*) represents numbers that classified malignant as benign. *False Positive* (*FP*) represents numbers that classified benign as malignancy. *True Positive* (*TP*) represents numbers that classified benign as benign.

Sensitivity represents the validity that classified malignant as malignant. *Specificity* represents the validity that classified benign as benign. *Accuracy* represents the whole validity. *PPV*

TABLE V. ACCURACY EVALUATION

	Sensitivity	*Specificity*	*Accuracy*	*PPV*	*NPV*
White Light	75.6	80.9	78.0	82.7	73.3
Dye	87.8	66.0	72.5	52.2	92.7
NBI	72.8	56.6	60.2	32.7	87.7
White Light + Dye	84.4	75.7	79.4	72.2	86.6
White Light + NBI	56.5	52.2	53.3	28.8	77.7
Dye + NBI	81.3	72.3	76.1	67.7	84.4
White Light + Dye + NBI	81.3	71.1	75.2	65.5	85.0
Poll Result	90.4	85.4	87.7	84.4	91.1

represents positive predictive value that classified malignant as malignant. *NPV* represents positive predictive value that classified benign as benign.

$$Sensitivity = \frac{TP}{TP+FP} \quad (4)$$

$$Specificity = \frac{TN}{FN+TN} \quad (5)$$

$$Accuracy = \frac{TP+TN}{TP+FN+FP+TN} \quad (6)$$

$$PPV = \frac{TP}{TP+FN} \quad (7)$$

$$NPV = \frac{TN}{FP+FN} \quad (8)$$

From Table IV, it is shown that the proposed method least misclassified the malignant polyps. In addition, Table V shows that both Sensitivity as validity of malignant polyp classification and PPV as predictive value of malignant polyp were obtained with high accuracy. When a malignant polyp was classified as a benign polyp, there would be a delay in polyp extraction that could become life-threatening. From these results, it is shown that the proposed method is useful for polyp diagnosis. Furthermore, the accuracy as the validity from all classifications shows high value in the proposed method. Error classification examples of benign polyp (a) (b) (c) and malignant polyp (d) (e) (f) are shown in Figure 5. A benign polyp has usually a round shape and a malignant polyp has a uneven shape with some feature on blood vessel. However, the polyps in Figure 5 have the opposite features and there is some possibility that this example is an incorrect classification result.

IV. CONCLUSION

In this paper, multiple CNN-SVM classifiers were constucted using three kinds of endoscope images taken by regular endoscope. The paper proposed a highly accurate classification method by integrating the results based on the voting processing. The effectiveness of the proposed method was confirmed via experiments using actual endoscopic images to classify malignant and benign polyps with CNN features and multiple SVM classifiers. As future work, some improvement is needed to reduce the misclassified polyps by increasing the number of dataset and constructing a specialized CNN model for endoscope images with fine tuning to get higher accuracy.

ACKNOWLEDGMENT

Iwahori's research is supported by Japan Society for the Promotion of Science (JSPS) Grant-in-Aid for Scientific Research (C) (23500228) and Chubu University Grant.

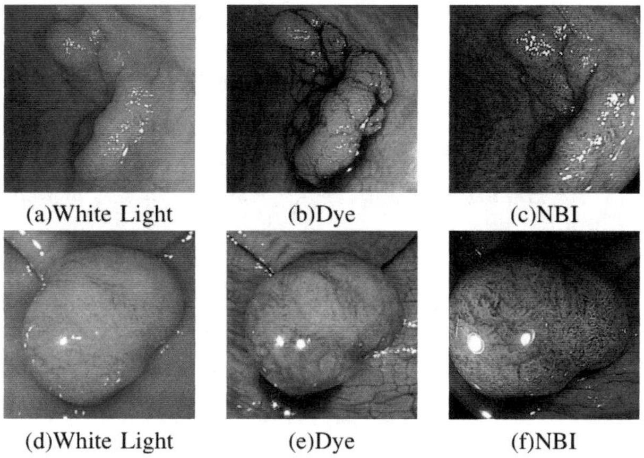

Figure 5. Example of Error Classification

REFERENCES

[1] Y. Mori et al., "Novel computer-aided diagnostic system for colorectal lesions by using endocytoscopy (with videos)." Gastrointestinal endoscopy, vol. 81, no. 3, 2015, pp. 621–629.

[2] M. Misawa et al., "Characterization of colorectal lesions using a computer-aided diagnostic system for narrow-band imaging endocytoscopy." Gastroenterology, 2016.

[3] H. Hiroaki, I. Yuji, and K. Kunio, "Automatic polyp detection from endoscope image using likelihood map based on edge information (in japanese)," in IEICE Technical Report, vol.115, no.401, 2015, pp. 193–198.

[4] U. Hiroyasu, O. Tsubasa, Yuji, Iwahori, and K. Kunio, "Automatic polyp region detection using watershed algorithm (in japanese)," in WiNF 2016, 2016, pp. B-22X.

[5] A. Sharif Razavian, H. Azizpour, J. Sullivan, and S. Carlsson, "Cnn features off-the-shelf: an astounding baseline for recognition," in Proceedings of the IEEE Conference on Computer Vision and Pattern Recognition Workshops, 2014, pp. 806–813.

[6] J. Donahue et al., "Decaf: A deep convolutional activation feature for generic visual recognition." in ICML, 2014, pp. 647–655.

[7] Y. LeCun, L. Bottou, Y. Bengio, and P. Haffner, "Gradient-based learning applied to document recognition," Proceedings of the IEEE, vol. 86, no. 11, 1998, pp. 2278–2324.

[8] B. Schölkopf and A. J. Smola, Learning with kernels: support vector machines, regularization, optimization, and beyond. MIT press, 2002.

[9] D. G. Lowe, "Object recognition from local scale-invariant features," in Computer vision, 1999. The proceedings of the seventh IEEE international conference on, vol. 2. IEEE, 1999, pp. 1150–1157.

[10] A. Krizhevsky, I. Sutskever, and G. E. Hinton, "Imagenet classification with deep convolutional neural networks," in Advances in neural information processing systems, 2012, pp. 1097–1105.

Defect Detection and Classification of Electronic Circuit Boards Using Keypoint Extraction and CNN Features

Yohei Takada Tokiko Shiina Hiroyasu Usami Yuji Iwahori

Department of Computer Science
Chubu University
Kasugai, 487-8501 Japan
email:{ytakada|shiina|usami}@cvl.cs.chubu.ac.jp
email:iwahori@cs.chubu.ac.jp

M. K. Bhuyan

Dept. of Electronics
and Electrical Engineering
Indian Institute of Technology Guwahati
Guwahati, 781039 India
email:mkb@iitg.ernet.in

Abstract—**This paper proposes a method for defect detection and classification of electronic circuit board by extracting keypoints without reference images. The final purpose is to distinguish a problematic defect, such as disconnection from a non-defect, dust in the manufacturing process et al. Keypoints are extracted from the electronic circuit board image, then a patch image is cropped using obtained keypoint information, such as the position. The cropped images are used as input to CNN (Convolutional Neural Network) and 4096-dimensional features are obtained in the final layer of the full connected layers. SVM (Support Vector Machine) is introduced for learning and classification using CNN features. The effectiveness of the proposed method is confirmed through a detection experiment using actual electronic circuit board images containing defects and by comparing the results with the previous method.**

Keywords–Defect Detection; Defect Classification; CNN; SVM; SURF.

I. Introduction

Electronic circuit boards are used as components of various precision instruments, such as computers and liquid crystal displays. Each layer is inspected after drawing and baking the mask pattern in the manufacturing process of the electronic circuit boards. There is Automated Optical Inspection (AOI) as a computer assisted automated visual inspection for circuit boards. The defect is judged from the loss rate of the lead wire portion in AOI, but the final goal is to determine if that defect is a true or a pseudo defect of the product. The inspections need to be done with high accuracy. The current AOI needs a subsequent final verification by the human eye to judge the existence of a defect. The human cost and variability of the inspection accuracy originating from individual checking ability are problems in the verification process. It is hoped to reduce this cost and to keep the accuracy for inspection with computer-aided defect inspection.

Defect types during the inspection consist of true defect and pseudo defect. True defects include chipping, breaking, protrusions, shorts, etc. True defects cannot be shipped as the products when these defects are found. On the other hand, pseudo defects have foreign matter adherence and stains and these can be removed after inspection. So, pseudo defets can be shipped as the product. If a true defect is erroneously classified into a pseudo defect, it becomes a problem. If a pseudo defect is erroneously classified as a true defect, the product will be discarded. Normal products are disposed of when a pseudo defect is erroneously classified as a true defect, and it causes reduction of production yield rate.

Papers [1] and [2] have been proposed to solve these problems using image processing. Paper [1] proposes a global defect inspection of defects by learning using Mahalanobis distance. Paper [2] supplies a current to the electronic circuit boards, and the defect is detected from the radiation position from the radiation infrared image by taking advantage of the characteristic that the short portion generates heat due to the leak current.

The works [3] - [4] have proposed the defect classification. Paper [3] classifies defect type using its shape informatio-nunder the assumption that the reference image is used for the classification. Paper [5] detects a candidate region of defect by taking the difference between the reference image and the test image. Feature quantities are obtained from the candidate region and two classes classification of true defect and pseudo defect is proposed using SVM. Mutiple subsets are constructed by random sampling of the dataset,thenn multiple classifiers are constructed based on each subsets feature. The data classification is performed by taking a majorityvote, and the stable accuracy is obtained if the number of learningdata is sufficient. However, it is necessary to prepare the reference images under inspection. The creation of the reference image requires positioning in units of pixels, and it costs much to create a reference image for each inspection image. Paper [4] proposes a defect classification method using Bag-of-Features as a method without using a reference image, while this paper deals with AVI (Automatic Visual Inspection) which is available to the simpler patterns of electronic circuit boards. The method cannot be directly applied to AOI.

This paper tries to improve the accuracy of detection and classification using features obtained by Convolutional Neural Network (CNN). The candidate defect region is extracted without reference image by keypoint extraction in defect classification, and features are extracted by inputting the cropped region into the CNN.

II. Types of Defect

True defect and pseudo defect are classified into several types depending on the color and shape of the defect portion.

A defect of the same type often has some variation based on the image, and this makes it difficult to classify it as a true or pseudo defect.

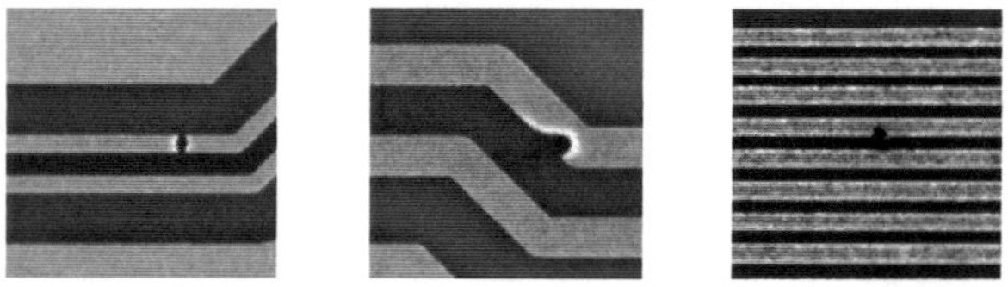

(a) Disconnection (b) Crack (c) Crack

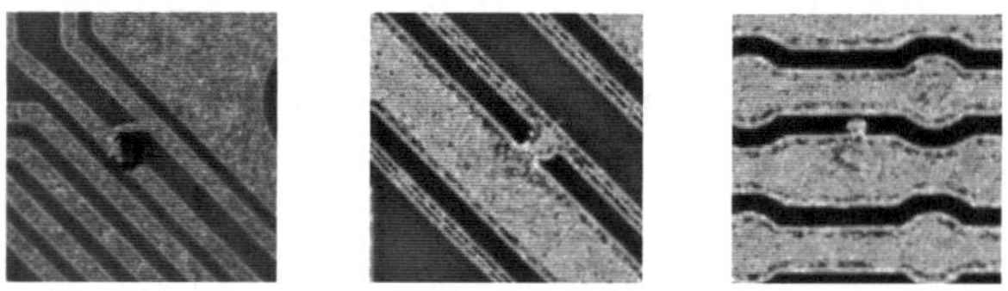

(d) Connection (e) Connection (f) Projection

Figure 1. Type of True Defects

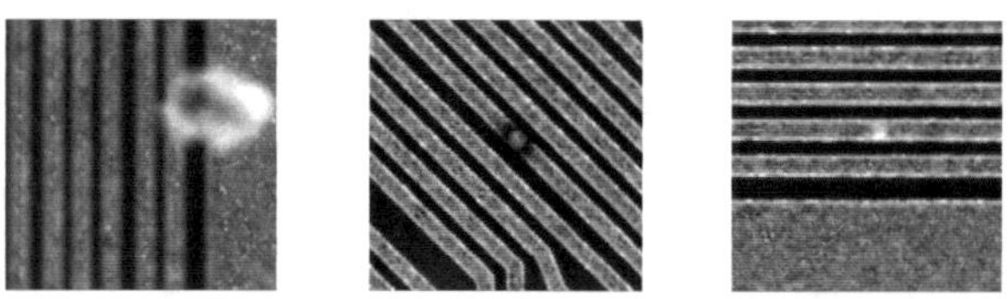

(a) Dust (b) Stain (c) Stain

Figure 2. Type of Pseudo Defects

It is confirmed that there is a difference in the intensity value of the edge portion in the crack defect as shown in Figure 1(b) and Figure 1(c). The connected part is thinner than the normal lead wire as shown in Figure 1(d), while a thicker part than the normal lead is observed in connection defect as shown in Figure 1(e). The appearance also differs even in the pseudo defect. It is confirmed that there is a difference in the radiance value of the defect part in the Figure 2(b) and Figure 2(c) which are stain defect. It is also confirmed that noise appears in the entire image.

III. Inspection Method Using Reference Image

In [5], a non-defect reference image is prepared for an image to be inspected. A difference is taken for each RGB channel and a binary conversion is performed on the difference image using a threshold value obtained from a discriminant analysis method. The defect region is detected by taking the logical sum of three binarized images (Figure (3)). Since the reference image should be aligned on a pixel-by-pixel basis at the time of creation and there may be multiple similar portions in the same electronic board, it takes cost to obtain the difference from the correct portion. The example result of defect detection using both inspection image and reference image is shown in Figure 3(c).

Feature quantities, such as maximum value, median value, mode value, and so on are extracted as a feature quantity from the detected defect region in each channel of RGB and HSV

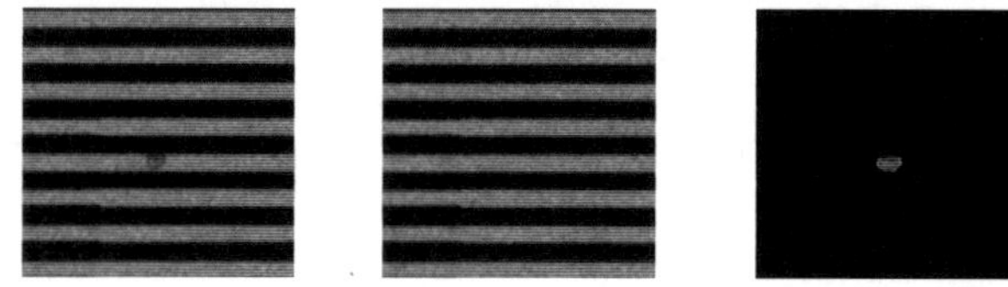

(a) Inspection Image (b) Reference Image (c) Result of Detection

Figure 3. Detection of Defect

(Hue, Saturation, Value) and so on. Subsets are created from the entire dataset using random sampling and multiple SVMs are constructed. The final result is decided by the majority vote using multiple SVMs.

IV. Proposed Method

The proposed method uses SURF, which is a keypoint extraction method, and extracts a defect candidate region without reference images. Features are obtained by inputting the extracted region to CNN, which is a feature extraction processing of Deep Learning. Both SVMs for defect detection and defect classification are constructed using the obtained features, and these SVMs perform defect detection and defect classification, respectively.

The procedure of the proposed method is as follows.

1) Convert the learning image to the HSV color representation system and detect the feature for the S channel using SURF.
2) Create a rectangle using the coordinates and scale of the obtained keypoint, and crop the image.
3) Label the image cropped from the defect portion or non-defect portion using the reference image.
4) Obtain features from the final layer of the full connected layer of CNN by inputting the cropped image to CNN.
5) Construct SVM for defect detection by using the features obtained from the defect portion and the features obtained from the non-defect portion.
6) Construct SVM for defect classification by separating the features obtained from defect region into true defect and pseudo defect.

A. Determination of Pseudo Defect Region Using Keypoint Extraction

SURF is a method to extract features which are invariant to the illumination change, the scale change or the rotation. Keypoints are detected by creating multiple DoG (Difference of Gaussian) images and detecting the local maximum value of intensity in SURF. The value of scale σ is also used to obtain the orientation of the keypoint. SURF is a rotationally invariant feature by normalizing direction in orientation. The gradient direction is determined within the circle region whose radius is obtained by multiplying the scale σ of the keypoint by six times.

SURF obtains the S channel after converting the input image to HSV color system. As a result, the S channel was adopted from the experience that the keypoint detected from the defect region gained the common point where the gradient strength becomes strong when obtaining SURF.

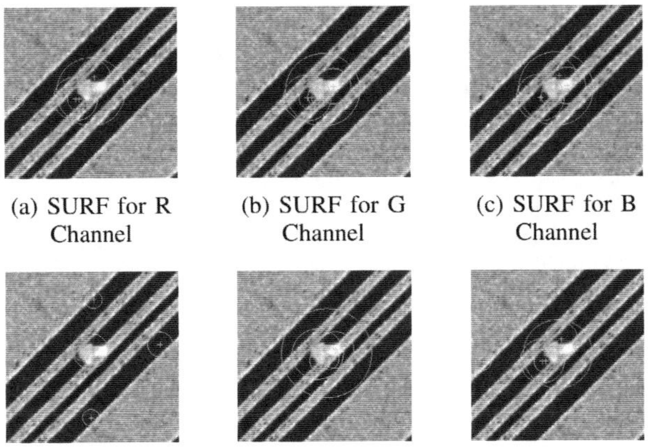

(a) SURF for R Channel (b) SURF for G Channel (c) SURF for B Channel

(d) SURF for H Channel (e) SURF for S Channel (f) SURF for V Channel

Figure 4. SURF Features

At first sight, observation shows that the keypoint is concentrated on the defect in the three channels of RGB (Figure 4(a), 4(b) and 4(c), but the keypoint was detected at the position deviating from the defect when the result is exactly confirmed with the mask image. It is confirmed that the keypoint concentrates on the defect at the result of the S channel (Figure 4(e)), and all five keypoints were detected on the defect region when the result is exactly confirmed with mask image. This characteristic was confirmed with more than 90% of dataset images.

B. Cropping Defect Candidate Image

Defect candidate images are cropped by SURF, as explained in Section IV-A. An image is cropped using a rectangle that encloses a circle with a radius of $6 \times \sigma$ used when orientation is determined by SURF. The number of keypoints used for a rectangle cropping in a test image is determined by the following procedure.

1) The keypoints detected from the learning image I_n is sorted in descending order of the gradient strength.
2) The keypoints are plotted in order of sorting for the mask image created from the learning image I_n and the reference image.
3) Record the number of the keypoint which is first plotted in the defect region of the mask image.
4) 1) to 3) are applied to all learning images, and the average value of the keypoint numbers recorded is used for cropping the rectangle in a test image.

True defect patches and pseudo defect patches are used for the learning with labelling.

Rectangle images cropped for the keypoint obtained using SURF are shown in Figure 5.

C. Feature Extraction Using CNN

Feature extraction is performed by inputting the image cropped using SURF in IV-B to CNN. AlexNet [6] is used as a pre-training model of CNN which structural concept is shown in Figure 6. Here, 4096-dimensional features which are obtained from the final layer of the fully connected layer (Layer FC7) are used for SVM learning as a transfer learning method.

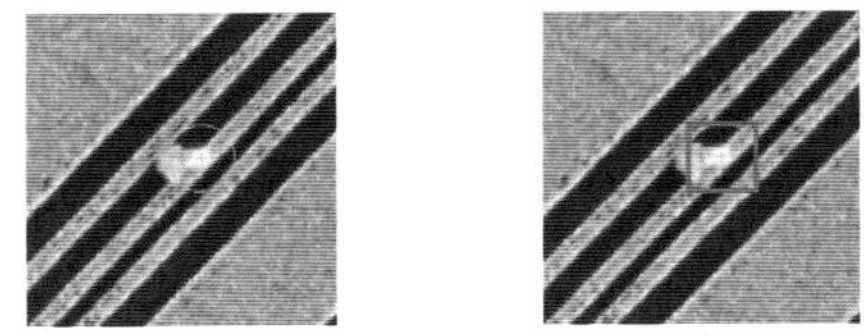

(a) Result of SURF (b) Cropped by rectangle

Figure 5. Cut by rectangle

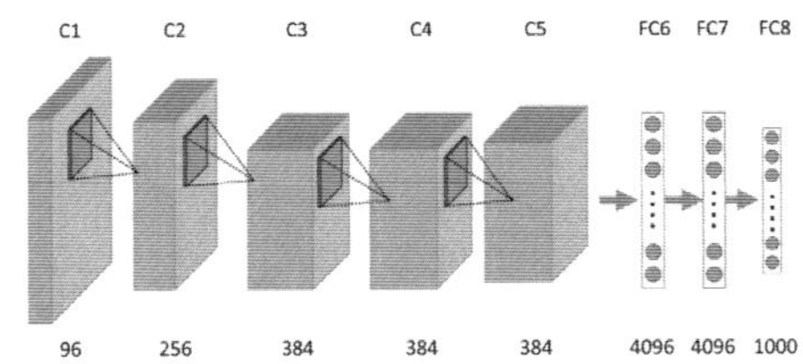

Figure 6. AlexNet

D. Construction of Classifier

SVM for defect detection is constructed using the defect patch and non-defect patch in the learning data. A linear kernel is used for defect detection SVM. The linear kernel is denoted by Equation (1).

$$k(\boldsymbol{x}_n, \boldsymbol{x}_m) = \boldsymbol{x}_n^T \boldsymbol{x}_m \tag{1}$$

The RBF kernel is used for constructing defect classification SVM. The RBF kernel is denoted by Equation (2). γ in Equation (2) is a parameter that controls the identification boundary. Here, as the value of γ increases, the boundary becomes more complicated.

$$k(\boldsymbol{x}_n, \boldsymbol{x}_m) = \exp(-\gamma \|\boldsymbol{x}_n - \boldsymbol{x}_m\|^2) \tag{2}$$

The performance of the final classification of the test image is shown in Table I according to the classification result using the classification SVM. It is important to reduce the rate of erroneously classifying a true defect as a pseudo defect.

TABLE I. FINAL JUDGMENT

Defect Patch in Image	Final Classification
Only True Defect Patch	True Defect
Only Pseudo Defect Patch	Pseudo Defect
True Defect Patch and Pseudo Defect Patch	Classify by Majority Voting
Non-Defect Patch	True Defect

V. EXPERIMENT

An experiment was performed to validate the effectiveness of the proposed method. Defect detection and defect classification are performed in two stages with the proposed method, that is, the experiment consists of detection and classification.

The dataset used for the experiment consists of 65 true defect images and 72 pseudo defect images.

A. Detection Experiment

The keypoints was detected by SURF on the defect image of the dataset, and SURF was obtained according to the number defined in the learning data in detection experiments. The results of obtained patches are shown in Table II.

TABLE II. NUMBER OF PATCH

Defect Patch	*Non-Defect Patch*
274	164

Detection and evaluation experiments were performed using the patch shown in Table II. The classifier is SVM, the kernel of SVM is a linear kernel, the parameter C of SVM is 1000 by GridSearch, and the evaluation method used is Leave-One-Out. Patches cropped from the same image were removed from the learning data for the test patch when Leave-One-Out is applied.

Precision, *Recall*, *F-measure* and *Accuracy* are calculated using the following equations.

$$\begin{aligned} Precision &= \frac{TP}{TP+FP} \\ Recall &= \frac{TP}{TP+FN} \\ F-measure &= \frac{2*Recall*Precision}{Recall+Precision} \\ Accuracy &= \frac{TP+TN}{TP+FP+FN+TN} \end{aligned}$$

TABLE III. EVALUATION OF DETECTION ACCURACY[%]

Precision	*Recall*	*F-measure*	*Accuracy*
89.05	84.14	86.52	82.64

It is confirmed that more than 80 percent of accuracy is obtained even without the reference image in inspection shown as Table 7.

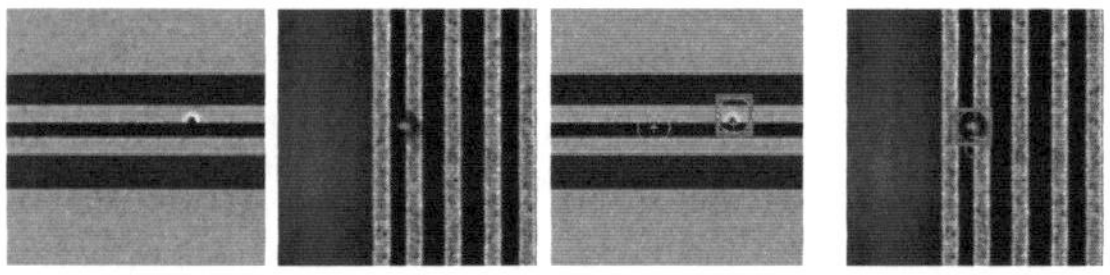

(a) True Defect (b) Pseudo Defect (c) Detect of True Defect (d) Detect of Pseudo Defect

Figure 7. Result of Detect

The detected images are shown in Figure 7. Figure 7(a) and Figure 7(b) show original images, and Figure 7(c) and Figure 7(d) show results of defect detection. The green circle in Figure 7 represents the keypoint that became a defect candidate. The red rectangle indicates the patch judged as a defect. It is shown from Figure 7 that the defect region can be cropped correctly.

B. Classification Experiment

The classification experiment was performed under the assumption that all detections made in V-A on the defect image of the dataset were successful. It is judged whether the patch is a true defect patch or a pseudo defect patch using only the defect patch from the cropped patch. The classifier is SVM, the kernel of SVM is RBF kernel, the parameter C of SVM is 1 by GridSearch, and the parameter γ of RBF kernel is 131. The evaluation method used is Leave-One-Out. The classification result of method [5] is shown when mask image is used at the test time for comparison. The number of learning images in the subset in method [5] is set to 50 as the number of datasets.

The result of classification are shown in Table IV.

TABLE IV. EVALUATION OF CLASSIFICATION ACCURACY[%]

Method	*Precision*	*Recall*	*F-measure*	*Accuracy*
Paper [5]	53.21	80.56	62.38	52.55
Proposed	86.11	67.39	75.61	70.80

It is confirmed that defect classification can be performed more accurately than method [5] despite using the defect detection method without reference images, which is shown from Table IV.

VI. CONCLUSION

This paper proposed a new highly accurate defect classification method without using reference images by introducing keypoint extraction and CNN feature extraction. The effectiveness of the proposed method was validated by an experiment for detecting the defect using actual images of electronic circuit boards. Defect detection without reference images was implemented by performing patch cropped using the keypoint extraction in the proposed method. As future work, there is higher accuracy of detection and classification.

ACKNOWLEDGMENT

Iwahori's research is supported by Japan Society for the Promotion of Science (JSPS) Grant-in-Aid for Scientific Research (C) (23500228) and Chubu University Grant.

REFERENCES

[1] S. Maeda, M. Ono, H. Kubota, and M. Nakatani, "Precise detection of short-circuit defects on tft substrate by infrared image matching," Systems and Computers in Japan, vol. 30, no. 12, 1999, pp. 72–84.

[2] M. Numada and H. Koshimizu, "A method for detecting globally distributed defects by using learning with mahalanobis distance," Journal of the Japan Society for Precision Engineering, vol. 75, no. 2, 2009, pp. 262–266.

[3] H. Rau and C.-H. Wu, "Automatic optical inspection for detecting defects on printed circuit board inner layers," The International Journal of Advanced Manufacturing Technology, vol. 25, no. 9-10, 2005, pp. 940–946.

[4] H. Inoue, Y. Iwahori, B. Kijsirikul, and M. Bhuyan, "Svm based defect classification of electronic board using bag of keypoints," in ITC-CSCC: International Technical Conference on Circuits Systems, Computers and Communications, 2015, pp. 31–34.

[5] H. Hagi, Y. Iwahori, S. Fukui, Y. Adachi, and M. K. Bhuyan, "Defect classification of electronic circuit board using svm based on random sampling," Procedia Computer Science, vol. 35, 2014, pp. 1210–1218.

[6] A. Krizhevsky, I. Sutskever, and G. E. Hinton, "Imagenet classification with deep convolutional neural networks," in Advances in neural information processing systems, 2012, pp. 1097–1105.

Internet of Things Patterns for Devices

Lukas Reinfurt[1], Uwe Breitenbücher,
Michael Falkenthal, Frank Leymann
Institute of Architecture of Application Systems
University of Stuttgart
Stuttgart, Germany
email: {firstname.lastname}@iaas.uni-stuttgart.de

Andreas Riegg
[1]Daimler AG
Stuttgart, Germany
email: {firstname.lastname}@daimler.com

Abstract—**Devices are an important part of the Internet of Things. They collect data from their environment with sensors and, based on this data, also act on their environment by using actuators. Many use cases require them to support characteristics such as being cheap, light, small, mobile, energy efficient, or autonomously powered. This creates constraints for available energy sources and leads to different kinds of operating modes. Based on existing terminology and additional examples, we describe these energy constraints and the operation modes in the form of Patterns. These Patterns are interconnected with other Patterns to form an Internet of Things Pattern Language that enables practitioners to find and navigate through proven solutions for their problems at hand.**

Keywords—Internet of Things; Patterns, Devices; Constraints.

I. INTRODUCTION

The development of the Internet of Things (IoT) is gaining momentum. Companies and research institutes create new technologies, standards, platforms, applications, and devices in rapid succession. As a result, it becomes increasingly hard to keep track of these developments.

We started creating IoT Patterns to help individuals working in this area [1][2]. By methodically collecting common problems and their solutions and abstracting them into Patterns, we are building up an IoT Pattern Language. These Patterns help others understand the core issues and solutions in the IoT space and provide them with the means to apply these solutions to problems in their own projects.

Devices are an important part of the IoT, as they are the point where sensors and actuators bridge the gap between the real world and its digital representation. To fulfill the vision of the IoT, a world where nearly everything works together to react and automatically adjusts to its environment, devices have to be ubiquitous. They come in all shapes and sizes and will be located not only in controlled indoor environments but also outside and in harsh conditions. For example, some of them are required to be mobile and are located off the power grid.

Such requirements lead to constraints in cost, size, weight, or available power and hence influence the choice of power source. Different power sources also require different operation modes. For example, Bormann et al. describe different energy sources and operation modes in their terminology for constrained-node networks [3].

Based on this terminology and additional sources describing the application of IoT devices in real world scenarios, we created six Patterns for IoT devices with different energy sources and operation modes. Devices can be ALWAYS-ON DEVICES, PERIOD ENERGY-LIMITED DEVICES, LIFETIME ENERGY-LIMITED DEVICES, or ENERGY-HARVESTING DEVICES, depending on the energy source they use. The energy source also influences a device's operation mode, thus it can be an ALWAYS-ON DEVICE or a NORMALLY-SLEEPING DEVICE.

The rest of this paper is structured as follows: Section II provides a short overview of previous work related to this paper. Section III briefly summarizes our understanding of Patterns and our previously published IoT Patterns. Section IV introduces six new IoT Patterns for devices and shows how they are connected among themselves and to the already presented ones. Section V describes three of the six new Patterns, namely PERIOD ENERGY-LIMITED DEVICE, ENERGY-HARVESTING DEVICE, and NORMALLY-SLEEPING DEVICE, in detail. Finally, Section VI provides a summary and outlook.

II. RELATED WORK

The Pattern concept was first introduced by Alexander et al. in the architecture domain [4]. Since then, the concept has been applied in other domains. Examples from IT include the Messaging Patterns by Hohpe et al. [5] or the Cloud Computing Patterns by Fehling et al. [6]. There has also been work on the Pattern writing process itself [7][8][9][10].

We presented our first five IoT Patterns, DEVICE GATEWAY, DEVICE SHADOW, RULES ENGINE, DEVICE WAKEUP TRIGGER, and REMOTE LOCK AND WIPE [1]. We later added three more Patterns, namely DELTA UPDATE, REMOTE DEVICE MANAGEMENT, and VISIBLE LIGHT COMMUNICATION [2]. These Patterns are not concerned with IoT devices themselves but do already mention the terminology by Bormann et. al [3]. They present a terminology for constrained nodes, constrained networks, and constrained-node networks. They describe some aspects of why and how different energy sources and operation modes occur, but not in the form of Patterns. The Pattern format used in this paper adds more to this description in form of the forces, the result section, and the benefits and drawbacks, as well as the interconnection with other Patterns.

Eloranta et. al published a Pattern Language for designing distributed control systems [11]. These Patterns focus on larger machinery and are not concerned with small constrained devices and the implications of these constraints.

Other Patterns in the IoT space exist which are not concerned with the devices themselves. Qanbari et. al present four Patterns for edge application provisioning, deployment, orchestration, and monitoring, which use existing technologies like Docker or Git that are not suited for constrained devices [12].

III. IoT Patterns Overview

The Patterns presented in this paper and our previous work follow the ideas of Alexander [4] and others [7][8][9][10]. As described in more detail in [1][2], we identified these Patterns by collecting material from product pages, manuals, documentation, standards, whitepapers, and research papers. Once reoccurring descriptions became evident, we grouped them and extracted the core principles into the more abstract Pattern format. The format is also described in more detail in [1][2] but, in short, is made up of the following elements: The **Name**, **Icon**, and **Aliases** help to identify the Pattern. The short **Problem** and **Solution** sections contain the core issue and steps to resolve it. The **Context** and **Forces** describe where the problem occurs and why it is hard to solve, while the **Result** section gives more details on the solution. Other relevant Patterns are listed as **Related Patterns**. Existing products which implement the Pattern and were used as sources are summarized under **Known Uses**. Table 1 provides an overview of our earlier Patterns, including a short summary of the problems they are solving and a brief description of how they solve it.

TABLE 1. OVERVIEW OF OUR PREVIOUS IOT PATTERNS

Device Gateway 	**P.:** You want to connect many different devices to an already existing network, but some of them might not support the networks communication technology or protocol. **S.:** Connect devices to an intermediary Device Gateway that translates the communication technology supported by the device to communication technology of the network and vice-versa.
Device Shadow 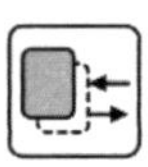	**P.:** Some devices are only intermittently online to save energy or because of network outages. Other components want to interact with them but do not know when they will be reachable. **S.:** Store a persistent virtual representation of each device on some backend server. Include the latest received state from the device, as well as commands not yet sent to the device. Do all communication from and to the device through this virtual version. Synchronize the virtual representation with the actual device state when the device is online.
Rules Engine 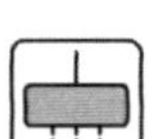	**P.:** Throughout its operation, a system receives a wide range of messages from devices and other components. You want to react in different ways to these messages. **S.:** Pass all messages received from devices through a Rules Engine. Allow users to define rules that evaluate the content of incoming messages or metadata about the message against a set of comparators. Also allow external data sources to be included in these comparisons. Let users associate a set of actions with these rules. Apply each rule on each message and trigger the associated actions if a rule matches.
Device Wakeup Trigger 	**P.:** Some devices might go into a sleep mode to conserve energy and only wake up from time to time to reconnect to the network. During sleep, they are not reachable on their regular communication channels. In some instances, other components might have to contact sleeping devices immediately. **S.:** Implement a mechanism that allows the server to send a trigger message to the device via a low energy communication channel. Have the device listening for these triggering messages and immediately establish communication with the server when it receives such a message.
Remote Lock and Wipe 	**P.:** Some devices might be lost or stolen. You want to prevent attackers from misusing the functionality of the device, or from gaining access to the data on the device or to the network through the device. **S.:** Make the device a managed device that can receive and execute management operations from the backend server. Allow authorized users to use the backend server to trigger functionality on the device that can delete files, folders, applications or memory areas, revoke or remove permissions, keys, and certificates, or enable additional security feature. Execute triggered functions as soon as the device receives them and provide an acknowledgment to the backend.
Delta Update 	**P.:** You want to reduce the size of messages containing sensor data without losing any information. **S.:** Store the last message send. Calculate the delta from the current data to this message. Also, calculate a hash of the current data. Send only the delta and the hash to the receiver. Let the receiver merge the delta with its current state and check, if it matches the received hash.
Remote Device Management 	**P.:** You want to manage a large number of devices remotely. **S.:** Set up a management server on the backend. Add management clients to the device which you want to manage. Send management commands from the server to the client and let the client execute these commands locally on the device.
Visible Light Communication 	**P.:** You need to use wireless communication in a crowded area, but you cannot use the crowded radio spectrum. **S.:** Use visible light for short distance wireless communication. Modulate messages into the light by turning the light on and off. Do it fast to not impede normal light usage and to be invisible to the human eye.

IV. Internet of Things Patterns for Devices

In this paper, we add six new IoT Patterns for devices, three of which are presented in detail in Section V. This section presents an overview of all of them in Table 2 and 3, including some additional explanations of the Patterns not further described in Section V.

Related Patterns are organized into two groups. The first group, *Energy Supply Types*, is summarized in Table 2 and describes Patterns based on different forms of energy sources a device might use. Which one of these is applicable depends on the use case and its environment. If for example, a device is required for a wearable use case, then a Mains-

POWERED DEVICE is not an option. But the environment of the use case might also not provide sufficient ambient energy for an ENERGY-HARVESTING DEVICE.

The second group, *Operation Modes,* is summarized in Table 3 and lists different Patterns based on a device's mode of operation. These often depend on the amount of energy available to the device. For example, if a device is an ENERGY-HARVESTING DEVICE, it will in many cases not have enough energy to be an ALWAYS-ON DEVICE and has to be a NORMALLY-SLEEPING DEVICE.

TABLE 2. OVERVIEW OF THE NEW IOT PATTERNS CONCERNED WITH DEVICE ENERGY SOURCES

Energy Supply Types	
MAINS-POWERED DEVICE 	**P.:** You need to power a stationary device, which requires a lot of energy. **S.:** Connect the device to mains power. (These types of devices do not have a direct limitation on energy. They are useful if batteries or energy harvesting do not provide enough power or are too maintenance intensive for the intended use case. They trade in more power for dependency on the grid and loss of mobility. They often are always-on but using other energy saving operation modes can lower energy cost.)
PERIOD ENERGY-LIMITED DEVICE (Section 0) 	**P.:** You need to power a device, which requires a fair amount of power. The device is mobile or located in a remote place. Moreover, mains power is not available. **S.:** Use a replaceable or rechargeable source of energy to power the device. Implement a notification mechanism that informs you when the power source is nearly empty. Replace or recharge the power source when needed.
LIFETIME ENERGY-LIMITED DEVICE 	**P.:** You need to power a device, which requires a small amount of power. The device is mobile or located in a remote place. You want to minimize maintenance. **S.:** Build an energy source into the device, which will last for the entire expected lifetime of the device. (Integrating a non-renewable energy source into a device can make sense if renewal is made difficult or impossible by the device's placement and if mains power is not available. The device should consume little energy and should have a known maximum lifetime. A normally-sleeping operation mode should be used to further maximize lifetime. Once the energy source is depleted, the device is useless, but until then it is low in maintenance and costs, simple and cheap to build, and highly independent.)
ENERGY-HARVESTING DEVICE (Section V.B) 	**P.:** You need to power a device with very little power needs. The device is mobile or located in a remote place. Its environment is stable and predictable. **S.:** Integrate an energy harvesting component, such as a solar cell, into the device. Use it to turn the energy available in the device's surroundings into power for the device. Use components and technologies optimized for low-power usage to make the most of the harvested energy.

TABLE 3. OVERVIEW OF THE NEW IOT PATTERNS CONCERNED WITH DEVICE OPERATION MODES

Operation Modes	
ALWAYS-ON DEVICE 	**P.:** You have a device with an unlimited energy supply and need to have it available and responsive at all times. **S.:** Leave the device turned on and connected at all times. (Leaving a device always on allows it to constantly take measurements and communicate with others, which may be required for some use cases. This requires more energy than other energy saving operation modes. Thus, being mains-powered or completely powered by energy harvesting is useful, or otherwise, maintenance will be high.)
NORMALLY-SLEEPING DEVICE (Section V.C) 	**P.:** You have a device with a limited energy supply. You want to minimize the power used by the device. **S.:** Program the device to disable its main components when they are not needed. Leave a small circuit powered which reactivates the components after a predefined amount of time has passed or when an event occurs.

These new Patterns do not exist in a vacuum. They are connected among themselves and to the Patterns which we previously presented [1][2]. Fig. 1 shows an overview of all the connections between the IoT Patterns. A black box in a row means that the Pattern represented by this row relates to the Pattern represented by the column in which the box is placed (the gray boxes show, where a Pattern is compared with itself). For example, in row four, a black box in column six shows that the ENERGY-HARVESTING DEVICE Pattern mentions the NORMALLY-SLEEPING DEVICE Pattern. The nature of the connection is not further elaborated in this figure but could be interesting for future research.

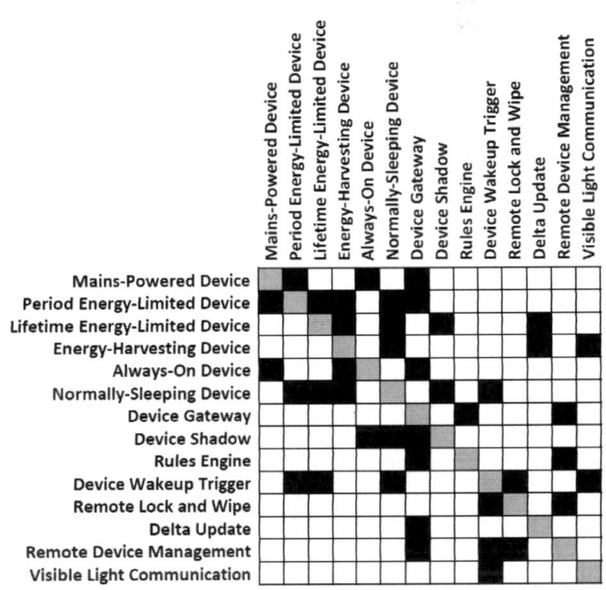

Figure 1. Connections between IoT Patterns.

As the applicability of the IoT device Patterns presented in this paper is heavily influenced by the particular use case, it seems reasonable to choose them as entry points into the IoT Pattern Language when designing an IoT system. Their selection then greatly influences the design of the remaining system by suggesting or forcing certain additional Patterns. For example, if a use case requires a PERIOD ENERGY-LIMITED DEVICE, then also being a NORMALLY-SLEEPING DEVICE will greatly enhance its energy efficiency. Adding a DEVICE SHADOW will make the overall system more robust and using a DEVICE WAKEUP TRIGGER will allow you to communicate with a NORMALLY-SLEEPING DEVICE in an instant if necessary.

In turn, if new devices should be added to an existing IoT system, the design decisions elaborated in the architecture of the existing system will dictate which kinds of devices can be added without modifications, or what modifications have to be made to support a specific kind of device.

V. DETAILED IOT PATTERNS FOR DEVICES

In this section, we describe three IoT Device Patterns in more detail. Out of the *Energy Supply Types* category we describe the PERIOD ENERGY LIMITED DEVICE and the ENERGY-HARVESTING DEVICE Pattern. From the *Operation Mode* category, we describe the NORMALLY-SLEEPING DEVICE Pattern.

A. PERIOD ENERGY-LIMITED DEVICE

Aliases: Rechargeable

Context: You have a device, which needs a fair amount of energy to work but does not necessarily require mains power, such as a device that takes regular sensor readings, communicates, and powers actuators. Besides, your use case dictates a specific location for this device which restricts available energy sources. For example, the device has to be mobile, wearable, or in a remote location.

Problem: You need to power a device which requires a fair amount of power. The device is mobile or located in a remote place. Moreover, mains-power is not available.

Forces:

- **Energy Needs:** The device needs a fair amount of energy to work. A LIFETIME ENERGY-LIMITED DEVICE is not an option if it needs more in its lifetime than current batteries offer in a reasonable form factor. An ENERGY-HARVESTING DEVICE is not an option if the device needs more power for a cycle than the harvesting generates between cycles.
- **Environmental Constraints:** Your use case enforces a specific location for the device. For example, the device has to be mobile or wearable, or the device location is in an area where mains power is not available. Thus, being a MAINS-POWERED DEVICE is not an option. Besides, an ENERGY-HARVESTING DEVICE is not an option if no suitable form of ambient energy source is available at the device's location.
- **Costs:** Replacing or recharging the power source is an option but has a cost associated with it, especially if the device is located in a remote or inaccessible location. For your use case, it makes economically and physically sense to do this in the time frame which allows the device to sustain its functionality.
- **Uptime:** You want to minimize the periods where the device is not operating because of power source renewal.

Solution: Use a replaceable or rechargeable source of energy to power the device. Implement a notification mechanism that informs you when the power source is nearly empty. Replace or recharge the power source when needed.

Result: Using a replaceable or rechargeable power source is a common occurrence in today's devices. Increasingly energy efficient electronic components now allow manufacturers to build devices which run on one charge for weeks to months, if not years. For the rest of this text, we equate a PERIOD ENERGY-LIMITED DEVICE with using batteries, as they are common in the domain of IoT. But for example, fuel for a generator is another valid form of a power source for a PERIOD ENERGY-LIMITED DEVICE.
Fig. 2 shows the lifecycle of a PERIOD ENERGY-LIMITED DEVICE. It can be roughly divided into three phases: Most of the time, the device operates normally and, thus, *discharges* the power source, as shown at the bottom. Once a certain threshold is reached, the device starts to *notify*, as shown at the top left. Then, the depleted power source is *renewed*, as shown at the top right, before the cycle begins again.

Batteries come in different forms and sizes and are renewable in two ways. The first way to renew power for a PERIOD ENERGY-LIMITED DEVICE is to replace depleted batteries with full ones. The replacement battery is either a new non-rechargeable battery or a recharged battery. In this case, it makes no difference to the device if the battery is rechargeable or not. If you recharge the battery, it happens outside of the device through a separate charger. Integrating this replacement mechanism into a device is straightforward. It requires a connector to which you attach the battery. An optional compartment housing this connector offers protection for the battery and the device internals from outside influences. The second way to renew the battery is to allow it to be recharged inside the device. This requires integrating a charging circuit into the device. When the battery is empty, you connect another energy source to the device to recharge the battery, for example, a power bank. Alternatively, you bring the device near to mains power where you can plug in a power supply. The complexity of the charging circuit varies depending on the type of battery and the desired recharge time. A slow charge circuit is simple because it cannot damage the battery and thus requires no end-of-charge detection. A fast charge circuit has to detect end-of-charge through voltage or temperature to prevent overcharging the battery. In this case, the battery has to be rechargeable but not replaceable. If it is rechargeable and not replaceable, replacing the battery when it malfunctions becomes difficult, but it allows for a tighter integration and closed housing. Depending on the intended use case of the device, you have to take care to shield it from its environment. Dust or waterproof battery compartments offer protection from outside elements. For integrated rechargeable batteries, nothing but the charging contact has to be accessible from the outside. This further prevents environmental factors of deteriorating the device.

Since the power renewal of the PERIOD ENERGY-LIMITED DEVICE requires another entity to act, the device needs a notification mechanism to trigger power source renewal, as shown at the top left in Fig. 2. If the device sends out messages, adding the battery status to these messages is one way to inform others about the device's battery status. Besides, a repeating light or sound indicating low energy is another option. You have to choose the notification threshold to allow time for power source renewal before it runs out to minimize downtime.

Benefits:

- **Independence:** The device is independent of the grid and of its environment. It has power regardless of power outages or bad weather as long as you replace its energy source in time.
- **Lifetime:** The power source does not limit the lifetime of the device if it is replaceable.
- **Cost:** The costs for the device itself and for its installation are low. A battery connector and compartment or a charging circuit do not add high costs and wires are not required.

Drawbacks:

- **Lifetime:** The power source limits the lifetime of a device if it is a rechargeable but not replaceable battery because aging batteries deteriorate with time and batteries have a maximum charge cycle count. This is not a problem if the maximum number of charge cycles allows the device to run until its intended end of life. Otherwise, making the battery replaceable solves this problem.
- **Costs:** You need to replace or recharge the power source in regular intervals which increase maintenance costs. Also being an ENERGY-HARVESTING DEVICE or a NORMALLY-SLEEPING DEVICE increases the interval length.
- **Durability:** The device has to support replacing or recharging the power source which requires access to the power source or the recharging contacts. If the device exposes these points to the environment they deteriorate in harsh conditions. One option is to build these points dust or waterproof but doing this does not offer full protection and increases costs. Wireless charging is another option which allows sealing the device.

Figure 2. Sketch of the PERIOD ENERGY-LIMITED DEVICE Pattern.

- **Uptime:** The device is not operational when you replace its power source instead of recharging it. Making the power source rechargeable besides being replaceable is one way to guarantee uptime. Another option is to have two power sources in the device, where it uses one as a backup while you replace the other one.

Related Patterns:

- **ENERGY-HARVESTING DEVICE:** One way to increase the time needed between power source replacements or recharging is energy harvesting. An example is adding a small solar cell, which trickle charges the battery.
- **NORMALLY-SLEEPING DEVICE:** A NORMALLY-SLEEPING DEVICE saves energy when the device is not needed. This can increase the interval length between power source replacement or recharging for PERIOD ENERGY-LIMITED DEVICES.
- **MAINS-POWERED DEVICE:** A MAINS-POWERED DEVICE can also be a PERIOD ENERGY-LIMITED DEVICE if it uses a battery as a backup in case of power outage.

Known Uses: One example of a PERIOD ENERGY-LIMITED DEVICE is the *Flic Wireless Smart Button*. It claims to last one year or more on its replaceable battery [13]. A similar device, *Logitech's POP Home Switch*, claims up to 5 years battery life from its replaceable battery [14]. *Sen.se's ThermoPeanut* is a wireless temperature sensor with a replaceable battery which lasts up to 6 months, depending on the frequency of sensor reading [15]. Another example is the *Nest Learning Thermostat,* which comes with a rechargeable lithium-ion battery [16]. The *Roost Smart Battery* is a replacement battery, which adds WiFi connectivity to smoke detectors. It notifies users via an app when the alarm is triggered or the battery runs low [17]. Besides, some MAINS-POWERED DEVICES are also PERIOD ENERGY-LIMITED DEVICES as they use batteries as a backup to increase their resilience against power outages. Examples include the DEVICE GATEWAYS from *SmartThings*, *Essence*, or *Afero*. They either include a backup battery or offer connection options for external batteries [18][19][20].

B. Energy-Harvesting Device

Aliases: Ambient Energy, Event Energy-Limited, Event-Based Harvesting

Context: You have a device that needs to be powered. The device needs only a small amount of energy to function. Besides, your use case dictates a specific location for this device which restricts available energy sources. For example, the device has to be mobile, wearable, or in a remote location.

Problem: You need to power a device with very little power needs. The device is mobile or located in a remote place. Its environment is stable and predictable.

Forces:

- **Location:** The device has to be mobile or is located at a remote place. Thus, it cannot be a Mains-Powered Device.
- **Effort:** Replacing or recharging a battery in frequent intervals is too much effort or not possible at all. Thus, using a Period Energy-Limited Device is not an option.
- **Energy Requirements:** The device needs very little energy to function.
- **Lifetime Energy Requirements:** The device needs more energy over its lifetime than current batteries can provide in a reasonable form factor without being replaced or recharged. Thus, using a Lifetime Energy-Limited Device is not an option.

Solution: Integrate an energy harvesting component, such as a solar cell, into the device. Use it to turn the energy available in the device's surroundings into power for the device. Use components and technologies optimized for low-power usage to make the most of the harvested energy.

Result: An Energy-Harvesting Device transforms ambient energy into electrical energy, as depicted in Fig. 3. Ambient energy can be in form of radiant energy (solar, infrared, radio-frequency), thermal energy, mechanical energy, or biomechanical energy. Each of these energy forms comes with its own benefits and drawbacks that have to be taken into account for each use case separately.

Figure 3. Sketch of the Energy-Harvesting Device Pattern.

Radiant energy in form of sunlight or other light sources is a common source of energy for Energy-Harvesting Devices. Miniature solar modules are able to harvest enough energy, even from indoor lights, to perpetually transmit a measurement a few times per hour. But especially when using sunlight, it has to be taken into account that it is only available for a limited time each day. Another form of radiant energy, radio-frequency, is produced by the many wireless communication technologies we use today and can also be harvested. Because it is purposely generated and heavily regulated, it is more predictable than other forms of ambient energy. However, to be usable, a sufficient level of energy density is required in the environment which might only be given in more populated areas. Mechanical energy can also be harvested. For example, a switch may generate enough energy when activated to be able to send several radio telegrams. Another example is a thermoelectric generator which is able to collect and transform thermal energy in form of temperature differences into electricity.

The availability of each of these forms of ambient energy depends on the environment of the use case. Not all forms might be available in all locations and the available energy might be too small to power a particular device. Besides, mobility has to be taken into account. If the device is fixed, then the availability of ambient energy can be measured and is fairly predictable. If the device is mobile, then the form and amount of available ambient energy can fluctuate widely.

Even though it might only supply a very small amount of energy, ambient energy can be used to power very energy efficient circuits and sensors and to transmit and receive small messages. An Energy-Harvesting Device can be powered directly if it uses very energy efficient components, but in many cases, the harvested energy will not be enough for sustained operation. In such cases, the ambient energy can be used to trickle charge a battery or capacitor. Once sufficient energy is collected, the device can then turn on and use it for a short period of operation. Another use is to supplement Period Energy-Limited Devices to increase the intervals between recharging.

As the harvested power is often so small, it is necessary for the device to use technologies which are optimized for ultra-low energy. This includes using components, such as microchips or sensors, which are very energy efficient. It also includes using communication technologies, such as wireless modules and even protocols and payload formats, which are optimized for ultra-low energy. Often, technologies are specifically created for this in mind, for example, the ISO/IEC 14543-3-10:2012 standard. But there are also examples of existing technologies, which have been adapted to be more energy-saving, such as IEEE 802.15.4, 6loWPAN, or CoAP.

Benefits:

- **Independence:** The device is independent of the electrical grid. Besides, it can be flexibly positioned because it does not require any wire.

- **Perpetual Energy:** Devices with very low energy requirements can be powered for as long as the energy harvesting components do not fail.
- **Cost:** The total cost of ownership of Energy-Harvesting Devices, which includes installation, operation, and management costs, is low. No cables have to be added during installation and battery replacement or recharging are either reduced in frequency or not necessary at all. Besides, the power used by the device is also free. Because there are no special infrastructure requirements, retrofitting an Energy-Harvesting Device is also easy.
- **Maintenance:** Maintenance can be reduced or is not necessary at all. This is especially beneficial if the device is located in inaccessible areas or if a lot of devices are operated.
- **Environmental Impact:** Energy-Harvesting Devices have a low environmental impact. The energy they harvest is freely available and energy wasting is not a problem. They also do not produce as much hazardous waste in form of old batteries as Period Energy-Limited Devices, but other components, including the energy harvesting components, might still be hazardous.

Drawbacks:

- **Dependence:** The device depends on the availability characteristics of the ambient energy source and its environment. These might be hard to accurately predict and control. If the environment changes it might no longer provide enough ambient energy for the device.
- **Energy:** Depending on the used technology, only small amounts of energy may be harvested from the environment. To get the most out of the available energy, high energy efficiency is necessary. This requires the device to consume very little energy during idle times, which can be achieved by making it a Normally-Sleeping Device. It also requires the device to be efficient when it is awake, which can be done by using low power components and technologies.
- **Fragility:** Depending on the form of ambient energy used, the components needed for energy harvesting might be fragile and not suited for all environments.

Related Patterns:

- **Period Energy-Limited Device:** Energy harvesting can be used to extend the intervals between recharging or replacing the energy source of a Period Energy-Limited Device.
- **Normally-Sleeping Device:** Energy harvesting may power Normally-Sleeping Devices if the harvested energy is only enough for short bursts of activity.

Known Uses: A common use of energy harvesting is found in devices which use passive RFID for communication. Here, the RF signal generated by the reader also powers the device [21]. Researchers are working on extending the capabilities of RFID powered device beyond responding with fixed data. An example is the *Wireless Identification and Sensing Platform* (WISP). It allows fully programmable 16-bit microcontrollers with attached sensors to be powered by RFID [22]. A device using WISP is the WISPCam, a passive RFID powered camera tag [23]. *EnOcean* created a patented wireless communication technology that is now standardized as ISO/IEC 14543-3-10:2012. It uses kinetic motion, solar, and thermal converters to create enough power for transmitting wireless signals. *EnOcean* also produces modules and products (mainly in the home automation sector) that utilize this technology. Many other companies have licensed the *EnOcean* technology and offer products [24][25]. *Freevolt* is another technology that harvests energy for low power devices from radio frequencies produces by broadcast networks, such as 2g, 3g, 4g, WiFi, and digital TV. The *CleanSpace Tag* is an air quality sensor which uses this technology to generate perpetual power for its lifetime [26].

C. Normally-Sleeping Device

Aliases: Sleepy, Deep Sleep, Hibernate, Duty-cycled, Normally-Off

Context: You have a use case which comes with size, weight, cost, or energy restrictions. For example, this is the case when the use case needs mobility or wearability. You use devices optimized to fit these restrictions. These devices are Lifetime Energy-Limited Devices, Period Energy-Limited Devices, or Energy-Harvesting Devices.

Problem: You have a device with a limited energy supply. You want to minimize the power used by the device.

Forces:

- **Limited Energy:** Having an Always-On Device is not an option since the device has a limited power source.
- **Energy Saving:** Saving energy decreases costs and is good for the environment but leads to constraints.
- **Component Use:** The device does not use every component continuously. Turning them off when not needed saves energy. But if these components have long startup times, the responsiveness of the device suffers.
- **Communication:** Turning of the communication module when not needed saves energy. But doing this manually takes too much effort, especially for remotely placed or large amounts of devices.

Solution: Program the device to disable its main components when they are not needed. Leave a small circuit powered which reactivates the components after a predefined amount of time has passed or when an event occurs.

Result: A NORMALLY-SLEEPING DEVICE cuts power to its main components for long stretches of time, as shown in Fig. 4. Good candidates for saving energy among these components are wireless communication modules, as they drain large amounts of power. Thus, NORMALLY-SLEEPING DEVICES are not able to communicate during their off periods. Other components, from processing units to individual sensors or actuators, are also disabled to add to these energy savings.

One component has to be active continuously to wake up the device. A clock component is able to reactivate power to the other components after a predefined amount of time, shown as the first active period in Fig. 4. This time is either absolute, for example, every full hour, or relative, for example, 5 minutes after the last active period ended. Another way to reactivate the turned off components is on events, shown as the second active period in Fig. 4. One option to do this is a small circuit which monitors a sensor and reactivates power when it reaches a predefined threshold. Or a DEVICE WAKEUP TRIGGER can be used to create such an event.

Once reactivated, the device resumes normal operation, as shown at the bottom of Fig. 4. For example, it saves the current sensor values and reestablishes a connection to a backend server. It uploads its state and processes messages which are waiting for it on the server. After the device has finished this process it returns to the sleeping state until the next period of activity.

Benefits:

- **Efficiency:** The device is more energy efficient because it is active only when needed.
- **Longevity:** Sleeping for long periods of time saves energy. This increases the maximum lifetime of LIFETIME ENERGY-LIMITED DEVICES. Besides, it increases the interval length between replacing or recharging the power source in PERIOD ENERGY-LIMITED DEVICES.

Drawbacks:

- **Intermittent Connectivity:** Communication with the device is intermittent. When it is sleeping, other communication partners cannot reach it. A DEVICE SHADOW is one option to allow others to communicate with an eventually consistent version of the device. On the device itself, not every component has to be off when it is sleeping. An example is a sensor which keeps collecting measurements that need to be sent to the backend eventually. The device has to store these measurements in a queue and sends them later when it activates the next time.

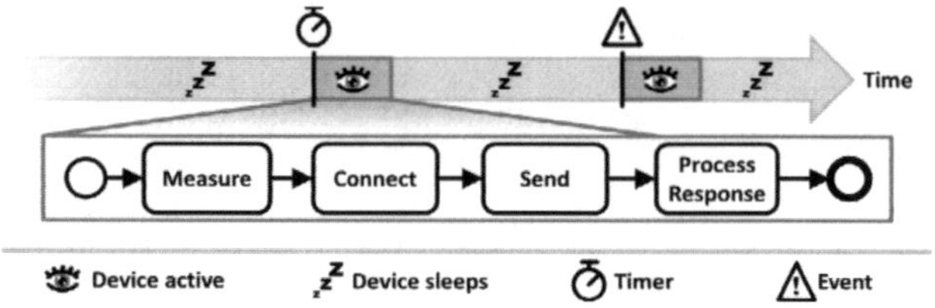

Figure 4. Sketch of the NORMALLY-SLEEPING DEVICE Pattern.

- **Timing:** In important cases, for instance for critical security updates, another component has to contact the device at once. Waiting for the NORMALLY-SLEEPING DEVICE to reconnect during its next activity window is not an option. A DEVICE WAKEUP TRIGGER is one way to get the NORMALLY-SLEEPING DEVICE to reconnect at once by creating an event that it listens to.
- **Energy:** Establishing a new connection for communication needs power. Sometimes it is more efficient to sustain an existing connection than creating a large number of new ones. This point depends on the chosen technology and the required communication frequency. You have to choose sleep schedules with this in mind.

Related Patterns:

- **ENERGY-HARVESTING DEVICE:** Devices which use energy harvesting as their source of power often also are NORMALLY-SLEEPING DEVICES. They sleep until they harvested the energy they need for a short period of activity.
- **DEVICE WAKEUP TRIGGER:** In situations when it is necessary to communicate with a NORMALLY-SLEEPING DEVICE outside of its regular communication windows, a DEVICE WAKEUP TRIGGER is one option. The DEVICE WAKEUP TRIGGER tells a disconnected device to reconnect at once.
- **PERIOD ENERGY-LIMITED DEVICE:** Being a NORMALLY-SLEEPING DEVICE extends the interval between replacing or recharging the power source in PERIOD ENERGY-LIMITED DEVICES.
- **LIFETIME ENERGY-LIMITED:** Being a NORMALLY-SLEEPING DEVICE extends the maximum lifetime of LIFETIME ENERGY-LIMITED DEVICES.
- **DEVICE SHADOW:** Using a DEVICE SHADOW allows other communication partners to retrieve the latest known state and to send commands to a currently sleeping device.

Known Uses: *Z-Wave* has so-called *sleepy devices*, which turn off to save energy and periodically wake up and reconnect. When reconnected, they inform other devices that they are listening for commands for the next seconds [27]. *Libelium's Waspmotes* support different operation modes to save power, including sleep and deep sleep modes which last from milliseconds to days. In these modes, they pause the main program and the microcontroller. Synchronous interrupts (periodic and relative programmed timers), or asynchronous interrupts (sensor readings or XBee activity) end these modes. Besides, they support a hibernate mode, where they cut power off from every part except the clock. The clock ends this mode after a predefined time with a synchronous interruption [28]. Other devices turn on for a brief moment if an event occurs. For example, the *Amazon Dash Button* turns on once a person presses the button. It connects to a WiFi network, places an order, and shuts off as soon as it receives a response [29]. The *PawTrax* pet tracker wakes up when it receives a text message, gets the current GPS position and returns it before it goes back to sleep. Besides, it has an option to return position data in set intervals [30].

VI. SUMMARY AND OUTLOOK

Devices are a central point of any IoT system, as they link the physical with the digital world through their sensors and actuators. They are also a starting point when designing IoT systems because they are directly influenced by the particular use case and the environment. Their selection then further influences the design of the IoT system as it has to cater to the different device characteristics.

To help individuals to design IoT systems that work with different kinds of devices, we presented six IoT device Patterns. Three of them were described in more detail. One of the energy source Patterns, PERIOD ENERGY-LIMITED DEVICE, describes a device which uses a replaceable or rechargeable power source. This allows it to be mobile but also requires some maintenance. Another Pattern in this group, the ENERGY-HARVESTING DEVICE, explains how devices can use harvest ambient energy for their power needs. From the category of operating modes, a NORMALLY-SLEEPING DEVICE can disable most of its components and sleep for some time to save energy. We also showed how these Patterns are interconnected, also with our previous Patterns.

In the future, we want to expand this selection of Patterns into a full IoT Pattern catalog and further refine their interrelations to form an IoT Pattern Language. This will also include new Patterns, which are concerned with device bootstrapping, device registration, communication between devices and platforms, data processing, and more.

ACKNOWLEDGMENT

This work was partially funded by the BMWi projects NEMAR (03ET4018B), SmartOrchestra (01MD16001F) and SePiA.Pro (01MD16013F).

REFERENCES

[1] L. Reinfurt, U. Breitenbücher, M. Falkenthal, F. Leymann, and A. Riegg, "Internet of Things Patterns," in *Proceedings of the 21st European Conference on Pattern Languages of Programs (EuroPLoP)*: ACM, 2016. in press.

[2] L. Reinfurt, U. Breitenbücher, M. Falkenthal, F. Leymann, and A. Riegg, "Internet of Things Patterns for Communication and Management," LNCS Transactions on Pattern Languages of Programming, 2017. unpublished.

[3] C. Bormann, M. Ersue, and A. Keranen, "Terminology for Constrained-Node Networks," IETF, 2014. [Online]. Available from: http://www.rfc-editor.org/rfc/pdfrfc/rfc7228.txt.pdf 2017.01.13

[4] C. Alexander, S. Ishikawa, and M. Silverstein, *A Pattern Language: Towns, Buildings, Construction*. New York: Oxford University Press, 1977.

[5] G. Hohpe and B. Woolf, *Enterprise Integration Patterns: Designing, Building, and Deploying Messaging Solutions*. Boston, Massachusetts: Addison-Wesley, 2004.

[6] C. Fehling, F. Leymann, R. Retter, W. Schupeck, and P. Arbitter, *Cloud Computing Patterns: Fundamentals to Design, Build, and Manage Cloud Applications*. Wien: Springer, 2014.

[7] G. Meszaros and J. Doble, "Metapatterns: A Pattern Language for Pattern Writing," *Third Pattern Languages of Programming Conference*: Addison-Wesley, 1996.

[8] N. B. Harrison, "The Language of Shepherding: A Pattern Language for Shepherds and Sheep," in *Software patterns series, Pattern languages of program design 5*, D. Manolescu, M. Voelter, and J. Noble, Eds. 1st ed., Upper Saddler River, NJ: Addison-Wesley, 2006, pp. 507–530.

[9] N. B. Harrison, "Advanced Pattern Writing: Patterns for Experienced Pattern Authors," in *Software patterns series, Pattern languages of program design 5*, D. Manolescu, M. Voelter, and J. Noble, Eds. 1st ed., Upper Saddler River, NJ: Addison-Wesley, 2006, pp. 433–452.

[10] T. Wellhausen and A. Fießer, "How to write a pattern?: A rough guide for first-time pattern authors," *Proceedings of the 16th European Conference on Pattern Languages of Programs*: ACM, 2012.

[11] V.-P. Eloranta, J. Koskinen, M. Leppänen, and V. Reijonen, *Designing distributed control systems: A pattern language approach*. Hoboken, NJ: Wiley, 2014.

[12] S. Qanbari *et al.*, "IoT Design Patterns: Computational Constructs to Design, Build and Engineer Edge Applications," *Proceedings of the First International Conference on Internet-of-Things Design and Implementation (IoTDI)*: IEEE, pp. 277–282, 2016.

[13] Shortcut Labs, *Flic: The Wireless Smart Button*. [Online]. Available from: https://start.flic.io/ 2017.01.13

[14] Logitech, *POP Home Switch Simple smart home control for the whole family*. [Online]. Available from: http://www.logitech.com/en-us/product/pop-home-switch 2017.01.13

[15] Sen.se, *ThermoPeanut*. [Online]. Available from: https://sen.se/peanut/thermo/ 2017.01.13

[16] Nest, *Nest Learning Thermostat - Install & Explore*. [Online]. Available from: https://nest.com/thermostat/install-and-explore/ 2017.01.13

[17] Roost, *Roost Wi-Fi battery for smoke and CO alarms*. [Online]. Available from: http://www.getroost.com/product-battery 2017.01.13

[18] SmartThings, *Architecture*. [Online]. Available from: http://docs.smartthings.com/en/latest/architecture/index.html 2017.01.13

[19] Essence, *WeR@Home Installation Guide* 2017.01.13

[20] Afero, "Hub Secure Hub Product brief," 2016. [Online]. Available from: https://developer.afero.io/assets/HubProductBrief.pdf 2017.01.13

[21] R. Want, "An introduction to RFID technology," IEEE Pervasive Computing, vol. 5, no. 1, pp. 25–33, 2006.

[22] J. R. Smith, *Wireless Identification Sensing Platform (WISP)*. [Online]. Available from: http://sensor.cs.washington.edu/WISP.html 2017.01.13

[23] S. Naderiparizi, A. N. Parks, Z. Kapetanovic, B. Ransford, and J. R. Smith, "WISPCam: A Battery-Free RFID Camera," *2015 IEEE International Conference on RFID (RFID)*, pp. 166–173, 2015.

[24] EnOcean, *EnOcean – The World of Energy Harvesting Wireless Technology.* [Online]. Available from: https://www.enocean.com/fileadmin/redaktion/pdf/white_paper/WhitePaper_Getting_Started_With_EnOcean_v1.0.pdf 2017.01.13

[25] EnOcean, *Energy Harvesting Wireless Power for the Internet of Things.* [Online]. Available from: https://www.enocean.com/fileadmin/redaktion/pdf/white_paper/White_Paper_Internet_of_Things_EnOcean.pdf 2017.01.13

[26] drayson, *RF Energy Harvesting for the Low Energy Internet of Things* 2017.01.13

[27] SmartThings, *Z-Wave Primer.* [Online]. Available from: http://docs.smartthings.com/en/latest/device-type-developers-guide/z-wave-primer.html 2017.01.13

[28] Libelium, "Waspmote Technical Guide," 2016. [Online]. Available from: http://www.libelium.com/downloads/documentation/waspmote_technical_guide.pdf 2017.01.13

[29] T. Benson, *How I Hacked Amazon's $5 WiFi Button to track Baby Data — Medium.* [Online]. Available from: https://medium.com/@edwardbenson/how-i-hacked-amazon-s-5-wifi-button-to-track-baby-data-794214b0bdd8 2017.01.13

[30] PawTrax, *Welcome to PawTrax.* [Online]. Available from: http://www.pawtrax.co.uk/ 2017.01.13

The Privacy Research Community in Computing and Information Technology

Charles Perez*, Karina Sokolova*

*PSB Paris School of Business, Chair D^3 Digital, Data, Design,
Paris, France
email:{c.perez, k.sokolova}@psbedu.paris

Abstract—**The technologies of information and communications are part of our day to day activities. From computers to smartphones and with the success of social media and the Internet of Things (IoT), we are now surrounded and fully part of a digital society that produces a big amount of data. In this context, privacy is raising importance in computing and information technology. In this article, we propose a study of the privacy research community. We examine over 13,646 articles published on privacy during the last ten years. We focus our analysis on co-authorship and identify the dynamics and key researchers of this domain.**

Keywords–Privacy, Information Technology, Bibliometry, Computer science, Survey, Co-authorship graph

I. INTRODUCTION

In European Union, privacy is considered to be a fundamental human right. During the last decades, with the rapid evolution of technologies, personalized services and big data, the interests in privacy rapidly grows and the privacy research community seems to expand. With the European legislation evolution and an introduction of "Privacy by Design" (PbD) notions applicable to all information systems [1], privacy research starts to englobe information system research and computer science: researchers currently work on bridging the gap between legal notions and information systems engineers to propose adapted solutions for modern systems design and evaluation [2]. Modern technologies, such as World Wide Web, mobile systems [3][4], Internet of Things (IoT) [5], data treatment and sharing [6] strongly impacts privacy research field and community. With the popularization of digital social networks and sharing services, user behavior regarding privacy evolves: privacy research field expands with the notions of user education, visibility and transparency [7][8]. Privacy becomes a large multidisciplinary research field treating legal and technological aspects, privacy models [9], design patterns [10], Privacy Enhancing Technologies (PET) [11][12][13], effective user interface [14], and much more. However, in our knowledge, no bibliometric research has been yet conducted on the study of the privacy research field community.

In this paper, we investigate the computing-related privacy research field by exploring the evolution of the community and co-authorship over the last 10 years. Our research is based on a set of 13,646 articles collected from the well-known Association for Computing Machinery (ACM) digital library in October 2016. We provide a set of statistics on this particular field and apply social network analysis techniques to better understand the evolution of this research community and identify the most relevant contributors.

The article is organized as follows. Section 2 presents the methodology used for data collection, general data analysis metrics and the co-authorship analysis. Section 3 highlights the obtained results: general dataset metrics and interpretation as well as co-authorship graph analysis results. We also compare the obtained results with the state-of-the-art works on other research communities. Section 4 presents related works and section 5 concludes this article.

II. METHODOLOGY

A. Data collection and preprocessing

We collected 13,646 publications from the ACM digital library [15] in October 2016 using the import.io software and a crawler setup for this purpose. All articles were published between years 2006 and 2016 and are a collection of conference proceedings and journal articles published by the ACM digital library and partner publishers. All of the collected articles mention 'privacy' either in the title, keywords or the abstracts. The following features were collected about the articles: the title, the abstract, the list of authors, the list of keywords, the number of downloads (6 weeks, 12 weeks and overall), the number of citations, the publisher and the publishing date (month and year).

When working with human generated data and scientific articles in particular, a few preprocessing steps are required for preprocessing. For example, it is a common observation that the same author is mentioned using different strings in different articles: "Heather Ritcher Lipford" and "Heather Richter Lipford", "Renè Mayrhofer" and "Rene Mayrhofer", "Alvaro A. Cardenas" and "Alvaro Cardenas" are observed in our dataset. To homogenize the authors' names, we first performed the following preprocessing steps using Regular Expressions: 1-Remove dots, 2-Replace dashes by simple spaces, 3-Remove all diacritical marks (e.g., 'è' becomes 'e'), 4-Remove titles and honorifics.

From the preprocessed authors list, we calculate the Levenshtein distance [16] between author names to measure potential misspellings that could not be detected by the four aforementioned techniques. Note that the Levenshtein distance between two strings is measured as the minimum number of basic operations (i.e., deletions, insertions or substitutions) needed to transform the first string into the second string. We found that most of errors (90%) can be detected by matching authors that have a Levenshtein distance below 2. A manual investigation of potential matches was performed to avoid any abusive match. Asian names were often found to be false positives due to the names' shortness (e.g., "Yun Zhang" and "Jun Zhang"). After resolving the entity disambiguation problem with authors, we finally obtained a total of 16,766 distinct authors for the 13,646 articles.

B. Dataset general statistics

1) Global measures: From the obtained dataset, we compute a set of metrics to have a vision of the broadness of the research field and its overall weight and interest. Given the total amount of contributors denoted $\mathcal{A}$ and the total quantity of contributions denoted $\mathcal{N}$, we compute the average number of contributions per author $\langle \mathcal{N}_a \rangle$ and the average number of authors per contribution $\langle \mathcal{A}_n \rangle$.

Since we analyze the last ten years of the field, we want to highlight the evolution of the field over time. For this purpose, we have computed a set of dynamic metrics, such as the number of articles per year y (denoted $\mathcal{N}_y$), the number of authors per year (denoted $\mathcal{A}_y$), the distribution of authors regarding their number of contributions and the authors publishing lifetime.

Concerning the distribution of authors regarding their number of contributions, we verify if our dataset respects the Lotka's law [17]. This law states that the number of researchers publishing exactly X contributions is a fraction of the number of authors publishing only one. This fraction is expressed by the equation 1.

$$Y = \frac{C}{X^k} \tag{1}$$

Where X is the number of publications, Y the relative frequency of authors with X publications, and k and C are constants depending on the specific field. It is admitted that the k parameter for bibliometrics is generally about 2.

The authors publishing lifetime L_a for a given author is a duration (measured in years) when the authors considered to be part of the research field. The lifetime L_a of an author in the research field is defined by equation 2.

$$L_a = 1 + (t_{out}(a) - t_{in}(a)) \tag{2}$$

Where $t_{in}(a)$ is the year of its first contribution in the domain (arrival time when the author is considered to be the new author) and $t_{out}(a)$ the year of its last contribution (leaving time). We also measure the average authors lifetime denoted $\langle L_a \rangle$.

C. Co-authorship analysis using graph theory

We propose to analyse the collaborations between authors by creating a co-authorship graph. In a first part, the graph is analyzed at the broad scale to obtain a general vision of the research field. In a second part, we deeply investigate the position of authors in the graph and characterize the importance of contributors using centrality metrics.

1) Graph construction and general metrics: The undirected weighted co-authorship graph is denoted $G(N, E)$ where each author is a node $n \epsilon N$ of the graph and each edge between two nodes is created when two authors are found to be co-authors of the same article. The edge is weighted by the number of the authors' collaborations: more the authors collaborated, the higher is the edge weight. In order to build the graph using the raw data harvested by import.io, we converted a list of authors of each article into a set of edges between all co-authors of the article using Talend Open Studio 'Extract, Transform and Load' (ETL) software.

First, we calculate density, clustering coefficient, degree distribution and average path length of the co-authorship graph to capture some general statistics of the privacy research field. The density of the graph reveals the probability that two given researchers of the privacy field collaborate together. It is measured as $d = {}^{2|E|}/_{|N||N-1|}$ where $|E|$ is the number of observed edges and $|N|$ the total number of nodes.

The local clustering coefficient reveals how likely the co-authors of a given author are also co-authoring papers together. It is measured as shown in equation 3.

$$C_i = \frac{2L_i}{k_i(k_i - 1)} \tag{3}$$

Where L_i represents the number of links between the k_i neighbors of node i. The local coefficient of clustering equals 0 if neighbors are not collaborating at all and 1 if all neighbors are collaborating with each other (they form a complete graph). The average clustering coefficient captures the general vision of how co-authors of a same author tend to collaborate at the general scope of the graph/research field. Average path length, diameter, degree distribution and other metrics are applied to the dataset but not discussed in this paper. For more information on social network analysis metrics, the reader can refer to [18]. All of the general metrics are compared to other fields in order to highlight specificities of the privacy research community.

In order to investigate the communities of researchers, we apply the modularity based clustering algorithm [19]. Note that all graph visualizations of this paper are performed using the Gephi visualisation software [20].

2) Algorithms to identify key authors: We apply several centrality algorithms to identify the key users of the graph. Centrality defines the importance of a node depending on its position in the graph [21]. We applied the following measure of importance: degree, weighted degree, betweenness centrality, closeness centrality and PageRank [22]. Degree measures the number of distinct collaborators (number of edges). Weighted degree highlights the number of collaborations (sum of edges weights). Betweenness centrality measures how intermediate a given node is in the graph. It is based on appearance of a node in the shortest paths between any couple of nodes in the graph. It can be interpreted as with a kind of diversity in collaborations. PageRank is built on the hypothesis that important authors are authors whose collaborators are also important (high number of links). It is an iterative process.

III. RESULTS

A. Dataset general statistics

The collected dataset contains 13,646 conference proceedings and journal articles from the ACM digital library having 16,766 distinct authors. Most of the collected articles were published by ACM (11,587 articles) and a minority was published by partner publishers, such as IEEE Press (256 publications), IEEE Computer Society (176 publications), Australian Computer Society Inc. (116 publications) and Consortium for Computing Sciences in Colleges (102 publications).

Fig. 1 highlights the number of the articles published every year by the privacy community. The blue line highlights the number of publications observed in our dataset; the orange dashed line is a linear trend-line. We observe that the field gained regularly in popularity and particularly between years 2007 and 2009 probably due to smartphones that cause many privacy and security concerns. We observe linear augmentation in yearly publications: the privacy field gains in the average 202 articles by year over the last ten years ($R^2 > 0.93$).

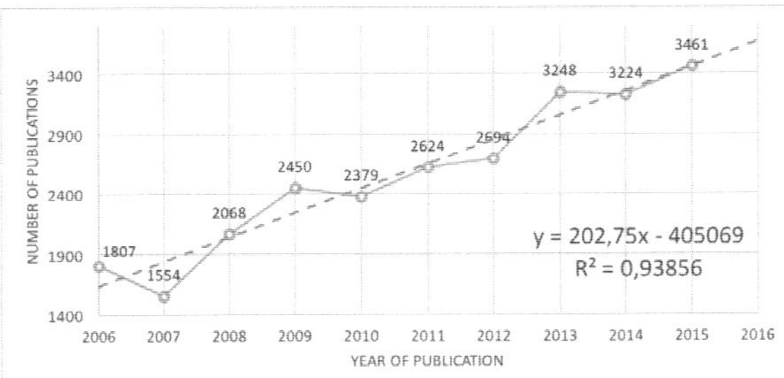

Figure 1. Evolution and trends in the number of published articles by year over the last ten years

Fig. 2 shows the distribution of authors regarding the number of articles they published (blue dots). A trend line is displayed as dashed yellow line. We observe that the decrease in publications by authors in the privacy community follows the Lotka's law with parameters $C = 28,424$ and exponent $k \approx 3$. We note that the exponent k is closer to 3 than to 2 as expected in well known bibliometrics datasets [17]. According to [23], this observation reveals that the privacy research field is a particularly productive community that is overestimated by the Lotka's law with exponent $k = 2$ and instead tends to follow the cube relationship ($Y = C/X^3$).

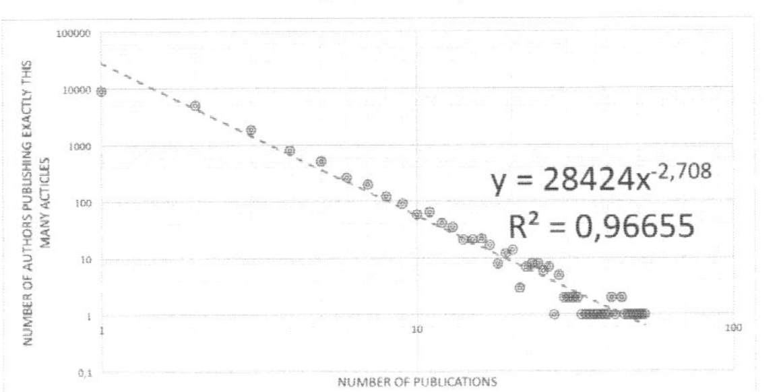

Figure 2. Research production in privacy field (logarithmic scale)

Fig. 3 shows the evolution of the authors in privacy community over the last 10 years. Fig. 3 shows the total number of unique authors by year, new authors and leaving authors. The new authors are the authors that publish their first article on the studied research topic at a given year. The authors are considered to be leaving the community if no article were published by the author after the given year. We observed that 15% of researchers have a 2 years delay between two publications, therefore we do not consider leaving authors for the years 2014 - 2015 as they could still publish in the near future and probably are still active in the community (e.g., working/reviewing/waiting decisions of papers). Even if the majority of authors are new authors, we observe that the community of republishing authors grows linearly: each year, the community gains authors and regularly keeps some of the new authors.

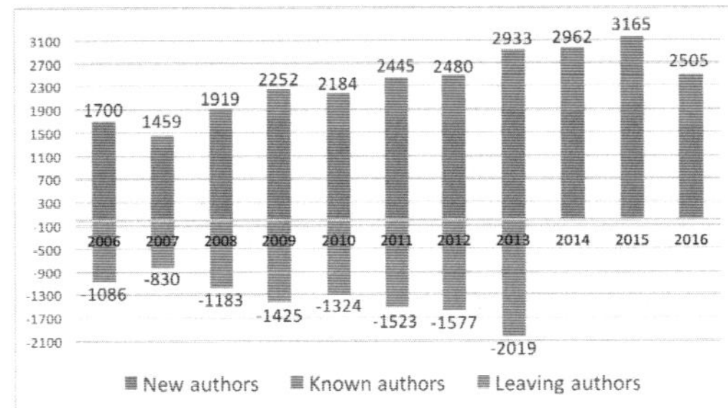

Figure 3. New, republishing and leaving authors by year.

Fig. 4 represents the number of authors according to their community publishing lifetime L. The publishing lifetime represents the number of years the author were observed in the community. The upper score indicates the number of incoming authors while the lower score indicates the number of leaving authors. We observe that most of the privacy authors (86,5%) had only a one year lifetime ($L = 1$), it means that the majority of the new authors are also leaving authors. Those authors could be researchers from different fields having short collaborations with the privacy community researchers. Fig. 4 depicts the number of researchers that stayed in the community more than a year. The minority of the authors leave the community in two years and approximately the same amount of authors were observed in the community during the full study period. Most of the privacy researchers contributes in the community for a period of 5 years ($\langle L_a \rangle = 5$).

We propose to have a closer look on the publication lifetime of the top 5 authors chosen by their lifetime and the number of published articles (Fig. 5). All the five authors are a part of the community from at least 2006 and are active publishers till 2016. Elisa Bertino (grey line) is the most productive author publishing in average 8 articles by year (publishing peak in 2009 with 18 published articles). Lorrie Faith Cranor (yellow line) and Ahmad Reza Sadeghi (orange line) in average publish 5 articles per year. Ninghui Li (blue line), Adam Lee (cyan line) and Ting Yu (green line) have an average publishing of 4 articles per year.

B. Co-authorship analysis

1) Large scale observations: Fig. 6 shows a global view of the obtained graph $G(N, E)$ composed of 16,766 nodes and 21,113 edges. One can observe a giant component that illustrates that most of privacy community has a core research community of collaborators and a set of isolated small connected

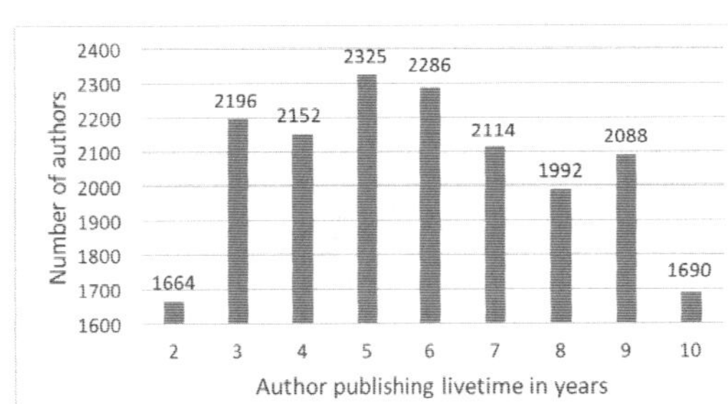

Figure 4. Number of authors according to their publishing lifetime L

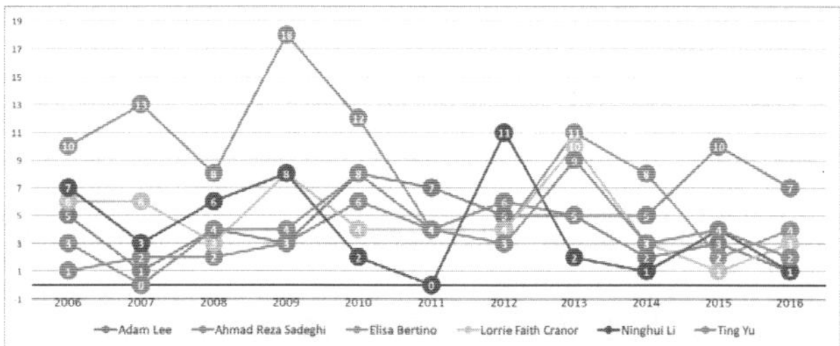

Figure 5. The publishing activity of the top 5 privacy authors for the last ten years

Figure 6. Privacy community co-authorship graph.

components (isolated collaborations). The giant component consists of 6,959 authors (41.5% of the total author number) and 11,373 collaborations (53,8% of total collaborations). An interactive graph of a subset of the privacy research community is available online at [24]. The density of the observed network is measured as $\approx$0.00015, which is relatively low but not surprising. This number illustrates that there is approximately 0.015% of chance that a random couple of researchers of the community has ever co-authored an article.We also observe a high number of connected components not belonging to the giant component (about 2,632). Most of these components are of size 2, 3 and 4 (small dots on the figure).

To get a better understanding of the specificities of the privacy research field, we propose to compare global characteristics of the graph to well-known co-authorship graphs of other research fields (i.e., Management, Physics and IT). The comparison features are displayed in Table I: number of authors, number of papers, average degree, main component size, main component percent, clustering coefficient, mean authors per paper, mean papers per author. We observe that Privacy research field is the unique sample that has a higher number of authors than the number of papers. This matches with the mean authors per paper feature that is significantly high in our dataset. This indicates that researchers of privacy research fields tend to publish with a higher amount of co-authors. This is certainly a proof of the particular dynamic of the field. However, we note that the average degree (number of collaborators by author) is relatively low compared to the mean authors per paper. This may reveal diversity in behavior between researchers (some having a very high number of collaborators versus some having a very few collaborators - see Fig. 7). The clustering coefficient is significantly high compared to the other research fields which reveals that if an author x publishes with author y and author z, it is very likely that y and z publishes also together. Note that this result is also partly due to the high number of co-authors per papers.

TABLE I. COMPARISON OF CO-AUTHORSHIP FEATURES FOR DISTINCT RESEARCH FIELDS

	Privacy	Management	Physics	IT
Number of authors $\mathcal{A}$	16,766	10,176	52,909	11,994
Number of papers $\mathcal{N}$	13,646	11,022	98,502	13,169
Average degree (collaborators per author)	2.5	2.43	9.7	3.59
Main component size	6,959	4,625	4,4337	6,396
Mean authors per paper $\langle \mathcal{A}_n \rangle$	3.32	1.88	2.530	2.22
Mean papers per author $\langle \mathcal{N}_a \rangle$	2.25	2.04	5.1	2.55
Main component %	41.5%	45.4%	85.4%	57.2%
Clustering coefficient	0.8	0.681	0.430	0.496
Reference	*Our study*	[25]	[26]	[26]

2) Authors characterization: We have applied the following centrality measures to the co-authorship graph: Degree, Weighted degree, Closeness, Betweenness and PageRank. Table II presents the top 5 authors according to the degree, weighted degree and PageRank. Three researchers (Elisa Bertino, Wei Wang, Adam Lee, Ahmad Reza Sadeghi) are highlighted in bold due to their apparition in top 5 of the three metrics. Table III shows top 5 authors according to the closeness and betweenness centralities where we observe 4 authors in common: Elisa Bertino, Michael Reiter, Ari Juels and Gene Tsudik (shown in bold).

The unweighted degree measures the total number of distinct collaborators for each author. The maximum degree of 68 is observed for Elisa Bertino; Ahmad Reza Sadeghi is observed to be the second most collaborative author having nearly half less collaborators (37 co-authors).

Fig. 7 shows the degree distribution representing the number of authors according to the number of unique collaborators they had during the last 10 years. A relevant ratio of authors (46%) collaborated with only 2 researchers and only a very small portion of authors collaborated with more that 15 researchers (0.5%). It is, however, more common to have a single collaborator (23.9%) than having three collaborators (16%). Considering only the giant component of the graph, most of authors have at least 3 collaborators and the average degree rises to 3.2.

It is interesting to note that authors having the highest

TABLE II. TOP 5 AUTHORS ACCORDING TO DEGREE, PAGERANK AND WEIGHTED DEGREE MEASURES

Rank	Author	Degree	Author	Weighted degree	Author	PageRank
1	**Elisa Bertino**	68	**Elisa Bertino**	138	**Elisa Bertino**	0.0023
2	**Ahmad Sadeghi**	37	**Adam Lee**	74	Wei Wang	0.0013
3	Wei Wang	31	Ting Yu	68	**Ahmad Sadeghi**	0.0012
4	**Adam Lee**	31	Li Xiong	66	**Adam Lee**	0.001
5	Ninghui Li	29	**Ahmad Sadeghi**	64	Mahesh Tripunitara	0.0009

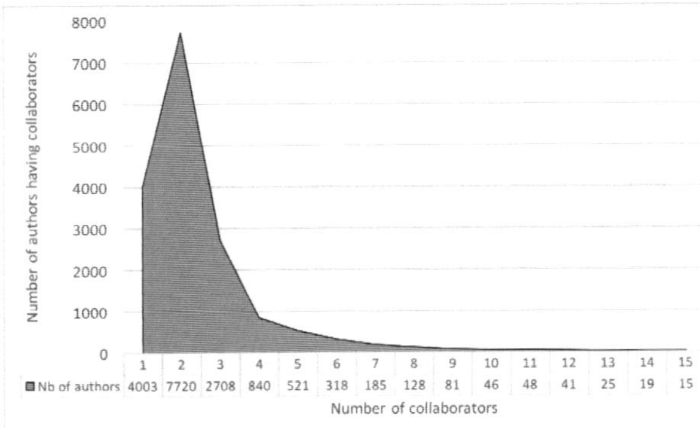

Figure 7. Authors and the number of unique collaborators (Degree distribution of the graph $G(N, E)$)

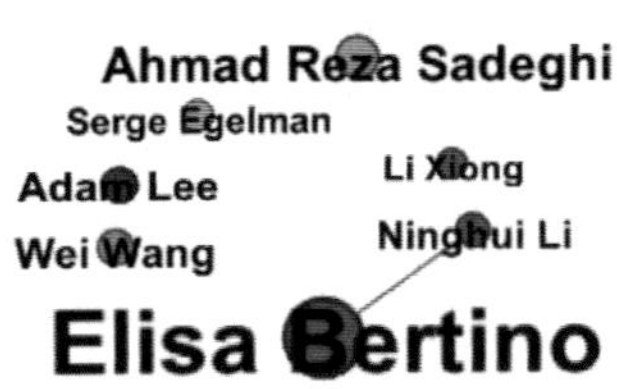

Figure 8. Author graph filtered by the node degree up to 25

number of collaborators do not collaborate with each other. Fig. 8 depicts the graph where nodes were filtered by degree to only keep track of authors having at least 25 unique collaborators. The size of the nodes shows the degree of the node before the filter is applied, authors names are proportional to the node size, the link shows the collaboration and the node colors indicated the modularity class (modularity class reflects the different clusters identified using the optimisation based algorithm). Elisa Bertino co-authored with only one researcher that has as many collaborators as herself (Ninghui Li with 29 unique co-authors). Ahmad Reza Sadephi, Wei Wang and Adam Lee both having 31 unique co-authors, Serge Edelman (27 collaborators) and Li Xiong (26 collaborators) never collaborate with each other.

The weighted degree represents the number of collaborations and not only the number of collaborators. Comparing to the degree ranking, we observe that Ting Yu and Li Xiong replaces Wei Wang and Ninghui Li at the top 5. Even if those authors have less unique collaborators (25 for Ting Yu and 26 for Li Xiong), their total quantity of collaborations is higher (68 for Ting Yu and 66 for Li Xiong): it means that they prefer long term collaborations with the same collaborators.

Fig. 9 represents the authors that collaborate the most with each other (more than 9 collaborations). The thickness of the edge corresponds to the edge weight and the node size

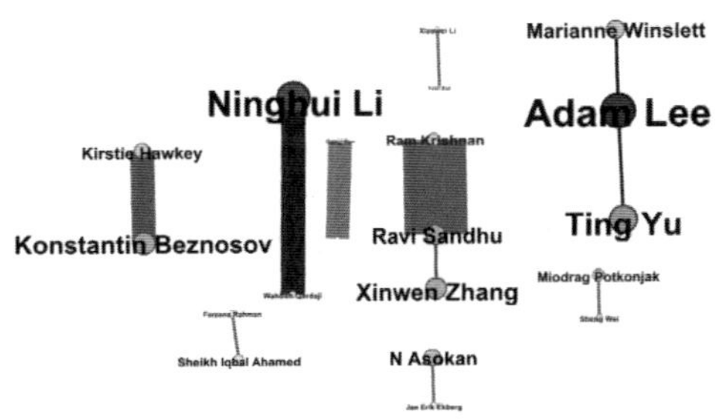

Figure 9. The most collaborative authors.

corresponds to the node degree before filtering. Ram Krishnan and Ravi Sandhu co-authored 12 articles that is the maximum value observed in our dataset. We observe that most of very strong collaborations occurs between couples of authors. Also we note that the privacy domain does not have any very strongly collaborative communities of size 3 or more.

PageRank measures the prestige of the author in the community. In our case, the top 4 authors are equivalent to the top 4 authors ranked according to unweighted degree (Table II). Mahesh Tripunitara replaces Ninghui Li on the fifth place: even if he has less collaborators and collaborations, he appears to be connected to more prestigious nodes.

Betweenness centrality measures how authors appear in between others. Regarding co-authorship, high betweenness can reveal an interdisciplinary researchers that are part of/in the middle between different communities (all belonging to a possible different clusters). Elisa Bertino and Ahmad Reza Sadeghi appear to be highly collaborative with a diversity of collaborators in terms of communities. We observe that Michael Reiter, Gene Tsudik and Ari Juels also appear in-between nodes probably due to a variety in their collaborators' interests (Table III).

Closeness centrality highlights the authors that are the closest to all other authors in the co-authorship network. That would highlight the authors that one would contact if one wants to relate to all/any other author of the network. We observe that the results are similar to the betweenness centrality: only Ahmad Reza Sadeghi is replaced by Peng Ning (Table III).

IV. RELATED WORKS

Social network analyses field gained considerable attention in bibliometrics to measure the evolution of research fields using graphs. Multiple types of bibliographical data may be modeled and analyzed as a directed/undirected and weighted/unweighted graphs. Thus, co-citation graph may be

TABLE III. TOP 5 AUTHORS ACCORDING TO BETWEENNESS AND CLOSENESS CENTRALITIES

Rank	Closeness	Betweenness
1	**Michael Reiter**	**Elisa Bertino**
2	**Ari Juels**	Ahmad Sadeghi
3	**Elisa Bertino**	**Michael Reiter**
4	**Gene Tsudik**	**Gene Tsudik**
5	Peng Ning	**Ari Juels**

built linking articles or authors that cite/are cited by other articles or authors; co-authorship graph links two authors if they co-published at least one article together; keywords graph links keywords that appears together in the same article, etc.

Co-authorship network is frequently used to study scientific collaborations and highlight the key actors of the field. Newman [27] studied co-authors in biomedical research, physics and computer science between 1995 and 1999 and highlighted the similarities between those networks. The authors of [28] studied mathematics and neuroscience between 1991 and 1998. In [29], authors studied scientometrics research collaborations (1980-2012). The authors of [30] analyzed all publications of the ACM Special Interest Group on Management of Data (SIGMOD) conferences between 1975 and 2002. In [31], authors analyses co-publications of ACM and IEEE conferences (1994 and 2000). Resent studies analyzed co-authors in computer science [32], eParticipation [33], industrial ecology [34], front-end of innovation [35] and digital heritage [36] to cite a few.

V. CONCLUSION

In this paper, we investigated the privacy research field from a computing and information technology perspective. We collected and analysed 13,646 publications published by 16,766 authors. We characterized this community with general statistics but also by analysing the underlying co-authorship graph. We show that the privacy research field is growing (up to 200 contributions by year), productive and strongly collaborative (about 2.5 collaborations per author) having high average number of authors per paper (3.32). Authors contribute to the community for an average time of 5 years. Using the co-authorship graph, we identified a set of authors that are key players of the field: Elisa Bertino, Wei Wang, Adam Lee and Ahmad Reza Sadeghi. Despite a strong activity, we highlighted that key authors of these fields do not often collaborate together. This work can be extended by qualitative analyses of the top communities and by topics evolution analyses.

REFERENCES

[1] A. Cavoukian, "Privacy by design: The 7 foundational principles," 2009.

[2] "Privacy and data protection by design – from policy to engineering," European Union Agency for Network and Information Security (ENISA), Tech. Rep., December 2014.

[3] J. Häkkilä and J. Mäntyjärvi, "Developing design guidelines for context-aware mobile applications," in Mobility '06: Proceedings of the 3rd international conference on Mobile technology, applications & systems. ACM, Oct. 2006.

[4] E. Chin, A. P. Felt, V. Sekar, and D. Wagner, "Measuring user confidence in smartphone security and privacy," in Proceedings of the Eighth Symposium on Usable Privacy and Security, ser. SOUPS '12. New York, NY, USA: ACM, 2012, pp. 1–16.

[5] C. Perera, C. McCormick, A. K. Bandara, B. A. Price, and B. Nuseibeh, "Privacy-by-design framework for assessing internet of things applications and platforms," CoRR, vol. abs/1609.04060, 2016.

[6] S. Yu, "Big privacy: Challenges and opportunities of privacy study in the age of big data," IEEE Access, vol. 4, 2016, pp. 2751–2763.

[7] K. Sokolova, M. Lemercier, and J.-B. Boisseau, "Respecting user privacy in mobiles: privacy by design permission system for mobile applications," International Journal On Advances in Security, vol. 7, no. 34, December 2014, pp. 110–120.

[8] F. Stutzman, R. Capra, and J. Thompson, "Factors mediating disclosure in social network sites," Computers in Human Behavior, vol. 27, no. 1, Jan. 2011, pp. 590–598.

[9] K. Harris, "Privacy on the go," California Department of Justice, Jan. 2013, pp. 1–27.

[10] M. Hafiz, "A collection of privacy design patterns," in Proceedings of the 2006 Conference on Pattern Languages of Programs, ser. PLoP '06. New York, NY, USA: ACM, 2006, pp. 1–13.

[11] G. W. van Blarkom, J. J. Borking, and J. G. E. Olk, "Handbook of privacy and privacy-enhancing technologies," 2003.

[12] G. D'Acquisto, J. Domingo-Ferrer, P. Kikiras, V. Torra, Y.-A. de Montjoye, and A. Bourka, "Privacy by design in big data: An overview of privacy enhancing technologies in the era of big data analytics," arXiv.org, Dec. 2015.

[13] Y. Deswarte and C. Aguilar Melchor, "Current and future privacy enhancing technologies for the internet," Annales Des Télécommunications, vol. 61, no. 3, 2006, pp. 399–417.

[14] L. F. Cranor, P. Guduru, and M. Arjula, "User interfaces for privacy agents," ACM Transactions on Computer-Human Interaction, vol. 13, no. 2, Jun. 2006, pp. 135–178.

[15] A. for Computing Machinery. Acm digital library. [Online]. Available: http://dl.acm.org

[16] V. I. Levenshtein, "Binary Codes Capable of Correcting Deletions, Insertions and Reversals," Soviet Physics Doklady, vol. 10, 1966, p. 707.

[17] A. J. Lotka, "The frequency distribution of scientific productivity," 1926.

[18] R. Alhajj and J. Rokne, Encyclopedia of Social Network Analysis and Mining. Springer Publishing Company, Incorporated, 2014.

[19] M. Newman, "Fast algorithm for detecting community structure in networks," Physical Review E, vol. 69, September 2003.

[20] M. Bastian, S. Heymann, and M. Jacomy. Gephi: An open source software for exploring and manipulating networks. [Online]. Available: http://www.aaai.org/ocs/index.php/ICWSM/09/paper/view/154 (2009)

[21] L. C. Freeman, "Centrality in social networks conceptual clarification," Social Networks, 1978, p. 215.

[22] L. Page, S. Brin, R. Motwani, and T. Winograd, "The pagerank citation ranking: Bringing order to the web." no. 1999-66. Stanford InfoLab, November 1999, Technical Report, previous number = SIDL-WP-1999-0120.

[23] D. J. d. S. Price, Little science, big science. New York: Columbia Univ. Press, 1963.

[24] K. Sokolova and C. Perez. Privacy co-authorship graph. [Online]. Available: http://www.charlesperez.net/privacy

[25] J. F. Acedo, C. Barroso, C. Casanueva, and J. L. Galan, "Co-authorship in management and organizational studies: an empirical and network analysis," Journal of Management Studies., vol. 43, 2006, pp. 957–983.

[26] M. Newman, "Scientific collaboration networks. i. network construction and fundamental results," Rev. E, vol. 64, 2001, p. 2001.

[27] ——, Who Is the Best Connected Scientist: A Study of Scientific Coauthorship Networks, E. Ben-Naim, H. Frauenfelder, and Z. Toroczkai, Eds. Berlin, Heidelberg: Springer Berlin Heidelberg, 2004.

[28] A. L. Barabasi, H. Jeong, Z. Neda, E. Ravasz, A. Schubert, and T. Vicsek, "Evolution of the social network of scientific collaborations," arXiv.org, Apr. 2001.

[29] M. Erfanmanesh, V. A. Rohani, and A. Abrizah, "Co-authorship network of scientometrics research collaboration," Malaysian Journal of Library & Information Science, 2012.

[30] M. Nascimento, J. Sander, and J. Pound, "Analysis of SIGMOD's co-

authorship graph," ACM SIGMOD Record, vol. 32, no. 3, Sep. 2003, pp. 8–10.

[31] X. Liu, J. Bollen, M. L. Nelson, and H. Van de Sompel, "Co-Authorship Networks in the Digital Library Research Community," arXiv.org, Feb. 2005.

[32] G. Cabanac, G. Hubert, and B. Milard, "Academic careers in Computer Science - continuance and transience of lifetime co-authorships." Scientometrics, 2015.

[33] E. Kaliva, D. Katsioulas, E. Tambouris, and K. Tarabanis, "Understanding researchers collaboration in eparticipation using social network analysis," Int. J. Electron. Gov. Res., vol. 11, no. 4, Oct. 2015, pp. 38–68.

[34] J. Kim and C. Perez, "Co-authorship network analysis in industrial ecology research community," Journal of Industrial Ecology, vol. 19, no. 2, 2015, pp. 222–235.

[35] G. H. S. Mendes and M. G. Oliveira, "Bibliometric analysis of the front-end of innovation," in 2015 Portland International Conference on Management of Engineering and Technology (PICMET). IEEE, Aug 2015, pp. 648–661.

[36] S. Münster and M. Ioannides, "A scientific community of digital heritage in time and space," in 2015 Digital Heritage, vol. 2, Sept 2015, pp. 267–274.

Domain-Oriented Design Patterns For Service Processes

Maik Herfurth
Hilti Befestigungstechnik AG
Global Information Technology
Buchs SG, Switzerland
email: maik.herfurth@hilti.com

Thomas Schuster
Pforzheim University of Applied Sciences
Pforzheim, Germany
email: thomas.schuster@hs-pforzheim.de

Abstract — **Business processes in the domain of service procurement have the potential to increase efficiency and reduce cost. These business processes are getting more complex since service providers and service consumers collaborate and interact in network structures. A precise description, modeling, analysis and execution of service procurement business processes for the implementation of process-oriented information systems is required to unlock these potentials and optimize network collaboration. In this article, we propose a pattern based approach for business process models to improve this collaboration systematically. The approach is based on patterns of service phases and service modules to increase efficiency and reduce cost.**

Keywords – service e-procurement; business process design pattern; service phase patterns; service module patterns

I. Introduction

The service sector is a fast-growing sector in all industrial nations and therefore, it has gained significant importance in all national economies [1]. Today, the strategic impact of services overruns products. With shifting the focus towards services and moving to a more service centric perception away from a product centric view, a new paradigm *service dominant logic* is postulated [2]. New business models are arising with cross-company network structures where service providers and service consumers act in service networks, so called *service chains* [3]. More and more companies outsource different areas and reduce the degree of company-internal value-add. More services are sourced externally and the meaning of service procurement is increasing exponentially. Service procurement becomes decisive for success and competition. A business process, which defines the control flows of service procurement, is called *service process,* a process object, which represents data flow is called *service object.* Within the network structures of service chains, the complexity of service processes is raising. New requirements of service-oriented procurement result from the definition of services because of the specific characteristics like immateriality and integrality, which determine the specific characteristics of transactions between service providers and service consumers. The use of modern information technologies like service-oriented architecture (SOA) for the electronic service processes of service procurement sounds quite promising. The efficiency and performance of service processes can be improved and cost can be reduced. Due to the increasing competition and cost pressure in the domain of service procurement, service processes leverage the improvement potential and come to the fore of companies. A systematic and structured approach for modeling and analyzing service processes based on patterns leads to a harmonization and integration of service processes and advantage transparency and structure. We develop two new patterns, namely, service phase patterns and service module patterns. Their application is presented based on examples and their advantages are outlined. The remainder of this article is structured as follows: in Section 2, we look at the current challenges of service procurement and motivate our approach. We look into design patterns and introduce Petri nets as a formal modeling language in Section 3. Service procurement design patterns are proposed in Section 4. In Section 5 and Section 6, we introduce two different design pattern types for service processes and motivate the advantages. Finally, Section 7 of this article concludes with findings and outlook on future work.

II. Challenges and Motivation

Today's service procurement processes of small and medium-sized companies are often characterized by heterogeneous and product-oriented business processes [3]. In contrast to products, services require interaction that is more personal and are more difficult to describe and to measure. Therefore, the procurement of services turns out to be more complex (1) due to process descriptions, (2) due to data descriptions and (3) due to process iterations, (4) due to unknown result of a service after a service request and (5) due to the individuality of services. A high amount of manual process tasks and therefore, missing automation can be observed [5]. Cross-company process structures are heterogeneous and the process and data flow design are influencing each other: an information asymmetry results out of different proprietary data formats and inconsistent data. The electronic procurement of services has still not reached a high level of maturity [6]. In summary, the following challenges can be observed:

- complex collaborative internal and cross-company business process models lead to high opacity, iterations and adjustment cost
- heterogeneous business processes, long process flows and use of different media lead to non-seamless processes

- heterogeneous data structures, different data formats and descriptions lead to non-integration and non-harmonization of data
- heterogeneous information technology (IT) landscapes with different interfaces lead to missing integration
- low maturity level of service process automation leads to long throughput times, redundancy of tasks and source of errors

Existing business process modeling methods for modeling, analysis and implementation of service processes aren`t matured enough and only cover partially the domain specific needs for service e-procurement. New methods for the harmonization, integration and standardization are needed:

- best practice based definition for understanding business processes and data
- harmonization and integration of business processes
- harmonization and integration of data
- integration of information systems

These challenges can be addressed by new domain-oriented design patterns. In this paper, we present a new domain-oriented design pattern approach based on the formal modeling language Petri nets. The Petri net based design patterns build up best practice knowledge and incorporate an integrated modeling approach for process and data structures. Design patterns provide an immediate benefit (1) by reducing design and integration efforts, (2) by encouraging best practices, (3) by assisting in analysis, (4) by exposing inefficiencies, (5) by removing redundancies, (6) by consolidating interfaces and (7) by encouraging modularity and transparent substitution [7].

III. BUSINESS PROCESSS DESIGN PATTERN

A *pattern* is a discernible regularity and the elements of a pattern repeat in a predictable manner. Patterns are an abstraction of a concrete problem observation, which was recognized due to its frequent appearance in a certain domain [8]. Hence, patterns result from experiences and behavioral observation. They represent identical modes of thought, design fashions, behaviors or courses of action, which can be repeated and reproduced. Software design patterns are introduced in the domain of software engineering. They are general solutions to solve a problem in a given context. Thus, a design pattern provides a reusable blueprint that may speed up the development of software [9] and is considered as a solution template for high quality software [10]. Software design patterns always represent solutions to common design problems in a given context [11]. Design patterns at architectural level provide solution templates at component level (e.g., as the pipes and filters pattern does). Object-oriented design patterns, on the other hand, typically show relationships and interactions between classes or objects, they are distinguished into creational patterns, structural patterns, behavioral patterns and concurrency patterns.

Design patterns can create substantial improvements of software quality and reduce costs associated to development and maintenance. Nowadays, design patterns are widely used since they capture and promote best practices in software design. Many catalogues for design patterns are known today, like patterns for software engineering from Gamma et al. [12] and patterns for the enterprise integration scenarios of software applications from Hohpe and Woolf [13].

Similarly, business process design patterns describe best practices for process models in a certain domain. These patterns are also based on empirical knowledge about process activity execution. Thus, business process design patterns are formalizing common structures of activities of process and data flows [14]. While a concrete pattern is bound to a specific modelling language, its abstraction is language independent and can be transferred to other business process modeling languages as well [12]. Specific patterns for the Petri net modelling language are outlined in the next subsection.

Barros et al. [15] define service bilateral and multilateral interaction patterns, which allow emerging web services functionalities like choreography and orchestration. Additionally, domain-oriented design patterns offer a flexible mechanism with clear boundaries in terms of well-defined and highly encapsulated parts being aligned with constraints of the considered domain [16].

A. *Petri net based process pattern*

Petri nets are a formal modeling language to model, analyze, simulate and execute distributed, discrete systems. Petri nets are bipartite graphs. Also, Petri nets can be used to model different levels of detail. Petri nets offer the modeling of static and dynamic elements, limited capacities of places and anonymous tokens to capture process objects. Petri nets are graphically represented by *tokens* (process objects), *places* (conditions), *transitions* (process tasks) and *directed arcs* (arrows). Places are containers for tokens and describe pre- or post-conditions for transitions. Places represent local conditions and describe static process components. Transitions describe dynamic process components and represent local state transitions [17]. As a formal and platform-independent modeling approach, *high-level Petri nets* allow for modeling with a precise description of individualized tokens. Hence, this can be used for the formalization of domain-specific process objects [18]. As a well-established modeling language, Petri nets have also been proposed to model process and data structures as mechanism for analysis and software-based execution of business processes. Especially, high-level Petri nets may be used as input for transformation to executable business processes.

Van der Aalst and ter Hofstede [19] define fundamental *Workflow patterns* based on Petri nets to formalize requirements of workflow languages and information systems. These patterns are further distinguished *into exception handling patterns*, *control flow patterns*, *data flow patterns* and *resource patterns*. Further existing examples for Petri net process patterns are given by *TimeNET* [20] (a software tool to model, analyze and control manufacturing systems based on colored Petri nets), *EXSPECT* [21] (a repository of tool for standardized business processes in logistics and production) or *CIMOSA* [22] (the modeling and analysis of cross-company value chains). To formally model supply chains as business processes, Liu et al. [23] are using Petri nets to define basic patterns of supply chains. Schuster [8] proposes resource assignment patterns and defines high-level resource nets.

IV. SERVICE PROCUREMENT DESIGN PATTERN

In the domain of service procurement, service suppliers and service consumers collaborate with each other. The collaboration itself can be considered as an instance of a service procurement process model. An instance of a service process model is described as a choreography of specific service phases, which comprise internal and cross-company service processes and service modules. The order of exchanged messages is predefined. Choreography is used to define a cross-company service process out of several independently orchestrated service processes (see Fig. 1). The interaction between several partners for the procurement of services based on the exchanged data is described [24]. The order of the exchanged data is pre-defined. Only valid orders of data between partners are allowed to be defined.

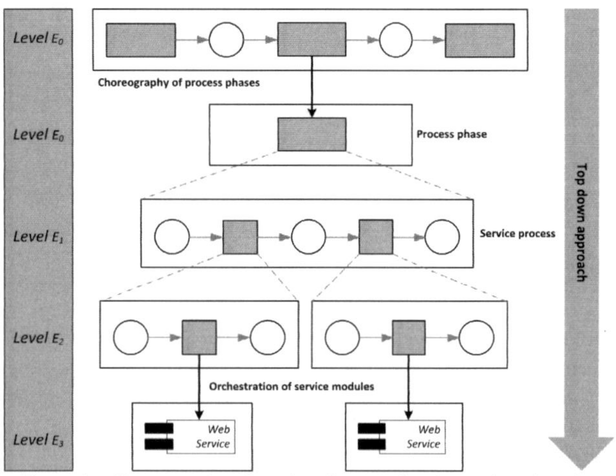

Figure 1. Choreography of service phases and orchestration of service modules on different abstraction levels

Based on our review of scientific literature [25] and empirical case studies [26], we derive new patterns for service e-procurement, which represent best practice of service procurement processes. We introduce the design patterns *Service Phase Patterns* (*SPP*) and *Service Module Patterns* (*SMP*) also supporting software architectures based on service-oriented architecture. These patterns define hierarchic structures and provide a structured concept for the modeling and implementation of service procurement process models. SPP and SMP ensure and precisely describe the order of message exchange and interaction in bilateral and multilateral service chains and constitute required process interfaces.

A sequence of SPP includes data flow, complex service processes and web services. SPP consist of SMP and are linked by internal and cross-company process interfaces. The choreography of SPP serves as a connector between orchestrations of SMP and their internal service processes. A concrete sequence of SMP is pre-defined. The combination of SPP and SMP results into global, cross-company service processes, which define the interaction of internal service processes accordantly.

The pattern-based application using SPP and SMP leads to a top-down approach from specific process phases down to detailed service process descriptions, executed by web services. The pattern-based approach enables a coordinated realization of service processes in information systems at the execution level. In a first modeling and description approach of service e-procurement process descriptions, we use Petri nets as modeling language to describe domain-specific service phases and service modules. Based on this definition, we further develop these patterns based on XML nets [27], a high-level Petri net variant.

V. DESIGN PATTERNS FOR CHOREOGRAPHY OF PROCESS FLOW AND DATA FLOW

Service procurement processes (between service providers and service consumers) are characterized by highly collaborative service processes. The collaboration is defined by specific process and data flows based on specific process interfaces. It can be observed that typical recurrent service procurement process models are characterized by a specific order of data flow and by specific service procurement types. These recurrent orders of process and data flow defining service procurement types can be described by patterns.

A. *Service Phase Patterns (SPP)*

SPP choreograph service procurement phases and therefore, the data flow in order to represent and manage cross-company interaction. The logic of process flow instances is determined as well. SPP are characterized by capsulated service procurement processes on a higher abstraction level. SPP configure different *service procurement types*. A service procurement type pre-defines a service process model, which represents a specific process flow occurrence for service procurement. The following service procurement types are defined:

- A planned need of a service is required and a frame contract does not exist.
- A non-planned need of service is required and a frame contract doesn't exist
- A planned need of a service is required and a frame contract exists.
- A non-planned need of service is required and a frame contract exists.

Based on a specific service procurement type, SPP can be configured to choreograph the data flow and process flow (see Fig. 2).

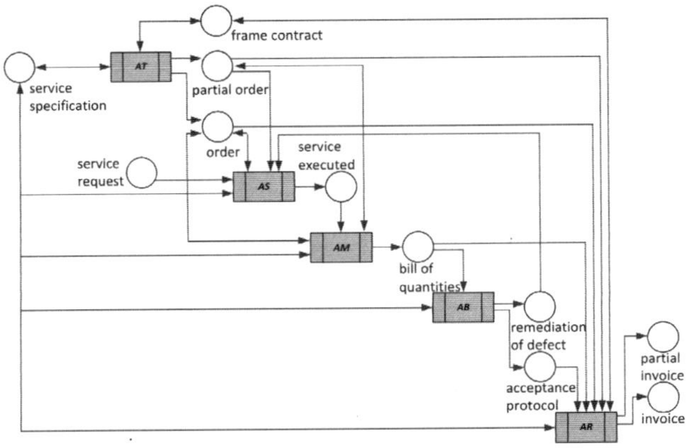

Figure 2. Service procurement type as choreography of SPP modeled as Petri net

B. *Definition and modeling of SPP with Petri nets*

SPP are transition-bounded service processes and are represented in a Petri net as a single transition, which can be extended to sub nets. *Service places* are defined by a set of service object-specific places, which are classified into *service object places SO, static and dynamic service interface places SI* and *service document places SD* (see Fig. 3).

Figure 3. Service object specified places *SO*, *SD* and *SI*

SPP represent a self-contained set of cross-company collaborative service processes. SPP are connected by cross company interfaces defined by service object-specific interface places *SI* and *SD*. SPP are represented graphically by a rectangle, which includes the service phase name (see Fig. 4).

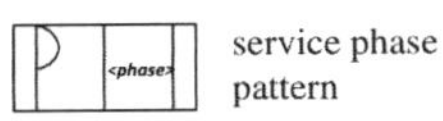

Figure 4. SPP modeled as Petri net

Domain-specific concepts for a formal modeling approach of service processes in the context of service e-procurement are also formalized based on high-level Petri nets. The transfer of the presented formalized concepts further enables communication and information context. SPP are further developed into formalized patterns based on high-level Petri nets with individualized and distinguishable tokens representing the service e-procurement-specific data transfer in information systems. Specific interfaces in collaborative and cross-company service processes represented by service process phases are identified, formalized and defined as patterns based on high-level Petri nets. The set of service object-specific places *SPS* are typified as object containers for service processes and defined as an XML net. *SPS* represent the complex data flow based on XML service objects to define the data and document exchange in collaborative cross-company service processes.

The set of typified service object specific places *SPS* is further distinguished into the set of service object places *SSO*, service interface places *SSI* and service document places *SSD*. The domain specific stereo types of SPP are proposed. SPP based on XML nets represent coarsened structures of capsulated service processes and SMP. SPP are defined based on specific, typified input and output places. They represent process patterns. SPP are defined based on the process and data flow of collaborative service e-procurement processes and consider the specific phases. Fig. 5 shows the example of the pattern of the service phase *Accounting AC*.

SPP are formally defined as the set *TSP* based on single transitions with dedicated service object-specific places. The sets of input places S_{SO}^{IN} and output places S_{SO}^{OUT} are assigned and consist of the sets of service object places *SSO*, service interface places *SSI* and service document places *SSD*. Each service phase $t_{sp_j}^{i}$ is defined by its internal structure, which enables the composition of service phases.

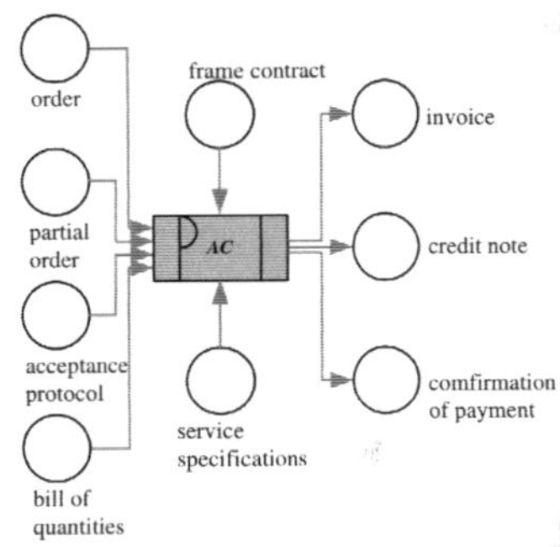

Figure 5. SPP example *Accounting AC* modeled as XML net

In case of a composition of two service phases $t_{sp_a}^{i}$ and $t_{sp_b}^{i}$, input and output places are melted together. The set of *TSP* is defined as single transitions of transition bounded sub XML nets *XN'=(S',T',F')* and service process modules $t_{SM}^{i} \in TSM$. The syntactical compatibility is a requirement for the composition of SPP.

C. *Advantages of SPP*

SPP for service processes of service procurement process models enable the following advantages:

- SPP choreograph service procurement phases and data flow and therefore, they define recurring process flow and data flow orders based on best practice in service procurement.
- SPP are defined patterns for the service procurement phases *specification, request, quotation, order, execution, measurement, acceptance* and *accounting*.
- SPP configure best practice service procurement types.
- SPP enable a pre-defined data flow. The order of exchanged data is prescribed for the definition of domain-specific standard for the interaction and data exchange for

partners [28]. The definition of specific data and process sequences provides the basis for required process interfaces in complex business-to-business (B2B) scenarios.

VI. Design Patterns for Orchestration of Process Flow and Data Flow

Collaborative service processes describe the interaction of service suppliers and service consumers on a detailed business process level. The pre-defined order of recurring service phases can be further structured into detailed service modules. These patterns of detailed service modules describe a recurring process and data flow characterized by specific process interfaces.

A. Service Module Patterns (SMP)

SMP are characterized by capsulated electronic service processes. SMP define orchestrations of their internal capsulated service processes. The process and data flow is orchestrated. The activities of these service processes are executed by web services for the horizontal and vertical integration of different information systems. One of the main characteristics of SMP is collaboration: the collaborative service process of a process participant is further capsulated into service modules.

B. Definition and modeling of SMP

Collaborative SMP are transition-bounded service processes and are represented in a Petri net as a single transition, which can be extended to sub nets. SMP define self-contained collaborative service processes of one collaboration participant (service supplier or service consumer). SMP are represented graphically by a rectangle, which includes the specific service phase name as well as the participant of the service process (see Fig. 6). The set of *SI* and *SD* are input and output places of service modules.

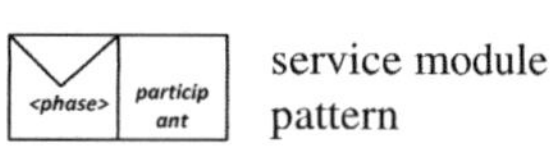

Figure 6. SMP modeled as Petri net

SMP are defined based on high-level Petri nets. SMP represent coarsened collaborative service processes of one process participant. The collaborative service process consists of several SMP representing all process participants and therefore, the entire service process of a SPP. SMP are connected via a set of input and output places *SPS* to model bidirectional interaction and communication patterns like *sending* and *receiving*. The internal structure of a service module is built by a coarsened service net and consists of a set of internal input and output places (S_{SM}^{IN}, S_{SM}^{OUT}) and internal transitions. The set of input and output places is defined as an internal *module interface* of a service module. The internal structure of a service module fulfills the requirements of a workflow net and soundness criteria [29]. A service module interface $S_{sm_1}^{IN/OUT}$ of one service module t_{sm}^1 can be melted with the service module interface $S_{sm_2}^{IN/OUT}$ of another service module t_{sm}^2. The set of service modules *TSM* is defined as single transition of a transition-bounded sub XML net *XN'=(S',T',F')* as part of an XML net and dedicated to one service process phase of the set of service process phases *TSP*. The syntactical compatibility of service process modules enables the composition of service process modules. Syntactically compatible service process modules have completely overlapping process interfaces. The composition of service process modules causes the melting of the common set of interface places. Based on a specific SPP, a capsulated service process can be further detailed into SMP to orchestrate the data flow and process flow (see Fig. 7).

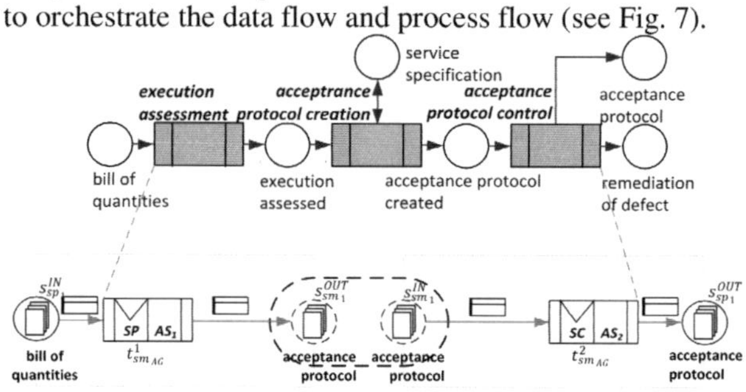

Figure 7. SMPs modeled as XML net

C. Advantages of SMP

SMP for service procurement processes enable the following advantages:

- SMP orchestrate the process flow and data flow and therefore, they define recurring collaborative service processes based on best practice in service procurement.
- SMP define patterns for the detailed service procurement processes *specification*, *request*, *quotation*, *order*, *execution*, *measurement*, *acceptance* and *accounting*.
- SMP enable a modularization concept for modeling and implementing collaborative service processes. The defined activities can be further modeled and implemented by web services.

VII. Conclusion & Outlook

We presented two new patterns SPP and SMP for the choreography of service phases and the orchestration of service modules in collaborative cross-company business process models. The design patterns are intended to describe recurring service process sequences based on observed best practices. SPP and SMP support the modeling and implementation of electronic service processes. SPP and SMP are defined based on a formal Petri net modeling approach for service e-procurement business process models.

Both the formal modeling language of Petri nets, as well as the service procurement domain-specific patterns lead to improved domain understanding, and support simulation based analysis as well as process implementation. The definition of SPP and SMP enables

- an *integrated, formalized modeling approach* of service processes and service objects.
- the modeling of *hierarchic service processes and modularization* of collaborative service processes.
- the definition and modeling of *service process interfaces*.

- a step-wise transformation of modeling to different *formalization levels*.
- the support of *distributed business processes* based on service oriented architecture (SOA).
- the validation of service process models.

As next steps, we further need to verify that these patterns meet the set of design specification and its intended purpose. We will also have to conduct further experiments to ensure the usability, the level of details and completeness of the defined patterns. We will evaluate our pattern approach by analyzing further service e-procurement use cases in order to validate the correctness and use of purpose of the pattern approach. We are planning to integrate the new defined patterns into a modeling approach for service processes, so called *Service nets*. The presented patterns SPP and SMP will be a part of the definition of Service nets. This modeling approach will serve as modeling support for collaborative service processes and distributed hierarchic service process models. The integrated modeling of service processes and service objects, the formalization of different levels of abstraction (hierarchy) and the modularization of service processes (interface design) will be addressed herein. The domain-specific extension of Petri nets is only based on a syntactical level without changing the semantic characteristics of Petri nets. Our pattern approach is based and developed on use cases of service e-procurement of industrial services. E-procurement of other service domains will also be analyzed and validated. The pattern approach can be transferred to further service process types different than procurement. Analog service process types are repair orders, return orders, warranty service orders and further ones. The pattern-based modeling approach will also further be used for simulation experiences and benchmarking of collaborative service processes of different service supplier and service consumer combinations.

REFERENCES

[1] A. Linhart, J. Manderscheid and M. Roeglinger, "Roadmap to Flexible Service Processes - A Project Portfolio Selection and Scheduling Approach", ECIS 2015, Paper 125, pp. 1-16, 2015.

[2] R. F. Lusch and R. Nambisan, "SERVICE INNOVATION: A SERVICE-DOMINANT LOGIC PERSPECTIVE", MIS Quarterly volume 39 (1), pp. 155-175, 2015.

[3] O. Kleine and R. Schneider (editors), "Service Chain Management in the industry – an approach for planning of cooperative industrial services", VDM Dr. Müller, 2010.

[4] L. R. Smeltzer and J. A. Ogden, "Purchasing Professionals' Perceived Differences between Purchasing materials and Purchasing Services", Journal of Supply Chain Management, volume 38 (19), pp. 54-70, 2002.

[5] M. Herfurth and P. Weiß, "Conceptual Design of Service Procurement for collaborative Service Networks", Collaborative Networks for a Sustainable World: 11th IFIP WG 5.5 Working Conference on Virtual Enterprises, PRO-VE 2010, France, pp. 435-442, 2010.

[6] P. P. Maglio and J. Spohrer, "Fundamentals of Service Science", Journal of the Academy of Marketing Science, volume 36 (1), pp. 18-20, 2008.

[7] R. J. Glushko and T. McGrath, "Designing Business Processes With Patterns", The MIT Press Cambridge, Massachusetts, 2005.

[8] T. Schuster, "Modeling, integration and analysis of resources in business processes", KIT Scientific Publishing, 2012.

[9] E. Gamma, R. Helm, R. Johnson, and J. Vlissides, "Design Patterns: Elements of Reusable Object-Oriented Software", Addison–Wesley, 1995.

[10] J. Arlow and I. Neustadt, "Enterprise Patterns and MDA", Addison-Wesley, 2003.

[11] E. Gamma and K. Beck, "Eclipse to be extended. Principles, Patterns and Plug-Ins", Addison-Wesley, 2005.

[12] E. Gamma, R. Helm, R. Johnson, and J. Vlissides, "Design Patterns: Elements of Reusable Object-Oriented Software", Addison-Wesley, 2001.

[13] G. Hohpe and B. Woolf, "Enterprise Integration Patterns: Designing, Building, and Deploying Messaging Solutions", Addison-Wesley Longman Publishing Co. Inc., 2004.

[14] O. Barros, "Business process patterns and frameworks: Reusing knowledge in process innovation", Business Process Management Journal, volume 13 (1), pp. 47-69, 2007.

[15] A. Barros, M. Dumas, and A. ter Hofstede, "Service Interaction Patterns", Proceedings of the 3rd International Conference on Business Process Management, France, Springer, pp. 302-318, 2005.

[16] D. Port, "Derivation of domain specific desing patterns", USC-CSE Annual Reasearch and Technology Week Presentations and Binder Materials, 1998.

[17] W. Reisig, "Petri nets – an introduction", Springer, 1982.

[18] J. Desel and A. Oberweis, "Petri nets in applied informatics: introduction, basics and perspectives", Business Informatics, volume 38(4), pp. 359-367, Vieweg + Teubner, 1996.

[19] N. Russell, A.H.M. ter Hofstede, W.M.P. van der Aalst, and N. Mulyar, "Workflow Control-Flow Patterns: A Revised View", BPM Center Report BPM-06-22, BPMcenter.org, 2006.

[20] A. Zimmermann, J. Freiheit, and A. Huck, "A Petri net based design engine for manufacturing systems", Journal International Journal of Production Research, volume 39 (2), pp. 225-253, 2001.

[21] W.M.P. van der Aalst and A.W. Waltmans, "Modeling logistic systems with EXPECT", in H.G. Sol, K.M. van Hee, Dynamic Modeling of Information Systems, pp. 269-288, 1991.

[22] M. Dong and F. F. Chen, "Process modeling and analysis of manufacturing supply chain networks using object oriented Petri nets", Robotics and Computer Integrated Manufacturing, volume 17, pp. 121-129, 2001.

[23] E. Liu, A. Kumar, and W.M.P. van der Aalst, "Managing Supply Chain Events to Build Sense-and-Response Capability", in D. Straub and S. Klein, editors, Proceedings of International Conference on Information Systems (ICIS 2006), Milwaukee, Wisconsin, pp. 117-134, 2006.

[24] M. Weske, "Business Process Management: Concepts, Languages, Architectures", Springer, 2007.

[25] M. Herfurth, A. Meinhardt, J. Schumacher, and P. Weiß, "eProcurement for Industrial Maintenance Services", Proceedings of Leveraging Knowledge for Innovation in Collaborative Networks: 10th IFIP WG 5.5 Working Conference on Virtual Enterprises, Greece, pp. 363-370, 2009.

[26] P. Weiss, M. Herfurth, and J. Schumacher, "Leverage Productivity Potentials in Service-oriented Procurement Transactions: E-Standards in Service Procurement", RESER Conference, Germany, pp. 1-22, 2011.

[27] K. Lenz, "Modeling and execution of e-business processes with XML nets", Dissertation J.W. Goethe University Frankfurt am Main, 2003.

[28] A. Grosskopf, G. Decker, and M. Weske, "The Process. Business Process Modeling Using BPMN", Meghan-Kiffer Press, 2009.

[29] W.M.P. van der Aalst, "Interorganizational Workflows: An Approach based on Message Sequence Charts and Petri Nets, Systems Analysis - Modeling – Simulation", volume 34 (3), pp. 335-367, 1999.